COMPETE OR FORFIET !

Strategies for Sustainable Competitive Edge in Pharma Product Patent Era

COMPETE OR FORFIET !

Strategies for Sustainable Competitive Edge in Pharma Product Patent Era

Subba Rao Chaganti

PHARMA BS

Pharma Book Syndicate

4-3-375, Ansuya Bhavan, Opp. Lane to Central Bank,
Bank Street, Hyderabad - 500 095 A.P.
Phone : 040 - 23445666, 23445622

Published by :

Pharma Book Syndicate

4-3-375, Ansuya Bhavan, Opp. Lane to Central Bank,
Bank Street, Hyderabad - 500 095 A.P.
Phone : 040 - 23445666, 23445622
E-mail: info@pharmabooksyndicate.com
info@thebooksyndicate.com &
anilshah@pharmabooksyndicate.com

ISBN : 978-93-89974-66-9

Preface

The pharmaceutical industry, which touches the lives of every human being, continues to be polarized with the big triad (North America, Europe and Japan) accounting for over eighty per cent of the total in value even today. The winds of radical change that is affecting the world are also affecting the pharmaceutical industry. Declining R&D productivity, vanishing exclusivities due to increasing patent expiries, determined governments of virtually every country on earth to contain the spiraling healthcare costs are driving rapid genericization of the pharmaceutical industry. Consequently the great divide between the big Pharma and the copycat generic companies is blurring. What was once upon a time unthinkable for a me-too generic company suddenly started looking plausible and possible! The little Davids are taking on the big Goliaths of the pharmaceutical industry with their paratroopers IV and patent challenges. The Goliaths too are planning counter offensive strategies such as authorized generics and patent extension among others.

These are most certainly the most difficult and yet exciting times for Pharma. All these significant changes are also creating new opportunities in their wake deconstructing the old business models giving rise to new. The new competitive spaces can broadly be classified into three: Innovation-led, International Generics and CRAMS. These are not separate watertight competitive spaces. They are rather seamless. It is as though the revered vertical integration model is turned into a modular model with a provision of 'join-the-pieces-when-you-can' modules. These modules are separate and yet are meshed closely facilitating a continuous flow. It is a recombinant business model wherein you build your own corporate genome adding, modifying your *capability genes*.

Compete of Forfeit presents the continuing adventure story of about thirty companies from the Indian subcontinents that are hell-bent on becoming competitive and staying competitive in the globalized world of Pharma. While the geographical origin of these players is India, the principles of their strategy and their business processes towards adaptation of change are universally applicable and therefore replicable.

In today's radically changing business environment of the world pharmaceutical industry, it is only a 24x7 news channel that can keep up-to-date to monitor, analyze and comment. It is not possible for any book to keep up with the pace of change as it is so rapid that even before you complete typing a page, some companies in some part of the world would have changed hands.

Every effort has been made to make the data presented in the book as up-to-the date as possible. Consider this for example: as this book has gone to the press, today (May 22, 2007), The Economic Times reported yet another major acquisition by an Indian company – Sun Pharma, one of the key players discussed on the book. Sun Pharma has announced that the company together with its subsidiaries, has signed a definitive agreements to acquire Taro Pharmaceutical Industries Limited, a multinational generic manufacturer with established subsidiaries, manufacturing and products across the US, Israel, and Canada. North America represents more than 90 per cent of Taro's sales of US$ 254 million in 2006. The US $ 454- million-acquisition strengthens Sun Pharma's position in the US and gives it access to over 100 ANDAs, and about 170-member strong experienced research team.

Compete or Forfeit, in sum offers valuable insights in terms of what needs to be done and more importantly how it can be done to achieve a higher degree of competitiveness in the brave new world of globalized Pharma by showing how a bunch of *never-say-die* companies are doing it successfully in some part of the globe.

Subba Rao Chaganti

May 22, 2007

Contents

List of Abbreviations

AIOF	Agenzia Italina del Farmaco (Italy)
APEC	Asia Pacific Economic Cooperation
ANDA	Abbreviated New Drug Application
ANDS	Abbreviated New Drug Submission
ASEAN	Association of South East Asian Nations
AFSSAPS	Agence Francaise de Sécurité Sanitaire des Products de Sante (French Agency for the Safety of Health Products)
BFAD	Bureau of Food and Drugs (Philippines)
CCMB	Center for Cellular and Molecular Biology
CDER	Center for Drug Evaluation and Research
CDRI	Central Drug Research Institute
COPD	Chronic Obstructive Pulmonary Disorder
COS	Certificate of Suitability
CRM	Customer Relationship Management
cGLP	Current Good Clinical Practice
cGLP	Current Good Laboratory Practice
cGMP	Current Good Manufacturing Practices
CRAMS	Custom Research and Manufacturing Services
CSIR	Council of Scientific and Industrial Research
DCI	Drug Controller of India
DCGI	Drug Control General of India

DMA	Danish Medical Agency
DMF	Drug Master File
DOE	Design of Experiments
DPCO	Drug Price Control Order
DRF	DR. Reddy's Research Foundation
DRL	DR. Reddy's Laboratories
DSIR	Department of Scientific and Industrial Research
ECOS	European Certificate of Suitability
EDMF	European Drug Master File
EDQM	European Directorate for the Quality of Medicines
EMR	Exclusive Marketing Rights
ERP	Enterprise Resource Planning
EU	European Union
EVA	Economic Value Added
FCCB	Foreign Currency Convertible Bonds
FDA	Federal Drug Administration
FDF	Finished Dosage Form
FDI	Foreign Direct Investment
FY	Financial Year
FYE	Financial Year Ending
GATS	General Agreement on Trade Related Services
GATT	General Agreement on Trade and Tariffs
HMO	Health Maintenance Organization
HMR	Hoechst Marrion Roussel
HPB	Health Protection Branch
HPFB	Health Products and Food Branch, Canada
ICMR	Indian Council for Medical Research
IDMA	Indian Drug Manufacturers Association

IICT	Indian Institute of Chemical Technology
IHC	Inspectorate of Healthcare (Netherlands)
IMB	Irish Medicines Board
IND	Investigative New Drug Application
INDA	Investigative New Drug Application
IP	Intellectual Property
IPA	Indian Pharmaceutical Alliance
IPR	Intellectual Property Rights
JV	Joint Venture
JVC	Joint Venture Company
MCA	Medical Control Agency
MCC	Medicines Control Council (South Africa)
MHRA	Medicine and Health Regulatory Agency
MCO	Managed Care Organization
MVA	Market Value Added
NAFTA	North American Free Trade Agreement
NAM	National Agency for Medicines (Finland)
NCE	New Chemical Entity
NCL	National Chemical Laboratories
NDDS	Novel Drug Delivery Systems
NDS	New Drug Submission
NME	New Molecular Entity
NPIL	Nicholas Piramal India Limited
NPPA	National Pharmaceutical Pricing Authority
OPPI	Organization of Pharmaceutical Producers of India
PAT	Profit After Tax
PBM	Pharmacy Benefit Management
PDA	Provincial Drug Administration (China)

PEPFAR	President's Emergency Program For AIDS Relief
PFI	Pharmaceutical Formulation Ingredients
PhRMA	Pharmaceutical Research and Manufacturers of America
R&D	Research and Development
ROCE	Return on Capital Employed
RONW	Return on Net Worth
SCM	Supply Chain Management
SIDC	State Institute for Drug Control (Czech Republic)
SNDA	Supplementary New Drug Application
SNDS	Supplemental New Drug Submission
SPARC	Sun Pharma Advanced Research Center
TGA	Therapeutic Goods Administration
TPD	Therapeutic Products Directorate (Canada)
TQM	Total Quality Management
TRIMS	Trade Related Investment Measures
TRIPS	Trade Related Intellectual Property Rights
UNIDO	United Nations Industrial Development Organization
WHO	World Health Organization
WTO	World Trade Organization

Chapter One

Compete or Forfiet !

The world pharmaceutical industry has been changing radically over the past few years. While the great divide in terms of the first world and the third world continues, the process of globalization is ushering in a new era of change where the participation by the second world (developing countries) and consequently their share is increasing slowly but surely for the past few years. This trend is likely to accelerate in the coming years. Consider these reasons for example:

- Healthcare costs are continuously under attack from the general public, governments of virtually every country and NGOs leading to pricing pressures and reduced margins.
- Weakening product pipelines, lower research productivity and ever-escalating costs of research and development activity.
- Number of blockbuster drugs losing their market exclusivities due to patent expiries.
- Increasing genericization as governments and payers are encouraging the use of generics in place of brand name drugs to cut down the healthcare costs in virtually every country.

Flatten or Flat Out!

The 650-billion dollar world pharmaceutical industry is slowly but certainly getting flattened. The first world countries – North America, Western Europe and Japan who account for a mere 16 per cent of world population have been accounting for over 85 per cent of world pharmaceutical production (and even consumption to a slightly lesser extent) for a long time now. That is changing, albeit slowly. What is responsible for this dramatic and significant change? The forces that are responsible for globalization are also responsible for making the pharmaceutical world flatter than ever before. And then there are some others specific to the pharmaceutical world.

Consider the forces that are shaping globalization. Thomas L. Friedman in his recent absorbing and insightful book *The World is Flat*, details the forces cogently. He lists ten forces that are shaping the process of globalization as we are experiencing to day and these are: ***The fall of the Berlin Wall on 11/8/89; Netscape Going Public on 8/9/95; Workflow Software; Open-Sourcing; Out-Sourcing; Off-shoring; Supply-Chaining; In Sourcing; In-forming; and The Steroids (Digital, Mobile, and Virtual – Anywhere, Everywhere Connectivity).***

Apart from these forces that are reshaping the world that we live in today, which is getting flattened (Thomas Friedman's book was the first to deal with the subject so succinctly), there are three more major forces or factors that are contributing the flattening of the pharmaceutical world. Consider these for example:

First, The Indian Patents Act of 1970 has played a vital role in helping the fledgling Indian pharmaceutical industry enhance the key competencies and enabled its proactive and progressive entrepreneurs achieve the world-class standards in organic synthesis and contract research. While the 1970 Indian Patents Act gave its pharmaceutical industry the time to nurture, its timely amendment of 2005 provided the ambitious players access to the lucrative markets of the first world. This is evident from the fact that Indian Pharma industry is poised to garner a third of the generic market and file one-third of the 500 anticipated ANDAs by next year. Indian

Pharma companies have already accounted for 25 per cent of the DMF submissions in the US.

Secondly, The Hatch-Waxman Act of 1984 simplified the FDA approval process of generic drugs. This and the subsequent cost-containment strategies and initiatives in healthcare by the US government have propelled the growth of the generic drug industry and helped in levelling the playing field. A number of generic drug manufacturers from the third world too were able to penetrate the remunerative US generic drug industry.

Thirdly, The Entrepreneurs who would level the playing field rather than waiting for it to be leveled have accelerated the flattening process. You would find useful strategic insights in this book – ***Compete or Forfeit,*** which describes the strategic planning process of some of the leading players in the Indian pharmaceutical industry who played an important part in levelling the playing field.

The New Competition - Newton's third law of motion that every action has an equal and opposite reaction is also applicable to the law of competition. Otherwise how do you explain the Para IV filings and the Authorized Generics?

The New Competition is best visualized in an old African Proverb:

> Every morning in Africa, a gazelle wakes up
> It knows it must run faster than the fastest lion or it will be killed
> Every morning a lion wakes up
> It knows it must outrun the slowest gazelle or it will starve to death
> It doesn't matter whether you are lion or gazelle
> When the Sun comes up, you better start running.

The race has begun and it is rather perpetual. The choice too is clear for there is only one choice. You have got to be a flattener to succeed in the new world economic order. You cannot wait for the field to get leveled or flattened. You have got to level it or flatten it for yourself. The message therefore is – Flatten or Flat Out!

Are you Leveling the Playing Field?

The pharmaceutical world is not flat. Not yet. Only three regions – North America, Europe (Western), and Japan which inhabit a mere 15 per cent of world population account for over 83 per cent of world pharmaceutical market. This is however, changing. A small number of entrepreneurial wizards who are hell-bent on leveling the playing field have been working hard to flatten the pharmaceutical world in myriad number of ways – mergers, acquisitions, filing of DMFs, ANDAs, strategic alliances, continuously upgrading their competencies to reach the critical mass – to stay competitive in the new economic order and a globalized market place. The key question is are you levelling the playing field or waiting for the field to be levelled?

Compete of Forfeit the story of a small of bunch of flatteners (about a dozen) and eighteen other firms who are followers or early adopters of these flatteners from India, and these are determined to flatten the pharmaceutical world by creating a world class technological and manufacturing infrastructure, and research and development capabilities. While the origin or roots of these champion-entrepreneurs is the Indian subcontinent, their strategic vision is not restricted to any one nation or region. Their mindset, outlook and business practices transcend the geographical borders making the world seamless. And therefore, all the elements of their strategies are applicable to all aspiring companies who want to enhance their competitiveness and are raring to compete, wherever they are situated be it China, Latin America, Africa, Russia or Asia.

Compete or Forfeit presents a detailed analysis of thirty companies some of whom have started proactively to enhance their competitive quotient to stay ahead of competition in the globalized Pharma world and others who became early adaptors and started improving their competitiveness. All of them have one thing in common - a clear vision of, which spaces they are competing for, what they need to do and whom they need to benchmark.

Compete or Forfeit is also a kind of progress report of the game plans and their outcomes. The book thus acts as a validation of this process of leveling-the-playing field and presents evidence that it is possible as demonstrated by these flatteners or levellers whose dogged pursuit is paying them very rich dividends. Consider their gains and contributions. Each of these thirty companies has achieved appreciable progress and is on course to realize their aspirations. Here's a sneak preview of some of their achievements. These thirty companies account for :

- Over 95 per cent of all US FDA approved manufacturing facilities
- Over 90 per cent of all manufacturing facilities that have approvals of leading international regulatory authorities such as UK MHRA, ANVISA of Brazil. TPD of Canada, MCC of South Africa, and others
- Over 95 per cent of all ANDAs and DMFs filed with US FDA
- Over 95 per cent of all International product registrations
- Over 80 per cent of all APIs manufactured in the country
- Over 95 per cent of all overseas acquisitions made by Indian pharmaceutical companies
- Over 90 per cent of all strategic alliances entered with international players across the Pharma value chain
- Over 80 per cent of all exports made to regulated markets
- Over 70 per cent of all exports made to semi-regulated markets

These are just a few indicators of what their strategic thrust has achieved. Just a few – about a dozen Indian drug majors and around eighteen followers achieved a major part of this. In all, slightly over thirty Indian pharmaceutical companies accounted for about 80 per cent or more of the total progress that has been achieved during the last six to seven years after the Indian government joined the WTO. That is what makes it more important and relevant to study the common thread that is running through their elements of a winning strategy.

The lessons one could learn from the experiences of and the success stories of pharmaceutical industry in this region would be valuable to pharmaceutical executives in the emerging economies as well as the developing economies, as the challenges and opportunities the new world economic order under the WTO regime offers, are similar in nature. The only elements that are dissimilar are the capabilities and the state or level of the current socio-economic situations between nations in these regions. But then, taking the bull of change by its horns can change these!

The discerning observer will certainly see a common thread running through their activities and outcomes and identify core elements of a strategy that can be replicated elsewhere. The case of the Indian pharmaceutical industry clearly shows that in the emerging Pharma space in the post-WTO scenario belongs to those who can build their competitive quotient (CQ).

That is what makes it more important and relevant to study the common thread that is running through their elements of a winning strategy. The book is structured into twelve chapters. Chapters one to four present an introduction and an overview of the world pharmaceutical industry and the changing scenario and an outline of competitive strategies being formulated and executed by the thirty Indian pharmaceutical companies of various sizes large, mid-cap and small competing in the three major, emerging and rapidly growing competitive spaces – innovation-led space, International generics space, and Custom Research and Contract Manufacturing space (CRAMS). Further, chapters five to twelve detail the winning game plans of these companies and attempt at unveiling the common thread of the grand strategy that differentiates these companies from the rest. The aim of these eight chapters is to present the readers in crisp, evidence based strategy to become and stay competitive in the hypercompetitive world of Pharma. To get to the roots of what it takes to succeed in the pharmaceutical market place in the era of globalization. The ten elements of the winning strategy that run through the game plans of all these thirty companies (strategic vision, reaching the critical mass, marketing focus, technology focus, integrating strategically, research focus, building intellectual capital, internationalization of business, alliance-attractiveness, and operational excellence) are discussed in twelve chapters:

1. Compete or Forfeit!
2. Brave New World of Pharma!
3. WTO and Pharmaceutical Industry
4. Competing for WTO Era: The Indian Experience
5. Strategic Focus
6. Critical Mass
7. Marketing Focus
8. Technology Focus
9. Research Focus
10. Global Mindset
11. Winners and Spectators
12. Winners' Checklist

While the book presents the case studies and analyses based on the Indian experience in improving the competitive quotient of pharmaceutical companies aspiring to succeed in the fiercely competitive pharmaceutical market place in a globalized world, the principles discussed and presented have universal applicability. They would be useful for everyone irrespective of geographical origin. It is axiomatic whether you are exploring international markets or not, you need to develop world class capabilities, because other world class companies from international markets are competing in your home market whether you like it or not. A global mindset is essential to survive and grow in the new economic order of globalization. That leaves us with two choices in this binary age. Compete or forfeit? It is not a dilemma. It is a choice. And it is mutually exclusive for if one is not competing he or she is certainly forfeiting.

Make the crucial decision now. Compete or Forfeit!

Chapter Two

The Brave New World of Pharma!

Welcome to the brave new world of Pharma.

Welcome to the brave new world of Pharma. The world where competition is not restricted to few days or weeks like the biggest sporting events be it Wimbledon, NBA National Championships, World Cup or even the biggest of them all - the Olympics – all of which are conducted with a periodicity of one to four-years. The competition in world pharmaceutical industry is 24×7 without a respite.

The world that is changing radically where competition is so intense that the little Davids of world pharmaceutical industry are taking on the Goliaths of the big Pharma with their paratroopers and patent challenges. The dramatic developments and advances that the biotechnology and life sciences are making in the field of healthcare makes the famous science fiction writers of yesteryears like – H G Wells, Jules Verne, Isaac Asimov look like science reporters (of the future) – making their predictions a reality!

Today's Pharma world offers tremendous opportunities to its inhabitants like Nature does to all its species. And hence the law of nature – that it is not the fittest or the fastest or the strongest of the species that survive, but the ones with the highest degree of adaptability – is applicable to pharmaceutical competitive scenario. How else can you explain the drug companies whose total turnover is less than the cost of developing a single drug from concept to commercialization of close to one billion dollars venturing into discovery research?

The brave new world of Pharma offers more to the innovative, and entrepreneurial, and the ones with initiative. Their old business models are deconstructed giving place to the new creating new opportunities in the process. The new competitive spaces are – innovative or brand-name drug space which is the most lucrative off all, the generics space generating a huge opportunity as the blockbusters of yesterday lose their market exclusivity and CRAMS space opening up a whole new planet of CROs and CMOs.

The US $ 650 billion dollar world pharmaceutical industry is highly polarized with nations the account for a mere 13 per cent of the population account contributing to over 80 per cent of the pharmaceutical output in the world in 2005. The generic drug industry thanks to the Hatch Waxman Act of 1984 in the US paving the way for faster genericization and the cost-containment strategies of governments of other regulated markets, has started to level the field for about twenty years and all that toil is bearing fruits now. Consider for example the fact that generic versions accounted for a massive 70 per cent of all the drugs listed in the 2005 Orange Book by US FDA.

The health care industry worldwide is undergoing a radical change. Under pressure from cost containment programs in virtually every market, the pharmaceutical industry has been forced to act, or rather react.

Companies in the West, which account for almost two-thirds of the world pharma market have reacted to the new tougher times in a variety of ways. Many have slashed costs by cutting staff. Some have divested unrelated businesses outside their core competencies. The more privileged blue chip companies have joined the scramble for merger partners or take-over targets. The once gentlemanly industry, in which hostile deals were virtually unknown, has turned vicious. What are the main reasons for these cataclysmic changes? Consider these:

- The world's leading pharmaceutical companies in the West had been achieving 15 to 20 per cent increases in profits each year during much of the 1980s. However, in the 1990s, their profits have been dwindling due to the open revolt of the people over the high cost of medicines. In the new millennium the growth rates continue to plummet. Valued at US $ 602 billion in 2005, the world pharmaceutical industry grew at only 6 per cent.
- In the US, Health Maintenance Organizations (HMOs), which are like private national health plans and Pharmacy Benefit Managers (PBMs), who buy drugs in bulk and distribute them mostly through the mail to members of their programs have been driving hard bargains. Result? Sharply reduced profit margins.
- In Europe too, state health plans have also demanded and received price reductions. In 1993, after Germany passed health care reform, the government spent 20 per cent less on drugs than in the year before. And containing healthcare costs is becoming an unending priority leading to increase in the usage of generics.

Further more, many of the products that fueled the strong growth of the yesteryears are reaching the end of the patent protection. In 2006 alone for example drugs with a 2005 sales value of US $ 21.2 billion would lose their market exclusivity due to patents expiry. When patents expire, generic brands rush in with low cost substitutes that may cost a mere tenth of the original. Consider these for example:

- Upjohn's Xanax, went off patent in 1993 and sales dropped from $ 624 million to $ 343 million within a year.
- Merck's best selling cardiovascular brand - Vasotec lost 65 per cent share of its prescriptions within six months of its patent expiry in 2000. Sales dropped from $ 2.31 billion in 1999 to 1.70 billion in 2000.

- The most drastic decline of all patent-expired blockbusters was probably of Eli Lilly's Prozac, the most widely known antidepressant in the world. Prozac lost two-thirds of its prescriptions in just one month after its patent expired in 2001.
- In 2003 Paxil, the antidepressant blockbuster of Glaxo SmithKline lost 40 per cent of its sales due to its US patent expiry.
- More recently Zocor, the cholesterol-reducing blockbuster drug of Merck that generated about sales of US $ 5.2 billion in 2004 and $ 4.38 billion in 2005 is going off patent in 2006. It is going to lose close to $ 4 billion in sales by 2010, estimate the analysts at Datamonitor.

In addition, pharmaceutical companies in recent years have not been coming up with new drugs to replace the high profit drugs going off-patent. Instead of producing breakthrough drugs to treat ailments such as AIDS, cancer and Alzheimer's Disease, they have been turning out more drugs that copy products already on the market. These are mere molecular manipulations and patentable innovations resulting in products with no significant therapeutic advantages. How else can you explain the development of so many fluro-quinolones, ace-inhibitors, SSRI agents etc?

The panacea of the moment is merger – the hope that bigger can be better. The new companies (post-merger), take the best of both firms and slash costs, mainly by cutting staff. Until pharmaceutical companies come up with breakthrough research products, they have to find other means for earnings and growth. One method is through mergers and acquisitions. During the last five years (2001-5) alone there were about 1,240 deals involving over 325 billion US dollars. Of those top 10 acquisitions, about six happened in the US. Novartis made three of those top ten acquisitions. The top ten acquisitions in 2005 included 4 European, 3 US, 2 Japanese and one Israeli firm with a total deal value of US $ 42.62 billion. Three of these top ten acquisitions were by the generic drug firms (Table 2.1). Truly generics are consolidating.

Table 2.1 Top Ten Acquisitions in 2005

	Acquirer	Acquisition Target	Deal Value US $ billion
1.	Sankyo Co (Japan)	Daiichi Pharmaceutical Corp (Japan)	7.70
2.	Teva (Israel)	Ivax Corp (US)	7.40
3.	Novartis (Switzerland)	Chiron Corp (US) (50% stake)	5.78
4.	Abraxis Bioscience (US) (formerly APP)	American Bioscience	4.17
5.	Allergan Inc (US)	Inamed (US)	3.10
6.	Sandoz– Novartis AG (Switzerland)	Eon Labs (US)	2.60
7.	Nycomed (Finland)	Nycomed Holding (Finland)	2.27
8.	Amgen (US)	Abgenix (US)	2.20
9.	Sandoz-Novartis AG (Switzerland)	Hexal Ag (Germany)	5.28
10.	Dainippon	Sumitomo Pharmaceuticals (Japan) Pharmaceuticals (Japan)	2.12

All these mergers will perhaps make pharmaceuticals the most international amongst major industries. The top ten drug companies in 1995 included five US, two British, one Swiss, one German, and one Swedish–American. The top ten companies ten years later in 2005 included six US, two British, one Swiss and one French.

The clear implication of all these mergers and acquisitions is that consolidation within the industry has only just begun. The internationally known consultancy firm, Baring Securities suggested in 1999 that within five years, the top ten pharmaceutical companies would control over 60 per cent of the world's pharmaceutical market. While they may not be accurate in their prediction, the trend of consolidation is certainly moving in that direction. The top ten drug companies accounted for 41.5 per cent of the total world pharmaceutical sales in 2005. The underlying motivation for this consolidation is not market share *per se*, but cost reduction.

The key criteria to be successful and competitive in the pharmaceutical industry are to have geographical reach, a strong product portfolio, a critical mass for R&D and financial strength.

The new giants are hoping to get many of their new products from biotech boutiques that have sprung up in the past decade particularly in the US. Bigger drug companies have been making deals with research-intensive firms to get marketing rights to the drugs they are developing.

Science Fiction Turning into a Reality

Ever since Watson and Crick discovered the double-helix structure of the DNA the excitement of the future prospects of biotechnology was palpable. Freeman Dyson prophetically announced that the dominant science in the twenty-first century would be biology. Dr. Francis Collins, director of US National Institute for Human Genome Research made predictions in the new millennium regarding the possibilities of genomic innovations within the next forty years:

- Expansion of molecular diagnostic tests
- Predictive tests for more than 20 genetic diseases
- Growth in number of molecular targeted therapies
- Pharmacogenomic markers tracking patients' responses to drugs
- New imaging probes to assess body functions
- Testing of populations for genotypes and creation of databases
- Tailored drugs for diabetes, hypertension, cancer and other chronic diseases
- Full applications of regenerative medicine (somatic cells for auto-grafts)
- Gene replacement therapy
- Characterization of genes involved in aging and clinical means to extend human life
- Comprehensive genomics based healthcare

Sounds like science fiction? We are already in this brave new world of the big Pharma and biotech convergence. What will be the impact of all these on pharmaceutical industry? The boundaries between biology and pharmaceutical sciences are gradually dissolving. This is evident from the ever-increasing number of alliances, tie-ups, mergers and acquisitions between the big Pharma and biotech companies. The number of research projects involving Pharma and biotech are also increasing rapidly.

Pharmaceutical Market – A Global Map

Over 80 per cent of the world's population lives in developing countries, yet their share of the global output is a mere 18 per cent. As a group, these countries still have a long way to go before they are fully integrated with the world economy.

The three largest markets: North America, Europe and Japan represent over 80 per cent of world pharmaceutical market while they account for a mere 13 per cent of the world population (Table 2.2).

Table 2.2 Population and Pharmaceutical Production

Country/Region	Share of Production	Share of Population
North America	30.9	4
Europe	30.4	7
Japan	20.9	2
Total	**82.2**	**13**
Rest of the World	**17.8**	**87**

Although the industry itself only began to assume importance after the Second World War, several of the world's major pharmaceutical companies can trace their lineage back to the nineteenth century. Roughly 60 countries now produce at least $ 100 million worth of pharmaceuticals each year.

The bulk of the world's pharmaceuticals are manufactured in a very few industrialized countries. The pattern of drug consumption is much the same: over three-quarters of all medicines are sold in industrialized countries.

Pharmaceuticals have clearly acquired an international character, but the industry is still not a global one, in the same sense as textiles, food processing or even steel.

The contrasts are equally great when the attention turns from countries to firms. Less than 50 multinationals account for over three-fourths of world's production and exports each year.

The top ten pharmaceutical companies in the world accounted for a whopping US $ 249.64 billion (44 per cent of world pharmaceutical sales) in 2005 (Table 2.3).

The largest among these in 2005 was Pfizer. The company's revenues in 2005 were $ 44.28 billion, an amount exceeding the entire pharmaceutical production of Latin America, Africa, India and China in that year.

Table 2.3 Top pharmaceutical companies — 2005 sales reflecting earlier mergers

Company	Country	$ Billion
1. Pfizer	USA	44.28
2. Glaxo SmithKline	UK	33.96
3. Sanofi-Aventis	France	32.34
4. Novartis	Switzerland	24.96
5. Astra Zeneca	UK	23.95
6. Johnson & Johnson	USA	22.32
7. Merck	USA	22.01
8. Wyeth	USA	15.32
9. Bristol Myers Squibb	USA	15.25
10. Eli Lilly	USA	15.25
	Total	**249.64**

The variety of products, which the industry produces, is another important feature. About 20,000 products are sold in large markets such as the United States and Japan. The number of products marketed in large developing countries like Brazil, India, China, South Korea and Mexico are over 10,000. Such a degree of product proliferation depends not only on product characteristics, but also on channels and methods of distribution, aspects of national policy and the promotional campaigns.

Not surprisingly, therefore, several products are available in each country to treat a particular ailment. However, not all are of equal importance. A single product may account for as much as a quarter of total sales in that segment.

Usually, the five largest suppliers may account for two-thirds or more of the domestic market. For certain diseases, the same products dominate markets throughout the world.

These characteristics, though few, suffice to attest to the industry's diversity and to suggest generalizations about important issues like public policy, corporate strategy and cost structures etc. The manufacturers in the pharmaceutical industry can be broadly classified into three categories:

1. Large, integrated corporations
2. Innovative companies
3. Imitative firms

Integrated Corporations

The integrated corporations are multinationals distinguishable in several ways. Firstly, they are exceptionally large; with annual sales of over $1 billion. Secondly, they place particularly high emphasis on product development, generating the New Molecular Entities (NMEs). Thirdly, these firms adhere to several well-defined methods of operation. They secure patents for their inventions at a global level. They market and distribute their products in a number of countries through subsidiaries or licensees. They purchase intermediate inputs only from approved vendors. They market their products under brand names and compete predominantly in the private market.

Innovative Companies

Innovative companies are easily distinguished from integrated companies. Annual sales of these companies are comparatively modest ranging between $ 300 to 800 million. They may be capable of developing and discovering NMEs. Their revenues are not sufficient to fund the massive research and development activity that drug discovery programs require. Their resources are not adequate to market and distribute their products even if they are able to develop an NME. The innovative firms, therefore, usually resort to licensing arrangements to market their products abroad. Innovative firms also enter into joint venture agreements for clinical research and product registration of their promising new product candidates with specialized developmental research companies or with other innovative and even integrated companies in other countries. Such strategies to overcome resource constraints are becoming increasingly common.

Innovative firms typically produce and market branded versions of patent-expired drugs in developing countries. The lack of significant research or distribution facilities does not mean that the innovative firms are excluded from foreign markets. Many are significant exporters, either selling drugs through their own channels or through international trading houses on the open markets. The logical progression for an innovative firm in the corporate or industrial evolution cycle is to become an integrated corporation. The more progressive innovative firms particularly in developing countries are increasingly advocating stronger protection for IPR.

Imitative Companies

Imitative companies are small in size and are usually family-owned enterprises. As they lack in-house research and developmental capabilities, they utilize technological and scientific knowledge developed by others to manufacture their products. The drugs they produce are patent-expired and they compete in the highly price sensitive markets. They often focus on specific regions and on highly price sensitive segments like institutional and tender business.

New Breed of Research Firms

There is a new group of firms emerging in the early 1990s consisting of small and medium-sized companies engaged in research-intensive activities. They are founded in order to exploit a single or smaller number of patents for the development of a unique drug.

The most important of these firms are engaged in genetic engineering. The drugs they produce are not usually NMEs, since they are generally identical, or very similar to substances, which occur naturally in the body. The best known of these firms are Biogen, Biotech and Genetech. All were founded at an early stage of product development as joint ventures between academic centers, venture capital entrepreneurs and integrated companies. Such firms typically incur operational losses at the early stages of operations since their research expenditures exceed revenues earned from royalties. A medium size research company typically would have a minimum of $ 100 million in operating revenues and a research expenditure of about 50 per cent.

These modern biotechnology firms may launch patented products at home and conclude licensing arrangements for overseas markets. Most become acquisition targets once their particular product is established in major markets. As a result, many are now becoming more closely integrated with the mainstream integrated pharmaceutical firms.

Out is *In*, In is *Out*!

What is the new panacea or the mantra for solving all the problems of reducing margins, escalating costs, falling productivities? Outsourcing of course! Outsourcing seems to be certainly in! Consequently in-sourcing (making one's own) of be it APIs, formulations, or even product development seems to be out if it is not cost-effective. Surely the trend seems to be out (sourcing) is in, and in (sourcing) is out!

Ever-escalating costs of research and development, declining levels of R&D productivity, never-ending pressures in containing healthcare costs by respective governments, and rapidly growing competition from generics – all these have been mounting pressure on the innovative drug companies. Hence the strategic recourse to outsourcing.

And the cost savings in outsourcing could be substantial. Whether it is contract research or contract manufacturing one could achieve a cost savings of 50 to 65 per cent by doing them in the Asian countries like

China or India who have been busy in creating a world class scientific and technological infrastructure ever since they opened their gates to WTO, by implementing product patents.

Time is literally money and lot more than that in case of drug discovery. Every day's delay in drug development could mean a potential loss of US $ 800,000 even for a non-blockbuster drug and for a blockbuster drug it could be a lot more, estimate the strategic consultancy firm Mckinsey.

Richard T Clarke, CEO of the 22-billion-dollar global drug major Merck during his recent visit in the first week of June 2006 to India said that his company has decided to outsource 35 per cent of its manufacturing process to countries such as China and India. Merck is targeting a 30 per cent reduction in costs through outsourcing and wants save US $ 1.2 billion in procurement and is restructuring accordingly. Merck, one of the most-admired companies in the world is even prepared to open its celestial gates of research to scientific talent from the developing world. Furthermore, the world's leading pharmaceutical company – Pfizer is aiming to save over US $ 4 billion in the next four years through strategic outsourcing!

Certainly, there is more to outsourcing than cutting down the costs. The five objectives of outsourcing part of research and development activity are:

1. Increase the scientists' time for focusing on key in-house research programs by outsourcing time consuming tasks
2. Control expenditure by reducing costs and optimizing R&D budgets
3. Multiplexing or increasing the ability to handle more projects as outsourcing enables parallel processing
4. Absorb and incorporate rapidly evolving technology at a faster rate
5. Access to a larger and more diverse pool of talent from around the world

The global outsourcing market is estimated to reach a whopping US $ 175 billion by 2010 with the major slice of about 57 per cent going to contract manufacturing of over-the-counter drugs and nutritional products. The opportunities for contract manufacturing of prescription drugs would be around 26 per cent and for contract research about 17 per cent.

While India and China are likely to ride the crest of the outsourcing wave, India does have an edge in the pharmaceutical sector. Consider for example that India has the maximum number of US FDA approved manufacturing facilities (over 104) outside the US. Indian Pharma companies accounted for over 30 per cent of all DMFs and 25 per cent of all abbreviated new drug applications submitted to US FDA in 2005 and this is likely to go up to 30 per cent of all ANDAs next year – amounting to a staggering 150!

That is the edge in terms of scientific and technological infrastructure, which is crucial for winning the outsourcing race. Even if Indian drug companies capture a 10 per cent share of the rapidly growing outsourcing business it would be much larger than the domestic industry. When you consider that a number of the Indian drug majors from whom leading pharma MNCs are outsourcing, are themselves outsourcing part of their requirements from smaller Indian companies to control costs; you know that outsourcing has arrived! The way to go seems to point to the fact that – Out is 'In' - and 'In' is out!

Demographic Effects

Pharmaceutical markets are being reshaped by two types of demographic trends – rates of population growth and changes in the age structure. Most countries fall clearly into either of the two groups, depending on the overall demographic pattern. In one group are countries the total population is constant or declining, while the median age is rising. In another group are countries experiencing a rapid increase in population although the median age is low and not increasing. Consider these facts:

- Population of many industrial countries is stagnating or is declining. Consequently, the aging process will be quite rapid in these countries. About half-of-all German population will be over 50 years old by 2010. The population of Canada, Italy and Japan are younger but aging rapidly.

- Aging process will be the fastest in a number of developing countries. While the share of the elderly and those over 45 will not rise significantly, the absolute numbers will soon exceed the totals for most industrialized nations. For example, by 2010 the number of Chinese over 65 exceed the total population of Western Europe today.
- In some of the developing countries like Kenya, Nigeria and Zaire the median age in 2010 will be less than half of the average in industrialized countries; In some cases the average age would be below 20 years.

Implications of Changing Demographics

These demographic trends are altering important features of drug markets. The frequency of drug consumption is rising most rapidly in markets where the population is aging. At the same time the pattern of consumption is changing. Chronic and degenerative diseases are prevalent after the age of 50 and are dominant among those over 60 years. The markets for medicines to treat these diseases are therefore growing.

The effects are different in the developing countries, where the population is young and increasing. Young people are subject to acute or infectious ailments. The need for drugs is particularly great among those under five years of age, to sustain vaccination programs against childhood diseases, prevention and treatment of vitamin and mineral deficiencies and treatment of cough and cold associated with infections. The unfavorable economic and social conditions, which prevail in many developing countries in turn result in poor hygiene and sanitation, increase the need for such drugs in this age group.

These demographic shifts are already changing the way governments influence the pattern of consumption. Over three-fourths of all drugs purchased in most developing countries are obtained through private rather than public channels. The increasing populations in these countries are unlikely to reverse this trend of inadequate systems of public support for health care in the foreseeable future. Regulators in industrialized countries too, are searching for ways to contain the costs of public health care and have chosen to focus on cost-effective reimbursement programs. The reasons for this decision are political as well as economic.

This regulatory regime in industrialized countries will definitely slow the growth of consumption, though the long-term effects may not be as severe as drug companies fear. Health authorities will have to search for significant savings in other areas of their budgets because spending on drugs accounts for only 8 to 15 per cent of the health care expenditure in industrialized countries. Eventually, the industry could even see its share of public health care spending rise, although the total amounts allocated for reimbursement programs will decline. This would be due to a stringent reduction in hospitalization, with its attendant high costs, and a preference for outpatient drug therapies, which are far cheaper.

How will these demographic trends and changing policies affect global markets? The general consensus is that the demand for drugs will grow rapidly. The share of the developing countries in the world market could also rise. This is due to the significant increases in populations of the developing countries. The second reason is the possibility of deceleration of sales in industrialized countries due to increasing generic substitutions, as governments are scaling back the reimbursement programs. While saying this, the graying of the population in industrialized nations with higher buying capacities and the impact of recent changes like Medicare D for greater coverage of the senior citizens under the health plans would be a counterbalancing factor, tending to retain the market share of the first world.

Demographics and Drug Consumption

Drug consumption among the elderly on the contrary is much lower in developing countries as their income levels are much lower. The frequency of drug consumption among the elderly, therefore, is substantially lower in developing countries as compared to developed countries.

Per capita sales of pharmaceuticals rose steadily from 1975 to 1984 in both industrialized countries and developing countries alike. Since then, however, the increment has been disproportionately higher in the industrialized world. Developing countries accounted for about 20 to 23 per cent of world sales in each year during 1975–84. Their share, however, has steadily fallen in later years and by 1990, less than 15 per cent of all pharmaceuticals were sold in developing countries. Developed countries accounted for the lion's share of 85 per cent. Even today the share of the developing countries is hovering around only around 17 per cent.

It is important to note that population increases, however rapid, do not by themselves lead to a substantial growth in pharmaceutical markets. Other factors such as income growth, higher priority for health care by governments, literacy levels and consequent awareness and importance attached to personal health are probably more important determinants.

Generic Explosion in the US

The generic pharmaceutical industry has seen many positive changes during the past twenty years. Generics in the US for example account for over half of all the prescriptions written in the US, the world's largest generic drug market accounting for close to half of all generic formulations sold.

The US market for generics is by far the largest. Valued at $ 6.5 billion in 1997, the generics have grown to a 40-billion large market in 2005. And the market is primed for even more spectacular growth. Three major forces are driving this positive trend. First, the patent expirations of blockbuster drugs in the next few years, and secondly, the continuing pressure of managed care and other cost-containment programs in the United States and international markets. The third driving force is the higher number of prescriptions filled with less-expensive generic alternatives. The new Medicare-D Program is a further boost to the increasing trend of generic prescriptions. In 2005 generics accounted for over 54 per cent of all prescriptions written and overtook the brand-name drug prescriptions for the first time.

A wide range of drugs continue to lose their market exclusivity due to patent expiry and most of these drugs are of great interest to the generic manufacturers. The extent and attraction of the generic market can be gauged when even the discoverers of these products are showing eagerness to join the generics bandwagon before generic manufacturers file their Abbreviated New Drug Applications (ANDAs).

Health care cost-containment is another reason. The whole issue of pricing has played a major role. HMOs, Managed Care Organizations (MCOs) and PBMs are mainly responsible for this acceleration of the already changing trends of prescription changes from branded to generic drugs.

In the past, under the health care insurance system, the user paid the fees and got the reimbursement from the insurer. There was no major incentive for health care deliverers, such as physicians and hospitals, to keep health care costs down.

Under the capitated system of health care, however, this is changing rather rapidly. MCOs, under the present system typically charge a flat fee upfront, for each insured person. With a low additional payment, they then provide all treatment. Thus MCOs have a vital interest in keeping down the use of expensive diagnostic and treatment procedures.

MCOs, in addition are showing a lot of interest in studying and adopting strategies to prevent morbidity in the insured persons. Pharmaco-economic studies too are increasingly being employed to examine the cost-effectiveness of pharmaceutical usage vis-à-vis other forms of treatment. Governments too are encouraging the use of generics.

As cost pressures become more acute and more blockbuster products come off patent over the next few years, the size of the North American generic market is set to expand sharply. Here is how some companies are preparing to meet the challenges of the future:

- Some of the leading Indian pharmaceutical companies like Ranbaxy, Lupin, Wockhardt, Dr. Reddy's Laboratories, Sun Pharma, Cipla and Glenmark are either entering into strategic alliances and are continuously acquiring off-shore manufacturing bases and brands to exploit the big opportunities that the American generics market has to offer.

- In addition some of the large and mid-cap companies Nicholas Piramal, Shasun, Divi's Labs and others have built up world class infrastructure for manufacturing and research and development and are entering into strategic tie-ups with international drug majors and generic companies for supplying APIs, FDFs, custom synthesis, and custom research – in fact across the whole spectrum of the Pharma value chain.

The global health care industry is undergoing a period of radical change, due to imposition of price control requirements. The major pharmaceutical companies are consolidating in order to cut costs and increase market share of ethical brands, whilst the generics market is expanding. The recent spate of mergers, acquisitions and genericization moves testify this.

Patent expiry of ethical products results in an extraordinarily rapid fall in market share. Generic competition is both extremely rapid and aggressive in price. Indian companies over the years achieved the cost advantage as compared to their western counterparts and are able to compete for the generic space and CRAMS space.

Generics in the European Union

The European generics market was around US $ 14.5 in 2005 and is expected to grow to $ 21.2 billion by 2010. Germany continues to be the largest generics market in Europe with about $ 6 billion followed by France and UK with around $ 4 and $ 3.2 billion in 2005. The ethical generics accounted for bulk of the sales with 83 per cent and OTC generics accounting for the rest of the 17 per cent. The major growth drivers for the accelerated genericization are patent expiries and cost containment strategies and policies by respective governments in the European Union. The outlook for generics continues to be bright in terms of growth and at the same time they are likely to face more pricing pressures than ever before, squeezing the margins.

Generics in Japan

The generics market is growing in Japan. The generics market is estimated was around US $ 3 billion in 2005. It is likely to grow faster than before as the country's MHLW (Ministry of Health and Labor Welfare) is embarking on a policy of reforms of health insurance and is encouraging generic prescriptions to contain increasing healthcare costs. The generics currently account for about 5.2 per cent of prescription sales by value and about 16.4 per cent in terms of volume.

Generic Drug Industry Prospects

The world market for generics was estimated to be around US $ 60 billion in 2005. It is expected to grow at 12 – 14 per cent per annum over the next four to five years for as many as 39 major drugs will go off patents by 2009 losing the branded industry an estimated $ 40 billion. The generic market is likely to reach a whopping US $ 90 billion by 2010. The generic industry in the world is consolidating in a significant way to exploit the big opportunity.

Changing Scenario

The pharmaceutical companies have to be global in a much tougher market. What Robert C. Holmes, Executive Director for Strategic Planning and Management at Astra Merck, presented a few years ago on the changing scenario of the drug industry holds good even today reminding us all once again that change is the only constant factor.

> The drug industry had been a very profitable gentleman's club. All could make money and there was no pressure on prices. The doctors determined the treatment. Then came the health care debate and a revolt against double-digit inflation. The whole industry's dynamics changed. It became more competitive. Now the people are very conscious of costs and the consumer is involved. So to cut costs health organizations, for example, look at the 12 ACE inhibitors, which control blood flow and pressure and may be put just two on the formulary and then negotiate the price of these two with the respective pharmaceutical companies. In the 1980s all 12 could sell profitably. The market for secondary products is disappearing. You have to be the first or second to the market. A second generation of somewhat better drugs that have fewer side effects

but are six times as expensive as the ACE inhibitors came to market in the 1990s with a much reduced potential. Until the 1980's a "me-too" drug could be brought out at lower risk than the trailblazer with prospects of selling very well (and with a patent that would last beyond the patent of the first drug). Peak-year sales of a late entrant could run into a billion dollars or more, but today the follow-on drugs best year would not exceed $ 500 million.

Survival of the Fittest

The competitive scenario is getting tougher today. It once again proves the old adage that *when the going gets tough, the tough get going.* The whole industry whether it is research based pharmaceutical industry or the generic industry seems to be seriously in a consolidating mode. Six generic companies catapulted their way into the top fifty pharmaceutical companies in 2005 and Teva the generic drug major made it to the top ten. The competing spaces are getting blurred and overlapped. Brand name drugs are entering the generic space through their own generic arms like Novartis with Sandoz, Pfizer with Greenstone and the generic companies are launching their own-patented products. The law of nature and the principle of evolution are applicable rather universally - whether it's a real jungle or concrete jungle, whether it is a case of evolution of a species or evolution of business - only the fittest survive!

A Look into the Crystal Ball

While it is extremely difficult to predict the exact future of the world pharmaceutical industry, a careful study of the past fifteen years reveals a clear enough picture of what is most likely to happen in the foreseeable future. Consider these ten trends:

1. The frenetic pace of change in the pharmaceutical industry worldwide will continue. The governments in industrialized countries will maintain the pressure to contain the health care costs. The pharmaceutical industries in these countries therefore will remain under severe pressure for margins.
2. The use of generics will increase in these countries, resulting in lower growth rates for pharmaceutical industry. The increasing use of generics will keep the pharmaceutical cake at a reasonably constant size.

3. The pharmaceutical industry, consequently, will continue to be in a consolidation mode. There will be more mergers and acquisitions. Pressures on margins, the large number of blockbuster drugs going off-patent and inadequate new product pipelines will drive industry towards even more acquisitions and mergers. The last fifteen years have seen over 1,280 mergers and acquisitions worth more than $ 600 billion. It's not over yet; there is more to come.
4. The world pharmaceutical industry is likely to defrag itself consequent to all these mergers and acquisitions. Analysts predict that about twelve to fifteen drug firms are likely to control close to two-thirds of the world pharmaceutical market in the next five to ten years.
5. The present imbalance of 80:20 Rule – the control of eighty per cent of pharmaceutical market by the industrialized triad is likely to tilt in favour of the developing countries. Developing markets, which currently account for only about 20 per cent of the total Pharma market will increase their share to a third by 2010, growing at 15–19 per cent as compared to the average growth rates of 7–8 per cent in the industrialized markets like the US, Europe and Japan.
6. In the coming years the protection for intellectual properties will be much stronger than in the past. Almost all countries with local pharmaceutical industries will join the WTO. Those who do not join will find it extremely difficult to survive the competitive pressures and will not have access to newer drugs.
7. The current biotech revolution will only accelerate and gain momentum further. The research pipeline of biotech companies will be very deep with an unprecedented promise to treat, hitherto-difficult-to-treat diseases. Genomics is another area, which will have a profound impact on the bio-pharmaceutical industry. It may eventually provide remedies for diseases like Parkinson's, Alzheimer's, Cancer, AIDS and other infectious diseases. Robert Thong, pharmaceuticals industry consultant with

Renaissance Worldwide, compares the current situation to the revolution in information technology 15 years ago, which saw a raft of computer giants swept aside by the new and faster kids on the block. He says, "There is a chance for the Microsofts and Netscapes of the pharmaceutical industry to emerge, but we don't know who they are yet!"

8. In addition to mergers and acquisitions, strategic alliances too will be on the increase, particularly in the area of biotechnology and genomic research. Scientists will be able to identify the precise molecular defect responsible for the disease state. They will also be able to develop the magic (molecular) bullet to set the defect right with great precision. These target-specific drug delivery systems will be the engineering marvels of our times. Companies that do not have these capabilities will naturally source the technology that will be needed for their own products to deliver what they promise.

9. In spite of the dramatic new medical advances and the unprecedented progress that the Human Genome Project has made, the rich and poor divide will remain. These advances may not be available to the third world. Those, who need them the most, may not be able to afford them even in the next fifty years.

10. In the past the generic companies used to wait for the patents on brand-name drugs to expire, but now they are being a lot more aggressive and proactive. They are bringing Para IV challenges to exploit the revenue generating opportunities during the 180-day exclusivity. The innovator companies too are adopting defensive strategies like launching their authorized generics and sNDA filings to protect their revenues from brands even after patent expiry. These generic wars are likely to intensify and escalate in the coming years.

Chapter Three
WTO and Pharmaceutical Industry

Pharmaceutical industry is research-driven. And pharmaceutical research is very expensive. It would cost around one billion dollars to develop a single drug from concept to commercialization. Further when you consider that the success rate of developing a drug is only one in five thousand that are screened the inherent risks in pharmaceutical research become clear. The gestation period of drug development too is very long. It takes anywhere between 7 to 10 years to develop and bring a new drug to the market.

That is why pharmaceutical industry in the world's highly regulated markets views the patent system as essential to its business model. An inventor is entitled to a limited period of exclusivity (deemed monopoly) typically twenty years. Such exclusivity permits high prices during which is the patent term; the consequent profit incentives provide the basis for the pharmaceutical industry to invest in the very costly development process that is necessary to bring new drugs to market. Patents, therefore, stimulate investment in scientific and technological development, producing innovations and benefits for society. In fact, the pharmaceutical industry in developed countries mainly US, Western Europe and Japan is primarily responsible for developing new drugs that have helped in increasing the quality of life and life expectancy of large percentages of the world's population.

History of IPR Protection – A Timeline

The history of IPR protection began in 1474 in Venice and the attempts to balance the protection of intellectual property continue even today. There have been many players – the governments, the corporate sectors in various countries, NGOs, social and political activists battling over, negotiating and litigating to achieve the best outcomes in IPR protection from their respective perspectives. Here are the important milestones in the history of IPR protection (Table 3.1).

Table 3.1 History of IPR Protection – A Timeline

Year	IPR Protection Initiatives
1474	The first patent law approved in history in Venice granted the inventors exclusive rights to produce their inventions for a limited period.
1883	Several countries signed the famous *Paris Convention* in Paris with three basic premises to operate in the International Industrial Property Protection: 1. Independence of patents and trademarks 2. Equal treatment for nationals and Foreigners 3. Priority Rights
1884	Paris Convention established an international office to conduct administrative procedures
1886	Revision of Paris Convention in Rome with an objective of protecting literary and artistic works. Creation of another international office. Paris Convention had undergone eight revisions: 1890 Madrid 1900 Brussels 1911 Washington 1925 The Hague 1934 London 1958 Lisbon 1967 Stockholm 1987 Madrid Paris Convention survived both the world wars as well as the creation of the World Trade Organization (WTO) in 1995 and is presently in force.

Table 3.1 *Contd...*

Year	IPR Protection Initiatives
1893	Merged the two international office to form the united office for the protection of intellectual property more commonly known as BIRPI (Bereaux Internatioanux Réunis pour la Protection de la Propriété Intellectuelle). BIPRI gave rise to the World Intellectual Property Rights Organization (WIPO) in 1970 with headquarters in Geneva.
1944	Creation of International Monetary Fund (IMF) and the World Bank (WB) with initial objectives of managing the international monetary system and to finance the projects that could reconstruct the economy of European countries devastated by the war.
1947	Creation of GATT (General Agreement on Tariffs and Trade), a milestone for multilateral negotiations with an objective of diminishing international trade barriers.
	The Rounds between the period 1947-61 played important role in reducing custom duties. 1947 Geneva Round resulted in 45,000 tariff concessions representing half of world trade 1949 Modest tariff reductions 1950-51 Torquay Round 1955-56 Geneva Round 1961-62 Dillon Round 1964-67 The Kennedy Round achieved an average tariff reductions of 35 per cent of industrial products, and modest reductions for agricultural products, and developed anti-dumping code 1973-79 The Tokyo Round formalized a series of agreements regarding: A. Technical barriers to trade B. Government procurement C. Subsidies D. Custom valuations E. Import licenses F. Anti-dumping practices 1986-94 The Uruguay Round, which is the most extensive one that culminated in the creation of World Trade Organization (WTO).
1995	WTO became functional acting as an organ of United Nations (UN) with Geneva as its headquarters.

GATT to WTO

The world economic scenario has been changing radically since the 1980s. After the crash of the 1970s, the world was shaken up by a profound capitalist reform backed up by the informatics and communications revolution. The IT revolution made simultaneous electronic connections between financial markets possible integrating the spatially decentralized productive processes. At the same time, other changes such as privatization, deregulation made the markets more flexible intensifying international competition for private capital. All these created rather phenomenal changes such as:

- Unification of financial markets nationally and internationally enabling the movement of capital rapidly
- Accelerated the formation of regional economic blocks
- Transnational mergers and acquisitions and
- The creation of the Group of Seven countries (G7) to coordinate the largest economies

The resultant new economic order came to be known as globalization making the borders of the nations porous. Technology has made geographical distances redundant. During this period some countries like Japan and some Asian countries enhanced their competitive quotient through clever use of intellectual property system.

United States put considerable pressure to organize The Uruguay Round to discuss issues related to international trade including services and intellectual property rights (IPR). This round focused on harmonizing international trade policies related to IPR and affected a series of national economic and trade policies that define competition rules within countries.

When the Uruguay Round began in 1986, the majority of developing countries did not grant patents for pharmaceutical products. However, over the years this situation changed substantially and many developing countries signed the 1994 GATT, became members of the WTO and implemented IPR protection by changing their national legislations accordingly. WTO had 147 countries as its members in April 2004.

WTO became functional in January 1995 with responsibilities for:

1. Administration of the new multilateral trade agreements
2. Provision of a forum for fresh negotiations
3. Settlement of disputes
4. Surveillance of national trade policies
5. Co-operation with other international bodies in drawing up of economic policies at the global level

The role of the WTO is much more extensive as it administers not only Multilateral Trade Agreements (MTAs) but also General Agreements on Trade-related Services (GATS) and Trade Related Intellectual Property Rights (TRIPS).

TRIPS Agreement and Pharmaceutical Industry

TRIPS Agreement is divided into seven parts composed of 73 articles. Part II contains the most important elements for Public health, especially in relation to access to medicines. The TRIPS Agreement defines the minimum standards in the filed of intellectual property rights that the WTO Member States must incorporate into their legislation. TRIPS has three broad components:

1. Parts I and II (containing Articles 1 to 40) set out the goals, objectives, and standards of IPRs.
2. Parts III, IV, and V (containing Articles 41 to 61) deal with the mechanisms of enforcement of IPRs.
3. Parts VI, and VII (contains Articles 62 to 73) focuses on specific needs of developing countries such as transitional arrangements, technology transfers, technical cooperation and the institutional arrangements of monitoring and review.

Before the TRIPS Agreement, the Paris Convention signatory countries could opt to extend or exclude patent protection for some technological fields, recognizing national autonomy to define the best strategy for social and economic development. After January 1995, WTO Member States lost the autonomy to choose the patent protection regime that would best benefit their social, economic and technological development as they all were required to comply with TRIPS, which meant granting protection to all technological fields, except for the exceptions stated in Article 27.

Articles 27 to 34 (section 5, Part II) of the TRIPS Agreement deal with the standards concerning the availability, scope and use of patents with the main provisions being:

1. Patents shall be available for any inventions whether products or processes in all fields of technology, provided that they are new, involve an inventive step and capable of industrial application
2. The term of protection must be a minimum of 20 years from the date of filing
3. The exclusive rights of the patentees include the right of making, using, offering for sale, selling or importing
4. Limited exceptions for such exclusive rights are possible
5. Compulsory licenses can be granted subject to certain conditions. A compulsory License is an authorization by a government to non-patentees to use the subject matter of a patent without or against the consent of the patentee
6. In case of infringements the burden of proof will be on the alleged infringer rather than on the right-holder

   Pharmaceutical and chemical industries are among those who need the patent protection most because their products are easily copied. The PhRMA (Pharmaceutical Research Manufacturers of America) estimate that they are loosing more than US $ 5 billion annually due to patent infringement in the developing world countries.

TRIPS Agreement Provisions Favoring Health Policy

TRIPS Agreement attempts to strike a balance between promoting access to the existing drugs and promoting R&D to develop new drugs. It addresses the major issues concerns such as access to medicines, compulsory licensing and parallel imports. Here are some of the more important provisions that impact the Health Policies of all the WTO Member States. TRIPS Agreement permits member countries (Article 30) to provide limited exceptions to the exclusive rights conferred by a patent. This article does not list the specific acts for which exceptions can be provided. What it says rather ambiguously is that such exceptions should satisfy certain conditions that do not *unreasonably conflict with a normal exploitation of the patent and do not unreasonably prejudice the legitimate interests of the patent owner, taking into account of the legitimate interests of third parties.* The three most significant and common exceptions, which most countries provided for in their national laws when TRIPS came into effect are: Parallel imports, early working and research and experimental use.

Table 3.2 TRIPS – Major Provisions Concerning Pharmaceutical Industry and Public Health

TRIPS Provisions	**Definition**
Article 65: Transitional Arrangements for adapting national legislation to the TRIPS Agreement	The WTO Member States have had the following deadlines since January 1995 to modify their legislation:
Article 66: Least Developed Countries	1. Developed countries: 1 year until January 1996
	2. Developing countries: 5 years until January 2000
	3. Least Developed Countries (LDCs): 11 years until January 2006
Article 65.4: Transition period to recognize patents in technological sectors not protected before the TRIPS Agreement (for example, patent protection in the pharma ceutical and chemical sector of several countries)	Developing countries have an additional 5-year period (until 2005) to recognize patents in the sectors pharmaceuticals and chemicals etc. For the LDCs the transition period could be extended for pharmaceutical products as per The Ministerial DOHA Declaration on TRIPS Agreement and the Public Health (WTO 2001)
Article 6: Exhaustion of rights Parallel imports or exhaustion of rights at regional and /or international levels	*Parallel* imports involve the import and resale in a country, without the consent of the patent holder, of a patented product which was put on the market of the exporting country by the title holder or in another legitimate manner

Table 3.2 *Contd...*

TRIPS Provisions	Definition
Article 30. Exceptions to Rights Conferred Bolar Exception (early working)	This exception allows a company to complete all the procedures and tests necessary to obtain market approvals for a generic product, before the original patent expires
Article 31: Other Use Without Authorizationof the right holder (Compulsory Licensing – TRIPS does not use the term *Compulsory Licensing.* Article 31 refers to use without authorization of the right holder and includes both – use by third party, what is usually called *compulsory licenses* and use by government)	Allows exploitation of a patented object, without the patent holder's consent through government authorization, but with remuneration (royalty payment)
Article 39: Data exclusivity and data protection	

Compulsory Licensing

Compulsory licensing can be issued by a national government on a number of grounds. Consider these for example:

- When a patent has not been locally exploited within a period of three years from the date of its original concession
- When public interests prevail over the individual interests of the patent holder. Public interest does not necessarily have to be at the national or federal level. This condition is consistent with article 31 of the TRIPS Agreement and can be applied in situations that fit the principles established in article 8
- When there is a national emergency whether it is in public or collective interest
- When voluntary permission has not been obtained to exploit the patent
- When there is an intermediate product or process that is patented and essential to produce the licensed invention, then, it is necessary to issue a CL for the immediate product or process (dependent patent)
- When there is lack of local production
- As a remedy to anti-competitive practices, such as cartels and dumping

A proper compulsory licensing system is of vital importance to deal with the negative implications of product patent protection on prices. It is one of the ways in which TRIPS attempts to strike a balance between access to current drugs and encourage R&D on new drugs. Granting a compulsory license to generic companies to produce a drug on a payment of royalty to the holder of rights drives competition, brings down the prices making medicines more affordable and accessible to the needy and at the same time encourages the research and development effort by the innovator companies that is so vital to bring newer therapies to the market.

Compulsory licenses have become a common feature of patent laws worldwide and over 100 countries provided for them even before TRIPS came into effect. UK adopted them in its 1883 Patents Act and granted compulsory licenses in about twenty cases relating to important products such as Chloromycetin, Librium and Valium between 1953 and 1971. USA also made extensive use of compulsory licensing particularly under its anti-trust legislation to remedy anti-competitive practices.

The MNCs, however, would not want compulsory licensing system, as the royalties payable through this system are grossly inadequate. The key question is how much is enough?

International NGOs such as MSF, CpTech and HAI have been drawing attention to compulsory licensing provisions of TRIPS to enhance access to medicines. What Penrose said in 1951 after a cost benefit analysis of the patent system is valid and relevant even today:

> The second method of reducing the cost of the patent monopoly is that of compulsory licensing.
>
> This is by far the most effective and flexible method and enables the State to prevent most of serious restrictions on industry. It could be used very effectively to undermine the monopoly power of several of the more powerful international cartels whose position is largely based on their control of the patent rights to industrial processes in the larger industrial countries; and it could be used to ensure that patented new techniques developed abroad are available to domestic industries wishing to use them.

Case 3.1 Compulsory licensing

The Canadian Experience

Canada has made the most effective use of compulsory licensing in pharmaceuticals. Canada granted patent protection for pharmaceutical products only since 1987.

In 1923, Canada introduced special provisions for compulsory licensing of patented products for pharmaceutical but the Canadian manufacturers did not make much use of it, as there was a restriction that the active ingredients had to be produced locally. The generic manufacturers were hesitant to undertake investments for basic manufacturing because the local market was relatively very small. Realizing this, the government amended its patent law in 1969 and eliminated the restrictive clause of local manufacture of active ingredients. Anyone could get a compulsory license not only to produce but also to import any drug produced with a patented process. The Canadian generic pharmaceutical industry received this very enthusiastically and achieved a substantial grew substantially in size riding piggyback on the increased number of compulsory licenses. The impact of compulsory licensing system is evident from the fact that Canada granted only 22 compulsory licenses between 1923 and 1969 and issued as many as 613 between 1969 and 1989.

Canada had a significant cost advantage during its compulsory licensing regime as it fueled competition. A study of 32 drugs under compulsory licensing in Canada but patented in the USA observed that the costs of these drugs as a percentage to the cost in thee USA was about 41.2 per cent in 1983.

Canada however abolished the compulsory licensing system in 1992 on joining NAFTA (North Atlantic Free Trade Agreement). Understandably, Canada has hardly used the compulsory licensing since 1992, and after having used CL effectively to its advantage, the country is advocating caution in the use of CL by other countries!

Case 3.2 Compulsory Licensing and the US

United States also has a rich experience of granting compulsory licenses particularly under antitrust legislation to remedy anti-competitive practices. US has granted more than 100 compulsory licenses in the past under its

Case 3.2 *Contd...*

patent law mainly to facilitate public non-commercial uses by the government. While this has been predominantly in the area of national defense, there were instances where it has used it to bring down the prices of medicines.

The most recent use of compulsory licensing in the US was in 2001, when there were a series of anthrax attacks and a fear of a possible anthrax epidemic. USA has initiated action to make ciprofloxacin, the most effective drug to treat anthrax more affordable to deal with the crisis. US government threatened Bayer, the German drug major and the patent holder of ciprofloxacin with the issue of compulsory license if it did not reduce the prices of its drug. Bayer complied with the US government's suggestion or threat and reduced the prices of its drug benefiting many people in the country.

It is interesting to note that neither the German government nor the European Union did anything to protest or issue any warning to impose trade sanctions on the US if it granted the compulsory license. Bayer however suggested that the US government should not grant a compulsory license in a measured and non-threatening manner.

There are other countries that have issued Compulsory Licenses to fight the HIV and AIDS crisis. Malaysian Government issued a Compulsory license in October 2003 to import antiretrovirals – didanosine 100mg and 25mg tablets; zidovudine 100 mg capsules; and a fixed dose combination of lamivudine 150mg + zidovudine 300mg tablets from Cipla the Indian drug major.

Mozambique also issued a compulsory license in April 2004 to the company Pharco Moazmbique Ltda., which presented a project for local production of a triple compound of lamivudine, stavudine, and nevirapine.

TRIPS Agreement and the Global Health Agenda

It was in 1996 at the 49th World Health Assembly (WHA) that the potential consequences from globalization and international trade agreements on access to medicines were discussed. Consequently, the WHO Action Program on Essential Drugs developed a strategic plan to identify issues related to access to essential medicines and pharmaceutical policy, within

WTO Agreements and to inform the Member States. The WTO launched its first publication on the TRIPS Agreement and Public Health – Globalization and Access to Drugs – providing detailed information to Member States regarding how to implement the TRIPS Agreement to maximize benefits and minimize negative impacts on access to medicines.

As can be expected, the Member States received the publication enthusiastically while the Pharmaceutical and Research Manufacturers (PhRMA) and the United States government called it misleading and biased. They also stated that this publication encouraged piracy of patented medicines and inadequate protection of IPR in the pharmaceutical sector by WTO Member States. The WHO in response to this criticism published a revised version of the document in 1999 and in the same year at the 52 WHA approved the Revised Drug Strategy (RDS) and recommended its Member States that they should ensure:

1. That public health interests will prevail over commercial interests
2. Flexibility and safeguard options in trade agreements aiming to guarantee access to essential medicines

The three most significant and common exceptions, which most countries provided for in their national laws when TRIPS came into effect are: Parallel imports, early working and research and experimental use.

Parallel Imports

Parallel imports are imports of patented products without the consent of the patent holder in the importing country. This is an important issue in pharmaceuticals particularly because the patented drugs are often sold at different prices in different countries at different prices. Thus parallel imports allow a country to shop around for the lowest price. The proponents of parallel imports argue that since the innovator has been rewarded through the first sale of the product, its patent rights have been *exhausted* and hence should not have any say in the subsequent *re-sale.*

A patent holder cannot legally stop imports of patented products offered for sale in another country. TRIPS provides (Article 28) the patent owner the exclusive right to prevent others from not only making, using, or selling the invented product or process in the country but also from importing from other countries. This is however subjected to its Article 6 on *exhaustion.*

Early Working (Bolar Provision)

The *early working* provision is popularly known as *Bolar Provision* in the US. It is known as Bolar Provision after the court case involving Roche, an MNC and Bolar Pharmaceuticals, a generic drug company in the US. The US Court ruled denied the right to develop and submit a generic product application to FDA for regulatory approval before the expiry of patent. The 1984 Hatch-Waxman Act basically overrules this court ruling and since then the early working has got its name as Bolar Provision.

Bolar provision is a very important to the generic drugs industry and it is important to understand its background. Patents provide market exclusivity to the innovator companies for a specified period of time. After the expiry of the patents, others can also manufacture and market the products. But the entry of generic drugs was very slow as the US FDA found out that in 1984, about 154 off-patent brand name drugs did not have any generic equivalents in the market. They identified FDA approval process and the patent law as the two main reasons for this rather slow process of genericization.

Before 1984, even the generic producers had to conduct their own studies and submit data about the safety and efficacy of their products. The generic producers had hardly the resources to under take such time consuming and costly studies. In addition, under the then existing patent law they could start the process of testing and submitting the data to FDA only after the patents had expired. To contain the healthcare costs and to encourage the generic drug industry which plays a significant role in reducing the prices of patent-expired drugs, the US government amended the Patent Act of 1952 and the Federal Food, Drug and Cosmetic Act to take care both the problems in 1984 and enacted The Drug Price Competition and

Patent Term Restoration Act in 1984 which is popularly known as the Hatch-Waxman Act. The Act made some path-breaking reforms that have been responsible for the rapid growth of the generic drug industry in the US. The most important features of the amendment are:

- Under the Bolar Provision of the Patent Act, non-patentees could start using the patented product for regulatory purposes even before the patent expiry
- Further, generic applicants were no longer required to repeat the clinical studies to prove the efficacy and safety of the product
- The generic applicants were permitted to rely on the innovators safety and efficacy data and were required to file only an Abbreviated New Drug Application (ANDA)
- They, however need to demonstrate that the generic product has the same active ingredient, route of administration, dosage form, strength and bioequivalence as that of the innovator drug

The Bolar provision is crucial for the progress of generic industry and the cost containment strategies for reducing healthcare costs by all governments. It permits the generic entry soon after the patents expire and allows benefits of lower prices to consumers without delay. Without this provision the generic companies will have to wait till the patents actually expire and then start the development work and make the necessary regulatory submissions to file their ANDAs. During the several months or even years that it may take to get the regulatory approvals for marketing their generic versions of the drugs the patentees will continue to enjoy the monopoly status for their products even after their patents expire and despite absence of any legal barriers to entry of generic versions.

The Bolar exception allows immediate marketing of generics after patent expiration, thus promoting competition with the innovator medicine with lower prices. Competition probably is the most powerful policy instrument for the reduction of drug prices. The average wholesale price of a generic drug drops to 60 per cent when there is just one competitor, and when there are ten competitors the price falls to 29 per cent. Canada too has successfully used the Bolar provision for many years to strengthen its national technological capabilities and build a buoyant generic drug industry.

Access to Medicines

Access to medicines is a major concern for the governments of all developing countries. Despite initiating a debate on the potential consequences on access to medicines from globalization international trade agreements at the 49th World Health Assembly, there was no progress. It was not until 1999 that the United Nations took a position this subject. The 1999 United Nations Development Program (UNDP) Report on Human Development addressed the issue of TRIPS Agreement and access to medicines.

During the WTO 3rd Ministerial Conference in Seattle, which took place from November 30th through December 3rd in 1999 some of the WTO Member States such as the European union, Hungary, Japan, Korea, Switzerland and Turkey proposed that the all the drugs on the WHO Essential Medicines List must be excluded from patentability. Otherwise developing countries should be allowed to give compulsory licenses for these medicines.

It took an immense crisis of the HIV/AIDS epidemic on the African continent, and the persistent efforts by NGOs, international activists, and a group of African countries, known as the African Group, to include a special session of the TRIPS Council about intellectual property and access to medicines. This was a milestone in the history of multilateral trade agreement system because it brought about a paradigm shift in WTO approach, recognizing that intellectual property rights were neither absolute nor superior to other fundamental rights.

Case 3.3 Pharma Patent Holders Vs. South African Government
The first clash between the pharmaceutical patent holders and the government authorities that occurred in South Africa in 1998 is also a landmark case. After President Mandela signed the South African Medicines

Case 3.3 *Contd...*

and Related Substances Act (Act 90/1997). The Amendment Act Provided for:

1. Generic substitution for drugs with expired patents
2. The establishment of a committee to regulate medicine prices transparently
3. Parallel imports
4. Establishment of an international competitive tendering system to assure provision of medicines

As soon as the Act was amended, the Pharmaceutical Manufacturers Association of South Africa along with 39 transnational pharmaceutical industries filed a lawsuit against the Government of Republic of South Africa in the High Court of Pretoria alleging that these changes violated the TRIPS Agreement and the South African Constitution bringing the Amendment to a grinding halt.

The Amendment Act was entirely consistent with the TRIPS Agreement provisions. It created a legal framework aiming to increase the availability of medicines at lower-costs in the country and improve the access to the medicines to the needy.

The litigation against South Africa included even the governments from other countries such as United States and the European Union, headquarters of the transnational pharmaceutical companies who are litigants. Together, they threatened to initiate trade sanctions if South Africa did not revoke the Amendment, which damaged the commercial interest of their industries. NGOs and representatives of the international campaign of access to medicines are also involved in the conflict. NGOs played a decisive role in mobilizing public opinion against the United States, whose position centered upon defending the commercial interests of its companies without considering the impact on human rights.

One of the main arguments of the activists is that 400,000 people died of AIDS during the suspension of the amendment, as they could not afford to pay for the treatment. They brought considerable pressure during the United States Presidential Campaign, and forced the US government to reverse its position against South Africa. In fact, the US government has gone step further. It even started later the PEPFAR program to improve access of HIV drugs for the poor.

It took three years of acrimonious debates, clashes and intense international pressure for the litigants to withdraw their lawsuit in April 2001 against South Africa.

The Case of South Africa is Groundbreaking for Three Reasons:

1. Exposed the conflict of interests and the tensions that exists between patent holders and the right of access to the medicines of poor people. It contributed to the debate on the public health implications of the TRIPS Agreement in different international forums
2. Demonstrated the power and necessity of international activism. A number of NGOs like Medicins Sans Frontiers (MSF) or Doctors Without Borders, Health Action International (HAI), Consumer Project on Technology (CpTech) and OXFAM rallied together to gather public opinion and support in United States and European Union against the actions pharmaceutical companies and forced them to withdraw the lawsuit
3. Roped in UNAIDS and WHO to demonstrate their relevance as supranational mediators in resolving the conflict of interests

Case 3.4 The Brazilian Experience with Compulsory Licensing

Brazil threatened to use the CL provision in order to obtain price reductions of four antiretroviral medicines (ARV) in 2001. The public pharmaceutical laboratories played an important role in implementing national drug policy in Brazil. The Instituto de Tecnologia de Fármacos, Oswaldo Cruz Foundation, and Ministry of Health were able to provide reference prices to the Ministry of Health in the price negotiations involving the Brazilian government and three transnational pharmaceutical companies – Merck & Co Inc, Roche and Abbott. Moreover, Ministry of Health has the capacity to reverse engineer some patented ARVs. The government was thus prepared to issue a CL in case of a deadlock. The negotiation resulted in considerable price reductions: 64.8 per cent for Indavir, 59 per cent for Efavirenz, 46 per cent for Lopinavir, Ritonavir, and 40 per cent for Nelfinavir, there by allowing the National AIDS Program to continue.

The Doha Declaration

Later in November 2001, during the Fourth WTO Ministerial Conference in Doha, Qatar, the development of the least developed countries (LDCs)

was discussed resulting in what is widely known as *Doha Declaration*. The Doha Declaration recognizes the gravity of the public health crises that affect the majority of developing countries and least developed countries, especially HIV and AIDS, tuberculosis and malaria, among others and their concerns related to the TRIPS Agreement and public health (Table 3.3)

The Doha Declaration was possible because the developing countries mobilized themselves and rallied around as one block and the strong pressure from international NGOs and the support of the public opinion they could gather around. More importantly the fact that the US and Canada had threatened to issue compulsory licenses against Bayer the German drug major the producer of ciprofloxacin, during anthrax scare and its use in biological terrorism.

Table 3.3 Doha Declaration on TRIPS Agreement and Public Health

Adopted on November 14, 2001
1. We recognize the gravity of the public health problems afflicting many developing and least developed countries, especially those resulting from HIV/AIDS, tuberculosis, malaria and other epidemics.
2. We stress the need for the WTO Agreement on Trade Related Aspects of Intellectual Property Rights (TRIPS Agreement) to be part of the wider national and international action to address these problems.
3. We recognize that intellectual property protection is important for the development of new medicines. We also recognize the concerns about its effects on prices.
4. We agree that the TRIPS Agreement does not and should not prevent members from taking measures to protect public health. Accordingly, while reiterating our commitment to the TRIPS Agreement, we affirm that the Agreement can and should be interpreted and implemented in a manner supportive of WTO members' right to protect public health and, in particular, to promote access to medicines for all.
5. Accordingly and in the light of paragraph 4 above, while maintaining our commitments in the TRIPS Agreement, we recognize that these flexibilities include: (a) In applying the customary rules of interpretation of public international law, each provision of the TRIPS Agreement, shall be read in the light of the object and purpose of the Agreement as expressed, in particular, in its objectives and principles. (b) Each member has the right to grant compulsory licenses and the freedom to determine the grounds upon which such licenses are granted.

Table 3.3 *Contd...*

(c) Each member has the right to determine what constitutes a national emergency or other circumstances of extreme urgency, it being understood that public health crises, including those related to HIV/AIDS, tuberculosis, malaria and other epidemics, can represent a national emergency or other circumstances of extreme urgency.

(d) The effect of the provisions in the TRIPS Agreement that are relevant to the exhaustion of intellectual property rights is to leave each member free to establish its own regime for such exhaustion without challenge, subject to the MFN and national treatment provisions of Articles 3 and 4.

6. We recognize that WTO members with sufficient or no manufacturing capacities in the pharmaceutical sector could face difficulties in making effective use of compulsory licensing under the TRIPS Agreement. We instruct the Council for TRIPS to find an expeditious solution to this problem and to report to the General Council before the end of 2002.

7. We reaffirm the commitment of developed-country members to provide incentives to their enterprises and institutions to promote and encourage technology transfer to least-developed country members pursuant to Article 66.2. We also agree that the least-developed country members will not be obliged, with respect to pharmaceutical products, to implement or apply Sections 5 and 7 of Part II of the TRIPS Agreement or to enforce rights provided for under these Sections until 1 January 2016, without prejudice to the right of least-developed country members to seek other extensions of the transition periods as provided for in Article 66.1 of the TRIPS Agreement. We instruct the Council for TRIPS to take the necessary action to give effect to this pursuant to Article 66.1 of the TRIPS Agreement.

Doha Declaration – Paragraph VI Problem

Before the TRIPS Agreement, A country can issue a compulsory license not only for manufacturing the drugs in the country but also for importing the drugs. Before the TRIPS Agreement, countries with insufficient manufacturing capacities could import patented drugs from developing countries like India, which have manufacturing capacities and did not introduce patent protection for pharmaceutical products.

After the TRIPS Agreement, since they have introduced patent protection for pharmaceutical products, under the TRIPS Agreement, these developing countries like India despite their manufacturing capabilities, are not permitted to produce new patented drugs unless they are specifically authorized to do so by getting a compulsory license. But a major limitation of such a compulsory license is that under Article 31 (F) of TRIPS, production will have to be predominantly for the supply of the domestic market of the member authorizing such use. Compulsory licensing cannot be granted in countries with manufacturing capacities exclusively or mainly to export to countries with no manufacturing capabilities.

Under the TRIPS Agreement, a country with manufacturing capabilities can resort to compulsory licensing to manufacturing drugs to meet her public health needs. But a country with no manufacturing capabilities cannot use the compulsory licensing provisions to *import* patented drugs to take care of her health care needs.

Doha declaration has rightly identified the problem and instructed the Council for TRIPS for an expeditious solution before the end of 2002. But the solution is not to be found easily. The differences between developed and developing countries over the scope of the solution, including the diseases and medicines covered, the countries to be eligible to import and procedures to be followed. They ultimately arrived at a compromise on August 30, 2003. The decision adopted by the General Council to be implemented in the light of shared understandings of Members was *the decision permits the countries producing patented drugs under compulsory license to export to those countries with no manufacturing capacities.*

However there are many strings attached to this decision limiting the extent to which it can be used. Rather than facilitating exports of drugs to improve the access to the needy, several hurdles, which act as a disincentive, have been put for such exports. Consider these for example:

- Two compulsory licenses – one in the importing country and another in the exporting countries for specified drugs and quantities are needed. Applicants must first try for a voluntary license before granting the compulsory license as per Article 31 of the TRIPS Agreement.

- The importing country (other than LDCs) will have to notify to the TRIPS Council and establish that it has insufficient or no manufacturing capacities for the product. The criteria for establishing insufficient manufacturing capabilities are not made clear. Countries such as India, South Korea with well-developed pharmaceutical industries may not be able to use such compulsory licenses to import drugs, which they may not find worthwhile producing domestically.
- The products exported should specifically be labeled and marked to prevent re-exports. This will increase the cost
- The exports under compulsory licensing should be used in good faith to *protect public health* and not be an instrument to pursue *industrial or commercial product objective.*

Simpler solutions were possible and in fact, WHO favored one based on Article 30 of TRIPS Agreement, which is administratively and procedurally simpler:

- No need for case-by-case compulsory licensing, which is time consuming and may involve litigations
- Only one compulsory license in the importing country. No need to rely on exporting country to issue a compulsory license
- Since the generic manufacturers would be free to produce for exports without any specific compulsory license, there would be greater competition among them, and hence, prices would be more affordable

Developing countries, particularly USA and members of PhRMA have all through been opposing a simpler solution. Their contention and apprehension are that if the solution is simple and easy to use, the generic manufacturers in countries like India can continue to do even after TRIPS Agreement what they have been doing before the TRIPS Agreement, which is produce patented drugs and export to other countries adversely affecting the MNCs of their intellectual property rights.

Data Exclusivity, The New Patent Extension Tool

TRIPS Article 39.3 obliges WTO Member States to protect clinical data made for registration purposes against *acts of unfair competition.* Members of PhRMA are claiming rather insisting that Article 39.3 requires the introduction of *data exclusivity provision* as operated in the EU or USA even by the developing countries that have joined the WTO. From acts of unfair competition *data exclusivity* and *data protection* are not the same.

Data exclusivity prevents the regulatory activity from making use of original clinical data submitted by the patentee for a set period, during which no authorization of generic medicines may take place. Data exclusivity therefore, provides a form of market exclusivity. What Article 39.3 requires is a form of data protection for preventing unfair commercial use of data by third parties. The intention of the TRIPS Article 39.3 is not to create a form of market protection.

The difference between *data exclusivity* and *data protection* can be seen clearly in the regulatory practices of the EU. The regulatory authority in the EU may not rely on the original clinical data submitted by the patent applicant during the period of data exclusivity granted, which is 6 or 10-years. Even on expiry of this period during, which no generic applications are assessed, the regulatory authority does not disclose commercially sensitivity data.

Professor Carlos Correa of the University, who has assisted the WHO in the area of health perspectives on TRIPS Agreement, wrote in 1999:

> The protection conferred to data submitted for the marketing approval of the product of the TRIPS Agreement has been another problematic issue in some countries. The Agreement does not oblige to recognize any kind of exclusivity on data submitted for approval, since the protection should be granted under the discipline of *unfair competition.* Once data on a new drug have been submitted, their use by a national health authority to study and approve a subsequent application on the basis of similarity does not entail a violation of the confidentiality obligation under the Agreement.

Moreover, data exclusivity does not meet the basic conditions indicated in Article 39.3 whereas clinical information, which is claimed to be protected under both Article 39.2 and 39.3. Article 39.2 sets down the criteria to define certain information as *undisclosed information.* Information that is secret and confidential in nature, which is not generally known and accessible to persons, is undisclosed information. However, the information and data the pharmaceutical and therapeutic properties of certain pharmaceutical products are widely published and therefore, represent part of *public knowledge* and hence cannot be claimed as *undisclosed information* by the patentee when a generic producer shows that their product is bioequivalent to the originator.

Data exclusivity provisions have implications for generic entry and hence for competition and prices. Consider this example:

> An innovative drug company after spending several years of clinical studies and millions of dollars discovered a drug *ARV-N* in 1995 and was granted a patent in 2005. The product may be introduced in developing countries even later say in 2010. With a 20-year patent term under TRIPS Agreement, the patent is supposed to expire in 2015 ending the market exclusivity and opening up the generic competition. But if the developing country provides *data exclusivity* for 10 years, then the generic applicants cannot use the clinical data before 2020 because generic companies do not have the resources to conduct such time consuming and expensive studies. Data exclusivity thus effectively extends the market exclusivity beyond the patent term.

The New Pressures

PhRma and USTR have been putting a lot of pressure on providing data exclusivity and data protection particularly after Doha Declaration. While the developed countries got their way in the Uruguay Round of multilateral the Doha Declaration gave some degree of flexibility to the developing countries in terms of compulsory licensing and improving access to medicines in case of public health crises. Data exclusivity continues to be a major issue in the USTR annual publication – Priority Watch – highlights inadequate clinical data protection in various countries.

The USA seems to be making up bilaterally for what it has lost multilaterally. In the recently concluded FTAs with a number of countries such as Jordan, Singapore, Chile, Central America, Australia and Morocco and other countries in Asia, Latin America etc. it places limits on the two flexibilities provided in the TRIPS Agreement – compulsory licensing and parallel imports.

United States also has been systematically imposing the threat of unilateral trade pressure through its omnibus Act – Section 301 of United States Trade Act, under which the United States Trade Representative (USTR) issues an annual report threatening foreign countries with trade sanctions for not protecting the intellectual property rights of the US companies.

Trade Blocks – Boon or Bane?

A *trade bloc* is a large free trade area or free trade area formed by one or more tax, tariff and trade agreements. A number of international – generally regionally based – economic blocs have been developed to promote trade between member states. There are several blocs, which have extended their arrangements beyond economic goals to political goals such as the European Union. A trade bloc is established through a trade pact covering different issues of the economic integration. Some of the more active trade blocs are listed in Table 3.4.

The main purpose of Free Trade Agreements or Trade Blocs is to secure trade liberalization. The common criticism about the FTAs is the danger that they can divert rather than create trade. In reality there has been little diversion and they have been encouraging wider trade liberalization. The advantages are that FTAs are quicker and easier to negotiate than multilateral agreements because fewer parties are at the table.

The disadvantages are that if the FTAs are not set up within right framework of policies, they can diminish rather than enhance economic welfare. They are not good vehicles of liberalization in sectors on which the parties outside the agreement have a major influence.

Table 3.4 More Active Regional Trade Blocs

Regional Trade Bloc	Member States
1. Asia Pacific Economic (APEC)	Australia, Brunei, Canada, Chile, Cooperation China, Hong Kong, Indonesia, Japan, South Korea, Malaysia, Mexico, New Zealand, Papua New Guinea, Peru, Philippines, Russia, Singapore, Taipei, Thailand, USA, Vietnam
2. Association of South East Asian Nations (ASEAN) Korea	Brunei, Cambodia, Indonesia, Laos, Myanmar, Philippines, Singapore, Thailand, Vietnam, South
3. European Union (EU) Asian Nations (ASEAN)	Austria, Belgium, Bulgaria, Cyprus, Czech Republic, Denmark, Estonia, Finland, France, Germany, Greece, Hungary, Ireland, Italy, Latvia, Lithuania, Luxembourg, Malta, Netherlands, Poland, Portugal, Romania, Slovakia, Slovenia, Spain, Sweden, United Kingdom
4 European Free Trade Association (EFTA)	Iceland, Norway, Switzerland, Liechtenstein
5. Caribbean Community (CARICOM)	Antigua and Barbuda, Bahamas, Belize, Dominica, Grenada, Guyana, Haiti, Jamaica, Saint Kitts and Nevis, Saint Lucia, Saint Vincent and the Grenadines, Suriname, Trinidad and Tobago
6. Economic Community of West African States	Benin, Burkina Faso, Côte d'Ivoire, Gambia, Ghana, Guinea, Guinea, Bissau, Liberia, Mali, (ECOWAS) Niger, Nigeria, Senegal, Sierra Leone, Togo, Cape Verde
7. Economic and Monetary	Cameroon, Central African Republic, Chad, Community of Central Africa Republic of the Congo, Equatorial Guinea, Gabon (CEMAC)
8. East African Community (EAC)	Kenya, Tanzania, Uganda
9. South American Community of Nations (CSN) Chile	Brazil, Argentina, Paraguay, Uruguay, Venezuela, Bolivia, Colombia, Ecuador, Peru,
10. Gulf Cooperation Council (GCC)	Bahrain, Kuwait, Oman, Qatar, Saudi Arabia, United Arab Emirates
11. Southern African Customs Union (SACU)	Botswana, Lesotho, Namibia, South Africa, Swaziland
12. Common Market for Eastern and Southern Africa (COMESA)	Sudan, Ethiopia, Eritrea, Djibouti, Comoros,

Table 3.4 *Contd...*

Regional Trade Bloc	Member States
13. North American Free Trade Agreement (NAFTA)	USA, Canada, Mexico
14. Eurasian Economic Community (EurAsEC)	Belarus, Kazakhstan, Kyrgystan, Russia, Tajikistan, Uzbekistan
15. Agadir Agreement	Egypt, Jordan, Morocco, Tunisia
16. Central American	Costa Rica, El Salvador, Guatemala, Honduras, Common Market Nicargua (CACM)
17. Pacific Regional Trade Agreement (PARTA)	Fiji, Kiribati, Marshall Islands, Micronesia, Nauru, Palau, Papua New Guinea, Samoa, Solomon Islands, Tonga, Tuvalu, Vanuatu,
18. African Economic Community (AEC)	All Regional Trade Blocks in the African Continent - ECOWAS, CEMAC'ECCAS, SACU, COMESA, EAC – will join into a common **African Economic Community** (**AEC**) by 2019
19. (MERCOSUR)	Brazil, Argentina, Paraguay, Uruguay, Venezuela
20. (ANDEAN)	Bolivia, Colombia, Ecuador, Peru
21. South Asian Association for Regional Cooperation (SAARC)	Afghanistan, Bangladesh, Bhutan, Bhutan, India, Maldives, Nepal, Pakistan, Sri Lanka

After ten years of existence of WTO, there are 148 Free Trade Agreements (FTA) and Economic Participation Agreements (EPA) in the world as of June 2006. The WTO has a membership of over 150 countries. Most of the WTO members if not all have also entered into FTAs with one or more blocs of countries. What is the reason for this duality of bilateral and multilateral negotiations?

The fundamental objective of an FTA is the elimination of tariffs and other trade barriers. At the same time it also bears characteristics of an EPA (Economic Partnership Agreement), which aims for a broader range of economic cooperation to enhance trade among the countries. EPA would include for example, provisions on intellectual property rights, harmonization of economic systems such as competition policies and movement of persons etc.

FTAs would facilitate replacement of inefficient domestic production with efficient foreign production, allowing consumers to purchase less expensive imported goods, which in turn enhances the economic welfare of the member countries. Even multilateral negotiations with WTO also can bring about such beneficial outcomes with a reduction or removal of trade barriers. Where is the need for a regional trade bloc like FTA?

FTAs globally are demonstrating that countries with real market power have an alternative to WTO and also help in keeping pressure on multilateral talks.

FTAs are a Boon	FTAs are a Bane
A. Provide political support for regional solidarity that may favor liberalization of trade. B. More efficient to negotiate with larger units, than with 101 small countries. C. A regional FTA can *lock- in* unilateral liberalization D. Regional liberalization may set the pace and build momentum for multilateral liberalization. FTAs internally help in dismantling import-substitution and externally help foster competitive liberalization E. Modern FTAs have multilateral rules on Foreign Direct Investment, competition policy and government procurement which WTO does not have	A. The greater market power that the larger trade blocs have may provide an incentive for higher trade barriers. However, Article 24 prohibits a customs union from raising barriers against outsiders B. Regional trade blocs may manipulate the details of regional trading arrangement with complica ted rules of origin for their own gain C. FTAs divert attention away from negotiating multilateral liberaliza tion. Since the political support of firms that stand to gain from exports is necessary to pass trade liberalization legislation, the firms that get what they want from FTAs may not be really keen on multilateral negotiations.

It is difficult achieve in the near future that what is the first best option of free trade for the globally system as a whole. The key question is whether the trade blocks are *stumbling blocs* for progress in the free trade or *building blocs* for free trade under WTO and in the era of globalization. One thing is certain. The geo-political rationale for FTA is only as good as the geo-political planners behind it.

Way Forward

Competitive liberalization may be the way to go. Consider these reasons: FTAs do two important things. Firstly, FTAs globally by demonstrating that countries with real market power have an alternative to the WTO help to keep pressure on the multilateral talks at the WTO. Secondly, at the domestic level FTAs by strengthening the pro-trade forces help to change the political economy dynamics and mobilize support for liberalization.

In the 2003 World Trade Report, the WTO authors suggested a test that might be applied in the case of particular FTAs to help us to judge whether the pact would likely to complement or compromise the WTO system. The two questions of the quick test are:

1. Are the two governments including any topics in the FTA that they would be unwilling to subject to negotiation in the broader multilateral system?
2. Would the two governments be prepared to extend their FTA to other countries if they wished to join?

Robert Baldwin cogently argues that it is initially easier for pro-trade forces to gain national agreement to free up the import regime with a small number of competitors, as in an FTA. Once the FTA enters into force, it further strengthens the position of the pro-trade forces and contributes to the weakening of the country's protectionist lobby – some of which will likely to go out of business as a result of the FTA's impact. As this process is repeated over time through successive trade deals, the pro-trade forces get stronger making the opposition to liberalization weaker.

Yusuf Hamied, chairman of Cipla, one of India's leading pharmaceutical companies expressed his concern on the way the TRIPS and access to medicines seem to be going in a statement released on November6, 2006 the following that reflects the concern of the developing countries:

Five years after Doha Declaration, the world has not upheld its promise to the poor and diseased.

The obstacles posed by the globalization of patents is still blocking access to medicines at affordable prices. Worse, whereas the Doha Declaration called for the WTO agreement on patents to be implemented in a manner conducive to access to medicines, in reality India was pressured last year into broadening the scope of patents and narrowing the scope of compulsory licensing – well beyond its obligations under the TRIPS Agreement. It is imperative that the original Doha Declaration of 2001 be passed in its original form, with a clause of compulsory licensing of all valid patents for all essential drugs required in the third world under payment of a nominal royalty to the originator. Unless this is done, newer drugs developed for HIV such as the integrase inihibitors and newer protease inhibitors will never be freely available at equitable prices.

The first world countries and the rest of the world have bipolar views on product patents, TRIPS Agreement and access to medicines. The views are based on mutual suspicion. What is needed is a paradigm shift from mutual suspicion to mutual trust. Only cooperation that is based on a trusting relationship can improve access to medicines and even a larger socio-economic progress that is very badly needed by the third world countries. After all when the third world progress the first world too will. encouraging the use of generics in place of brand name drugs to cut down the healthcare costs in virtually every country.

Chapter Four

Competing for WTO Era: The Indian Experience

The Indian pharmaceutical industry is one of the most closely regulated industrial sectors in India. The government not only controls prices of formulations and bulk drugs but also controls the profitability of pharmaceutical companies.

The industry is characterized by a high degree of proliferation. Over 9,000 Pharma units produce bulk drugs, intermediates and formulations. Many of these units are low-cost single product firms servicing regional markets with low technology bulk drugs and generic formulations. They have very small market shares. The top 250 companies account for over 75 per cent of pharmaceutical production.

The industry produces over 456 bulk drugs, 525 intermediates and 60,000 formulations and has been a net exporter for over ten years now.

Life before GATT

The Indian pharmaceutical industry has developed significantly since the early 1970s. Prior to this, multinational companies dominated the industry with their superior technological base (mostly import-dependent) and marketing strengths. They had a strong control on the availability and prices of drugs, with the result that drug prices in India were considerably higher than they are now and in fact were comparable to prices in the developed world.

DPCO 1969 (Drug Price Control Order) was the first step taken by the government towards encouraging self-reliance in drug technology and availability. DPCO established retail ceiling prices for certain drugs. Indian companies that manufactured these drugs were, however, exempted from price control for as long as five years.

The second major step towards increasing self-reliance in the drug industry was the introduction of the Indian Patents Act of 1970. This has resulted in fundamental structural changes within the industry. The Act recognized only process patents and not product patents. This allowed companies to copy a drug using different process routes without payment of royalty or license fees to originators.

Indian Pharma companies with lower labour and operational costs were able, for the first time, to manufacture international drugs (discovered elsewhere in the world) and sell them cheaper than the MNCs could. Multinationals had to adhere to international patent regulations and were restricted to their own proprietary drugs.

Multinationals, for almost 25 years, have largely steered clear of the Indian market with the exception of a few companies like Glaxo, Hoechst (Aventis now) etc. As drug prices were fixed at levels that were at times about 4 per cent of prices in developed markets, multinationals stopped introducing their new products and stopped selling products that were priced too low. As a result, the top ten MNCs accounted for a mere 17.7 per cent per cent of the market in 2005, down from 80 per cent in 1970. The top ten Indian drug companies garnered about 31 per cent in 2005 (Table 4.1).

Table 4.1 Top ten companies: MNCs Vs Indian

MNCs

Rank	Company		Rs. Billion Sales	Market Share
1.	Glaxo SmithKline		111.61	5.43
2.	Sanofi Aventis		47.70	2.32
3.	Abbott		47.34	2.30
4.	Novartis		37.34	1.82
5.	Pfizer		24.91	1.45
6.	Wyeth		24.91	1.21
7.	E. Merck		22.96	1.12
8.	Parke Davis		16.09	0.78
9.	Astra Zeneca		15.13	0.74
10.	Solvay		11.13	0.55
		Total	**364.24**	**17.72**

Indian sector

Rank	Company		Rs. Billion Sales	Market Share
1.	Cipla		114.12	5.56
2.	Ranbaxy		91.09	4.43
3.	Nicholas Piramal		86.18	4.20
4.	Sun Pharma		69.00	3.36
5.	Zydus Cadila		50.00	2.43
6.	Dr. Reddy's		49.84	2.43
7.	Aristo		48.09	2.34
8.	Alkem		45.51	2.22
9.	Lupin		42.20	2.05
10.	Micro		39.60	1.93
		Total	**635.63**	**30.95**

Source: Data derived from the Retail Store Audit of IMS ORG-MARG, March 2005

Life after GATT – Two Scenarios

What will life after GATT be for the Indian pharmaceutical industry? Will it be better or worse off? Can Indian companies continue their growth path, the way they did during the "process patent only" period of the 1970s and after? Or will the multinationals rule the roost in the new product patent regime after 2005? How many companies are going to survive the advent of GATT?

Dr. Heinz Redwood, in his study on 'New Horizons in India – The consequences of Product Patents in India' presents the expectations, predictions and predilections of life after GATT in the Indian pharmaceutical industry in two mutually contradictory scenarios of the future (Table 4.2) – 'Sunset and Sunrise.'

Table 4.2 Two Scenarios

Sunset Scenario

Many of the Indian-owned pharmaceutical companies which are grouped under the IDMA (Indian Drug Manufacturer's Association), supported by many politicians and consumer activists, present a 'Sunset Scenario'. They opposed product patents and think that it will spell the doom of the Indian pharmaceutical industry. Under this scenario, there will be a drug price explosion as soon as product patents are recognized. Imports will soar. Exports will dry up. The Indian-owned pharmaceutical companies will be largely wiped out by multinational patent power with its accompanying exclusivity of marketing. There will be a reversal of fortunes from being a net exporter to an import-dependent industry.

Sunrise Scenario

By contrast, the members of the Organization of Pharmaceutical Producers of India (OPPI), who include all research-based multinational drug companies operating in India and a number of progressive, forward-looking Indian pharmaceutical companies present an optimistic 'Sunrise' scenario. They are supported by a significant number of independent experts and observers.

The 'Sunrise' scenario projects the impact of full patent protection as a galvanizing force for pharmaceutical industry in India. It foresees:

- A fundamental change of attitude towards India on the part of multinationals, with a renewed willingness to invest and conduct R&D locally after decades of clamping down on Indian commitments.
- Increased collaboration between multinationals and Indian companies in the development and marketing of patented drugs.
- The transition of the more advanced Indian companies from a drug copying culture to a research-based strategy with its own aspirations to eventual multinational status.

The advocates of both scenarios are striving to enlist the most important player in the political triangle – the Indian government – on their side. The proponents of the 'Sunset scenario' appeal to the government to maintain status quo of the Indian Patents Act of the 1970. The advocates of the 'Sunrise scenario' on the contrary pleaded that the government could ensure a bright future for the Indian pharmaceutical industry only by implementing TRIPS with dedication and determination.

Whether a strong IPR for pharmaceutical industry results in a 'Sunset' or a 'Sunrise' is not pre-ordained. It is largely in the hands of those who shape events – namely, the Indian pharmaceutical companies, multinational groups and the Indian regulatory authorities.

If the government decides to promote a strong and research-based pharmaceutical industry in India, then watertight patent protection is a must. The second pre-requisite is some degree of relaxation of its severe controls and introduction of new measures for raising the profitability levels to encourage risk-taking research.

Taking the sum of pre-tax profit and R&D expenditure as an indicator of 'available revenue', the level in Indian drug firms (as a percentage of sales) is about one-third of that in Japan, and one-fifth that of the global pharmaceutical level. The Indian figure is not adequate for investment in innovative R&D.

Not a Knockout Bout!

Indian companies will not be knocked out by patent protection, if they adapt their corporate strategy to it. Multinational companies too, on their part will not find bonanza conditions on their Indian doorstep. At the same time, reasonable opportunities are arising in India at a time when a severe squeeze in profits is being suffered due to cost containment strategies and policy reviews in Europe and North America. Collaboration, rather than confrontation, will ensure success for both. A number of strategic alliances are already taking place between the more progressive Indian companies and multinationals to exploit the market opportunities in a mutually beneficial manner.

India already possesses the necessary technological infrastructure and scientific talent for original pharmaceutical R&D. It is not scientific genius that is in short supply, but cash flow. The Indian government, therefore, can encourage both Indian and foreign industry by changing the ground rules sufficiently to provide the necessary incentive for investment in pharmaceutical innovation and research under patent protection. Only then, it can convert the barriers of inadequate cash flow for research and innovation and create gateways.

Generics – The Big Opportunity in the post–WTO Regime

The market for off-patented generic formulations in the world is estimated grow to $ 83.9 billion (estimates by Visiongain 2005) from the present $ 44 billion by the year 2010.That is roughly about ten times the present size of the Indian pharmaceutical market. US alone accounts for close to one-half of this huge generic-pie. Typically, the US imports nearly 80 per cent of its generic drugs. Given the proven track record of the Indian pharmaceutical industry in bulk actives and drug intermediates, it is reasonable to assume that at least Indian Pharma companies could serve ten per cent of the emerging business. That would mean a whopping $ 8 billion. The generic penetration in the European Union too would grow significantly in the near future, as more and more governments in Europe are encouraging the use of generic drugs in order to contain health care costs.

Large Window of Opportunity

The US generics market, which has so far been catered to largely by Italian and Spanish companies, is set to open even further after tightening of European Patent laws with the adoption of Supplementary Protection Certificate (SPC). In the past, companies were allowed to produce patented drugs on a small or pilot scale, in order to generate samples for the regulatory authorities. The samples now have to be submitted four years before the drugs go off-patent, and so the adoption of the SPC in effect chokes the US market for the new generics off, for European producers. Italy will had to stop production of these bulk generics by 1997, and Spain, a smaller producer, by 2002. Europe accounts for 80 per cent of bulk generic sale in U S and Italy alone accounts for 80 per cent of this. There are only two major independent US producers of bulk generics, Gaines Inc. and Wyckoff Chemical Company Inc. They account for only 10 per cent of US generic sales.

Once the European supplies dry up, there is a large window of opportunity available for Indian drug companies to enter. The Indian companies have many advantages over their counterparts in other developing countries. They have a proven track record in process development skills and a number of manufacturing facilities that are approved by US FDA. The game plans of some of the Indian drug companies like Ranbaxy, Dr. Reddy's Labs, Lupin, Wockhardt, Sun Pharma, Cipla and others clearly indicate their focused approach to exploit the generic opportunities in North America and Europe.

The strategy adopted by these companies to exploit opportunities in the rapidly expanding markets for off-patent generics in North America and Europe is twofold. Firstly, some companies are creating beachheads in these difficult-to-enter markets through acquisitions of small generic and over-the-counter companies and US FDA approved manufacturing facilities. Ranbaxy, Wockhardt, Lupin and Sun Pharma have already entered these markets this way, with Ranbaxy leading the pack.

The second strategic approach of Indian companies to enter and conquer foreign shores is by teaming with local partners to gain faster access to markets and to share the high costs of product development, registration and marketing. Cipla has formed a strategic alliance with five generic majors for marketing its generic formulations in North America. Cipla's alliances cover a long pipeline of over 140 generic products. Lupin has chosen Merck Generics as its partner for marketing its generic versions of sterile dosage forms of cephalosporin molecules that would go off patent soon. Nicholas Piramal too has formed a joint venture with Swiss-based Siegfried Pharma to penetrate the generics markets in European Union and North America.

The third strategic initiative taken by more aggressive Indian drug companies is Para IV filings like Dr. Reddy's Laboratories and Ranbaxy.

Four Opportunities for MNCs

Now that the new patent law is in place, the market place is on its way to become a level playing field for MNCs. Here are the implications:

The Indian pharmaceutical market is likely to grow rapidly. Volumes will increase as healthcare spending rises and health coverage improves from the current 33 per cent of the population. Prices too will continue to rise although the government will be reluctant to let them soar. The industry has been lobbying for gradual but complete decontrol so that it can be internationally competitive.

The rate of growth, however, will depend on the extent of decontrol, health care coverage, overall economic growth and opening of the health care insurance sector.

Mckinsey, one of the top international management consultancy firms specializing in strategic issues, identified four opportunity areas for MNCs to exploit in India in the post-GATT era.

McKinsey's Prescriptions to MNCs

1. **The Domestic Market:** MNCs operating in India need to be aggressive in tapping into the rapidly growing Indian drug industry. They may have to make some strategic and operational changes to expand market share rapidly. They have to be marketing oriented. They need to reconsider the product mix strategies depending on what the market needs rather than offering just what their parent company produces. Glaxo is already following an India-specific strategy. Its acquisition of Biddle Sawyer is a market-specific one. Pfizer has been adopting a different pricing strategy for some of its new molecules. MNCs need to consolidate their presence in key therapeutic segments that are rapidly growing and expand their market share.
2. **Sourcing of Bulk Actives and Intermediates :** Indian bulk drug industry has progressed very rapidly over the years with

over 800 manufacturers, some of whom have world class developmental and manufacturing skills in organic synthesis and process re-engineering technology. Furthermore, low infrastructural and manufacturing costs make it an attractive sourcing base for bulk actives and intermediates. MNCs can source all their requirements of their mature, off-patent bulk actives and intermediates, which are under cost pressure in their home countries.

3. **Sourcing of Formulations for Export to Developing Countries:** MNCs can use India as a sourcing base and export off-patent generic formulations to developing nations cost-effectively.

4. **Out-Sourcing Research:** India has the largest English speaking scientific talent in the world with over 200 universities and 2000 research institutes. MNCs which can tap into the rich scientific base of India can out-source part of their research and collaborate with Indian institutes. The low cost-structure of research in India can help MNCs to meet the challenges of ever increasing cost containment pressures in their home markets. HMR (Aventis now) for example, within months of selling its established research centre in India to Nicholas Piramal has gone into a collaborative arrangement in the research area with Nicholas Piramal itself.

That may sound like a generic prescription to companies operating in a "branded generic market" that will evolve into a "branded market" in the coming product patent regime. Very often, the broad strategy or 'what to do' is known. The Business Press accelerates the process of this knowledge and insights of strategic moves by publishing the success stories of leading players in all industries. Success, however, increasingly depends on knowing 'how to do it' and 'on how effective one is in doing it'.

McKinsey's Prescription to Indian Drug Firms

A. Consolidate market penetration.
B. Achieve higher levels of productivity.
C. Stick to the knitting – stay more focused on core businesses.
D. Expand related businesses by making separate subsidies ensure operational freedom.
E. Enter into strategic alliances or collaborations to create international and global presence.

Opportunity Horizon

The opportunity horizon for the progressive Indian drug companies is indeed very wide. Indian companies are low cost producers. Consider these opportunities on the horizon for Indian companies:

1. Marketing of branded generic formulations in home country.
2. Marketing of bulk actives and intermediates in home country in addition to captive consumption.
3. Marketing of branded generic formulations in countries with intellectual property protection.
4. Marketing of bulk actives of off-patented drugs in highly regulated markets with strong intellectual property protection.
5. Marketing generic formulations of off-patented drugs in regulated markets with strong IPR protection.
6. Marketing branded generic formulations of difficult-to-make, off-patent-yet single-source drugs in regulated markets with strong IPR.
7. Marketing formulations of patented drugs through licensing arrangements in home country and select international markets.
8. Custom synthesis for bulk active substances of patented and off-patent drugs under secrecy agreements with multinational firms.
9. Contract research arrangements with multinational companies, who are on the look out for outsourcing some steps of research.
10. Developing New Chemical Entities (NCEs) through indigenous drug discovery programs.

Future Positive!

The wide opportunity horizon by itself should convince the skeptics about the opportunities in the product patent regime. The future for Indian pharmaceutical industry can be very optimistic for the positive minded. Consider these facts for example:

- India's process developmental skills are very well known by now. The technological capabilities too are evident from the fact that India exports pharmaceutical substances, drug intermediates and dosage forms of off-patent drugs not only to the developing and third world countries with little or no IPR protection, but to the highly regulated first world countries as well. There are over 104 manufacturing facilities in India today, which are approved by the US FDA, which is the largest number outside the US.
- In less than three years after launching the 'drug discovery programs', two companies – Dr. Reddy's Labs and Ranbaxy have developed and filed international patents for new chemical entities. They have completed pre-clinical research and are entering the clinical research phase. Other companies like Wockhardt, Lupin, Torrent and Glenmark have also entered the discovery race and are on the lookout for alliance partners to share the developmental and international registration costs and efforts.
- With a large pool of scientific talent comparable to the best in the world, huge manufacturing infrastructure and process development skills that are world class, Indian pharmaceutical industry is on the threshold of emerging as a leader among the developing countries in pharmaceuticals. A strong protection of IPR would only facilitate and accelerate this process.
- The process of change in the coming product patent regime in India will be a gradual one. It had started before 2005 and will stretch beyond 2015. Only by 2015, we will have a patent regime that is in conformity with the industrialized world.

- The market for off patent branded generics will remain far bigger than for patented drugs even in 2015. Even in the highly industrialized world, where almost the entire patentable research is taking place currently, more prescriptions are written for off-patent products than for patented drugs. In the UK for example, prescriptions for off-patent drugs are around 60 per cent. In Germany they are around 54 per cent and even in the US, as many as 54 per cent of the prescriptions are written for off-patent drugs. In India, it is estimated that prescriptions for off-patent drugs would account for over 80 per cent even in 2015. The growth in value terms however will be higher, because even if ten per cent of the prescription business is switched over to research based products (which are usually priced ten times more than the current alternative treatment norms), it would mean higher growth in value terms over the ten year period. The industry, therefore, would witness faster growth rates because of increased consumption and because some higher-priced drugs will enter the prescription market.
- The transition time or preparation time in real terms for adopting, adapting and adjusting to the changing marketing environment is considerable. The beginning, of course has to be made now. It is not too late. There is no more room for complacency and the complacent.
- The MNCs will not have a field day either, though their growth rates would start climbing from 2005 onwards as some of the leading multinational pharmaceutical companies have already started an India-specific strategy. They will also introduce new products to defend their therapeutic segments aggressively. Some of them would introduce new molecules through their newly formed 100 per cent subsidiaries to realize higher prices. However, since patented drugs will not have more than 20 per cent share even in the next ten to fifteen years, the market need not

necessarily be tilted in favor of multinationals. Companies, whether Indian or multinational, have to compete aggressively for improving their slice of the cake. No automatic advantage for any sector.

- In the coming product patent regime, the marketplace will be a level playing field. A level playing field on which only players of a certain level will be successful. There are qualifying criteria for entry as well as for victory. For those who are well prepared to compete it would be a level playing field. And for the Rip Van Winkles of the Indian pharmaceutical industry, who are just out of their long deep slumber, it could be a minefield.

A case in point: Indian Pharmaceutical Industry

A careful analysis would reveal a common thread, a carefully crafted strategy behind the actions and responses of some leading Indian pharmaceutical companies. One can identify ten essential elements that are common from the game plans of these determined players. The ten essential elements of their winning strategies are detailed in Table 4.3 – Perfect Ten: Elements of a Winning Strategy.

The Indian pharmaceutical industry today is probably in its most challenging phase ever. It had shed its most protective armor (Indian Patents Act, 1970) and is in the process of opening its markets wide for product patent protection and stronger IPR regime. The industry is gearing up to meet the challenges and has already some achievements to its credit. Consider these for example:

- Indian drug industry ranked fourth in volume terms and thirteenth in value terms in 2005.
- Exports accounted for 40 per cent of the total industry output which is valued at US $ 8 billion in 2005.
- Accounts for 25 per cent of the total ANDAs filed in the world's largest generic market – the US in 2005.
- Filed close to 30 per cent of all DMFs in the US in 2005.

- Maximum number of US FDA-approved facilities outside the US .
- Ranbaxy – an Indian Drug Major moved up into the top ten generic companies in the world.

Change – rapid change – can be seen in the Indian Pharma market, be it in industry structure, strategic approaches or tactical moves. In fact change is already quite palpable. McKinsey, one of the world's leading strategic consultancy firms in its report projected that Indian pharmaceutical industry would reach Rs. 1,000 billion in sales by 2010.

Yesterday's mighty companies are yielding their hard earned market shares to the once-fledgling companies, which show initiative in the emerging specialty segments.

A careful look into the high profile initiatives that have been launched by some of the more aggressive companies reveals a shrewd strategy of organizing their marketing operations around specific therapeutic segments.

The marketing-mix too, has been undergoing rapid changes. Some of the fastest growing companies are those who have reinvented the marketing-mix through fresh tactical approaches like reaching a large customer base through scientific seminars, symposia, sponsorship of medical conferences and scientific information services that are not essentially product-related, etc.

Competition in the Indian pharmaceutical industry has always been severe as there are more number of players and the nature of the market being braded generic. What makes the competition even tougher is that more and more MNCs are likely to step up their activity and compete more intensely as the market becomes more of a level playing field. So far they have not been very active except for a few companies like Glaxo SmithKline, Aventis etc. The MNCs such as Merck, Bristol Myers Squibb, Eisai and a few others, who are not currently present till recently have set up wholly owned subsidiaries to launch their new products, outsource some of their more important products and even to enter into custom research, custom synthesis, and clinical research.

It is difficult to predict at this point of time the precise impact of GATT on the Indian Pharma industry. Based on the experiences of other developed countries that have accorded product patent protection over the past two decades, experts opine that:

- Proliferation of companies would be checked. The number of companies would dwindle.
- Some of the more efficiently run smaller companies would be acquisition targets for the newly entering MNCs or large Indian companies on an expansion spree.
- Smaller companies with good manufacturing facilities would do contract manufacturing for the more aggressive, larger marketing companies.
- New product introductions would be reduced and restricted to new products under licensing arrangements.

Like dinosaurs threatened by cataclysmic changes, companies often find it impossible to cope with a radically altered environment. It is only the fittest that survive. To seize the opportunity in any changing scenario, four broad principles are important:

1. An understanding of how competition for the future is different.
2. A process for finding and gaining insight into tomorrow's competition.
3. An ability to energize the company top-to-bottom for what may be a long and arduous journey towards the future.
4. The capacity to outrun competitors and get to the future without taking undue risks.

Companies, therefore, need to raise their antennae higher to spot, track and monitor the signals of change. Like in war, in business too forewarned is forearmed!

The challenges faced by the Indian drug industry are at two levels. One is at the functional level of marketing, which essentially revolves around the improvement of operational efficiency and effectiveness. The other is at the organizational level. Marketing is not to be viewed in the relatively narrow functional level but in a much broader perspective encompassing the whole organization. This holistic view of marketing has been emphasized by management practitioners as well as by theoreticians. Consider these for example:

The key questions for the senior management towards meeting the future challenges are:

- Is our action agenda mostly offensive or defensive?
- Are we devoting too much energy to preserving the past and not enough to creating the future?
- What percentage of our improvement efforts (quality, customer service, innovation, and operational excellence) focuses merely on catching up with our competitors?

Catching up is necessary, but it is not going to turn an also-ran into a leader. Defending today's leadership is no substitute for providing tomorrow's leadership, and market leadership today certainly does not equal market leadership tomorrow. This requires clear, well-defined answers for these key questions.

- What will be the basis for your competitive advantage in the future?
- Where will your margins come from in the future?
- In what product/markets will you participate in the future?

Some Indian drug companies have started asking these questions about the future and have been gearing up to meet the challenges involved. A careful analysis of the high-profile initiatives taken by some aggressive Indian Pharma companies like Ranbaxy, Cipla, Dr. Reddy's, NPIL, Sun Pharma, Lupin, Wockhardt, Zydus Cadila, Glenmark, Aurobindo, Matrix, Divi Labs, and others suggests that there is a pattern, which emerges from their game plans. There is a common thread that runs through their carefully woven strategies. There may be some differences in the relative importance given to various strategic elements. Here (Table 4.3) is a broad outline of their action agenda for effectively competing in the post-GATT era.

Table 4.3 Perfect Ten: Elements of a Winning Strategy

1	**Strategic Vision** A vision is only an idea or an image of a more desirable future for the organization, but the strategic vision is an idea that it in effect jump-starts the future by calling forth the skills, talents and resources to make it happen. A strategic vision essentially does four things. **A.** It attracts commitment and energizes people across the organization. **B.** It creates meaning in employees' lives. **C.** It establishes a standard of excellence. **D.** It bridges the present and future.
2	**Reaching the Critical Mass** It is essential for any company to reach a critical mass in terms of size to effectively generate and leverage resources. In the new economic order, where entry barriers are slowly dissolving, the level and intensity of competition are bound to increase significantly. Unless a company achieves a critical mass in terms of sales and profits, a dominant position in select key markets, it would not be able to compete effectively and make strategic investments required for future growth.
3	**Marketing Mindset** Achieving a dominant position in a therapeutic segment requires a focused marketing strategy like careful selection of product-mix in terms of both width and depth, superior customer service programs, target specific communication strategies etc., in relevant therapeutic and prescriber segments. Above all, one needs a strong customer- orientation.
4	**Upgrading Technology** Upgrading technology is a must not only for growth, but vital even for survival in the rapidly changing pharmaceutical industry in India. Up-gradation of manufacturing facilities to international regulatory standards like US FDA., U.K. MHRA and Canadian HPB (Health Protection Bureau) are essential prerequisites to export pharmaceutical substances and formulations to these countries respectively.
5	**Focusing on Research** Pharmaceutical industry is highly research -intensive. Process development is an area where Indian companies have excelled over the years and have brought the country a net-exporter status to the drug industry. The R&D investment is a tiny 1.5 percent on average by Indian pharma companies as compared with the 12 to 18 percent by multinational companies abroad. As the product patent protection era ushers in, the introduction of newer drugs will be reduced to a trickle.

While basic research (considering the cost of developing a new molecule is over US $ 800 million) is unaffordable in India, increased R&D effort is a must even to assimilate transfer of technology and to pursue applied research. Some of the more progressive Indian pharma companies have taken the initiative and are stepping up their R&D effort. Some companies Ranbaxy, Dr.Reddy's, Wockhardt, Lupin , Cipla and Sun have even started allocating significant resources to discovery research effort.

6 Integrating Strategically

Strategic integration - be it backward integration to manufacture pharmaceutical substances by a manufacturer of formulations or a forward integration to manufacture formulations by a manufacturer of pharmaceutical raw materials – offers a distinct competitive advantage. Control on input costs, continuous supply, quality and even unique customer perceptions are some of the important advantages that strategic integration offers.

7 Internationalizing the Business

The importance of earning valuable foreign exchange in today's business can never be over emphasized. Large markets and remunerative prices are the major motivating factors that drive companies for export performance. Leading Indian drug companies, who have gained strong foothold in international markets for their bulk actives, are slowly shifting their emphasis to more value added formulation exports. Some others Like Ranbaxy, Sun, Dr.Reddy's, Wockhardt, Lupin , Torrent etc., have started registering their branded generic formulations and marketing them in South East Asia, Africa , CIS and US, Europe and Japan.

8 Attracting Alliances

Collaborate to compete seems to be the new stratagem in the international business arena. In a research-intensive industry like the pharma industry, more and more strategic alliances are being formed every day. To pool up resources and to compete cost effectively by optimization, alliances are important. They are also powerful sources of synergy. Glenmark for example entered into a strategic alliance with Merck Generics and Dr. Reddy's forged an alliance with GSK to market their authorized generics.

9 Adding Economic Value

Technology upgradation, R&D effort are highly investment intensive. They require huge outlays of capital. International operations too, require large up front investments for product registration and marketing thrust. A company that is profit making, with an impressive track record, clearly defined and well crafted strategy and a high degree of transparency in its transactions can attract huge investments from the capital markets. In the final analysis, the key determinant of effectiveness or success is a healthy bottom line. This can be achieved only by a systematic approach to all aspects of business and uncompromising standards in operations across the business. Generating surplus is essential and only companies with high profitability can invest strategically for future growth.

10. Operational Excellence

Since a core competence is most decidedly a source of competitive advantage, a company must invest considerable amount of time, effort and resources in building a portfolio of core competencies. There are five important steps involved in building core competencies:

A. Identifying existing core competencies
B. Establishing a core competence acquisition agenda
C. Building core competencies
D. Deploying core competencies and
E. Protecting and defending core competency leadership.

These are the essential elements of the winning game plans diligently crafted by those Indian Pharma companies, which have understood the full implications of the post-WTO scenario.

All of them are gearing up to meet the emerging challenges which will have to be faced. While the game plans are easily understood and appear deceptively simple (since the model is available), transforming and translating these into an action plans is very difficult. It takes one hundred per cent commitment, determination and total support from the top management to make it happen!

Enhancing CQ

What it takes to succeed in today's fiercely competitive world of Pharma that is changing not just rapidly but radically? How can one become competitive enough to survive and grow in the globalized pharmaceutical world, which understands only international harmonization and not the current stage in which a country may be in the development cycle, unless forced, like in the case of DOHA declaration in terms of providing access to the medicines in an epidemic or pandemic or a healthcare emergency? While there are no clear-cut or right answers for these questions a careful observation and analysis of the changing landscape of the pharmaceutical world provides very useful and meaningful insights into what needs to be done and what can be done to achieve the C Q (Competitiveness Quotient) for succeeding in the brave new world of Pharma and continuously enhancing it.

Chapter Five
Strategic Focus

Strategy, the dictionary defines, as a carefully devised plan of action to achieve a goal, or the art of developing and carrying out such a plan. Strategy, therefore is the ultimate responsibility of every business leader. Companies succeed when they get it right. Companies fail when they get it wrong. Tony Manning in his small yet profound book – *Making sense of Strategy* cogently argues that:

> The purpose of a leader is to create a context in which people will perform to their full potential. This *mental space* is where they discover and test themselves and where they reveal (or conceal) their magic. Context is a product of conversation.

He adds further and says that organizations then, are managed conversations. People inside them talk to one another all day long about what they must do and how they do it. Behind every successful business there is leader who has a clear idea of what his or her organization could become and what has to be done to accomplish. A strategic vision is imperative for success. A business leader who can inspire his troops and rally support for realizing the dreams and the potential of the organization manages these conversations through sharing them appropriately and often enough.

There is no more powerful engine driving an organization towards excellence and long-range success than an attractive, worthwhile and achievable vision of the future that is widely shared.

Vision plays an important role not only in the start-up phase but also in an organization's entire life. Vision is a signpost pointing the way for all who need to understand what the organization is and where it intends to go. Sooner or later, the time will come where an organization needs re-direction or perhaps a complete transformation, and then the first step should always be a new vision, a wake up call to everyone involved with the organization that fundamental change is needed and is on the way.

Top executives are increasingly seeking strategic input from the lower rungs of the corporate ladder, and find that broader participation helps translate vision into reality. Participation is important in strategic setting, because unless the strategy is 'owned', vision will not become 'action'. The key to strategic success, therefore, is to gain broad commitment through participation in the strategic process. This does not mean that strategy should be an exercise in Athenian democracy. It does not mean management by consensus.

Whatever model for formulating and implementing strategy your organization employs, the strategic process offers great opportunities for participation. Strategic process provides a common road map for participation, which becomes increasingly important, as the organization grows bigger and more complex with a number of strategic business units spread across a number of locations.

Strategic process is essentially a sequence of logical steps for collecting and analyzing information and drawing inferences. It is very important to have a clear idea of the various roles people play in the strategic process right from managing director on down the line.

Organizations that are successful in implementing strategy have redefined the role of middle managers to include significant strategic responsibility. Although middle managers have different responsibilities and roles in implementing strategy, one connecting thread is the shared responsibility for effectively communicating strategy to subordinates. Furthermore, it is essential that people feel they are contributing to the vision. Another important strategic role for middle management involves them in setting the vision for their own units. Ideally, strategy should cascade down through the organizational hierarchy.

No doubt, broadening involvement adds complexity to the strategic process. But creating and living by a vision is a social act. A vision that does not touch every employee's head, heart and hands remains an idea in waiting. For vision to come alive, participation is needed.

Five Elements for Success

Companies that have achieved uncommon success in creating and transforming vision into a reality possess five common elements, which are crucial for success.

1. **A common strategic language :** Strategic language means a common vocabulary of expression that every one across the organization understands.
2. **A simple and specific strategy :** Strategy should be simple and specific enough to be carried around in everyone's head and not in a three ring binder. Any strategy entombed in a thick, three ring binder will never rise from the dead.
3. **Managed participation :** Managed participation involves clearly defining roles and creating opportunities for managers and other key contributors to participate in the strategic process. That is why many companies are creating cross-functional taskforces to stimulate creativity and commitment to resolve key strategic concerns.
4. **Motivated work force :** Motivated work force keeps vision an ongoing vital, vibrant influence. The management has to provide enthusiasm and motivational climate so that, managers across the organization want to get involved. Participation should not come as a command performance.

5. **Chief Executive's role :** The involvement of Chief Executive is the most crucial success factor. Without his personal involvement and encouragement in every step along the strategic path from the creation of strategic vision to action planning, vision will not become a reality.

Corporate mission statements – sometimes called value statements, vision statements, credos or principles – are the operational, ethical and financial guiding lights of companies. They are not simply mottos or slogans; they articulate goals, aspirations, dreams, behavior, culture and strategies of companies more than any other document.

The mission or vision statements of successful, exciting and powerful companies are not just concepts or philosophies or mere intentions that are nice to have. They have true values and clear, well thought out ideas that help them meet, exceed the corporate financial, social and emotional goals. They also stake out a 'right way to do', in case of any dilemma or crisis.

That is perhaps why managers, in an international study conducted sometime ago, covering twenty-five "corporate tools" such as customer surveys, pay-for-performance, total quality management and re-engineering, used mission statements more than any other tool. Managers like mission statements because they make a difference between success and failure.

A mission or vision statement is to a company what the constitution is to a nation. It is an excellent, much revered and often imitated set of values. It has worthy goals and aspirations. Sometimes you reach them. Some times you don't. But you always try because it is the right thing to do.

Impact of Vision Statements

Vision or mission statements describing what a company is doing and what it stands for can have a stabilizing and reassuring effect on employees and investors. Mission statements usually have two parts. The first part is declaration of the company's strategic intent. The second part describes the enablers. They tell everyone how the mission or vision will be accomplished, and what values and principles the company and its employees will use to guide them day-to-day into the future.

Five Basic Rules

There are five basic rules for writing an effective vision and mission statement:

1. Keep the mission statement simple. Not necessarily short, but simple.
2. Involve all the key contributors in preparing the mission statement. Involvement helps to get people on board. It gets them excited as they have a stake in its fulfillment. Allow companywide involvement.
3. Always ensure that the wording and tone reflect the company's personality or what the company would like to be.
4. Exposure and reach are vital. Share the mission statement in as many creative ways as possible. Keep it in front of people constantly.
5. Above all, live by the mission statement. Use it as guiding light. Judge employees by how well they adhere to its tenets. Management must say it and live it.

A brief analysis of the vision statements, their action plans and programs of about thirty companies in the Indian pharmaceutical industry is presented here and in the later chapters which will provide very useful insights into the strategic planning process of a pharmaceutical company that is keen on becoming competitive in the new globalized pharma world.

Here are some thirty examples of vision and mission statements articulated by some of the leading Indian pharmaceutical companies. Many of them are official vision or mission statements. Some are widely communicated than others and shared across their companies. All of them however, have concepts, game plans, strategies, goals or dreams straight out of the horses' mouths – all of them are either statements made by their respective CEOs in interviews to the business press or in corporate advertisements, brochures and annual reports.

Some of them are in the form of specific corporate goals in the short and medium term. Some goals are even for the long term. Others are value statements, principles and game plans. All of them clearly communicate what the company is or does or what it intends to do. They all are declarations of their strategic intents. A careful analysis of the vision statements would give the reader very useful insights into the strategies, beliefs, convictions and indeed the character and personality of the organizations.

The globalized Pharma world is at once highly competitive and demanding and offers tremendous opportunities. Broadly speaking, there are three major competing spaces in the new pharmaceutical world order.

A. *Innovation-Led* space is the first and most difficult to achieve and it takes the best and the brightest of the pharmaceutical world to exploit opportunities in this huge opportunity area. Not only it is the largest but also is greatly responsible for all progress made in the pharmaceutical world either directly or indirectly. In fact the entire industry is revolving around it. The other two spaces are also created as spin-off opportunities based on the progress that the innovation-led pharmaceutical companies have been making.

B. The second space is the rapidly growing *International Generics* space the growth drivers of which are patent expiries and ever-increasing cost-containment strategies of virtually every government in the world of healthcare. It is not just that enthusiasm is contagious, even cost-containment seems to be as infectious.

C. Cost-containment is also like a chain reaction and it is creating a new competitive space called *CRAMS* (Contract Research and Manufacturing Services). It has not spared even the most prolific innovators of the past. Globalization of pharmaceutical industry certainly has arrived and CRAMS is its buzzword and operational phrase. What outsourcing is to IT (Information Technology) industry, CRAMS is to the pharmaceutical industry.

The thirty companies that we discuss throughout this book have a clear knowledge and understanding of these competitive spaces and opportunities they present and accordingly are charting their courses and action agendas.

These thirty companies are divided into three groups – A, B, and C based on their Vision statements communicated either in their annual reports (2005-06), or websites, presentations to investors or in their interviews published in the print media.

The companies in *Group A* (Table 5.1) expressed their strategic intent in clear terms that they would like to carve our place in the innovation-led global pharmaceutical space. Companies in *Group B* (Table 5.2) are competing in the rapidly growing generic drug space in the international markets and are determined to become international generic companies. Companies in Group C (Table 5.3) would like to achieve the partner-of-choice 'status' in the fast expanding CRAMS space.

This classification or grouping of companies is done to essentially understand and gain insight into the process of their strategy formulation and it is not conclusive. These groups are not watertight compartments either. They are rather seamless. A company from one group would plan to move into the next group or compete in the other space once it attains the critical mass required and realizes its current strategic vision. It is more of a corporate evolutionary process.

Group 'A' Companies: Competing for Innovation-Led Global Pharma Space

All the ten companies in Group 'A' are clearly aspiring to become innovation-led international pharmaceutical companies of distinction. Each company has set specific goals depending on the current stage they are in but all of them are investing their efforts with a clear focus on reaching the goal post of a research based pharmaceutical company. The Vision statements reflect those commitments and their action plans and operations amplify these commitments. The multiple strands of the common thread that runs through their strategic intent are vertical integration, world-class technological infrastructure for manufacturing and research and continuous strategic benchmarking. The vision statements of the ten companies in our study are presented in brief in Table 5.1.

Table 5.1 Group 'A' Companies Strategic Vision: Innovation-Led

Company	Strategic Vision
1. Ranbaxy	The company's vision is to achieve significant business in proprietary prescription products by 2012 with a strong presence in developed markets. It also aspires to be amongst the top 5 generic players with US $ 5 billion in sales by 2012
2. Dr. Reddy's Laboratories	To become a discovery-led global pharmaceutical company
3. Sun Pharma	To become a research-based international pharmaceutical company
4. Lupin	To be an innovation-led transnational pharmaceutical company.
5. Nicholas Piramal	To become the most admired Indian pharmaceutical company with leadership in market share, research and profits by: • Building distinctive sales & marketing capabilities • Evolving from licensing to globally launching our patented products • Inculcating a high performance culture • Being the partner of choice for global pharmaceutical companies Always adhering to values, based on obligations as the trustees of customers, employees, shareholders and society
6. Zydus Cadila Healthcare	In our vision to lead: One of India's leading healthcare players, they aim to be a global research-driven company by 2020 1. To achieve sales of US $ 400 million by 2006 2. To be a top ten global generic company with a strong R&D pipeline and sales in excess of US $ 1 billion by 2010
7. Wockhardt	Wockhardt is a global, pharmaceutical and biotechnology company that has grown by leveraging two powerful trends impacting the world of medicine – globalization and biotechnology Preparing for change before change beckons. Harnessing the power of innovative research. Providing high quality medicines for a healthier world.
8. Biocon	To be an integrated biotechnology enterprise of global distinction.
9. Glenmark	To emerge as a leading integrated research-based global pharmaceutical company.
10. Torrent Pharma	• Committee to total customer care by delivering world class products and services • To be the leader in pharmaceutical industry.

Ranbaxy before GATT, Strategic Vision during the Transition Period

Ranbaxy has clearly been the intellectual leader of the Indian pharmaceutical industry. What separates Ranbaxy from the rest of the industry is its ability to spot change and assess its impact quickly.

When the Indian drug industry was viewing exports as a necessary evil (to get import licenses), Ranbaxy thought otherwise. It considered exports as an opportunity as early as the 1970s. Since drug prices are higher in overseas markets, exports offer an opportunity for higher price realizations for the price controlled Indian drug industry.

Again in 1992, when the entire Indian industry was raged against the Dunkel draft, which advocated a strong product patent regime, Ranbaxy accepted the new era as an evolution that every company had to be ready for. The logic was simple. You cannot be a global player by following one set of rules in your home country and another in the developed markets.

As early as 1992, Dr. Parvinder Singh, the chairman of Ranbaxy had articulated the company's vision to be a research based international pharmaceutical company with a turnover of $ 1 billion by 2003. He knew that highly successful companies use their mission statements to 'gather the troops' and affect a new corporate culture and behavior. He was probably the only chief executive in the Indian pharmaceutical industry, who used to communicate through the monthly missives, 'from the CEO's desk' – directly with each employee highlighting the objectives of the organization as well as his concerns.

The Year after Implementing GATT

Today Ranbaxy's vision is once again reaffirmed its pledge:

> To achieve significant business in proprietary prescription products by 2012 with a strong presence in developed markets. It also aspires to be amongst the top 5 generic players with US $ 5 billion in sales by 2012.

To translate these objectives into reality and to optimize value creation, the company has adopted a multi-pronged strategy. Entering high potential new markets with value-added product offerings and actively seeking overseas acquisition opportunities in the US and in Europe will be the major thrust areas for Ranbaxy in the coming years.

Together, with the commitment of – 10,000-strong multicultural work force, Ranbaxy continues to aggressively pursue its mission to become a Research-based International Pharmaceutical Company.

Dr. Reddy's Labs before GATT, Strategic Vision during the Transition Period

Dr. K. Anji Reddy is a visionary. He dreamt of putting India on the bulk drug map of the world in the early eighties by reverse engineering patented molecules. Having achieved that, in the early nineties he dreamt once again. This time it is about putting India on the drug discovery map of the world. He succeeded again when Dr. Reddy's Laboratories became the first-ever Indian drug company to license an NCE to a multinational. The company has changed its focus at the right time to formulations and never looked back ever since. The company's mission clearly indicates its research bias. The company's Mission and Vision Statements in 1998 were:

Our Core Purpose:

To help people lead healthier lives

Our Vision:

To become a Discovery-led Global Pharmaceutical Company.

Our Values:

We strive for excellence in everything we think, say and do

The Year after Implementing GATT

Today in 2006, the vision statement of Dr. Reddy's reflects the same commitment confidence and the dramatic progress they made over these ten years. The company would like to become an innovation led global pharmaceutical company and is well on its course.

Sun Pharma before GATT,

Strategic Vision during the Transition Period

Right from inception Sun Pharma has chosen the path of least resistance. It has focused on specialty segments. The company firmly believes that the road less travelled need not necessarily be long. Mergers and acquisitions have been the major growth drivers for Sun Pharma. To sustain growth, the company has created six strategic business units in 1998, which had focused on different therapeutic and prescriber segments. Sun Pharma has also concentrated on exporting bulk actives of specialty drugs and marketing of branded generics in international markets. Here are the highlights of Sun's strategic vision of 1998:

1. To be among the top 5 pharmaceutical companies in India by 2005.
2. Focus on low volume, high value specialty drugs.
3. Use a dedicated field force for each specialty segment.
4. Maintain a first-mover advantage by quickly introducing new formulations by reverse engineering new drug molecules.
5. Accelerate growth through mergers and acquisitions.
6. Look for small Pharma outfits that have expertise in high value specialty drugs.

The Year after Implementing GATT

The company's reaffirmation of its vision and renewed commitment are palpable in this rather picturesque narrative statement:

> The Sun Pharma of tomorrow will have brands registered in major markets of the world, and in most markets, promoted by high quality field force. In India, we expect to retain leadership in our key therapy areas, and reach leadership in newer therapy areas that we entered after 1997.
>
> In key international markets across Asia, South East Asia, Russia, China, the Middle East, LATAM, and Africa we would be a strong specialty company with prescription driven sales with a strong network and

established company equity and therefore would be an excellent partner for any company seeking to license out products across markets.

In the high value generic markets of the US we expect to become a respected generic company, with portfolio comprising of both complex and simple-to-file generics, building an edge with technology and the cost advantage of vertical integration. While we have recently completed our fourth acquisition in the US, we believe there are excellent opportunities in the US generic space, where we can affect a turn around and add value to a business. We have about $ 400 million earmarked for acquisitions in the US generic and drug discovery space.

Our innovation-based R&D programs, we recently de-merged into a separate company. The new R&D Company will have projects covering new molecules and novel drug delivery in late phase human trials over the next few years, which it may seek to license out.

Sun Pharma further sharpened its focus with the creation of 17 marketing teams to achieve a higher degree of promotional focus to as many as twenty-three specialty prescriber segments.

Lupin before GATT,
Strategic Vision during the Transition Period

Lupin's strategy can be described in one word – Focus. The company focused first on the anti-tubercular market in India, which accounts for half of the T B cases in the world. It has integrated backward and gone whole hog to become a leading anti-TB player in the world. The next area of focus for Lupin has been the huge $ 10 billion world cephalosporin market, in which a number of major molecules were going off patent in the next few years. The company has become a fully integrated cephalosporin player to become competitive. It has made strategic acquisitions and alliances to ride the first wave of generic cephalosporins in the US and Europe. Lupin has set itself a very ambitious goal of achieving $ 1 billion in sales by 2003 which is still alluding the company. It has upgraded technologically to a world-class level and has been focusing on research to become a vertically integrated international generic company. The salient features of its strategic vision and mission were:

Mission :

To be an Innovation-led Transnational Pharmaceutical Company.

To Achieve this, Lupin had a Clear-Cut Game Plan:

1. To upgrade technology to a world-class level.
2. To build process and product development capabilities that are internationally competitive.
3. To globalize the business and become a major player in the generics market.

Lupin had a Three-Tier Plan to Achieve this:

To identify drugs with difficult chemistry and high technological barriers that are shortly going off patent in the first stage

A. To pre-empt competition in catching the generic 'first wave'.
B. To leverage its research and technological strength to develop non-infringing processes for those drugs.
C. To build large capacities so as to achieve cost competitiveness in the second stage.
D. And to penetrate the global market with the product and add value through strategic alliances in the third stage.

The Year after Implementing GATT

In 2006, Lupin is still focused but is expanding beyond a leading integrated player in anti-TB segment and cephalosporins and crafted a winning strategy for regulatory markets and is on a fast track to become an innovation-led transnational pharmaceutical company.

Nicholas Piramal before GATT,
Strategic Vision during the Transition Period

Six acquisitions and seventeen strategic alliances in 10 years. That should describe the strategic vision of Nicholas Piramal. The company believes in having a large number of products in its portfolio instead of depending on a few strong brands. It would like to grow by individual companies while others grow by individual products. The company has recently in 1998 filled an important gap in its overall strategy – focus on research and development – through its acquisition of the Hoechst Research Centre at Mumbai. Nicholas Piramal is the only Indian pharmaceutical company, which is planning to be a leading player in the counter drug market in addition to the prescription drug market. It has also very big plans to set up clinical research facilities in India. The company's strategic vision in 1997 was:

A. To be among the top three health care companies in India by the year 2000.
B. To achieve this through strategic acquisitions and takeovers.
C. To stay focused on mainstream products and diversify into niche markets through strategic alliances and joint ventures with people who are leaders in their fields.
D. To increase exports by entering the market for generic formulations for off-patented products abroad.
E. To upgrade manufacturing facilities to international standards.
F. To be a major player in the domestic market for OTC pharmaceuticals.

The Year after Implementing GATT

Nicholas Piramal continued its acquisition spree even in the new millennium and acquired the brand portfolio of ICI pharmaceuticals in India, and Avecia Pharmaceuticals in the UK. The company's strategic vision currently is to become the most admired Indian pharmaceutical company with leadership in market share, research and profits by building distinctive sales and marketing capabilities.

Zydus–Cadila Health Care before GATT, Strategic Vision during the Transition Period

Almost ten years ago, Pankaj Patel, the Managing Director of the Zydus–Cadila Health Care has clearly articulated the goal of his company in his vision statement:

> To become one of the top three Indian Pharma companies, become a regional player in five to seven years and a global player by 2020.

The strategic vision of the Zydus group was to create a Performing Organization through:

A. Increasing market share
B. Internationalization of business
C. Technology transfer and upgradation
D. Human resource development and
E. Cost leadership

The building blocks for these are the 3 E's, namely – Enrich, Empower and Excel.

The salient features of Zydus's action plan were:

A. Focus on drugs, which are growing fast.
B. Strengthen the product portfolio with niche products.
C. Enter into strategic alliances to co-market new molecules in India.
D. Enhance research capabilities by entering into joint ventures with international and national research institutes and companies engaged in research.

The Year after Implementing GATT

A look at the performance of the company testifies for the umpteenth time in business history as to what strategic focus can lead to when it is backed by execution. Zydus Cadila would like to leverage the strengths of its vertically integrated business model and explore inorganic opportunities to realize its strategic vision. The company's vision statement in 2006 reiterates their pledge to become *a research-driven global pharmaceutical company by 2020.*

The goal for the immediate term that is the current fiscal year (2006-07) is to achieve revenues of US $ 400million. And the company aims to be among the top ten global generic players with a strong R&D pipeline and sales in excess of US $ 1 billion by 2010.

Wockhardt Before GATT, Strategic Vision During the Transition Period

Habil F. Korakhiwala, Chairman of Wockhardt always believed that speed is necessary for staying ahead, which is what competition is all about. He has certainly ensured this, for Wockhardt has always been ahead of the industry in terms of profitability. He has steadfastly built Wockhardt into one of the Indian drug majors, which is ready to compete in the post-GATT era. His strategy has been a classical one. The company has regained its focus by pulling out of unrelated diversifications into real estate and put a hold on its hospital and diagnostic businesses at the suggestion of McKinsey, the leading international consultancy firm specializing in strategic issues. It is also one of the biggest spenders on R&D in India. Wockhardt was bang on target on its key strategic objectives during the late 1990's:

A. To achieve Rs. 10 billion in sales by the year 2000.

B. To reach a critical mass through acquisition and organic growth. Set aside Rs. 2 billion for acquiring pharmaceutical brands and companies.

C. To progressively increase investment in R&D, build infrastructure and create a competent research team that is capable of entering drug discovery program. The immediate focus areas for research are - Novel drug delivery systems, Biotechnology products, New drug discovery. To achieve this the company planned to invest 4–5 per cent of sales on R&D

D. To give a new thrust to globalization of business by setting up joint ventures and entering generic markets in the US and Europe through acquisitions

E. To pursue brand building aggressively in the home market to achieve the coveted 5th position in the industry.

F. To pursue a low cost and command a high premium strategy for products.

G. To introduce hepatitis-B vaccine by 1999.

The Year After Implementing GATT

When you look at the company's vision statement of 2006 you would not only recognize the significant achievements Wockhardt had made over these years but also see the renewed spirit of the organizations to make its own place in the globalized Pharma world. By being proactive. By preparing change before change beckons. By harnessing the power of innovative research.

Biocon

Biocon is the new member of the, Ivy League, of the Indian Pharma. Biocon clearly is the leading player from India with global aspirations in the biopharmaceuticals space. The company's mission is to become an integrated biotechnology enterprise of global distinction.

The company understands what it takes to achieve this and embarked on a journey towards achieving excellence in creating and gaining:

- Intellectual assets through discovery research and development
- State-of-the-art manufacturing capabilities
- Internationally benchmarked quality and regulatory systems
- New medical insights through disease-specific clinical research
- Customer relationships through outstanding products and services
- Human resource development through training, mentoring and empowering
- Research and partnership management

Glenmark

Glenmark is certainly the new kid on the block of the Indian drug majors. Started twenty-eight years ago, Glenmark has been showing a steady progress but did not belong to the top league. Ever since Mr. Glen Saldana the present CEO took charge of the operations a few years ago, he has put his world vision of the Pharma business into practice. The strategic focus of the company is clearly on the bull's eye – the heart of the pharmaceutical business that is discovery-led. The strategic vision of *emerging as a leading integrated research-based global pharmaceutical company* is confirmed by every single move by the company over the last few years.

Torrent Before GATT, Strategic Vision During the Transition Period

Torrent has been the first Indian pharmaceutical company to exploit the opportunities in specialty therapeutic segments like psychiatry, cardiology and gastroenterology. It has become a trendsetter and a role model to other companies like Sun Pharma and Intas. Many other Pharma companies are now focusing on these specialty segments. Torrent later embarked on a massive business diversification program into unrelated areas like power generation and manufacturing of cables and consequently lost its pre-eminent leadership position to Sun Pharma in the specialty segments of neurology, psychiatry and even cardiology.

The company has, however, regained its focus and is planning aggressively to build up its Pharma business to become a major player. It has also built a state-of-the-art research and development facility and launched its drug discovery program and has met with an early success in developing a NCE in cardiovascular area. Torrent in the late 1990's described itself as 'the great Indian tomorrow.' The company's strategic objectives were:

A. To reach the leadership position.
B. To become the most integrated Pharma company in India.
C. Focus on exports.
D. Step up research and development activity and launch drug discovery program.
E. To gain access to new products, technologies and markets through strategic alliances.

The Year After Implementing GATT

The company has achieved what it has planned and a lot more. Its 2006 vision statement clearly states that the company is determined to achieve leadership position and pledges its commitment to total customer care by delivering world-class products and services.

Group 'B' Companies: Competing for International Generics Space

All the ten companies in the Group 'B' have a common goal. They all want to become leading international generic companies. This strategic focus is at once the guiding post and the major driver of all their action programs and plans which we will explore and analyze in the later chapters. All the ten companies in the group are vertically integrated and are constantly investing in upgrading technology. The top five companies in the group have proven skills in process development and formulation development. Their product portfolios are very wide and deep. The others in the group too have world-class manufacturing infrastructure.

Table 5.2 Group 'B' Companies Vision: International Generics

Company	Strategic Vision
1. Cipla	• To retain the leadership position in domestic market and expand international business by leveraging its technological advantage • To continue the focus on result-driven research work to develop and enhance know-how for new drug delivery systems and manufacturing processes for both APIs and formulations
2. Aurobindo Pharma	• An integrated healthcare company with major thrust in APIs for both regulated and other global markets and significant presence in custom synthesis and specialty generic formulations • Aspire to be a leading provider of pharmaceuticals to both brand and generic pharma industry • Shall achieve it by creating a competitive advantage in chemistry through innovation, cost structure and constructive partnerships

Company	Strategic Vision
3. Matrix Laboratories	To be an innovative and integrated partner in the global pharmaceutical industry.
4. Orchid	To become an integrated pharmaceutical corporation of global scale and standing with a comprehensive coverage from discovery to delivery.
5. Ipca Laboratories	To be a fully integrated pharmaceutical company with world class manufacturing facilities approved by all the leading regulatory authorities in the world. The company's major thrust is on exports.
6. Alembic	To become a knowledge-driven global pharmaceutical company with the highest level of operational excellence in all spheres.
7. Claris Life Sciences	Vision: To be one of the world's leading and most admired pharmaceutical companies in the global generics industry. To continually create value and bring pride to their share-holders, partners, customers and the community at large. To preserve earth's most precious resource - human lives.
8. J.B. Chemicals	The company is committed to healthcare, quality manufacturing and innovative research with basic values like Industry, Integrity and Innovation.
9. Unichem Laboratories	To be a global pharmaceutical company with increasing focus on innovative research and developed markets.
10. Strides Arcolabs	To become a significant global Pharma company in difficult-to-manufacture and innovative domain

Cipla Before GATT,
Strategic Vision during the Transition Period

Technology and marketing are the core competencies of Cipla. Cipla has built an enviable manufacturing infrastructure in the Indian pharmaceutical industry. Its process development skills too are among the industry's best. Its strategic vision amplifies its values and objectives. In 1997, the company has set itself these goals:

A. To achieve technological leadership in the domestic market.

B. To achieve quality not to just meet the regulatory requirements but to meet the ultimate requirement of quality – the requirements of the customer and the market place.

C. To exploit the opportunity that the liberalized environment has given the Indian companies by using the technological strengths to expand overseas.

D. To set up at least one production base in each region and then leverage these bases through technical tie-ups and franchising agreements. Initially all these tie-ups or joint ventures will manufacture and market only formulations. Once these international markets take shape, the ventures will move into the manufacture of bulk drugs through backward integration. Cipla will provide the required technology.

E. To achieve over one third of turnover through exports by the year 2000.

The Year After Implementing GATT

Cipla has achieved every single one of these objectives. Today in 2006, The company continues to maintain its leadership position in the domestic market. Exports contributed one-half of its Rs. 32.36 billion sales in the year ending March 2006. Cipla is one of a handful of Indian Pharma companies that have achieved a steady growth with improved profitability for fifteen years in a row. The company continues its strategic focus on:

- Retaining its leadership position in domestic market and in expanding its international business
- Working through partnerships and strategic alliances to sustain its steady business growth in the future
- Leveraging its technological advantage developed over 70 years and sharpen its competitive edge
- Result-driven research work to develop and enhance know-how for new drug delivery systems and manufacturing processes for both APIs and formulations

Aurobindo Pharma

Started as a manufacturer of semi-synthetic penicillin bulk actives in 1986, Aurobindo Pharma had grown to become a leading player in the Indian pharmaceutical industry in less than two decades. Constantly improving its business model, the company is well on its way to realize its strategic vision of becoming a leading provider of pharmaceuticals to both brand and generic Pharma industry by creating a competitive advantage in chemistry through innovation, cost structure, and constructive partnerships.

Matrix Laboratories

Matrix (formerly known as Herren Drugs) is a manufacturer of Active Pharmaceutical Ingredients (APIs). It acquired Medicorp Technologies and Vorin Laboratories (a subsidiary of Ranbaxy Laboratories) in 2002. The company clearly defined its mission and vision and stormed into the big league in the Indian pharmaceutical industry in a short time. By 2006, the company has established its presence in international markets including the regulated ones and is cruising on its strategic trajectory to become an innovative and integrated partner in the global pharmaceutical industry. The recent acquisition of a majority stake in Matrix by Mylan Laboratories, a leading international generic company is indicative of the capabilities of Matrix.

Orchid Before GATT,
Strategic Vision During the Transition Period

Orchid has started as a 100 per cent export-oriented bulk drug manufacturer with focus on cephalosporins. It has built a world class manufacturing facility and been exporting its bulk actives to major international world markets including US and Europe. Having reached a turnover of Rs. 2.4 billion in the fiscal 1997 with exports of bulk actives and drug intermediates, the company planned a major expansion program in bulk drugs and integrated forward into formulations. The essence of its strategic vision in the late 1990's was:

1. To become the most integrated Cephalosporin producer in the world.
2. To achieve cost leadership.
3. To diversify into all the six basic process technologies.
4. Product strategy with an eye on patent protection trends.
5. To create world class manufacturing facilities.

The Year After Implementing GATT

Orchid is certainly emerging as a global pharmaceutical company with established research, manufacturing and marketing capabilities. The company is vertically integrated with presence across the pharmaceutical value chain. The company made significant investments since 2001 to enter and expand into regulatory markets.

The discerning analyst would observe the consistency in both performance and the continuous strategic focus in the company's vision statement of 2006: To become an integrated global pharmaceutical player of distinction with a comprehensive coverage from discovery to delivery.

Ipca Before GATT,
Strategic Vision During the Transition Period

What are the three most important areas of focus at Ipca? Backward integration in bulk drugs. Brand building in marketing of formulations. Export thrust. These three areas have helped Ipca reach a critical mass of Rs. 3.3 billion in fiscal 1998. The company has embarked on a major product diversification plan. It is expanding its therapeutic coverage with a massive new product launch plan: about ten new introductions per year. It had already introduced ten new products in 1998 and ten more in 1999. Here are the strategic objectives of the company:

1. To achieve a sales turnover of Rs. 3.3 billion in 1998–99.
2. To extend the therapeutic coverage through aggressive new product introduction.
3. To grow at a minimum rate of 20 per cent per annum.

4. To concentrate on exports of bulk actives and drug intermediates to developed markets.
5. To target developing markets in South East Asia, Africa, Middle East and the CIS for formulation exports.
6. To optimize the capacity utilization through contract manufacturing, approved by international regulatory authorities for select overseas companies at its facilities.

The Year After Implementing GATT

The company has more than fulfilled its growth objectives during the next five years. The company continues to build its manufacturing infrastructure to exploit the emerging opportunities in the CMO space reiterating its strategic vision in 2006 to become a fully integrated pharmaceutical company with its manufacturing facilities approved by all leading regulatory authorities in the world as the company's major thrust is on exports.

Alembic

Incorporated in 1907, Alembic is one of the oldest pharmaceutical companies in India. In 2006, the company has embarked on a major change program. The company is redefining a host of paradigms in terms of markets, positioning and manufacturing. It is trying to synergize new learnings, new investments to propel growth in the new economic order. The company has a very ambitious vision of becoming a knowledge-driven global pharmaceutical company with the highest level of operational excellence in all spheres.

Claris Life Sciences

Claris started its operations on April 1, 1999. The company was founded by a team of scientists, pharmaceutical specialists and management experts and has global tie-ups and networking with research laboratories and pharmaceutical companies across the world. The company is focusing on a niche segment where the number of players is not many owing to the complexities of products and technology involved. The company 's customers include government institutions, and large corporate hospitals and international AID agencies as its products - sterile injection products are used in operation rooms and ICUs (intensive care unit).

J B Chemicals

J B Chemicals and Pharmaceuticals Limited is a vertically integrated pharmaceutical company from India manufacturing bulk drugs, intermediates and formulations in cardiovascular, anti-amoebic, anti-ulcerant and NSAID (Non-Steriodal Anti-inflammatory Drugs) therapeutic areas. The company currently generates over half of its turnover from international markets. Today, the company has emerged as a contract research and manufacturing partner of some of the international pharmaceutical giants. J B Chemicals is planning to further consolidate its position in CRAMS space and leverage its power of integration across the value chain to emerge as a significant player in the international generics arena.

Unichem Laboratories

Unichem Laboratories is a fully integrated Indian pharmaceutical company, which was founded in 1944. The company has been investing for the past few years on enhancing its research and developmental capabilities to compete in the CMO space in addition to catering to its own growth requirements. All its expansion plans are consistent with its strategic vision of becoming a global pharmaceutical company with increased focus on innovative research and developed markets.

Strides Arco Labs

A global top five producer of soft gelatin capsules, Strides Arco Labs has set its sights high on the world pharmaceutical market in the globalized environment that is beyond soft gelatin capsules. The company has created a platform to provide full service to global Pharma players in the regulated markets. The company made all the right moves to become a partner of choice like investing in R&D, creating world class manufacturing infrastructure, regulatory competencies and win-win partnerships with international drug majors.

Group 'C' Companies: Competing for the CRAMS Space

The ten companies in Group 'C' are vying with each other in competing for the fast expanding CRAMS (Custom Research and Contract Manufacturing Services) space. These companies have built a manufacturing structure that is contemporary and many of them received approvals from international regulatory authorities such as US FDA, UK MHRA, MCC of South Africa, TGA of Australia and ANVISA of Brazil etc. The rest are in the process of receiving them as they built their plants complying with the international regulatory requirements. Some of the companies are already planning to enter into specialty generics and gradually building their capabilities to participate in the discovery research by providing the customized solutions. The key to success in the CRAMS business is world-class technological and research infrastructure, scientific capabilities and cost efficiencies.

Table 5.3 Group 'C' Companies Vision: CRAMS Partners-of-choice

Company	Strategic Vision
1. Jubilant Organosys	• To be among the top 10 most admired companies • To maintain and acquire the First or Second leadership position in chosen areas of business in India • To expand position of leadership in India to establish global presence • To continuously create new opportunities for growth in strategic businesses • To continuously achieve a return on invested capital of at least 10 points higher than the cost of capital
2. Divi's Labs	A Vision to Excel: To maintain leadership in custom synthesis of APIs and Intermediates for healthcare and life sciences industry and to be one of the top companies world-wide in this domain to develop generic APIs for the late cycle needs of the industry.
3. FDC Limited	To be a globally acclaimed generic pharmaceutical company.

Company	Strategic Vision
4. Shasun Chemicals	Shasun carries out custom manufacturing of off patent drugs for MNCs like Eli Lilly, GSK, Boots and Reliant Pharma. Long term nature of supply contracts assures Shasun of stable revenues. Thrust on US markets to increase with large outsourcing opportunity in bulk as well as formulations.
5. Dabur Pharma	A specialty pharmaceutical company that develops, manufactures and markets oncology products with manufacturing operations located in India and UK and marketing operations world wide. The company is uniquely positioned to compete in the rapidly growing and extremely attractive oncology market.
6. Ind-Swift Laboratories	• To emerge as one of the most profitable pharmaceutical companies in India, enhancing value for user, consumer, community and shareholder value. • Ind-Swift intends to increase its presence in the international scene • The Group is concentrating on the CRAMS business which is supported by world class research and manufacturing facilities
7. Dishman Pharmaceuticals	To develop as a contract research outsourcing (CRO) and contract manufacturing outsourcing (CMO) partner of choice in the global pharmaceutical and chemical industries, whilst continuing to be a leading supplier of QUATs and specialty chemicals, intermediates and APIs.
8. Natco Pharma	Innovative and active across the entire spectrum in pharmaceuticals – from basic research, bulk actives and intermediates to finished dosage forms and clinical research.
9. Nectar Life Sciences	To become a preferred contract manufacturer for leading pharmaceutical companies with the impetus coming from domestic as well as global markets
10. Suven Pharma	In the business of design, manufacture and supply of bulk actives, drug intermediates and fine chemicals, catering to the needs of global life sciences industry with products fulfilling customers' needs and expectations.

Jubilant Organosys

Jubilant Organosys has positioned itself as a strong player and partner of choice in the rapidly growing CRAMS space. The company has developed and acquired key competencies that are crucial for success to become a leading player in the contract services – like strong presence across the value chain, world class manufacturing infrastructure with approvals from leading international regulatory authorities and robust relationships with global customers.

The company's strategic approach has a clear focus: win-win partnerships, creation of incremental value by moving up the value chain, differentiation through innovation and economies of scale. The company in 2006 is among the top 35 companies in the Indian pharmaceutical industry.

Divi's Labs

Started as Divi's Research Centre Private Limited in October 1990, the company began its operations in 1991 as a research consultancy organization for developing commercial processes for APIs and intermediates. The company supplied process technology on turnkey basis to several generic drug manufacturers. Later in December 1994, the company was converted into a public limited company changing its name to Divi's Laboratories and entered into manufacturing of APIs and intermediates. The company has been targeting the regulated markets and accordingly built a world class manufacturing and R&D infrastructure and got approvals from leading regulatory authorities of the world. The company earns over 80 per cent of its revenue from international markets. The company's focus is clearly and sharply on the CRAMS space and wants to be the partner of choice for some of the global pharmaceutical majors.

FDC Limited

Formerly known as Fair Deal Corporation, FDC limited has a history spanning over seven decades. The company made a modest beginning in 1936 marketing vitamins and other formulations. It started its manufacturing operations in 1949. FDC has many firsts to its credit over the years. The company had always adapted itself to the changing vicissitudes and today's FDC has modern facilities approved by leading regulatory authorities across the world and is exporting to over fifty countries. The company's attitude can be seen from its welcome sign on its home page, which says - *Where state-of-the-art facilities meet ground-breaking APIs and formulations.* The company is striving to be a global player in the generics space.

Shasun Chemicals

Shasun started in 1976 as an API manufacturer of Analgin has gradually evolved into a vertically integrated player in pharmaceuticals with global aspirations. Shasun has been improving its competitive quotient over the years and consolidating its position year after year to emerge as a leader in the CRAMS space. The company has built its manufacturing structure to meet the international regulatory approvals and received several from the leading regulatory authorities of the world like US FDA, UK MHRA, and TPD of Canada etc.

Dabur Pharma

Dabur Pharma Limited, a public limited company incorporated in 2003 is an associate company of Dabur India Limited, a 250-million healthcare company incorporated in India in 1884. Dabur Pharma operates in Europe and some other international markets through its wholly-owned subsidiary Dabur-Oncology Plc. The company is a vertically integrated specialty pharmaceuticals company focusing on oncology. The company's strategic vision is to achieve a significant position in the global oncology therapeutic area.

Ind-Swift Laboratories

Promoted as a joint venture by the Swift Group of Chandigarh, India with the Punjab State Industries Corporation Limited (PSIDC), the Ind-Swift Group went public in 1977 and focused on API manufacturing.

The company built world class manufacturing infrastructure, obtained approvals from the leading regulatory authorities in the world and is emerging as a dependable supplier of APIs to global majors in regulated markets and leading pharmaceutical companies in other international markets. The company's strategic vision is clearly focused on becoming a leading player in the CRAMS space.

Dishman Pharmaceuticals

After achieving a leadership position in the QUATs (Quaternary Ammonium and Phosphonium Compound) business, Dishman Chemicals Private Limited integrated forward to manufacture drug intermediates and APIs and became a public limited company in February 1997. The company clearly defined its strategic vision of becoming a leading player in the fast expanding CRAMS business. The company has successfully bagged some long term supply arrangements for its APIs and intermediates with some of the leading international pharmaceutical companies.

Natco Pharma

Natco Pharma, started in 1981 had been through ups and downs during the past two decades. The company had built huge manufacturing infrastructure, became the preferred partner in contract manufacturing services to some of the Indian drug majors and was marketing a wide range of products in diverse therapeutic categories in the Indian market. The company's key competitive advantage was in manufacturing sustained release oral dosage forms. But some how the company had excess unutilized capacities and was unable to sustain its marketing activities and sold its product portfolio in domestic market to Sun Pharma in 1998. In the post-GATT Era, however, the company has refocused its vision and bounced back with renewed vigor. Natco Pharma in 2006 is a vertically integrated pharmaceutical company with world-class infrastructure across the Pharma value chain. The company has set its goal to become an innovative and active player across the Pharma value chain – from drug discovery to bulk actives to dosage forms development and manufacture and clinical research.

Nectar Life Sciences

Formerly known as Surya Medicare, Nectar Life Sciences is among the largest manufacturers and exporters of cephalosporins and semi-synthetic penicillins. Its manufacturing facilities are located at the foothills of Himalayas. The compnay earns 25 per cent of its revenues from non-regulated markets currently and is planning to enter the regulated markets in less than two years. The company Nectar Life Sciences is upgrading and expanding its manufacturing facilities to world-class level as it is targeting the regulated markets. The company's strategy is also to diversify its product portfolio into non-antibiotic segments.

Suven Life Sciences

Suven Pharmaceuticals Limited, which was started in 1989 as a private limited company was converted into a public limited company in 1995 with a new name Suven Life Sciences and with a new scope and hope. The company has renewed its focus to become a prominent player in the CRAMS space building competencies across the value chain including discovery research and clinical research. In 2006 the company is emerging as a leading NCE development company. Suven is one of the very few companies, which develops and supplies intermediates starting from Phase I till launching. The recent agreement with Eli Lilly the global pharmaceutical major in the area of custom research reinforces that the company is right on course to realize its strategic vision.

A Common Thread

The strategic vision of all these companies indicate that they are pursuing the strategic path of transforming their organizations from their current branded generic or international generic company stages to ultimately becoming research based pharmaceutical companies or to become partner-of-choice in the rapidly growing CRAMS space. The key elements of the strategic vision of all these companies are to:

A. Achieve a critical mass to generate investible surplus.
B. Upgrading technology to a world-class level.
C. Become a vertically integrated player to achieve control on costs, quality and strategy.
D. Export thrust and international marketing capabilities.

E. Stepping up of investment in R&D.

F. Establish a strong presence and become competitive across the value chain.

When the strategic approaches are similar, what separates the winners and the "also-rans" is superior levels of competence, sheer will to win the race, stamina to sustain and, above all, executional capabilities to translate vision into reality!

Vision 2020

What is the ultimate goal of a generic manufacturer in a developing country like India? When you ask this question you are likely to get three types of responses.

- Some of the leading organizations would like to be research-based or innovation-led global pharmaceutical companies.
- A few others would like to compete in the generic space that is rapidly growing and become international generic companies with respectable to strong presence in both lucrative first-world or developed markets and other international markets.
- A few companies would like to position themselves as 'partners-of-choice' or preferred partners in the CRAMS (Contract Research and Manufacturing Services) space that is expanding fast.

Whatever be the space in which a company chooses to compete, every company wants to become an integrated company competing across the value chain. At least ten to fifteen of the Indian Pharmaceutical companies are planning and preparing themselves to become research based pharmaceutical companies of global standing. And then there are others who are trying to be among the top ten international generic companies. The remaining companies are competing to create their own place in the fast-cramming CRAMS space.

The journey or the transition, or perhaps the metamorphosis from a generic manufacturer to a research-based international pharmaceutical company is tough and arduous to say the least. The evolutionary process (Figure 5.1) would take anything between 20 to 25 years provided one works towards this goal with unflinching determination. It can take a minimum period of ten years for a generic manufacturer to graduate into a branded generic company and to an international generic company with the right investment and the right capabilities. From an international generic company to a research-based international pharmaceutical company, it could take anywhere between ten to fifteen years with the right combination of competencies, capabilities, strategies and investments.

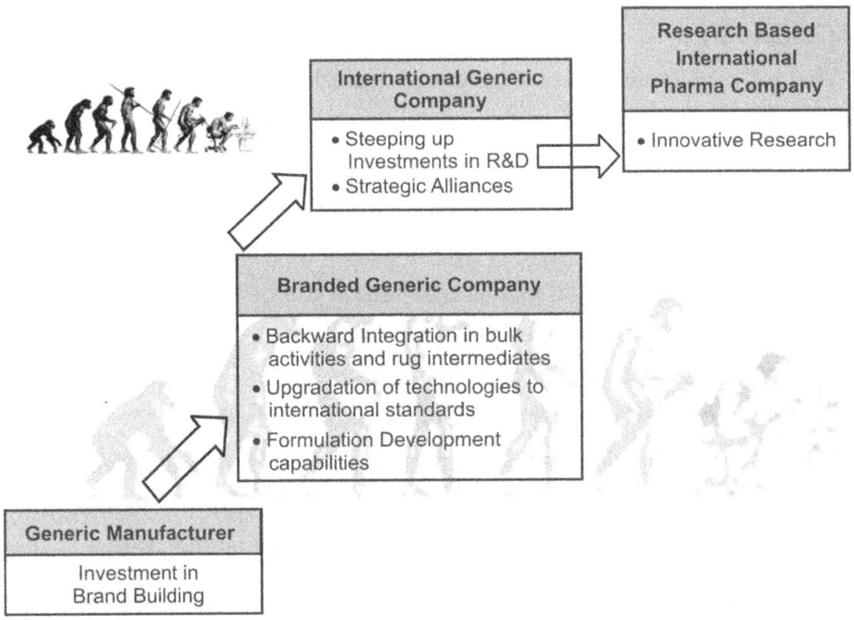

Fig. 5.1 Evolution of a Research Based Pharmaceutical Company

There seems to be a well-defined hierarchy of goals in the pharmaceutical industries of the developing world. All firms virtually start off either as manufacturers and marketers of formulations or bulk actives and drug intermediates. Then they integrate backward or forward depending upon the point from where they started, to become fully or vertically integrated pharmaceutical companies.

Vertical integration gives a significant and sustainable advantage to a pharmaceutical firm. It gives them control on costs, timely availability and quality of inputs. The underlying assumption here, of course, is that the integrated firm has a more cost-effective process. Superior technology, therefore, holds the key to successful integration.

Barring Teva, the Israeli drug major, there are not many international generic companies that are fully integrated. Many of them outsource their raw materials and here lies the big opportunity. Indian drug companies, which have developed very good process development skills over the years, can compete very effectively in international generic markets.

That is why many of these leading Indian drug firms have been pursuing vertical integration very aggressively to succeed in the highly competitive international generic markets. Ranbaxy, which has already become a vertically integrated international generic company, has reset its goal: to be among the top five international generic companies in the world with US $ 5 billion in sales by 2012.

What is common between the leading drug firms like Ranbaxy, Cipla, Dr. Reddy's, Sun Pharma, Lupin, Wockhardt, Zydus Cadila, Aurobindo Pharma, Glenmark, Orchid and the others in terms of their strategic content and intent?

Vertical integration. Virtually every one of these firms and others with aspirations to becoming international generic companies and research-based international pharma companies have been vying with each other to become vertically integrated. This is because vertical integration helps lower costs, achieve economies of scale and raise the capital cost barriers.

Economies of Scale

The unit cost of a product (or operation or function that goes into the production of a product) declines as the absolute volume per period increases. Lupin has achieved significant advantages due to economies of scale to become a world leader in the anti-TB segment. Orchid has achieved similar benefits to become one of the most sought after producers of cephalosporins in the world, mainly due to its backward integration. Biocon is doing it with statins. Ranbaxy, by virtue of its vertical integration among other strategic moves, has become India's largest pharmaceutical company.

Economies of scale also help in creating entry barriers, particularly when there are economies in vertical integration, when the firms operate in successive stages of production and distribution. In the pharmaceutical industry, there are significant economies of scale for a vertically integrated company. The raw material costs account for anywhere between one-third to one-half of the production costs. A vertically integrated firm can, therefore, achieve considerable control on input costs. The new entrant consequently must be either integrated or face a cost disadvantage, as well as foreclosure of inputs or markets if most established competitors are integrated. Consider the case of the cephalosporin market. A number of blockbuster molecules have gone out of patent during the last few years and more number of blockbuster molecules would be going to be out of patent in the next few years. The most integrated companies in the cephalosporin segment such as Orchid and Lupin are going to reap a rich harvest in this huge opportunity.

Backward Integration

Backward integration means that a manufacturer of finished dosage forms starts producing key raw materials like bulk drugs and intermediates. This gives the integrated firm the necessary control over costs, quality and timely availability of its inputs. It also helps the firm to lower its production costs and put pressure on competitors, who cannot afford such integration.

In the case of backward integration, the volume of captive consumption of the firm contemplating backward integration must be large enough to support an in-house production unit. Otherwise the firm faces the dilemma of whether to sell the extra output to its competitors in the domestic market or to export to reap the economies of scale in producing the inputs.

Forward Integration

Forward integration means that a bulk drug manufacturer starts manufacturing the end use applications of products – finished dosage forms or formulations, generic or branded. In the case of forward integration, the firm is competing with its purchasing firms. Forward integration, thus helps the company to enhance value addition and allows it to charge a premium for its products. The firm can achieve higher margins for its products and a higher rate of return on its investment due to higher price realizations.

Forward integration can often allow the firm to differentiate its product more successfully because it can control more elements of production processes. The race for developing novel drug delivery systems for out of patent drugs by some leading Indian drug firms amply illustrates this.

Vertical Integration

Vertical integration stated simply, means that a firm is integrated both forward and backward. Vertical integration in the drug industry has important generic benefits and costs. They apply to both forward and backward integration.

Backward integration helps the firm lower costs and forward integration helps raise price realization. Vertically integrated firm, therefore, can reap double benefits.

Economies of scale are at the core of vertical integration. International generic companies have a strategic need to achieve low-cost production and higher price realization. They have a two-pronged approach for enhancing value-addition. They place greater value and emphasis on achieving economies of all types.

A second potential benefit of vertical integration, proposed by Michael Porter in his brilliant treatise "Competitive Strategy", is that it provides a tap into technology. In some circumstances it can provide close familiarity with technology in upstream or downstream (or both) businesses; a form of economy of information so important as to deserve separate treatment.

Formulation manufacturers integrate backward into making bulk drugs and bulk drug manufacturers integrate further backward into intermediates to gain better understanding of this essential technology.

Manufacturers of bulk drugs integrate forward into formulation to enhance value-addition by improving margins and by expanding business as a whole.

One company that has become vertically integrated in the real sense is Ranbaxy. It has a clear strategy to support its global brand building for 25 products with its own low cost bulk actives about ten years ago. This puts Ranbaxy in an enviable position, because there is hardly any international generic company, which is so fully integrated and operates in as many markets. The company is able to command higher margins in both bulk drugs and formulations, because it controls costs throughout the value chain. That is what has made Ranbaxy the ninth generic company in the world. It is this distinct competitive advantage which will drive its generic business in the US and Europe and help it achieve its objective to be among the top five generic companies in the world with US $ 5 billion in sales and a significant business in proprietary prescription products in developed markets by 2012.

Key Issues

Vertical integration can reduce uncertainty of supply and hedge the firm against fluctuations in prices. At the same time, it is important to ensure that internal transfer prices reflect market realities. Porter strongly suggests that products should pass from unit to unit within the integrated company at transfer prices reflecting market prices to insure that each unit will manage its business properly. If transfer prices differ from market prices, one unit will be subsidizing the other compared to what it could be achieving on the open market. One unit will be better off and the other worse off as a result. The managements of the upstream and downstream units may then make decisions, which reduce efficiency and harm the competitive positions of the units.

Integrate to Succeed

Vertical integration gives the firm competitive advantage over the un-integrated firm, in the form of higher prices, lower costs and even lowers risk. Thus the unintegrated firm must integrate or bear a disadvantage. The new entrant to the business is forced to enter as an integrated firm or face the consequences. The more significant the benefits of net integration, the greater the pressure on other firms also to integrate. If the capital investment required for vertical integration is significant, the necessity to integrate will raise an entry barrier.

Quasi-integration

Quasi-integration, as the name suggests is establishment of a relationship between vertically related businesses that is somewhere between long-term contracts and full ownership. Common forms of quasi–integration are:

A. Minority equity investment
B. Loans or loan guarantees
C. Exclusive dealing agreements
D. Cooperative R&D

Many of the thirty pharma companies discussed in this book are among the most integrated branded generic companies. Between them, they manufacture as many as 200 bulk drugs and a number of intermediates in addition.

Competitive Advantage

Vertically integrated pharmaceutical companies in India have a distinct competitive advantage that is sustainable. Many overseas generic manufacturers out source their bulk requirements, whereas a vertically integrated manufacturer can achieve lower costs of production. This is a definite competitive advantage leading to either higher margins or more competitive prices to penetrate the market.

Many of these leading Indian drug companies have demonstrated the benefits of vertical integration. Dr. Reddy's process innovation skills and consequent cost advantages are well known to the pharmaceutical world. Through highly cost-effective alternative, non-infringing processes for products like ibuprofen, norfloxacin, ciprofloxacin etc., the company has demonstrated that these products can be marketed at unbelievably lower prices. Lupin has achieved similar successes in the anti-tubercular segments with rifampicin and ethambutol and now it is repeating the same in the cephalosporins segment. Wockhardt has achieved the distinction of becoming one of the largest producer of dextropropoxyphene and is planning to do the same with vitamin B12.

IPCA's success with the bulk active of the most widely prescribed anti-hypertensive molecule – atenolol is due to its ability to integrate right up to the basic stage. There are many examples of similar successes by other companies.

Vertical integration provides competitive advantage for a company irrespective of its competitive arena. Even in case of international generic companies vertical integration provides the competitive edge. The leading international generic companies are merging, acquiring or allying with other companies to integrate their operations and become more competitive.

The companies competing in the CRAMS space too are doing the same to reach the scale of economies and become the partner of choice by becoming integrated companies so that they can offer their services across the total spectrum of the value chain of contract research and manufacturing services.

In all the groups the discerning analyst would find a common thread. And that is either all the companies have already achieved vertical integration to a certain degree or taking all the steps to become a vertically integrated company in their respective competitive spaces across the pharmaceutical value chain.

As Dr. Parvinder Singh, the late chairman of Ranbaxy observed, "the fact is that if you control bulk, you also control cost, quality and strategy."

Three Major Opportunities, Three Major Competitive Spaces

The new globalized Pharma has thrown open three major competitive spaces which offer huge opportunies. Table 5.4 presents a summary of the three major competitive spaces that these thirty Indian pharmaceutical companies are targeting to explore and reap rich rewards.

Table 5.4 Competitive Spaces, Key Competencies

Competitive Space	The Opportunity	Key Competencies
Innovation –Led global Pharma company	Very large. Close to 90 per cent of the world US $ 650-billion.	• Vertical integration covering chemistry skills for developing molecules to developing dosage forms • Drug discovery skills right from screening the compounds to preclinical studies to clinical studies through all the four phases • Patenting skills • Regulatory environmental understanding and product registration skills • Marketing skills • Fund-raising capabilities either through operational excellence or mobilizing the funds from venture capitalists, markets etc.
International Generic Company	US $ 60-billion large and rapidly growing across the world due to increasing patent expiries of a number of block buster drugs till 2010 and increasing pressure from the governments of various nations to contain the healthcare expenditure.	• Strong chemistry skills to develop non-infringing processes. • Product developmental capabilities to develop innovative dosage forms • Strong regulatory capabilities • Thorough understanding about patents and how to file them. • Vertical integration to achieve sustainable competitive edge and cost leadership • World class manufacturing infrastructure with approvals from all the leading regulatory authorities in the world

Competitive Space	The Opportunity	Key Competencies
CRAMS Contract Research and Manufacturing Services)	CRAMS business is estimated to be US 175-billion large and growing at ten per cent annually. A. Custom Synthesis B. Custom Research C. Clinical Research D. Contract Manufacturing of OTC Healthcare Products, Generic Formulations	• Discovery capabilities for custom research • Capabilities to recruit clinical investigators, institutions, and patients • Data management capabilities • Capabilities of statistical analysis • Strong chemistry skills • Product development capabilities • World class manufacturing infrastructure with international approvals from leading regulatory authorities in the world • Skills to build and manage win-win strategic alliances • Cost leadership

Chapter Six

Reaching The Critical Mass

Critical mass is the market share, which a firm must obtain in order to become fully competitive on price and cost. To be fully competitive, a firm must achieve critical mass in all key functional areas like marketing and manufacturing infrastructures, technology base, research and developmental capabilities. It is also important to attain the critical mass within a reasonable span of time, the faster the better. Time overruns lead to cost overruns and creates strong pressures, resulting even in the abandonment of the venture itself.

What is critical to the whole business of critical mass is making a realistic estimate of the critical mass itself. The critical mass, for example, for an international generic company is a sales turnover of $300 million. This explains probably why some of the leading Indian pharmaceutical companies were chasing an objective of Rs. 10 billion in sales by the turn of the century that is during the transition period granted to India when it signed GATT. The critical mass for a research based pharmaceutical company is over $ 1 billion. Ranbaxy and Lupin aimed to achieve $ 1 billion by 2003. Ranbaxy achieved it a few years ago and Dr. Reddy's a few months ago and Lupin along with other Indian and drug majors like Wockhardt, Sun Pharma, Nicholas Piramal, Aurobindo Pharma are still chasing it.

At the same time, a number of firms sought to enter the Indian Pharma industry, apparently without having anticipated the very high start-up costs and the very large development and marketing service costs. Natco's failure to anticipate these and reach the critical mass quickly has forced it to put its most profitable formulations business on the block. Natco, however has currently refocused its strategy and is on a resurgent trail. Orchid, on the other hand, reached the critical mass in real quick time and is planning to integrate vertically to become even more competitive. Its success depends on whether it can attain the critical mass quickly enough in the fiercely competitive formulations business as it had in the cephalosporins bulk actives. The new Kids on the block who aspire to become innovation led pharmaceutical and biopharmaceutical companies of global distinction are Glenmark and Biocon. Aurobindo Pharma, and Matrix Laboratories too made dramatic progress and are serious contenders for their place in the international generics space.

Companies who are hell-bent on reaching the critical mass in time are turning themselves into predators. They are pursuing a very aggressive strategy of acquiring companies, manufacturing facilities, brands and even research centers. The new rule to reach the critical mass is simply this: If it takes time to create and you have no time, buy it!

Critical Mass, the Prerequisite

First, for a company to be successful in the pharmaceutical industry, it has to reach or acquire a critical mass and scale in those core therapeutic areas where it intends to focus.

Secondly, it has to have a broad production line that includes a range of products and services that can really deliver health care solutions.

Thirdly, to be successful, firms must effectively access and serve customers.

Fourthly, cost competitiveness is going to be very critical in today's environment of cost-containment.

The next is to have highly customer-driven processes, so that they are structured to succeed. Decision-making must be market driven, so that you can make decisions much more quickly and you can make those decisions in the context of a strategy and knowing where you are going.

What is Critical Mass?

Simply stated, critical mass is an amount necessary or sufficient to have a significant effect or to achieve a result.

While it is difficult to determine precisely the critical mass for Indian drug companies, based on international experience, it is possible to arrive at a ball park figure. The critical mass, for example, to become an integrated international generic company would be around $ 300 million in annual sales. It is only at this volume that the company can sustain the costs and investments required for being competitive and competent in international generic markets. The critical mass for a research-based international pharmaceutical company would be much higher – over $ 1 billion in annual sales, since the costs and investments needed would be significantly more.

Acquisition Route

Mergers and acquisitions have promoted growth for over a century in the West, most of all in corporate America. It is clear that mergers and acquisitions have become a staple of the world pharmaceutical industry. The many transactions that have been concluded in the last five years amply testify to this.

The Indian drug industry too seems to have been caught by the acquisition and merger bug. Nicholas Piramal, Ranbaxy, Sun, Wockhardt and Dr. Reddy's have been on the prowl and account for most of the drug industry mergers and acquisitions (companies as well as brands), in India during the last three years.

History shows that acquisitions are one of the surest ways of accomplishing ambitious corporate growth targets with acceptable returns.

Buying a business can be favorably compared with expanding an existing line of products, starting up an entirely new venture or entering into a halfway arrangement such as a joint venture, passive investment or marketing alliance. Compared with these alternatives, buying an established business can be a preferable development strategy for four key reasons:

1. **Less risk :** Established businesses that are acquired have a developed customer base, a verifiable financial track record and a demonstrated product line. The prospective acquisition has long ago passed the most risky phase of corporate life, the start-up.
2. **Infrastructure for growth :** The acquired company's plant, technology, reputation and employee base provide the buyer with a readymade infrastructure. The potential for growth is significantly enhanced if the buyer uses this infrastructure more effectively than the original owner.
3. **Conservation of capital investment :** Most extensions of existing product lines require significant operating capital beyond an initial investment. In contrast, as a stand-alone investment, many acquisitions produce income and positive cash flow immediately. Financing corporate growth can be easier via acquisition itself as predictably, contributing funds to pay for debt service and to provide shareholder returns, respectively.
4. **Control :** Alternatives to an acquisition – joint ventures, passive equity investments in third parties and marketing/distribution alliances – require less capital, but offer reduced control. The potential acquirer's return on its investment would depend on someone outside its own corporate organization.

Strategic Alliances

Necessity, as in the case of invention, is the mother an alliance too. The basic reason behind any alliance is a strong need for gaining access to products, markets, technology, know-how and even capital.

Alliances between companies, whether they are from different parts of the world or different ends of the supply chain, are facts of life in business today. 'Collaborate to compete' and 'Co-Opetition' have become signs and symbols of business today.

The Indian pharmaceutical industry is no exception. From being a highly protected environment until recently, Indian industry, particularly the pharmaceutical industry, seems to be in a tearing hurry to get into the alliance mode. How else can any one explain the sudden increase in alliances with both Indian and foreign companies?

The top ten Indian drug companies have forged into as many as 63 alliances with leading international players during the last three to four years. Out of these, just two companies, Nicholas Piramal and Zydus, have entered into 30 alliances as on date. Nicholas Piramal is clearly dependent on its alliances for growth. The company expects to achieve 50 per cent of its turnover from alliances within two years.

Alliances do not guarantee success. An alliance is like a marriage. The success of an alliance depends on how competent, open, understanding and mutually dependent each alliance partner is. In the absence of mutual respect and importance, alliances are no more than fleeting encounters, lasting only as long as it takes one partner to establish a beachhead in a new market. Others may become a prelude to a full merger. What is of paramount importance in making an alliance successful is 'being a good partner'. It has become a key corporate asset.

In today's global economy, a well-developed ability to create and sustain fruitful collaborations is a significant competitive advantage.

Why Are Alliances On The Increase?

The basic reason behind any alliance is to achieve synergy. To optimize utilization of resources. To do more with less. Here are nine important reasons for this unprecedented increase in alliances or partnerships in the pharmaceutical industry the world over.

1. Stagnant growth rates in many markets.
2. Slowing down of population growth rates (or even no-growth) in many industrialized countries.
3. Continuous escalation of costs in manufacturing, marketing and other areas.
4. Huge costs of research and development.

5. A number of blockbuster drugs that fueled the growth in the previous decade coming off-patents.
6. Not enough potential blockbuster drug candidates in the new product pipeline of companies.
7. Shortening of product life cycles due to intense competition.
8. Increasing pressure from cost-containment programs in virtually every market.
9. Eroding profit margins resulting from direct or indirect price controls by various governments.

All these changes in the marketing environment of the global health care industry are most likely to result in a greater harmony between the needs of Pharma producers in the developed world and the developing world. Research-based Pharma companies in the developed world will be even more selective in setting up off-shore manufacturing bases. There will be a sharp increase in the number of marketing alliances and technology transfers between multinational companies that do not want to manufacture locally and the local generic companies that do not have product development capabilities.

Generic companies in developing countries will look for alliances that help them in upgrading their technology base and to gain market access for their pharmaceutical substances and generic formulations.

Alliances – The Indian Scenario

India has all the features to become one of the most attractive alliance partners for prospective suitors. Consider these reasons:

- India has the potential to become one of the largest bulk drug manufacturers in the world. This is crucial, as the biggest single development since the late 1990s has been the growth of the generic market in the advanced countries. Moreover, all these countries continue to reel under the pressure of rising health care costs and cost-containment strategies of their respective governments. They are likely to out-source off-patent generic drugs and formulations from low cost producers that meet their quality.

- The key success factor in the generic market is low cost manufacturing of bulk actives, drug intermediates and generic formulations. India is strong on both counts.
- Further, India is a large market with a growing middle class that is over two hundred and fifty million large. This is almost the size of the population of the whole of Europe. Increasing living standards of the urban middle class and the rural population make it a potentially attractive market, despite its present per capita consumption of $ 5 per annum, which is the lowest in the world.
- A number of brand-name drugs are going off-patent in the next five years. This will increase the opportunities for significant revenue growth in the generic drug market.
- There is considerable pool of highly trained scientific personnel. The cost of conducting research in India is considerably lower than in developed countries like USA, Germany, France, UK and Japan. The costs of conducting pre-clinical tests too, are extremely low when compared to the developed countries. A rough estimate puts the cost of conducting clinical trials at about eighty per cent lower than in the US. India, thus can be very attractive to those MNCs that are looking for out-sourcing part of their research and development work.

Why Ally?

Almost all companies enter alliances out of need. A company may have the technology, but lack an important piece of the puzzle, such as market access. Alliances help the partner companies get a head start in tapping new business opportunities and overcome obstacles. The key questions to ask before deciding on an alliance are:

- Why do you need a partnership?
- With whom you want to collaborate?
- How are you going to combine your core competencies with your partner-to-be?
- How will you structure your relationship or alliance?

The international experience suggests that there are nine strategic factors that drive alliance formation.

1. **Changing Customer Demands :** Customer demands in many markets are changing. Consider for example that in the highly industrialized countries in Western Europe, North America and in Japan, the cost-containment drives by the respective governments are creating new opportunities for low cost generic drugs on an unprecedented scale. Many of the research-based pharmaceutical companies are making new strategic moves to meet the challenges either by starting their own generic companies or by allying with generic companies or by sourcing generic drugs from low cost manufacturers in developing countries.

   A number of leading Indian companies like Ranbaxy, Dr. Reddy's Laboratories, Lupin, Wockhardt, NPIL, Torrent and Cipla have been forming multi-level alliances with well-known MNCs. The salient features of these alliances are:

   - Collaborative research in select areas.
   - Sourcing of off-patent generic drugs – bulk actives and formulations.
   - Access to new products, markets and technology.

2. **Sharing of R&D costs :** The pharmaceutical industry is research-led. Research is very risky and expensive. High financial stakes, escalating R&D costs and cutthroat global competition have fueled a number of collaborations based on research. Out-sourcing of research too is on the increase. The major purpose of this is to optimize resource utilization, reduce costs and speed up the development process.

   Take for example the three recent research-based alliances between Indian Pharma companies and their international partners:

   - Glenmark's alliance with the global generics major Merck KgaA
   - Alliances with international generic companies for marketing their ANDAs in the US generic markets by Cipla, Orchid, Dabur etc.

- Long-term supply agreements of APIs and FDFs to International drug majors by Wockhardt, Nicholas Piramal, Shasun Chemicals among others
- Dr. Reddy's strategic alliance with Merck for authorized generics

3. **Sharing of knowledge :** Companies that are focused can capture new developments through alliances without reducing their focus. A number of drug firms, the world over, are allying with highly specialized developmental firms in areas like biotechnology, novel drug delivery systems etc. Alliances between Pharma companies and governmental research institutions like IICT and CDRI to share assets and fill knowledge gaps are also increasing.

4. **Achieving economies of scale :** Alliances can achieve the economies of scale needed to amortize investment and improve profitability. Alliances between Ranbaxy and Glaxo SmithKline in the area of research and development, Nicholas Piramal's with international drug companies for contract manufacturing and custom research and Wockhardt's alliances with international Pharma majors for contract manufacturing to achieve considerable economies of scale.

5. **Enhance scope of economies :** Companies can dramatically enlarge the scope of their operations through alliances. Consider for example the multi-level strategic alliance between Ranbaxy and Eli Lilly, in 1990's that covered two 50:50 joint ventures, collaborative research in select therapeutic areas, manufacturing and marketing of generic drugs and formulations in the US, India and South East Asia. Companies with well-defined strengths can, through tie-ups like these, enter new business areas more effectively and enhance the scope of economies significantly.

Development-based alliances can generate a steady stream of product enhancements in branded generics, generic drugs and formulations.

6. **Converting Barriers into Gateways :** However formidable the position of a company in its home market may be, the company may not be able to market its major or mature products equally well in all the international markets. More so in the case of companies in developing countries trying to enter the advanced countries like the US, UK, France, Germany, Japan etc. That is why the number of alliances between some leading Pharma companies and the generic companies in the US and Europe is increasing. Consider the following alliances in progress:
   - Zydus Cadila with Mallinckrodt Generics
   - Dr. Reddy's Labs with Merck for authorized generics
   - Glenmark with Merck KgaA Generics for dermatology range
   - Natco Pharma with Akorn for marketing their ANDAs in the US generic market
   - Orchid with Apotex, Par, Purepac and others for marketing generic formulations in the US
   - Cipla's marketing arrangement to enter the US generic market with its huge product basket with a number of American generic companies

   All these alliances are trying to get an access to the very lucrative, difficult-to-penetrate North American generic market. They are all trying to get a foot in the door by creating a beachhead through these alliances.

7. **Pre-empting the Competitive Threats :** You can pre-empt and blunt the competitive threats by a time-tested method through alliances. Remember? If you cannot beat them, join them!

8. **Using Excess Capacity :** A small number of companies in India are preparing themselves to enter into manufacturing alliances with some well-known multinational companies to soak up their excess capacities.

9. **Minimizing exit costs :** Companies can use tie-ups, collaborations and alliances to minimize the costs of leaving a business sector by establishing an alliance with a competitor and becoming a partner.

Reaching the Critical Mass

Companies, in order to achieve success, have to reach critical mass in all key areas of their business. A pharmaceutical company, for example, has to achieve the critical mass in market share, sales turnover, technological and manufacturing infrastructure, research and developmental capabilities etc. Some of the leading Indian pharma companies like Ranbaxy, Dr. Reddy's Laboratories, Nicholas Piramal, Lupin, Wockhardt and Sun Pharma are pulling out all stops to reach the critical mass.

The basic strategic approaches which are being adopted by all these companies to reach critical mass are somewhat similar in nature. These are:

1. **Extending Therapeutic Coverage :** Companies need to extend the slice of their served markets. They need to enter the new therapeutic areas and new customer segments to increase market share.
2. **Aggressive New Product Planning and Introduction :** The rate and success of new product introduction is crucial to improve, consolidate and defend one's market position in a given therapeutic segment.
3. **Market Coverage :** Entry and penetration of new geographical markets is vital for improving the overall sales of the company. Many of these successful companies very ambitiously chase export targets.
4. **Building and Upgrading Technological and Manufacturing Infrastructure :** If you want to compete in international markets or with international players in your own market, you need to deliver world class products and services. Upgrading technology is a must.

5. **Research and Developmental Capabilities :** It is also important to create and upgrade research and developmental capabilities for transforming from an imitative culture to an innovative one.

Winning Moves

The thirty companies that are selected for this study have been preparing vigorously to compete in the brave new world of globalized Pharma. Their corporate workouts are indeed very rigorous. Their strategic approach is to reach the critical mass in all key functional areas that are crucial for success in the product patent regime. All these successful companies have been following four broad strategic routes. These strategic highways are:

A. **Mergers and Acquisitions :** The fastest way to reach the critical mass is of course the M&A route. Mergers and acquisitions provide instant access to products, markets and technology. The sudden flurry of mergers and acquisitions across the industry and across borders clearly indicates the rush companies are in to achieve the critical mass.

B. **Strategic Alliances :** Another route that is brisk enough, if not as fast as mergers and acquisitions to reach the critical mass is through strategic alliances. The alliance route too, helps gain a faster access to products, markets and technology. In the case of acquisitions you own them and, in the case of alliances, you share them. No wonder that there is a dramatic increase in the number of alliances forged by Indian companies of late, now that the product patent era is a reality.

C. **New Products :** New products are the lifeblood of any business. Twenty-one of the thirty companies discussed in this study, have been pursuing very aggressive new product introduction strategies. They account for a fifth of all new products introduced in the Indian pharmaceutical industry during since 1998. Between them they have introduced 128 new products, which account for a quarter of the industry's new product sales during the previous year.

D. Expansion Strategies : Business expansion into new markets, whether they are new therapeutic segments or new geographical markets, is vital not only for growth but is essential even for survival. And business expansion strategies, by definition, require structural adjustments and changes to manage complexities of growth and diversification. Re-engineering of business processes and even organizational structures, therefore become necessary. These companies have been quick to adopt a dynamic approach towards structuring their operations.

Group 'A' Companies: Competing for The Innovation-Led Space

The ten companies in Group 'A' who made their strategic intent clear that they would compete for the innovation-led space, together gathered a critical mass of Rs. 177.39 billion which includes their international sales and the sales by their wholly owned subsidiaries internationally. The total number of acquisitions made by them is thirty-seven and the number of strategic alliances that they entered is over sixty-one. The motivation for these acquisitions and alliances is to gain or improve access to technology, markets, products, drug-discovery capabilities, manufacturing bases, capacity expansions, and customers. In other words, to strengthen their competitiveness and capabilities across the whole spectrum of the Pharma value chain.

Table 6.1 Group 'A' Companies Critical Mass

Company	Sales in FYE March 2006 Rs. Billion
1. Ranbaxy	51.02
2. Dr. Reddy's Laboratories	24.30
3. Sun Pharma	18.06
4. Lupin	16.60
5. Nicholas Piramal	15.82
6. Zydus Cadila Healthcare	15.07
7. Wockhardt	14.10
8. Biocon	7.93
9. Glenmark	7.57
10. Torrent Pharma	6.92

Table 6.2 Group 'A' Companies Mergers and Acquisitions (2000-06)

Company	Acquisitions	Purpose and Impact
1. Ranbaxy	8 acquisitions between 2002 and 2006 in France, Germany, Spain, Romania, Netherlands, South Africa and the US	To consolidate its position in the European and South African generic markets. To gain access to new technology platforms.
2. Dr. Reddy's	5 acquisitions between 2001 and 2006 in Germany, Spain and Mexico.	To gain market access, and consolidate its position in the European generic market. To strengthen its CPS business and consolidate the API business in regulated markets
3. Sun Pharma	4 acquisitions between 2004 and 2006 in the US, Hungary.	To expand manufacturing and activities in the US and consolidate its position in the US generics market. To create a manufacturing hub for its foray and consolidation in the European specialty generics market
4. Lupin	NA	Looking for acquisitions
5. Nicholas Piramal	8 acquisitions between 2001 and 2006 in India and UK	To beef up its contract manufacturing business. To gain access to generics business in regulated markets and new technology platforms, and new B2B customers To reinforce its manufacturing capabilities overseas
6. Zydus Cadila Healthcare	3 acquisitions between 2001 and 2003 in India and France	To extend therapeutic coverage and to improve market share in India To gain rapid market access to the French and European generics market
7. Wockhardt	4 acquisitions between 2003 and 2006 in UK, Germany, Ireland and France	To consolidate its already strong position in the UK generics market and improve presence in European generics market
8. Biocon	One acquisition in the US	To strengthen its research and development capabilitiesin the drug discovery area
9. Glenmark	4 acquisitions between 2004 and 2006 in Brazil, Argentina and South Africa	To consolidate its position in LATAM and South Africa
10. Torrent	One acquisition in Germany	To gain market access and build Pharma its position in the German and European generics market

Table 6.3 Group 'A' Companies Strategic Alliances

Company	Strategic Alliances (2000-06)	Nature and Purpose
1. Ranbaxy	3 alliances	To enhance product assess and to improve Market access
2. Dr. Reddy's	6 alliances	Research and Development To enhance product access and market access To improve Research and Development capabilities
3. Sun Pharma	NA	
4. Lupin	6 alliances	To gain and improve market access, out-licensing, and supply arrangements of anti-TB drugs
5. Nicholas Piramal	11 alliances and tie-ups	Product access through in-licensing, contract manufacturing and co-development of processes and products
6. Zydus Cadila	8 alliances	Contract manufacturing, co-marketing, and co-development
7. Wockhardt	8 alliances	Contract manufacturing and in-licensing
8. Biocon	3 alliances	Research and Development
9. Glenmark	12 alliances	Co-development of products, marketing, in-licensing
10. Torrent Pharma	4 alliances	Research and Development, in-licensing, and co-marketing

RANBAXY

Ranbaxy has a very clear idea of the critical mass it wants to reach to become a research-based international pharmaceutical company with $ 1 billion by 2003. The company has been aggressively pursuing a strategy of internationationalizing its business and consolidation of its domestic market position. It has worked out a detailed plan till 2003 for achieving the $ 1 billion target. Mergers and acquisitions are an important element of its growth strategy. Consider these facts :

A. *Mergers and Acquisitions:* Ranbaxy has taken over Croslands Research Laboratories through a merger in 1996. By this, Ranbaxy gained an instant access to the fast growing therapeutic segments of dermatalogicals and orthopaedics. It has also added a turnover of Rs. 760 million to its sales and 0.6 per cent share of the Indian pharmaceutical market through this merger. Furthermore, the product-mix acquired has higher gross margins.

Ranbaxy needed something more to boost its market share in the domestic market and consolidate its position. It therefore acquired Gufic's prescription business comprising the leading amoxicillin brand 'Mox' (sales over Rs. 300 million) and other anti-bacterial and dermatological brands in 1997. This acquisition helped in consolidating Ranbaxy's leadership position in the largest therapeutic segment of antibiotics in the Indian Pharma industry and reinforced its dermatological portfolio with the 'Zole' range from Gufic.

In September 1996, Ranbaxy acquired Ohm Laboratories, the New Jersey-based manufacturer of OTC formulations. This has given the company a faster access to the rapidly growing and lucrative North American generics market, which is a very important priority for Ranbaxy.

The market for off-patent generic formulations has also been growing in Europe. Ranbaxy acquired Rima Pharmaceuticals of Ireland, in November, 1996 to exploit marketing opportunities in the European Union, the second largest market for pharmaceuticals in the world.

Not satiated with these acquisitions, Ranbaxy is looking for more. This time it is looking for brand acquisitions. It is not keen on plants and labour as it has got them in plenty. The company has set up an internal M&A cell, which has identified 15–20 brands for acquisition worldwide. The company has also set aside a whopping $ 150 million to fund these acquisitions. Table 6.4 presents the recent acquisitions of Ranbaxy.

Table 6.4 Ranbaxy's Recent Acquisitions

	Acquired	Purpose and Impact
1.	Veratide, the second largest brand with 2002 annual sales of € 3 million in the calcium channel blocker plus diuretics category in Germany for € 5 million through its German subsidiary Basics Gmbh.	To strengthen its product portfolio in the chronic disease segment and reinforce its position in the Europe's largest generic market.
2.	The generic business of RPG Aventis in France in 2003.	To establish its presence in one of the most important European generic markets.
3.	The generic portfolio of 18 products belonging to the Spanish pharmaceutical company EFARMES SA, through its WOS – Ranbaxy S L, Barcelona in July 2005. EFARMES is a leading company in the development of pharmaceutical products on its own and on exclusive customized basis.	To consolidate its position in the rapidly growing US $ 700 million-dollar Spanish generic market that is fifth largest in Europe.
4.	Allen S.p.A, a division of the unbranded generic business of Glaxo SmithKline (GSK) in Italy through its Italian subsidiary – Ranbaxy Italia S.p.A. in March 2006.	To strengthen its position in the US $ 420-million large Italian generic market that is growing at 49 per cent.
5.	96.7 per cent stake in Terapia, the largest independent generic company in Romania for US $ 324 million in March 2006.	Ranbaxy acquired through this Terapia's two manufacturing units, bioequivalence centers, and sixty products, thirty percent of which are registered in 15 countries. More importantly Ranbaxy has gained access to 4000 pharmacies and 450 hospitals in Romania. Ranbaxy wants to make this its European manufacturing hub and consolidate its position in the rapidly genericizing market in Europe.
6.	Ethimed NV, the top-ten generic company in Belgium the seventh largest market in Europe and Netherlands the sixth largest market.	To gain a firm foothold and reinforce its position in European generics market
7.	Acquired patents, trademarks and automated manufacturing equipment for Senetek PLC's proprietary disposable autoinjector for self-administration of parenteral drugs, including epinephrine.	Access to new technology platform for delivering injectible drugs and new products to gain a competitive advantage.
8.	Acquired South Africa's fifth largest pharmaceutical firm Be-tabs Pty Ltd for US $ 70 million in November 2006.	To achieve considerable synergies and strengthen the company's foothold in South Africa. Ranbaxy is already present in 45 of the 50-odd countries in Africa.

Almost all of Ranbaxy's recent acquisitions are in Europe. The company is bullish on Europe as it acquired three companies in just one week during March 2006 to consolidate its position in three rapidly growing generic markets such as France, Italy, and Romania. The company is looking for more.

B. *Strategic Alliances :* The North American generic market is the highest priority for Ranbaxy. It is next only to the Indian market in terms of importance. To gain a faster access to this rather tough-to-enter market, Ranbaxy has chosen the alliance route. The company has already entered into two marketing alliances in North America. To consolidate its position in the domestic market, the company is planning to tie-up with some small domestic companies for marketing some of its low volume products.

Table 6.5 Ranbaxy's Strategic Alliances

Alliance with	Purpose and Impact
1. Zenotech, India for marketing Zenotech's oncology and cytotoxic injectible products under Ranbaxy label on a non-exclusive basis in certain key international markets like LATAM including Brazil, and Mexico, and in Russia and other CIS markets.	Access to products in the rapidly growing Oncology therapeutic area.
2. Ferring Interernational, Switzerland, a biopharmaceutical company for co-marketing its product – Desmopressin, (a structural analogue of Arginine vasopressin indicated for Nocturia) in India.	Product access to reinforce its leadership position in Urology therapeutic area.
3. A 70:30 J V with CIH (Community Investment Holdings) South Africa christened as 'Sonke Pharmaceuticals Pvt. Limited.'	To market and sell Ranbaxy's range of ARV (anti-retroviral) products in South Africa.

The strategic alliances of Ranbaxy are essentially in the areas of product access, market access and co-marketing.

C. ***New Product introductions :*** Entered respiratory and asthma segments with a number of new products – Dry Powder Inhalers (DPI), and Metered Dose Inhalers (MDI) thus becoming the first company to launch the entire range of inhalers based on hydro-fluoro-alkane (HFA) propellants. The company also introduced Rheohaler, an innovative DPI devise which is convenient to use and demonstrates better drug deposition rates vital for respiratory medication. In the HIV segment, the company introduced a new combipack Virolis E. Its new product Suncross became one of the top 30 introductions during the year in India.

D. ***Expansion Strategies :*** Ranbaxy has always been highly strategic in restructuring its operations and re-engineering its business processes. Its management structure is quite unique – with the world divided into four geographical regions, each headed by a regional director. In the domestic market it has created nine independent marketing divisions to achieve a marketing focus even as it is undertaking a major product diversification strategy to extend its therapeutic coverage.

DR. REDDY'S LABORATORIES

The metamorphosis of Dr. Reddy's Labs from a bulk drug company, known for its copying skills, to an innovative drug firm is a result of clear thinking, strategic vision, unflinching determination and careful business planning. The company has been dexterously planning to achieve a sustained growth to generate the investible surplus necessary for building world class research and developmental capabilities. Dr. Anji Reddy is emphatic when he says that future growth will rest on the foundation of research, which will be fueled by the formulations business. The bulk drug business will play an important supportive role.

A. ***Mergers and Acquisitions :*** The Company chose the brand acquisition route rather than that of acquiring companies. Its logic is that when you acquire companies, you are likely to inherit the field force and distribution net work, with a different value system and work culture. The integration of these may create problems for companies with adequate manufacturing and marketing infrastructure, leading to redundancies and mismatches. Hence the focus is on brand acquisitions.

DRL's first brand acquisitions were the Hyderabad-based SOL Pharma's Riflux and Clamp in 1996. These acquisitions filled the gap in the company's product portfolio and reinforced the company's position in gastro-intestinal and anti-infective segments. Close on the heels of this was the acquisition of Becelac from Pfimex Laboratories, which is an essential co-prescription brand. Later in 1998, the company acquired five brands from the Calcutta-based Dolphin Laboratories. The company expects to achieve a turnover of Rs. 200 million from these acquisitions in fiscal 1999.

Table 6.6 Dr. Reddy's Acquisitions

Acquired	Purpose and Impact
1. Group Pharmaceutical's entire range of six dental brands in an all cash deal worth around Rs. 300 million in 2001. The company also acquired Group Pharma's marketing rights to Fittydent denture adhesive and denture-cleaning system which was under license from Fittydent International, Austria.	These seven brands through acquisition and marketing rights made Dr. Reddy's dental product portfolio to sixteen and made the company the leader in the dental segment.
2. Trigenesis Therapeutics Inc., the US-based skin care company for US $ 11 million 2004. The company will also make the contractual payments during the course of development of products and technology platforms, as well as royalties on sales to Skye Pharma and Silva foam of UK as per the existing agreements with Trigenesis.	Will facilitate entry into the US $ 6-billion-large dermatology market in the U S and $ 8-billion-large world dermatological market with the product and technology access obtained through the Trigenesis acquisition
3. Roche's API business in with its order books and the state-of-the-art, US FDA approved manufacturing facility at Cuernavaca, Mexico for US $ 61 million in November 2005	Will enable Dr. Reddy's Custom Pharmaceutical Services Business from the present US $12 million to 100 million within fifteen months
4. betapharm Group, Germany's fourth largest generics pharmaceutical company for an all cash deal of € 483 million in March 2006 in the largest international acquisition made by an Indian company.	With a portfolio of 145 products and several more in the pipeline, this acquisition will not only give Dr. Reddy's a firm foothold in the largest generics market of Europe, but also enable its pan European strategy. Betapharm had a turnover of € 164 million in 2005.
5. Laboratories Litaphar, SA, the Spanish generics pharmaceutical producer for € 3.5 million in July 2006. Litaphar was started in 2001 and has recorded annual sales of € 1 million.	The acquisition will facilitate Dr. Reddy's entry into the rapidly growing generics market in Spain.

B. *Strategic alliances:* The most important strategic alliances of the company are research-based and therefore are significantly different from the rest of the industry. Its alliance with the Danish drug major – Novo Nordisk has been at once path-breaking and torch-bearing.

Path-breaking, because it was the first of its kind, wherein an Indian drug company has licensed its NCE to a multinational for consideration of upfront milestone payments, undertaking further development through the clinical phases of research and product registration and marketing after the drug is approved in international markets. Torch-bearing, because it has already become a sort of role model in the effort to contain the huge and almost unaffordable costs of drug discovery to other aspirants in the Indian drug industry, who have launched their own drug discovery programs.

DRL has also formed an equity-based marketing joint venture in Brazil with a local company to access the Latin American market. It is about to finalise a joint venture in China with a local partner, involving manufacturing and marketing. The company has already a joint venture – Reddy-Biomed in Moscow – covering the CIS markets.

Table 6.7 Dr Reddy's Strategic Alliances

Alliance with	Nature and Purpose
1. CliniTec International, the UK-based privately owned full service contract research organization located in Windsor with presence over thirty countries worldwide including India, South Africa and the Middle East. It provides clinical research support services to the pharmaceutical, biotechnology and medical device companies.	Joint development of an anti-cancer compound DRF 1042 belonging to the topoisomerase inhibitors class of compounds for use as potential treatment of various types of cancer. Dr. Reddy's will retain the commercialization rights for the US and the rest of the world excluding CliniTec's territories for most of Europe. Dr. Reddy's will also retain the exclusive rights to supply the commercial quantities of the drug.

Alliance with	Nature and Purpose
2. Merck, the global drug major	To sell the authorized generic versions of Merck's Proscar (2005 sales US $ 600 million) and Zocor(2005 sales US $ 4.5 billion) subject to a 180-day exclusivity upon their patent expiries.
3. Rheo Science A/S	Co-development of balaglitazone which is set to move up to Phase II clinical trials. Dr. Reddy's will keep its full rights for North America, Japan and the rest the world except Europe (excluding Russia and CIS) and China.
4. Argenta Discovery Ltd, the UK Based privately held drug discovery and development company.	Joint development and commercialization of a novel approach to the treatment of chronic obstructive pulmonary disease (COPD). Both companies agreed to jointly collaborate up to funding the proof of concept.
5. ICICI Venture Capital Fund Management Company, and Citi-Group Venture Capital International Growth Partnership Mauritius Limited	Together formed an integrated drug development company called Perlecan Pharma Private Limited with capital commitment of US $ 52.5 million, in a path-breaking de-risking strategy. Dr. Reddy's has transferred to Perlecan all the rights of four NCEs in the area of cardiovascular and metabolic disorders. Perlecan is managed by an independent board of directors and will accelerate the development of the assets upto Phase II a, and there after seek out licensing, co-development or joint commercialization opportunities.
6. Torrent Pharma	For exclusive commercialization of four of Torrent's– two (Omez and Omez-D) in gastro-intestilnal segment and two in cardio vascular segment - Listril (Lisinopril) and Listril Plus (Lisinopril and Hydrochlorthiazide) in Russia.

While the trend in the industry is to create therapeutic and prescriber segment-specific marketing divisions, DRL had followed a different strategy. It had merged two existing marketing divisions – Stangen and Genesis to achieve greater customer coverage. The company's 560-strong field force had achieved an enviable reach, covering customers across different prescriber segments during mid-90s. The company has more than tripled its sales force today and provides focused marketing services in a number of therapeutic areas with its seven marketing divisions.

SUN PHARMA

Sun Pharma entered the pharmaceutical industry through the niche route of specialty segments fifteen years ago. The specialty segments, which were considered as a 'path of least resistance', have now become a 'path of most resistance'. They are getting crowded by the day, with more and more players joining the fray. The highly ambitious Sun, like its most aggressive peers, has been pursuing all major strategic routes to move up the ladder in the Indian drug industry and indeed, to become one of the integrated international pharmaceutical companies.

A. ***Mergers and Acquisitions:*** Sun's acquisition spree started in September 1996, when it acquired a controlling stake in Gujarat Lyka, the Rs. 520-million manufacturer of bulk actives of semi synthetic anti-bacterials. This has been a part of the grand strategy of Sun, to become a vertically integrated firm. To expand its capacities for bulk actives, it has also acquired Knoll's bulk drug manufacturing facility at Ahmednagar in Maharashtra in 1996.

Further, the company had acquired M J Pharma in January 1997. M J Pharma holds regulatory approvals from the Medicine Control Agency (MCA) of the UK for all its manufacturing lines, and from the US FDA for cephalosporin capsules.

Sun has took over through a merger towards the end of 1997 the Chennai-based TDPL, an integrated pharmaceutical company with a turnover of Rs. 600 million and gained an immediate access to large new therapeutic segments such as gynaecology, paediatrics and speciality segments like oncology and anaesthesiology. It had also acquired in the bargain the R&D center of TDPL at Chennai, which has considerable process development skills. Having acquired and built a sizeable manufacturing infrastructure Sun has started looking for brand acquisitions.

The company had acquired almost the entire basket of the Hyderabad-based Natco's prescription brands to extend its therapeutic coverage and to consolidate its position in select speciality segments. The total turnover of the acquired brands in 1998, the year of acquisition, was around Rs. 520 million. All these acquisitions have catapulted Sun into the top ten of the Indian pharmaceutical industry (monthly rank of 8 in November 1998 as per ORG Retail chemist audit).

Sun had also gained an immediate entry into the opthalmic segment and an instant customer franchise, when it acquired Vadodara-based Milmet Laboratories, the Rs. 100 million firm specialising in opthalmic preparations.

Sun had also picked up a controlling stake in the Michigan-based Caraco Pharmaceuticals to gain a faster access to the North American generic market. Sun-Caraco has already got eighteen approvals in the US and four more are in the pipeline. Here are the details of Sun Pharma's acquisition spree:

Gujarat Lyka	1996
Knoll's bulk drug facility	1996
M J Pharma	1997
Caraco	1997
TDPL	1997
Natco's brands	1998
Milmet	1998

Table 6.8 Sun Pharma's Acquisitions in the new Millennium

Acquired	Purpose and Impact
1. Two brands from Women's First Healthcare, USA in 2004	Entry into a new segment and reinforcement of its product mix in the world's largest generic pharmaceutical market - US
2. Formulation plant at Bryan, Ohio, USA in 2005.	Beefing up of manufacturing capabilities in the US.
3. Manufacturing operations of Able Labs, New Jersey, USA in 2005 for US $ 23.5 million through Sun Pharmaceuticals Inc. Michigan, the wholly owned subsidiary of the company.	A Sq Ft manufacturing facility in the US with special suits for manufacturing controlled substances. Strengthens the company's ability to compete in the generic space of controlled substances. Also gained access for the intellectual property for the products being manufactured by Able.
4. ICN Company Limited, a Hungary based pharmaceutical company, which is a division of Valeant Pharmaceuticals International, USA in 2006.	Gained a manufacturing facility in Europe with access to a product portfolio and a 30 per cent market share of a controlled substance in Europe.

B. ***Strategic Alliances :*** Sun has not yet chosen the alliance-route. The company has only marketing and sourcing arrangement with the South Korean drug major – KGCC (Korean Green Cross Corporation) for marketing certain blood products in India.

C. ***New Product Introductions :*** Sun has been very aggressive in launching new products since the beginning. The company introduced as many as 32 new products during the year 2005-06.

D. ***Expansion Strategies:*** Sun has been the first Indian drug firm to create and organize its business around stand-alone strategic business units dedicated to one or more therapeutic and prescriber segments to achieve a sharper marketing focus. This has been one of the major contributing factors to its success in speciality segments. Today a number of leading Indian pharma companies follow this strategy of creating speciality-oriented marketing divisions or SBUs. Sun has further consolidated its structure and created seventeen strategic business units catering to neuro-psychiatry, cardiology, nephrology, diabetology, gastro-enterology, respiratory disorders, orthopaedics, gynaecology, paediactrics, oncology, anaesthesiology, opthalmology, critical care and ENT.

LUPIN

Lupin, like Ranbaxy has been chasing a critical mass of $ 1 billion since 2003. Its priorities too are the rapidly expanding generic markets in the US and Europe. All its moves in domestic as well as international markets are centered round gaining as quick an access as possible to new markets, products, facilities and technologies.

A. ***Mergers and Acquisitions:*** The acquisition bug has bitten Lupin too rather recently. It has acquired Eli Lilly's cephalosporin plant in Puerto Rico, essentially to cut short the time-to-market and gain a first-mover advantage in the soon-to-go off-patent cephalosporins in the US. As a part of its internationalization of business, Lupin is looking for some more acquisitions in the US, Europe and China. It has set aside $ 10 million to fund these acquisitions.

B. ***Strategic Alliances :*** Lupin is determined, rather hell-bent on making it big in the generic markets in North America and Europe. All its alliances – with Merck Generics, PRI, Fujisawa and the more recent joint venture with MOVA – are aimed at achieving synergies between Lupin's integrated manufacturing capabilities and the marketing savvy of overseas partners.

Table 6.9 Lupin's Strategic Alliances

Alliance With	Nature and Purpose
1. Glaxo SmithKline, Philippines	Promoting Lupin's anti-T B Product range in Philippines
2. Aspen Pharma Care Holdings, South Africa	50:50 J V to develop, manufacture, and globally market (except in the US, India and South Africa Trade) select anti-TB products. The J V aims at creating synergies between Lupin's traditional strengths in Anti-TB formulations and APIs and Aspen's experience in Anti-retrovirals and MDR-TB business
3. Ranbaxy Laboratories	Licensing arrangement for marketing Lupin's anti-T B range in the severely affected West and North African markets like Nigeria, Ghana, Ivory Coast, Cameroon, Algeria, Chad, Mauritius and Congo
4. Kyowa Pharmaceuticals Industry Co Ltd, (KPICL), Japan	Marketing arrangement for entering the fast growing generics market in Japan. KPICL will conduct the bio-studies, obtain regulatory approvals and market products developed and manufactured by Lupin.
5. Chester Valley Pharmaceuticals, US	Lupin Pharmaceuticals Inc. (LPI), US entered into agreement with Chester Valley Pharmaceuticals in the US to promote Atopictavi non-steroidal cream to paediatricians
6. GDF (Global Drug supply Facility)	Supply arrangement with Global Drug supply facility, the procurement agency that supplies anti-TB drugs in the high-burden countries identified by WHO.

C. ***New Product Introductions:*** Lupin has been planning to extend its therapeutic coverage from anti-TB drugs and cephalosporins to other segments. The company launched seven new generic products. It also launched a new Herbal division in 2004 with a portfolio of 19 products which will be promoted ethically.

D. ***Expansion Strategies :*** Lupin has one of the largest medical detailing forces in the country – to promote the company's products. It has six divisions to increase the strength and flexibility of product promotion. Currently the focus is on cardiology and critical care. The general division focuses on anti-TB drugs and anti-bacterials and other products.

NICHOLAS PIRAMAL

Acquisitions and alliances drive Nicholas Piramal's business strategy. Ajay Pirmal entered the pharmaceutical industry through the acquisition route. He acquired Nicholas Laboratories in 1988 and grabbed every opportunity that came along. He stormed into the top-ten league in Indian drug industry in ten years – entirely through acquisitions.

A. ***Mergers and Acquisitions :*** Five acquisitions in ten years (1988–1998) to reach a critical mass of Rs. 5.42 billion. Acquired the Indian subsidiary of Roche in 1993 and increased market share by 0.6 per cent. Took over Sumitra Pharmaceuticals, the Rs.600-million bulk drug manufacturer in 1995 to achieve backward integration. Acquired the Indian subsidiary of Boerhinger Mannheim in 1996 and increased market share instantly by 0.5 per cent. These acquisitions have given the group an increased market share, extended therapeutic coverage to more profitable speciality segments like cardiology, neuro-psychiatry, oncology, haematology etc. The acquisition of Boerhinger Mannheim has given access to (and the leadership position) the new rapidly growing diagnostics business virtually overnight. The group has acquired what has been missing in its strategy – a research and development facility – from Hoechst India in 1998. This acquisition takes Nicholas Piramal one more step towards becoming a fully integrated pharmaceutical company. Nicholas Piramal's acquisition logbook would read like this:

Company	**Year of acquisition**
Nicholas	1988
Roche	1993
Sumitra Pharma	1995
Boerhinger Mannheim	1996
Hoechest's R&D Centre	1998

Table 6.10 Nicholas Piramal's Acquisitions in the New Millennium

Acquired	Purpose and Impact
1. Rhone Poulenc India from Aventis Pharma in September 2001	To expand the company's therapeutic coverage and increase market share in India.
2. Pharmaceutical operations of ICI India in March 2002	To strengthen their position in cardiovascular segment in India.
3. Global Bulk Drugs and Fine Chemicals Pvt. Ltd in November 2002	To reinforce the API developmental and manufacturing capabilities to consolidate its position in the CRAMS space
4. Completely acquired Sarabhai Piramal Pharma from Sarabhai International in December 2003	To extend therapeutic coverage and increase market share in India
5. Canere Actives and Fine Chemicals, an Indian chemicals company in March 2004	To expand its API and drug intermediate capabilities and capacities
6. UK-based Rhodia's inhalation anesthetics business in January 2005	To gain access to a new technology platform and to strengthen its CRAMS capabilities
7. Pharmaceutical custom synthesis business of UK based Avecia Ltd. In October 2006	To strengthen its position in the CRAMS space
8. Morepeth, U K based drug manufacturing and distribution facility of Pfizer Inc. in June 2006	To beef up the manufacturing capabilities and consolidate its position in the CRAMS space

B. ***Strategic Alliances :*** Nicholas Piramal has also been working to build a manufacturing infrastructure that is comparable to the best in the world, even while acquiring companies with the insatiable appetite of a predator. The company has been planning these moves essentially to become an attractive suitor for an alliance. And an attractive if not irresistible suitor, it has certainly become. How else can you explain seventeen alliances in five years? Sales from alliances currently account for a third of the company's total sales. Nicholas Piramal is planning to achieve half of its total sales from alliances within two years from now.

Table 6.11 Nicholas Piramal's Recent Strategic Alliances

Alliance With	In-licensing Agreements for
1. Gilead, USA	*Ambisone*, a biotech product
2. Chiesi, Italy	*Curosurf*, a Lung surfactant for babies born prematurely
3. Biogen Idec	*Avonex*, for multiple sclerosis
4. Pierre Fabre, France	*Exomega, Kertyol S*, Dermo-cosmoceutical products
5. Ethypharm, France	Paracetamol Flash Tab, Taskte-masking Dispersible paediatric tablets
6. Genzyme, USA	*Synvisc*, for Pain treatment in osteo-arthritis
7. Biosyntech, Canada	New Gel-based products for cartilage regeneration

C. ***New Product Introductions:*** All these alliances and acquisitions give the company an enviable access to new products. Nicholas Piramal, after acquiring Roche has introduced sixteen speciality products of Roche in India. The company has also got the right of first refusal for marketing in India for all new products developed by Boerhinger Mannheim. All these alliances, covering a wide range of therapeutic segments in both prescription and over-the-counter drug categories, offer a tremendous scope for introducing new products. New product access in the product patent regime, once it is implemented in India by 2005, is the main reason for the alliance-driven strategy behind Nicholas Piramal's grand plan. The company introduced 32 new products in FY2005-06. Sales from new products launched during the last two years were Rs. 687.4 million.

D. ***Expansion Strategies :*** Nicholas Piramal has consolidated all its acquisitions and structured its marketing operations around 15 divisions including two franchisee divisions. The divisions provide a focused approach with a disease management orientation. The divisions are focused on market leadership in selected areas. The size of the company's field force is one of the largest in the industry. The joint venture with the OTC major Reckitt Colman India has led to the formation of a separate company. Furthermore, Nicholas Piramal has taken a number of strategic initiatives to emerge as a leading CRAMS player (Table 6.12).

Table 6.12 Nicholas Pirmal's CRAMS Initiatives

Agreement With	Nature and Purpose
1. AMO (Advanced Medical Optics)	Exclusive outsourcing partner for select AMO eye-care products for global markets including USA, Europe and Japan
2. Allergan, USA	Long-term API contract up to October 2011 for two high-value anti-Glaucoma APIs
3. Astra Zeneca, UK	Global partnership for developing, scaling up API processes and commercial manufacturing on product-launch for Astra Zeneca,
4. Pfizer, USA	Developmental partnership with Pfizer for its animal health division for developing processes and providing scale-up batches for Phase trials and commercial manufacturing on product launch

ZYDUS–CADILA HEALTH CARE

Zydus–Cadila Health Care has set its sights high right from day one, when the Cadila split, or restructuring as they would like to call it, became inevitable in 1995. The company set itself the objective of consolidating its position in the domestic market first and to go global by setting up joint ventures abroad. The company has set itself a formidable goal of reaching US $ 1 billion by 2010, which means a four-fold growth in five years.

A. *Mergers and Acquisitions :* The first step that the Zydus group took in consolidating the domestic business has been the acquisition of the ailing Indon Pharmaceutical Works Limited and turning it around into a performing, speciality- focused company.

Zydus acquired German Remedies in India, created a distinct entity for it and expanded its therapeutic coverage to gynaecology, respiratory and oncology segments.

Zydus later picked up a 30.7 per cent stake in Carnation Nutra-Analogue Foods Limited, the manufacturers of Nutralite, which is India's largest selling margarine currently enjoying a market share of over 60 per cent.

In 2003, Zydus acquired Alpharma, a prominent generic company in France in its first international acquisition, formed a wholly owned subsidiary in – Zydus France SAS and gained access to one of the fast growing generic markets in Europe.

B. *Strategic Alliances :* At Zydus, strategic alliances are the primary drivers of growth. It has formed as many as thirteen strategic alliances to gain access to new products, markets, technology, research and development. Three of these have been joint ventures, whose scope involves manufacturing, marketing and product development. The joint venture partners are KGCC of Republic of Korea (recombinant vaccine for hepatitis-B), BYK Gulden of West Germany (manufacture and marketing of bulk active - Pantoprazole and its formulations). And the German drug major Bayer AG (a separate joint venture to market the products of Bayer and Zydus in India).

Zydus has become even more aggressive in the new millennium and here is a synopsis of its strategic alliances:

Table 6.13 Zydus Cadila's Strategic Alliances

Alliance With	Nature and Purpose
1. Mallinckrodt Pharmaceuticals, US	Tied-up with Mallinckrodt, a business unit of Tyco Healthcare and one of the leading American generic firms through Zydus Pharmaceuticals Inc., US for developing, manufacturing at its Ahemdabad in India facility that is US FDA approved and register the generic formulations (ANDAs). Mallinckrodt will market and sell these products once approved under a joint Mallinckrodt-Zypharma label in the US.
2. Bio-Sidus, a business unit of the Argentina drug major - Sidus	Entered into a strategic alliance through its group company German Remedies for marketing the generic version of the biotech drug – Filgrastim in Argentina. There are more products in the pipeline.
3. Mayne Group Ltd, a leading player in specialty pharmaceuticals from Australia	The strategic intent of the MOU signed by Zydus Cadila with Mayne Group is to set up a manufacturing JVC to explore opportunities, construct a facility for selected cytotoxic formulations and APIs in India.
4. Zambon Group of Italy	The MOU covers a wide ranging areas for cooperation like research and development, contract manufacturing of fine chemicals, APIs and FDFs and marketing of pharmaceutical products both generics and ethical formulations in Europe and India
5. Evolupharm, the second largest 'Groupment' (a bargaining group with a large network of pharmacies)	Entered through Zydus France SAS for gaining access to 2,250 more pharmacies to reinforce its existing marketing efforts.
6. Altana Health Care	Entered into a JV at Mumbai for manufacturing pantoprazole inter mediates
7. Sarabhai Animal Health	J V with Sarabhai Animal Health achieved a turnaround in its operations and became profitable in the fiscal 2005-06
8. IICT (Indian Institute of Chemical Technology), Hyderabad, Andhra Pradesh, India	Drug discovery

In addition to these, Zydus Cadila closed as many as eleven contract manufacturing deals with innovation and generic Pharma majors in the US and Europe having a peak revenue potential of US $ 23.6 million. Zydus Cadila knows that alliances are the way to go in the era of globalization.

C. ***New Product Introductions :*** Zydus has introduced 34 new products in FY 2005-06. The company has been a frontrunner in new product launches for many years.

D. ***Expansion Strategies:*** Zydus re-engineered its management structure and business processes to become a performing organization. They have introduced the SBU concept to achieve a relentless focus on bottom line. Domestic marketing of formulations is divided into 10 teams focusing on different segments including generics. They have, in addition, created an agro-vet division and a cosmetic division. International marketing, manufacturing and bulk drugs have been made into three strategic business units.

WOCKHARDT

Wockhardt has a clear focus. It is a determined player in the fiercely competitive Indian pharmaceutical industry. Determined to become a vertically integrated international pharmaceutical company. The company has been using a judicious blend of acquisitions and alliances to reach the objective.

A. ***Mergers and acquisitions:*** Wockhardt acquired in December 1995, the Chennai-based R R Medi Pharma, a manufacturer of intravenous fluids. This strategic acquisition has helped Wockhardt in more ways than one. Firstly, it helped the company cut its cost of transportation of intravenous fluids in the southern region. Secondly, it has given the company an instant access to the market in the South. Thirdly, it has expanded its manufacturing capacities. This is now rechristened as Wockhardt Health Care. Wockhardt acquired Merind through a merger in 1997. This has pushed Wockhardt into the top ten of the Indian pharmaceutical industry by adding 0.8 per cent market share. It has also helped consolidate its position as a vertically integrated player. Wockhardt, with this merger, has become one of the major manufacturers of vitamin B12 in the world. This merger has also given the company an immediate market access to the rapidly growing Diagnostics business.

In addition, Wockhardt has made two strategic acquisitions abroad. It has acquired two generic companies – Accumed in the US and Wallis Laboratories in the UK. With these, Wockhardt has created beachheads in the two most important regions North America and Europe – to exploit opportunities in the fastest growing and most lucrative generic markets in the world.

Table 6.14 Wockhardt's Recent Acquisitions

Acquired	Purpose and Impact
1. C P Pharmaceuticals, Wales, U K, the second largest generics market in Europe in 2003.	Consolidates its position in UK.
2. Esparma GMBH, Germany, the largest Generics market in Europe in 2004. Gains a foothold in the largest generics market in Europe and increases its presence across Europe.	Gains a foothold in the largest generics market in Europe and increases its presence across Europe.
3. Pinewood Laboratories Limited, the largest and fastest growing branded generic pharmaceutical company in Ireland for US $ 150 million in 2006.	Significantly enhances the product portfolio, customer base and market access and consolidates the company's top-ten position in the UK. Pinewoods acquisition complements the company's overall product portfolio covering virtually all dosage forms.
4. Negma Laboratories, the innovative Pharma company in France for US $ 265 million.	Ownership of the intellectual property of 172 patents of Negma Laboratories in France. Access and presence in the osteoarthrits and hypertension theraeputic areas in France. Negma Laboratories recorded sales of $150 million in 2006.

Wockhardt made four acquisitions in Europe making it the company's major region accounting for over half of the total sales of about US $ 200 million. Wockhardt with its most recent acquisition of Pinewood in Ireland consolidates its strong top-ten position and move up further in UK.

B. *Strategic Alliances :* The strategic alliances that Wockhardt formed are synergistic with its acquisitions. The basic purpose of all these alliances and acquisitions is to mutually reinforce its strategies of increasing market share, extending therapeutic coverage and gaining access to new products, new markets and new technologies. The alliances, whether they are formed in the domestic or overseas markets, should meet these objectives. Its two alliances with Japanese companies strengthen its product portfolio in two of its important segments – wound care and pain management. Its alliance with Rhein Biotech involves technical know-how in the emerging field of biopharmaceuticals. Or consider for instance, its two strategic alliances with Ferrings in Europe and the more recent one with the North American generic firm, Sidmak Inc. Both these alliances are to gain access to the generic markets in the highly industrialized and highly regulated markets in the West.

In the new millennium Wockhardt has sewn a number of alliances majority of which are contract-manufacturing arrangements (6 out of 9) leveraging the world-class manufacturing infrastructure with approvals from all the leading international regulatory authorities that the company had built over the years.

Table 6.15 Wockhardt's Strategic Alliances

With	Nature and Purpose
1. Astra Zeneca	Contract manufacturing of Tenormin and Inderal
2. Cell Therapeutics	Contract manufacturing of Arsenic Trioxide
3. G W Pharmaceuticals	Contract manufacturing of Sativex
4. Lab Aguettant	Contract manufacturing of Apomorphine
5. Schering Plough	Contract manufacturing of Insuvet
6. Smith & Nephew, UK	Contract manufacturing of Ametop Gel
7. Eisai, Japan	Exclusive marketing arrangement of Methycobal
8. Daiichi, Japan	Exclusive marketing arrangement of Cymin
9. Bristol	Marketing arrangement

C. ***New Product Introductions :*** Wockhardt launched the generic terbenafine on the first working day after patent expiry in the UK thereby getting a head start. Likewise, its wholly owned subsidiary – Esparma Gmbh launched lamotrigene on the first working day after patent expiry in Germany. In India Wockhardt launched its human recombinant insulin – Wosulin and Wosulin device. Wockhardt continues to introduce key new product through in-licensing arrangements.

D. ***Expansion Strategies :*** Wockhardt has five marketing divisions to retain focus on customer and therapeutic segments as it has a very large product portfolio. In addition, it has a veterinary division for marketing its products for animal health care.

BIOCON

Biocon was first started as a joint venture with Biocon Bio-chemicals Limited of Ireland for manufacturing certain enzymes for the brewery industry in 1978. The J V was terminated in 1999 and Biocon changed its tacks to a fast track and emerged as the leading biotechnology company from India with a global presence. The company changed its name to Biocon Limited in 2003 and entered into the capital markets in 2004.

Biocon today is a vertically integrated biopharmaceutical company with world-class manufacturing and R&D infrastructure. The company has established Asia-Pacific's largest manufacturing facility for recombinant-human insulin and has product mix comprising of oncology, cardiovascular and anti-diabetic drugs. The company is a leading manufacturer of statins, which are lipid lowering drugs belonging to the world's leading therapeutic category.

Biocon has reached a critical mass of Rs. 7.93 billion in the fiscal 2005-06 and is following the classical strategy of acquisition and collaboration to become more competitive in its pursuit of becoming a leading integrated biopharmaceutical company of global distinction. Consider its game plans for example:

- Acquired the I P assets of Nobex Corporation for US $ 5 million. This strategic acquisition provides the company with valuable I P platform and complete ownership of the oral insulins and oral BNP programs. It also brings with it a novel platform technology that encompasses 300 plus patents based on oral peptide delivery in the metabolic and cardiovascular segments. The company plans to leverage these proprietary assets through a combination of licensing and co-development partnerships, which fit its innovation strategy for future, like a glove.
- Collaborative program with CIMAB of Cuba for a monoclonal antibody BIOMAB EGFR which has recently completed a two-year clinical trial for head and neck cancer.
- Partnering in product development with Vaccinex, USA.
- Joint PhD studies at Karolinska Institute at Sweden.
- Partnering in product development with the Centre of Molecular Immunology (CIM), Havana.

Biocon has set up two group enterprises to cater to contract research services – Syngene and Clingene. Syngene has become one of India's leading custom research providers already across the value chain. It has gained acceptance as a leading research hub for the biggest names in the global Pharma industry. Clingene, a CRO boasts the first lab in India to be accredited by CAP (College of American Pathologists) and NABL (National Accreditation Board for Testing and Calibration Laboratories).

GLENMARK

Incorporated in 1977 as a pharmaceutical company headquartered in Mumbai, Glenmark has set its sights high on the international horizon only in the new millennium. What a progress it has made in the past five years! Remarkable indeed in every which way you look at its performance. Today the company is a vertically integrated pharmaceutical company and seems determined to become a discovery led international company.

A. ***Mergers and Acquisitions :*** The company has put into action every strategic move in a copybook style to perfection. A quick look at how the company is reaching the critical mass required to realize its vision would convince even the skeptic observer about its strategic intent and ability to deliver. Consider its acquisitions first:

Table 6.16 Glenmark's Acquisitions

Acquired	Purpose and Impact
1. Laboratorios Klinger of Brazil in 2004 through Glenmark Pharmaceutica, its wholly owned subsidiary (WOS).	To consolidate its position in Brazil, the largest Latin American market
2. Bouwer Bartlet Private Limited, a generic marketing company in South Africa with a product basket of 22 products in the dermatology area	To penetrate the South African market and establish its presence in the dermatology segment.
3. Rights to seven branded generics from P D Pharma in South Africa.	To consolidate its position in the dermatology segment in South Africa
4. Servycal, S A in Argentina	To enter the Argentinian market and consolidate its position in the LATAM. Filed 19 dossiers with ANVISA and obtained eleven product registrations. Registered sales of US $ 17.26 million in the fiscal 2005-06.

To enter the Argentinian market and consolidate its position in the LATAM. Filed 19 dossiers with ANVISA and obtained eleven product registrations. Registered sales of US $ 17.26 million in the fiscal 2005-06.

Glenmark started with a focus on dermatology therapeutic area, became a leading player and expanded into other therapeutic areas. Its strategic acquisitions are in line with its core strengths and other key therapeutic areas that are rapidly growing. Acquisitions have contributed significantly to Glenmark to become a Rs 7.57 billion vertically integrated pharmaceutical company that it is today.

B. ***Strategic Alliances :*** Glenmark in just three years entered into as many as nine alliances with international players of various sizes and competencies to reach its goals. Its alliances are mainly to penetrate the regulated markets like the US and Europe and in the drug discovery area. A glimpse at its alliances would give an insight into what Glenmark is up to:

- Tied up with several generic players in the US for supplying APIs
- In-licensed four generic formulations for marketing in the U S.
- Signed a unique royalty deal for US $ 27 million to build US dermatology portfolio with Paul Capital Partners' Royalty Fund, a leading international healthcare investment fund limited.
- Entered into a collaboration agreement with InvaGen Pharmaceuticals Inc. for the joint development, filing and marketing of seven generic pharmaceutical products for the US market.
- Formed a strategic alliance with Lannett Company Inc. for exclusive marketing and distribution arrangements in the US generic market.
- Entered into a product development and marketing agreement with K V Pharmaceuticals in the US for developing eight generic products for regulatory approval and marketing in the North American market. The licensed products include both paragraph 3 and paragraph 4 ANDA filing opportunities. The scope of the alliance goes further for developing and licensing additional generic ANDA products and certain branded specialty products, which may incorporate Glenmark's proprietary platform of controlled technology.
- Concluded a deal covering development and marketing with Merck Generics, Europe through its wholly owned subsidiary Glenmark Pharmaceuticals, UK for a portfolio of 8 dermatology products. Both Merck Generics and Glenmark will market the products once approved.

- Entered into another agreement with Merck KgaA, the generic arm of the German drug major covering development, registration and commercialization of Glenmark's NCE GRC 8200, a DPP IV Inhibitor for Type 2 diabetes for North American European and Japanese markets. The partners will share commercialization rights for other markets in the world. Merck KgaA will bear the cost of ongoing studies and will be responsible for planning, managing and sponsoring the developmental activities in the future. The value of payments could total up to € 190 million including a € 25 million upfront payment and various milestone payments upon successful development and launch of mono therapy and combination products based on GRC 8200.
- Collaborating with Forest Laboratories in the US through Glenmark Pharmaceuticals SA, Switzerland, its WOS for the development, registration and commercialization of a NCE for treating COPD and asthma. Forest will make an upfront payment to Glenmark upon initiation of the agreement and other milestone payments if the development and commercialization of the product is successfully completed. Forest will market the product in the North American market while Glenmark retains the rights for the rest of the world.
- Napo Pharmaceuticals Inc., Japan entered into a collaboration with Glenmark to develop and commercialize 'Crofelemer', Nappo's novel antidiarrheal compound for India and 140 other countries mainly in the developing world. Napo has granted developmental and commercialization rights to Glenmark.

Glenmark would supply the APIs and finished formulations to its alliance partners and is providing custom research services or participating in joint or co-development programs. All these will have a very positive impact in reaching the required critical mass in generating the investible surplus that is vital for fueling its growth plans.

C. ***New Product Introductions :*** Glenmark launched 40 new generic drugs and captured the first mover's advantage in nine first generics.

D. ***Expansion Strategies :*** The Company entered thirteen new countries in FY 2006 and in-licensed novel products.

TORRENT

Started as a specialty focused company, Torrent achieved leadership position in Neuropsychiatry and Cardiovascular therapeutic areas by mid-1990s. Later, the company diversified into other areas like power and seemed to have lost focus losing the leadership position to Sun Pharma in these areas. In the new millennium Torrent bounced back with renewed vigor and is pursuing an aggressive strategy to reclaim what it has lost. Its aggression is not limited to the domestic formulation market but to the rapidly growing international generics market and the innovation led international pharmaceutical market. Here are some of its more prominent winning moves:

- Torrent acquired Heumann Pharma GmbH & Co Generica KG, the generic arm of Pfizer, the world's leading Pharma Company in November 2004 through its German subsidiary Torrent Pharma GmbH. Heumann, the 90-year old brand enjoying good equity with the physicians in Germany has 315 marketing authorizations, 135-strong field force covering 24,000 physicians and 14,000 pharmacies. This will give Torrent an instant access to the German generic market and a strong foothold in Europe, which is the second largest generic market in the world. Furthermore, Torrent has an MHRA UK-approved plant in Indrad, Gujarat, India. The product portfolio of Heumann is in synch with Torrent's therapeutic focus like CNS, Cardiovascular and Gastro-intestinal and Anti-infectives.
- Torrent signed a research collaboration agreement with Astra Zeneca, one of the global drug majors in a project aimed at discovering novel drug candidate for the treatment of hypertension. Both the companies will fund the research project jointly in equal proportion. The agreement envisages success-based R&D milestone payments to Torrent, and also royalties based on the commercialization of the drug candidate. Torrent will have the co-marketing rights for India.

- Torrent entered into a marketing tie-up with Tasly, a Pharma group in China for marketing their 'Cardiotonic' in India. Talsy will market Torrent formulations in China.
- Torrent has set up subsidiary companies in Brazil, Mexico, Philippines, Australia, Japan and Australia and in the process of setting up one in South Korea to beef up its international operations.
- Torrent signed an agreement with Novo Nordisk India to establish a new, dedicated formulation and packaging facility for Insulin, exclusively for Novo Nordisk.
- Torrent signed a non-exclusive agreement with Dr. Reddy's Laboratories Limited (DRL) for licensing and supplying the formulation of one of Torrent's best selling drugs 'Domstal O' in the Gastro-intestinal segment. Torrent Pharma would license the dossier and marketing authorization for the formulation to DRL initially for Russia, which would later be extended to other CIS countries. The scope of this agreement extends to two more products in Cardiovascular segment for 'Listril' and 'Listril H.'
- Torrent started six more specialty marketing divisions to facilitate successful launches of more new products in the areas of CNS, Cardiovascular, Gastro-intestinal, Diabetology. The total number of marketing divisions is now eleven with a total sales force of over 2,000.

Torrent is exploring all avenues to become a leading player in the international arena by beefing up its domestic operations, acquisitions, expanding its world class manufacturing and R&D infrastructure which are now globally recognized.

Group 'B' Companies: Competing for The International Generics Space

The combined sales of the ten companies in Group 'B' are about Rs. 98.82 billion. These sales are consolidated net sales for the FY 2005-06 and include their international sales, and the sales of their wholly owned international subsidiaries. They made 13 acquisitions during the period 2001-2006 and entered into 31 alliances. The basic purpose of all these acquisitions and alliances is to strengthen their competitiveness across the whole spectrum of Pharma value chain. The strategic objective of these alliances and acquisitions is to gain and improve access to markets, technology platforms, process and product developmental capabilities, distribution and marketing of their formulations in international markets, supply arrangements of their APIs and intermediates etc.

Table 6.18 Group 'B' Companies : Critical Mass

Company	FYE March 2006 Rs. Billion
1. Cipla	32.36
2. Aurobindo Pharma	15.02
3. Matrix Laboratories	11.58
4. Orchid	8.88
5. Ipca Laboratories	7.53
6. Alembic	6.65
7. Claris Life Sciences*	4.00
8. J.B.Chemicals	4.81
9. Unichem Laboratories	4.66
10. Strides Arcolabs	3.33

* Company's projection for the year ending December 2006

Table 6.19 Group 'B' Companies : Mergers and Acquisitions

Company	Acquisitions	Purpose
1. Cipla	NA	
2. Aurobindo Pharma	3	To create a beachhead in the US generics market with a manufacturing and warehouse facility. To improve access and reinforce its position in the European generics market
3. Matrix Laboratories	4	Improve market access in the European generics market. Access to new technology platforms. To augment manufacturing capabilities.

Company	Acquisitions	Purpose
4. Orchid	3	To strengthen its R&D capabilities, access to technology.
5. Ipca Laboratories	NA	
6. Alembic	NA	
7. Claris Life Sciences	NA	
8. J.B.Chemicals	NA	
9. Unichem Laboratories	NA	
10. Strides Arcolabs	2	To gain market access and strengthen the manufacturing infrastructure

Table 6.20 Group 'B' Companies : Strategic Alliances

Company	Alliance	Nature and Purpose
1. Cipla	6	Marketing generic formulations in the US Supply of APIs to International drug majors Development of biopharmaceutical product
2. Aurobindo Pharma	1	Improve market access and presence
3. Matrix Laboratories	2	To gain market access and long-term supply agreement of ARVs and other products
4. Orchid	8	Strengthen R&D capabilities Marketing of formulations in the US Generics market Co-development of processes and products
5. Ipca Laboratories	4	To supply APIs, FDFs to international generic companies and Pharma majors
6. Alembic	NA	
7. Claris Life Sciences	3	Marketing of generic formulations in the European markets
8. J.B.Chemicals	NA	
9. Unichem Laboratories	2	Marketing generic formulations in the US
10. Strides Arcolabs	6	Access to new technology platforms Marketing of generic formulations in the US Improve market access

CIPLA

Cipla's technological strength is widely acknowledged both in India and abroad. The company, over the years, has built an enviable manufacturing structure. Many of its manufacturing plants have been approved by all major international regulatory authorities. Its product portfolio too, is both wide and deep, covering various therapeutic and prescriber segments. The company, naturally is not keen on acquisitions.

The process of internationalization began only a few years ago at Cipla. It has made rapid progress within these three years. It has formed several strategic alliances with overseas partners, essentially to gain market access. The basic structure of all these alliances is that Cipla provides technology and products and the alliance partners abroad provide marketing support and distribution net work. Some of these alliances could culminate in full-fledged joint ventures involving local manufacturing, once they make the required progress.

Cipla entered into many alliances (covering over 140 products) in the past three years for supplying its APIs with some leading international innovative drug companies and for supplying ANDAs to some of the major international generic pharmaceutical companies in the regulated markets. Consider these for example:

- Entered into an agreement for supplying APIs to Pfizer and Merck.
- Entered into a deal with US-based Akorn Inc. to develop and supply a generic anti-infective drug. Cipla will develop and supply the drug and Akorn will make the regulatory submissions and clinical development. Akorn will pay Cipla the development fees as per milestones reached. Akorn will have exclusive marketing rights for the United States.
- Entered into a strategic alliance with Watson the US generic major to develop and commercialize generic products in the US.
- Tied up with Ivax of TEVA for supplying APIs covering about fifty products the most recent one being a pediatric drug in US market.

- Tied up with Bangalore-based biotechnology firm Avestha Gengraine Technologies (Avesthagen) for a biopharmaceutical development program.

Cipla reached the critical mass of Rs 32.36 billion in the fiscal 2005-06 by achieving consistently higher growth rates in the domestic formulation market and its thrust on exports. In the Indian pharmaceutical market the company dislodged the *numero uno* of many years – GSK and achieved the coveted leadership position in certain months during the year.

Cipla has been a very aggressive player in terms of new product introductions. In fact, it has been one of the first-movers in almost all its new product introductions. That explains the large product portfolio it has and the kind of customer franchise it enjoys. It introduced 55 new products in the year 2004 alone.

AUROBINDO PHARMA

Started in 1986 for manufacturing semi-synthetic penicillin bulk actives, Aurobindo Pharma Limited has come a long way in a very short time for it has planned an aggressive strategy only in the new millennium. In five short years it catapulted itself into the top six of the pharmaceutical league table in India and became a force to reckon with on the international generics scene. Today in 2006, Aurobindo Pharma has thirteen manufacturing facilities many of which have approvals from leading international regulatory authorities, strong chemistry skills for developing non-infringing processes and competent product development skills. The company has reached a critical mass of Rs 15. billion to fuel its growth engine towards becoming a leading provider of products and services across the value chain to the innovative and generic pharmaceutical companies globally. The company has followed the classical path of creating a world-class manufacturing infrastructure and develop scientific capabilities and strategic acquisitions. Here are the highlights:

- Acquired a controlling stake of 79.39 per cent in Rannit Pharma.
- Acquired a manufacturing and warehousing facility in Dayton, New Jersey, US located in the heart of Princeton Life Sciences

customers – a beachhead for its foray into the world's largest generic market.

- Acquired through Aurex Generics, UK, its wholly owned subsidiary the UK-based Milpharm Limited which owns over a hundred MAs (marketing authorizations) across diverse therapeutic areas like CNS, cardiovascular, GI, diabetology, antifungal, anti-bacterial, oncology etc., by UK MHRA and has annual sales of about £ 7.7 million.
- Acquired Pharmacin International BV, a Netherlands based generic pharmaceutical company from Jenim and Jonghoud International through its wholly owned subsidiary Agile Pharma BV in Netherlands in December 2006. Pharmacin had sales over € 6 million for the year ended December 2006.

The company has remodeled its strategy and is sharpening its focus on regulated markets and drug development and its renewed strategic thrust is palpable in all its moves, which we will review, in subsequent chapters.

MATRIX LABORATORIES

Matrix Laboratories catapulted itself into the limelight in Indian pharmaceutical industry in the new millennium. The company seemed to be in a hurry to achieve the critical mass and moved into the top fifteen companies pretty fast. The company followed a strategy of acquisitions and alliances most of which happened in 2005. Here are the details:

Table 6.21 Strategic Acquisitions of Matrix

Acquired	Purpose and Impact
1. 95.5 per cent share in Docpharma, Belgium through its subsidiary Matrix Laboratories NV for US $ 263 million.	Provides market access to select European markets like Belgium, Netherlands, Italy and France where Docpharma has a presence. Gives access to a 130-strong Docpharma product portfolio in Europe. Helps the company in becoming a strong vertically integrated player in the international generics market and achieving economies of scale.

Acquired	Purpose and Impact
2. Controlling stake in Concord Biotech Limited, an Ahmedabad-based biotechnology company.	Gives a strategic foothold in the largest and growing market of statins. Provides access to US FDA-approved commercial scale fermentation manufacturing capacities. Above all provides the required synergies for Docpharma operations and strengthens the company in the CRAMS segment.
3. Controlling stake in Mchem Group, China through a share purchase agreement (SPA)	Would help Matrix to achieve end-to-end capabilities through both forward and back ward integration across the value chain. Improves access to China and other emerging markets and helps to consolidate its position as a leading player in the CRAMS space.
4. 43 per cent stake in Explora Laboratories S.A, a technology platform company in Switzerland engaged in the research and development of APIs and intermediates through chemical, biochemical and fermentation processes.	Access to Explora's scientific capabilities would accelerate the entry of Matrix into high potential growth areas such as oncology, and corticosteroid segments. Explora's platform technology would help Matrix strengthen its contract research and manufacturing for the multinational branded formulation companies.

Matrix also entered into a strategic alliance in April 2005 with South Africa's largest pharmaceutical manufacturer and a major supplier of branded as well as generic pharmaceutical products to the southern African and selected international markets with a group turnover of US $ 321 million in the fiscal 2004. The alliance aims at a long-term relationship between both the companies and covers two joint ventures in both the countries. The salient features of this alliance are:

- The first JVC christened as Astrix laboratories Limited is a 50:50 joint venture located in Inida will manufacture APIs required by Aspen Pharmacare, South Africa. Matrix would license the product technology for the APIs (mainly ARVs) on a non-exclusive basis. Aspen will source these APIs from Matrix. Matrix will receive US $ 36 million from transfer of assets, technology and IP in ARVs.

- As part of the agreement, Matrix will pick up a 50 per cent stake in Fine Chemical Corporation (FCC), South Africa, which is a wholly owned subsidiary of Aspen for US $ 20 million making FCC a JVC of Aspen and Matrix in South Africa. FCC has a US FDA-approved manufacturing facility with over 25 DMF filings, good customer base and expertise in handling oncology, controlled substances and high potency APIs. The alliance achieves the required synergies to become more competitive as there is no overlap between the products of Matrix and FCC.

Matrix having achieved all this in a short span of time became an attractive suitor for the international generic major – Mylan Laboratories of USA which acquired a controlling stake of 71.5 per cent in Matrix in August 2006 for US $ 736 million.

ORCHID

Orchid has reached a critical mass of Rs. 2.4 million in the fiscal' 97 as a 100 per cent export oriented bulk drug manufacturer, focusing only on cephalosporins till now. The company is undertaking a major product diversification program in bulk actives by entering into other high value bulk drugs and intermediates like anti-virals and next generation cephalosporins.

The company had planned in the late 1990s to integrate forward into value-added formulations of cephalosporins and non-cephalosporins to accelerate its chase for critical mass, to become a vertically integrated international pharmaceutical company. Today in 2006, Orchid has become a vertically integrated pharmaceutical company with competencies across the Pharma value chain from development to delivery. The company has its step on the pedal continuously accelerating during the past seven years and reached a critical mass of Rs 8.88 billion with a presence across 28 countries with its focus clearly on regulated markets. The company's strategy to reach the critical mass is a judicious mix of acquisitions, alliances, new product and new market expansions. Here is a sneak preview of its game plans:

- Acquired 100 per cent stake in Bexel drug discovery company in the US to strengthen its research capabilities.
- Entered into various strategic alliances covering distribution and marketing in the US, Europe, Australia and other regulated markets with the leading generic players like Apotex, Par Pharmaceuticals, Stada, IVX, Actavis, Mayne Pharmaceuticals spread over a product portfolio of 41 products that include both cephalosporin and non-cephalosporin, non-antibiotic products.
- Signed a long-term master research and development agreement with the global Pharma major – Pfizer for new animal health products.
- Acquired Mano Pharma, a specialty branded generic formulations marketing company in India to boost up its domestic marketing activities.
- Set up a 50:50 manufacturing and marketing JVC with North China Pharmaceutical Corporation (NCPC), the largest pharmaceutical group in China with a proposed investment of US $ 25 million. The JVC – NCPC – Orchid Pharmaceuticals Co Ltd will be based in Shijiazhuang.
- Signed a contract with Biovitrum AB, Sweden, one of the largest biopharmaceutical companies in Europe to undertake medicinal chemistry work to support certain drug discovery activities of Biovitrum AB.

IPCA

Ipca has a strong presence in the anti-malarial, anti-emetic and cardiovascular segments. It also has a strong international presence and supplies drugs and intermediates to Teva of Israel, Sintofarm of Italy and Hoechst Celenase of the US. The company is planning to add to this list of prestigious clients even a more prestigious client – Merck of the US.

The company has created a new marketing team to step up its new product launches and improve its market share. It introduced 12 new products in the domestic market in the fiscal 2006. New products are the key drivers of growth at Ipca.

ALEMBIC

Incorporated in 1907, Alembic Limited is one of the oldest pharmaceutical companies in India that is making sincere efforts to adapt to the changing pharmaceutical scenario. Adaptability has been a great strength to the company as it has survived many changes during the past one hundred years and managed to be in the top-twenty league. The difference now is that it has set its sights high on the pharmaceutical world at large foraying into international markets with an unprecedented vigor. Alembic has reached a critical mass of Rs. 6.65 billion in sales during the fiscal 2005-06.

Alembic has a well-knit net of distribution arrangements, agency tie-ups and end-user tie-ups covering 75 countries globally. Department of Scientific and Industrial Research (DSIR) has recognized the company's R&D unit since 1975. Bio Arc, the R&D unit of Alembic is into custom research offering a wide range services. The company's manufacturing infrastructure too is of world-class with approvals from major regulatory authorities in the world and is geared up to compete in the rapidly cramming CRAMS space.

CLARIS LIFE SCIENCES

In less than six years from its commencement of operations, Claris Life Sciences has built up strong regulatory and registration capabilities with over 1,000 product dossiers filed in various countries, six ANDAs in the US, and 40 Marketing Authorization Applications (MAA) in Europe and Australia. The company's products are supplied to hospitals in over 65 countries worldwide. The company has reached a critical mass of over Rs. 4 billion in sales by end of December 2006. The company has been able to attract an investment of US $ 20 million from the Carlyle Group, the Global private equity firm based in Hong Kong to fund its global expansion plans. The company entered into strategic tie-ups for gaining access to generic markets in regulated markets. Consider these for example:

- Entered into a strategic alliance with the STADA Group for marketing and distributing its four products in select European markets such as Belgium, Italy and France
- Tied-up with Copyfarm, the Danish Kroner firm for marketing its products in Finland
- Signed a cooperation and supply agreements with PlasmaSelect for marketing its injectable anaesthetic products in Germany and Europe

J B CHEMICALS

Originally formed as a partnership firm in the name of Unique Pharmaceutical Laboratories the company was converted into a public limited company in 1976 with a new name – J B Mody Chemicals & Pharmaceuticals and was rechristened as J B Chemicals & Pharmaceuticals in 1985.The company manufactures bulk actives, drug intermediates and formulations in a number of therapeutic areas like cardiovascular, anti-amoebic, anti-ulcerant, NSAID and anti-rheumatic drugs. International sales account for over 52 per cent of the company's total sales from exports to about fifty countries across the globe.

The company is a leading player in the anti-amoebic and cardiovascular areas in the domestic market and ranked 38 in Indian pharmaceutical industry.

The company today is vertically integrated with manufacturing facilities approved by international regulatory authorities like US FDA, UK MHRA and TGA, Australia. J B Chemicals built a very good R&D infrastructure and research capabilities. Having reached a critical mass of Rs. 4.81 billion in the fiscal 2005-06, the company is planning to compete in the CRAMS space as well to accelerate its growth.

UNICHEM LABORATORIES

Unichem Laboratories Limited, a fully integrated Indian pharmaceutical company was founded in 1944. The company went public in 1962. Currently the company is involved in the synthesis, development, manufacturing, marketing and export of drug intermediates, APIs, and formulations for both human and veterinary health care. The company has a state-of-the-art manufacturing infrastructure with international regulatory approvals from US FDA, South African MCC etc. For the year ending March 2006 the company achieved a sales turnover of Rs. 4.66 billion with international sales contributing to over 16 per cent of the total.

In 1996, Unichem merged its group companies Unisearch and Unichem Exports and revisited its strategy to become competitive in the globalized Pharma world. The company is focusing on international sales with region-specific strategies and is keen on entering regulated markets for marketing APIs, generic formulations and branded generics in some markets. The company tied up with two generic companies in the US- Lannet and Pliva for marketing its generic formulations since 2005. The company is planning for more such alliances.

Unichem has three marketing divisions in India – Unisearch focusing on cardiovascular and diabetes therapeutic areas, Unichem Pharma concentrating on pain management, Gastro-intestinal, and anti-infectives and Neu Foreva catering to CNS disorders. The company has launched 20 new products including brand extensions in India to improve its share and rank.

STRIDES ARCOLABS

In just over a decade, Strides Arcolabs has stormed into the top league of exporters of pharmaceuticals from India. The company during the past few years has positioned itself to capture a greater share of the regulated markets. Strides Arcolabs manufactures a wide spectrum of ethical pharmaceutical products, OTC products and nutraceuticals in a wide range of dosage forms – soft gel capsules, hard gelatin capsules, dry and wet injectables at its world class manufacturing facilities with various international regulatory approvals. The company has also launched global initiatives to promote products for HIV/AIDS, tuberculosis and malaria. Strides has used strategic acquisitions and alliances and product and market expansion strategies to reach the critical mass. With manufacturing facilities spread over the globe including the regulatory markets, the Company has a presence in sixty countries of which Latin America is its strongest market today. Here is a snapshot of Strides' winning moves:

- Entered into an agreement to set a worldwide joint venture company with Accu-Break Pharmaceuticals Inc., US for developing generics using the patent-pending technologies of Accu-Break.
- Tied up with Abdi Ibrahim, the leading pharmaceutical company in Turkey to start a 50:50 joint venture to market a range of specialty pharmaceutical products developed by Strides in the Turkish and neighboring markets.
- Formed a JVC with Akorn Laboratories in the US – Akorn-Strides and submitted ten ANDAs for generic formulations in the US. The alliance covers product development, manufacturing and marketing generic formulations in the US. Strides develops the products and Akorn files the ANDAs with the US FDA and markets them upon approval.
- Received approval from the US FDA for two of its ARVs (Anti-retrovirals) under the expedited review provisions of the PEPFAR (President's Emergency Plan for AIDS Relief) program.
- Strides is included in the WHO list of pre-qualified suppliers of fixed dose combinations of anti-HIV generic drugs.
- Entered into a strategic alliance with Cellopharm, a leading Brazilian distributor of hospital products.
- Partnered with Infabra, a well-entrenched marketer for OTC products in Brazil.

- Acquired 90 per cent holding in Medigene Pharmaceuticals Private Limited.
- Stepped up its investment in Strides Latina SA to 67 per cent.
- Acquired Drug Houses of Australia (Asia) Pvt Ltd (DHA), one of Singapore's largest generic pharmaceutical manufacturers for $ 19.7 milllion through its subsidiary Strides Singapore from Haw Par Healthcare the present owner of DHA in October 2006.

Group 'C' Companies: Competing for the CRAMS Space

The ten companies in Group 'C' together have reached a critical mass of Rs. 32.23 billion in the FY2006. The total number of acquisitions made by companies in the group is 5 and the number of alliances entered is 16. The purpose of these alliances is to strengthen their capabilities to become more competitive in the CRAMS space.

Table 6.22 Group 'C' Companies Critical Mass

Company	Sales in FYE March 2006
1. Jubilant Organosys*	7.89
2. Divi's Labs	3.92
3. FDC Limited	3.77
4. Shasun Chemicals	3.49
5. Nectar Life Sciences	3.10
6. Dabur Pharma	2.68
7. Ind-Swift	2.32
8. Dishman Pharmaceuticals	2.16
9. Natco Pharma	2.07
10. Suven Pharma	0.83

* sales from pharmaceutical CRAMS business only, business from Industrial polymers not included

Table 6.23 Group 'C' Companies Mergers and Acquisitions

Company	Acquisitions	Purpose and Impact
1. Jubilant Organosys	2 in the US	To strengthen its position in the CRAMS business
2. Divi's Labs	NA	
3. FDC Limited	NA	

Company	Acquisitions	Purpose and Impact
4. Shasun Chemicals	One in the UK	To strengthen the CRAMS capabilities with two manufacturing sites in the UK and Scotland
5. Nectar Life Sciences	NA	
6. Dabur Pharma	NA	
7. Ind-Swift	NA	
8. Dishman Pharmaceuticals	1 in Europe	To strengthen its R&D capabilities
9. Natco Pharma	1 in the US	Retail drug store to foray into distribution of its generic formulations
10. Suven Pharma	1 in the US	To gain access to technology

Table 6.24 Group 'C' Companies Strategic Alliances

Company	Strategic Alliances	Nature and Purpose
1. Jubilant Organosys	NA	
2. Divi's Labs	NA	Although the company did not enter into any strategic alliances, Divi's has a number of supply agreements in the area of Custom synthesis and API-supplies and intermediates to some of the global drug majors
3. FDC Limited	Two	Marketing generic formulations in the US
4. Shasun Chemicals	Five	Spanning the Pharma value chain. Cover API supply, custom research and custom syntheis
5. Nectar Life Sciences	NA	
6. Dabur Pharma	Three	Across the CRAMS value chain and marketing generic formulations in the US
7. Ind-Swift	NA	
8. Dishman	Four	Development and supply arrangement of Pharmaceuticals, APIs and Intermediates
9. Natco Pharma	One	Marketing generic formulations in the US
10. Suven Pharma	One	Pre-clinical research

JUBILANT ORGANOSYS

Jubilant Organosys acquired Target Research Associates Inc. USA, a clinical research company for US $ 33.5 million to drive its CRAMS business. The company also acquired a 64 per cent stake in the US based Trinity Laboratories and its wholly owned subsidiary Trigen Laboratories for US $ 12.3 million and gained access to a US FDA approved facility and a pipeline of ANDAs to fuel its growth plans. The company's pharmaceutical business across the spectrum of CRAMS reached a critical mass of Rs. 7.9 billion in the fiscal 2006. The company developed world-class infrastructure, regulatory capabilities and an expanding base of customers from the regulated markets to achieve this. The company is planning to consolidate on these gains and plans to do even better in the coming years.

DIVI'S LABS

Divi's Labs has a very clear focus. Custom synthesis and CRAMS. The company that started manufacturing of APIs and intermediates towards the end of 1995 has built a state-of-the-art manufacturing and research & development infrastructure, received certifications for ISO-9002, ISO-14001, OHSAS-18001, WHO GMP, EOS, and US FDA approval. The company has reached a critical mass of Rs. 3.92 billion, 17 DMFs (likely to increase to about 25 by end of fiscal 2006-07). The company's main focus is on exports, which contribute to about 90 per cent of its revenues, most of which is from regulated markets.

Divi's is the largest producer of peptide building blocks and is poised to leverage this strength in the billion dollar global market for peptides. The company is also the first one to develop and manufacture synthetic carotenoids, a segment that is growing rapidly.

Divi's Labs seems determined to achieve leadership position in each generic product they manufacture (among the top three in the world) and expand the custom synthesis business through mutually reinforcing relationships that are sustainable over the long haul.

FDC LIMITED

Started in 1936, FDC, which is one of the oldest companies in India, has become adept at adapting to changing vicissitudes in Indian pharmaceutical industry. The company is bracing itself to meet the challenges of the globalization and product patent era. The company has built a manufacturing infrastructure of world standard and received many international regulatory approvals. Exporting to around fifty countries in the world, FDC has reached a critical mass of Rs. 3.77 billion in the year ending March 2006 and is foraying into the US generic market through the alliance route. Here are some of the company's initiatives:

- Signed an exclusive development and supply agreement with Akorn Inc. a leading marketing company of ophthalmic drugs with a market size of $ 170 million in the US. FDC will fund the development of these drugs, manufacture them while Akorn will be responsible for marketing. FDC will receive 60 per cent and Akorn 40 per cent of the gross profit generated from the sale of these two products.
- Entered into a non-exclusive licensing agreement with GILEAD Sciences Inc. for production and distribution of Viread (Tenofovir Disproxil Fumarate) to 95 low-income countries around the world. This agreement allows FDC to manufacture both API and the finished product.

Forbes Asia October 2006 issue has ranked FDC as one of the 200 best under-a-billion companies' with sales of less than $ 1 billion with solid top and bottom line gains and potential for more success.

SHASUN DRUGS

Shasun Chemicals and Drugs has been working on moving up the value chain from an API supplier to a preferred partner for global Pharma majors across the whole CRAMS spectrum. The company is investing in upgrading technology, R&D capabilities to achieve cost leadership and moving towards becoming a 'one-stop-shop' for its clients' needs. The company has followed the alliance route since 1995 and here is its trail of growing alliances in a networked Pharma world:

- 1995: signed technology and joint marketing agreement with Nagase & Co, Japan for S + Ibuprofen

- 1997: entered into a technology agreement with Clinicotech, UK for S + Naproxen
- 1999: singed a joint venture agreement with Austin Chemical Company, USA for process development and custom manufacturing for MNCs
- 2001: entered into an arrangement with Eastman Chemical Inc, USA for the manufacture of MAP
- 2002: singed a letter of intent with Eli Lilly, the global drug major for supply and manufacture of an anti-TB drug

Shasun after reaching a critical mass of Rs. 3.49 billion in the fiscal 2005-06, decided that alliances are not enough to fuel its growth plans and shifted gears into the acquisition mode and made its first acquisition. Shasun acquired Rhodia Pharma Solutions, part of the French Group Rhodia S A in January 2006 for US $ 35 million. The deal brings into Shasun's fold two manufacturing sites at Dudley, England and Annan in Scotland, besides Rhodia's development and custom manufacturing services. The acquisition thus will expand the company's manufacturing and customer base and strengthens its position in the CRAMS space.

NECTAR LIFE SCIENCES

Nectar Life Sciences is undergoing a major transformation from an API player in antibiotic and cephalosporin segment to an integrated player of Non-Cephalosporins and Non-antibiotics firm to compete in the CRAMS place. The company has built a state-of-the-art manufacturing and R&D infrastructure and got some international regulatory approvals and awaiting some more. The company has clocked Rs. 3.1 billion in the fiscal 2005-06. The company has a wholly owned subsidiary in Sri Lanka.

DABUR PHARMA

Dabur Pharma is clearly following the strategic path of the Indian drug majors like Ranbaxy and Dr. Reddy's Labs. The company's focus is clearly on the world oncology market and has built a portfolio of 34 products covering both APIs and finished dosage forms. Dabur entered UK through its wholly owned subsidiary – Dabur Oncology Plc and is planning to follow the alliance route to tap the regulated markets. To realize its aspirations in the oncology generic market and leverage its R&D and manufacturing competencies Dabur has chosen the alliance route and entered into three major alliances.

- Signed an agreement with Abbott Laboratories, one the largest marketers of injectables pharmaceutical products in the US. Dabur under this exclusive, long-term alliance will develop and manufacture prescription generic oncology products and Abbott will market them in the US.
- Entered into another strategic alliance with Hospira, a leading supplier of generic injectables drugs in the US.
- Signing up a major collaboration with a leading British Institute for fundamental research in cancer vaccines and diagnostics to explore the possibilities of developing NCEs with anticancer potencies.

IND-SWIFT LABORATORIES

An emerging API player, Ind-Swift Laboratories has positioned itself as a primary supplier of bulk actives to regulated markets. Hitherto focused on markets with little or no IPR protection, Ind-Swift is steadily building up a platform based on manufacturing R&D capabilities of international standards. The company has six cGMP-compliant plants and a product basket of 18 molecules (20 more in the pipeline). Ind-Swift is certainly on growth path. The company recorded a sales of Rs. 3.23 billion in the fiscal 2005-06.

The company is now focusing on regulated markets to accelerate its growth and evolve into a full service provider in the CRAMS space. Ind-Swift has entered in March 2006 into contract research agreements with two leading European Pharmaceutical Companies for the molecules with the market size of over US $ 8 billion to be completed in the next 18 months.

The company is aiming for a 40-45 per cent of its bottom line from CRAMS business in the next two to three years.

DISHMAN PHARMACEUTICALS

Known for its quats business Dishman has positioned itself as a 'preferred partner' of global pharmaceutical companies in the CRAMS segment that is rapidly growing. The company therefore follows a research-centric strategy and already procured more than a dozen Contract Research assignments and fifteen more are in the final stage of negotiations. The company follows the globally accepted Safety, Health and Environmental Policies (SHE) and received the coveted ISO: 14001 and OHSAS:18001 certification. The company generated Rs. 2.16 billion in sales in the fiscal 2005-06.

Dishman acquired Carbogen AMCIS AG, a research-based company in Switzerland from Solutia Europe SA for US $ 75 million in August 2006. All the intellectual property, patents, trademarks, customer contract as well as employees of the pharmaceutical services business are a part of this acquisition. This acquisition gives Dishman three world-class research and development facilities in Switzerland providing seamless solutions to the world's leading pharmaceutical and biotechnology companies. With this acquisition the company's ability to serve the entire drug life cycle of 15-20 years is greatly enhanced.

Earlier to this in February 2006, Dishman acquired Io3S Ltd of Bern, Switzerland through its wholly owned subsidiary Dishman Switzerland Ltd. IO3S is the only Company in the world in the field of consultancy and research in Ozone based chemistry. It has a fully developed laboratory as well as a pilot plant for Ozone based reactions. IO3S has created a strong IP, having serviced major global Pharma MNCs and specialty chemical companies. This acquisition is a step in the right direction for strengthening its position in CRO and CMO strategy.

Dishman also entered the alliance route and forged alliances in its pursuit to become the preferred partner. Here is a brief account of its alliances:

- Executed various agreements with Arab Company for Drug Industries and Medical Appliances (ACDIMA) for setting up a joint venture project initially to manufacture 20 APIs for marketing in the Arab world and exporting them. ACDIMA is promoted by 18 Arab nations for economic development of these nations through setting up of projects in various fields including manufacturing of raw materials for pharmaceutical industry. Dishman will hold 51 per cent of the equity and ACDIMA, a government body and a local partner will hold the rest.
- Entered into an agreement with leading British company Nu SCAAN, for development and manufacture of bulk actives for Neutraceutical products.
- Formed a 50:50 J V with Schutz GmbH, Germany, a company engaged in marketing and distribution of the bulk drugs and fine chemicals to create Schutz Dishman Biotech Pvt. Ltd. This acquisition gives the company a foothold in the largest generic market in Europe.
- Created a 50:50 J V with Adiman's Ventures Ltd in U K a firm engaged in trading and marketing products in U K and Europe.

Dishman is certainly changing gears to change its pace in the race to become the preferred partner in the CRAMS segment.

NATCO PHARMA

Natco, the mid-size, vertically integrated pharmaceutical company is driven by global aspirations. Accordingly it built manufacturing infrastructure with state-of-the-art facilities for APIs and finished dosage forms that are approved by international regulatory authorities like US FDA. The company is focusing on world oncology generic market. Here are some of its key strategic initiatives:

- Entered into a strategic alliance with the US-based Akorn Inc. for supply of APIs for two injectable oncology drugs and finished dosage forms for three ANDAs in oncology and anti-emetic segments whose combined market size is over $ 1.3 billion in 2006.

- Acquired a majority stake of 75 per cent in a retail drug store with annual sales of $ 20 million in Newark, New Jersey, USA. Natco identified Pharma retail as a key area for growth and would go in for more such acquisitions. The company intends to sell its generic drugs through retail stores directly.

SUVEN PHARMA

Established as Suven Pharma in 1991 and rechristened as Suven Life Sciences in 2003, the company is clearly focused on the fast growing CRAMS space. The company has set up a U S subsidiary – Suven Life Sciences LLC, USA and has acquired the assets of New Jersey-based Synthon Chiragenics Corporation, who is a world leader in carbohydrate-based chiral technology for pharmaceuticals in 2003. it is a significant step for Suven in its aspiration to emerge as a leading full spectrum provider of discovery research related services.

Suven signed an agreement with the global Pharma major Eli Lilly to collaborate on the pre-clinical research of molecules in the CNS therapeutic area. Suven will receive payments from Lilly and potentially downstream payments if the identified candidates are selected by Lilly.

Outlook for Strategic Acquisitions and Alliances

Acquisitions and alliances are here to stay. The thirty Indian drug companies in this study made 55 acquisitions and entered into as many as 108 alliances during the last three to four years. Most of these are marketing alliances to gain access to new products. Many Indian companies have started pursuing a very aggressive strategy to introduce new products before the product patent regime arrived. Some alliances cover manufacturing, technology transfer and collaborative research. A few of them are even equity-based.

Another major focus of more than half of these alliances is the penetration of the difficult to enter but highly lucrative North American generic market for off-patent drugs and the rapidly growing European generics market. Whatever are the objectives and the duration of these alliances, being a good partner has become a key corporate asset. How to become a good partner may be a matter of pure and simple common sense. But the only thing common about common sense these days is that it has become so uncommon. It is, therefore, worth reiterating what Rosabeth Moss Kanter emphasized in her HBR article sometime ago as the eight 'I's for an enduring relationship.

Eight 'I's

Indeed, the best organizational relationships are, like the best marriages, true partnerships that tend to meet certain criteria. These are relationships, where both partners are strong and have something of value to contribute to the relationship. The eight 'I's of an enduring, fruitful relationship are:

1. Individual excellence
2. Importance
3. Interdependence
4. Investment
5. Information
6. Integration
7. Institutionalization
8. Integrity

Reaching the Critical Mass

Companies have taken all the possible strategic routes to reach the critical mass. They seem to have, literally and figuratively, left no stone unturned and no path unexplored. They have pursued all winning ways like:

A. Mergers
B. Acquisitions of businesses, facilities and brands
C. Strategic alliances including joint ventures
D. Extension of therapeutic coverage
E. Expansion of customer coverage
F. Exploration of new shores

Unless a firm reaches a critical mass of investible surplus, it cannot fuel its growth strategies. In the final analysis, what is critical to the whole business of critical mass is reaching it!

Chapter Seven

Marketing Focus

Marketing focus needs a marketing mindset which is viewing the entire business from the customers' point of view. When the sole purpose of the whole business is to 'create' and 'keep' a customer, can marketing be seen as only a functional area in an organization? Peter Drucker emphatically declared that :

> There is only one valid definition of business purpose: to create a satisfied customer. It is the customer who determines what the business is. Because it is its purpose to create a customer, any enterprise has two – only two basic functions: Marketing and Innovation.

Marketing mindset has to become the philosophy of an organization. It must permeate throughout the organization. Customers should be able to see, touch, feel, taste and experience the marketing orientation and mindset of an organization. How can one cultivate the marketing mindset? One possible way is to clearly define and identify the criteria that determine the marketing mindset and set objectives for each of these. While measurement of attitudes is not possible, one can infer and indeed measure the degree of marketing orientation, disposition or even the mindset of a company through observable behavior in the marketplace and the outcomes. Consider these criteria for a starter, which can be used as indicators of gauging the marketing mindset:

- Market share and growth
- Brand building capabilities
- Focus on therapeutic segments
- Size of the participated market
- Product portfolio and product strategies
- Strategy for key markets including overseas markets
- Customer franchise and satisfaction

Evaluating or taking stock of where the organization stands against these criteria is an essential first step. Only when you know where you stand, you can plan and decide where to go and which way to go. As a second step, benchmark the intra and inter-industry best practices for each of the criteria.

Marketing therefore is an organizational responsibility and should not be viewed as just that of one functional area. That is the essence of marketing mindset. The managers of General Electric, the world's largest corporation said it best: "Marketing is too important a function to be left to the marketing department alone".

Pharmaceutical industry the world over is research-led and marketing-driven. The drug markets can be broadly classified into two categories – the innovative and the imitative. The innovative markets are single source product-markets, which are the terra firma of research-based drug companies. The imitative markets are the multi-source product-markets or branded-generic markets with inadequate protection for intellectual property rights. While the competition is very intense in innovative markets, it is both intensive and extensive in nature in imitative markets.

Competition, therefore, is doubly fierce in imitative markets. When competition is fierce it is marketing that calls the shots. We are not referring to marketing in the narrow functional sense here. Neither are we undermining the importance of research or technology, which are the key success factors in the pharmaceutical industry. What we are referring to is the marketing attitude of the organization as a whole or the classical marketing concept that pervades the entire company. In other words, we are referring to the extent of customer focus and the disposition of the company to serve the customer.

Product Portfolio

One of the most important aspects of value creation inside a corporation is the management of product portfolio. A strongly positioned company should have products that are highly capable of generating cash today and others that show potential and promise for value creation over the next three to five years. Then, there should be some products and businesses that are in embryonic stage today that can be potential winners 10–15 years from now.

Companies that have a balance of all the three horizons are well poised to work towards the maximization of economic value in a long-term perspective. Consider how some of the leading Indian drug companies are faring against this marketing mindset backdrop.

Brand Building

Some years ago, the editor of the Journal of Marketing Research asked Larry Light, a prominent advertising research professional, for his perspective on the future of marketing in the next three decades. Light's analysis was at once perceptive, instructive and even prophetic.

> The marketing battle will be a battle of brands – a competition for brand dominance. Businesses and investors will recognize brands as the company's most valuable assets. This is a critical concept. It is a vision about how to develop, strengthen, defend and manage a business. It will be more important to own markets than to own factories. The only way to own markets is to own market-dominant brands.

This explains why a number of companies are in a rush to acquire brands with a strong presence in the market and brands that strengthen their presence in their therapeutic segments of focus. In retrospect, it may look simple but it takes time to build brands or businesses but to buy them, it only requires cash. It has taken a long time for the companies to recognize this seemingly simple truth. Brand building, of course, becomes a continuous activity once you acquire brands or businesses. Consider the spate of brand acquisitions over the years in the Indian pharmaceutical industry:

- Ranbaxy acquired Gufic's leading brands like Mox, Suprimox and others to strengthen its pre-eminent position in the anti-infective segment.
- Dr. Reddy's Labs acquired Riflux and Clamp from Standard Organics and Becelac from Pfimex to reinforce their position in anti-ulcerant and anti-infective segments and to enter the essential co-prescription segment of vitamin B complex. They have also acquired five more brands from Dolphin Laboratories to reinforce their presence in anti-infective and gastro-intestinal segments and to enter the new haemostatic segment.
- Nicholas Piramal acquired a number of leading over-the-counter brands like Strepsils, Sweetex, Cherana and Burnol from Boots and Dettol and Disprin from Reckitt & Colman through innovative joint ventures to establish a strong OTC presence.
- Nicholas group also acquired a number of leading prescription drug brands from Ambalal Sarabhai Enterprises through another creative joint venture Sarabhai Piramal.
- Nicholas Piramal acquired the entire prescription drug portfolio of ICI in India.
- SmithKline Beecham (Glaxo SmithKline now) in India acquired Crocin, the leading OTC analgesic anti-pyretic brand of Duphar Interfran.
- Sun Pharma acquired a bevy of brands covering a wide range of therapeutic segments from Natco. The total sales of these

acquired brands were around Rs. 520 million at the time of acquisition in 1998.

- Sun Pharma acquired two brands in the Woman's Healthcare segments in the USA.

Marketing Focus

Marketing capabilities of a company are measurable because there are a number of precise metrics such as market share, growth, therapeutic focus and coverage, brand-building capabilities (even in a branded-generic market the relative market share indicates the strength of a brand), customer franchise and growth rate. These companies realize that they have to achieve an optimum balance between extension of therapeutic coverage and customer focus. That is why many of them (twenty-one out of the thirty companies discussed in this book, as they have domestic marketing operations) have been restructuring their marketing operations in India and sharpening their focus around therapy-specific marketing teams or task forces. The total number of marketing divisions or teams that they have between them is around 126. The average size of the sales force in this group is the highest in the country.

Group 'A' Companies and Marketing Focus

The ten companies in 'Group A' barring Biocon have essentially reached their critical mass by building their branded generic business in the domestic market. Many of them simultaneously pursued the business opportunities in international markets for their APIs, branded formulations through strategic alliances, acquisitions of brands, manufacturing facilities and even the generic businesses in select overseas markets. These companies have been extending their therapeutic coverage by introducing new products consistently year after year. They participate in all major chronic and acute therapy areas with renewed focus in chronic therapy areas as these segments are growing more rapidly than others. Their marketing mindset and focus can be seen from what they have achieved so far in the Indian pharmaceutical market. Consider these facts:

- These ten companies accounted for close to 26 per cent of the total domestic formulation market sales of over Rs. 257 billion in July 2006 (MAT).
- They have about 150 brands among the industry's top 500 brands (Table 7.3)
- These 150 brands contributed close to one-half of the total sales of these companies and 12.7 per cent of the total industry's sales of Rs. 257 billion in the same period
- These ten companies have created a total of 90 marketing teams to achieve the critical balance between customer focus and therapeutic coverage extension
- The average size of the field force of these companies is in excess of 1200 which is significantly larger than other companies in the Indian pharmaceutical industry

Table 7.1 Group 'A' Companies : Domestic Market Share.

Company	Branded Formulation Sales in India Rs. billion	Market Share Per cent
1. Ranbaxy	13.02	5.10
2. Dr. Reddy's Laboratories	5.91	2.30
3. Sun Pharma	8.39	3.30
4. Lupin	5.90	2.30
5. Nicholas Piramal	11.15	4.50
6. Zydus Cadila Healthcare	8.98	3.50
7. Wockhardt	4.61	1.80
8. Biocon	0.09	0.03
9. Glenmark	3.16	1.20
10. Torrent Pharma	4.99	1.90

Source : Data derived from IMS-ORG Report July 2006

Table 7.2 Group 'A' Companies : Therapeutic Focus

Company	Marketing Teams (Number)	Therapeutic Focus
1. Ranbaxy	9 marketing divisions	Anti-infectives, Cardiovascular, Diabetology, Urology, Nephrology, Anti-Retrovirals, Pain Management, Lipid Regulators, Dermatology, Neuro-psychiatry, Gastroenterologicals, Nutritionals,
2. Dr. Reddy's Laboratories	7 marketing divisions	Cardiovascular, Diabetology, Gastro-intestinal, Urology, Nephrology, ENT, Dental, Nutritionals, Oncology, Critical Care, Anti-infectives, Dermatology
3. Sun Pharma	17 marketing divisions	Cardiovascular, Interventional Cardiology, Diabetology, Neuro-psychiatry, Gastro-intestinal, Respiratory, Opthalmologicals, ENT, Gynecology, infertility, Oncology, Critical Care, Dermatology, Pain Management,
4. Lupin	6 marketing divisions	Anti-TB, Anti-infective, Cardiovascular, Diabetology, Respiratory, Neuro-Psychiatry, Pain Management, Herbal Remedies
5. Nicholas Piramal	15 marketing divisions	Cardiovascular, Diabetology, Neuro-Psychiatry, Nutritionals, Pain Management, Cough and Cold, Gastro-intestinal, Anti-infective,
6. Zydus Cadila	10 marketing divisions	Antiinfectives, Cardiovascular, Diabetology, Gastro-intestinal, Gynecology, Neuropsychiatry, Pain Management, Respiratory and Nutritional
7. Wockhardt	5 marketing divisions	Pain Management, Cardiovascular, Diabetology, Nutritional, Vaccines, Anti-infectives, Neuro-Psychiatry, Biopharmaceuticals
8. Biocon	2 marketing divisions	Cardiovascular, Lipid Regulators, Diabetology, Biopharmaceuticals
9. Glenmark	8 marketing divisions	Dermatology, Diabetology, Cardiovascular, Pain Management, Cough and Cold,
10. Torrent Pharma	11 marketing divisions	Cardiovascular, Diabetology, Neuro-Psychiatry, Anti-infective, Gastro-intestinal, Pain Management

Table 7.3 Group 'A' Companies : Brand-building in Domestic Market

Company		No. of Brands of Top Brands Among Industry's Top 500 brands	Annual Sales Rs. Million
1.	Ranbaxy	33	8,803
2.	Dr. Reddy's Laboratories	10	2,796
3.	Sun Pharma	16	2,522
4.	Lupin	14	2,385
5.	Nicholas Piramal	27	5,875
6.	Zydus Cadila	22	5,185
7.	Wockhardt	15	2,379
8.	Biocon	None	None
9.	Glenmark	6	873
10.	Torrent	8	1,798

Data Derived from IMS-ORG Report July 2006

Ranbaxy

Ranbaxy, the largest Indian pharmaceutical company, has moved to the coveted 2nd position in the domestic formulations market. It has a market share of 4.9 per cent of the Rs. 257 billion large domestic formulation market. The company has achieved this through a strategic recipe of organic growth, brand acquisitions and a merger.

The company has a distinct leadership position in the anti-bacterial segment which is the largest in the Indian drug market, accounting for about one-fifth of the total market. The company has built its brands through a well planned, consistent strategy. Today it has 33 brands (Table 7.4) among the top 300 of the industry. These thirty-three brands account for about 68 per cent of the company's total domestic formulations' sales of Rs. 13 billion. The company's marketing orientation is evident from the fact that it is able to manage and build a large and diverse product portfolio and build many major brands out of them.

The company pursued a fully integrated strategy to build 25 global brands of major molecules that are going off patent a few years ago and launched many of these brands in all its key branded-generic markets.

Table 7.4 Ranbaxy's Top Brands in India

Brand	Sales Value in Fiscal 2005-06 Rs. Million	Brand	Sales Value in Fiscal 2005-06 Rs. Million
1. Cifran	885	18. fortwin	162
2. Sporidex	878	19. Keflor	151
3. Mox	801	20. Covance	140
4. Zanocin	475	21. Loxof	139
5. Revital	440	22. Calmpose	132
6. Volini	402	23. Cilanem	132
7. Storvas	370	24. Vericof	127
8. Cepodem	312	25. Histac	121
9. Verorab	298	26. Zole F	119
10. Oframax	288	27. Efrobax	119
11. Moxclav	272	28. Covance D	118
12. Ricona	204	29. Mobizox	117
13. Ranbiotic	203	30. Romilast	116
14. Roscillin	195	31. Enhancin	109
15. Cifran CT	180	32. Simvotin	105
16. Silverex	177	33. Pioglar	103
17. Carveta	167		

Data derived from IMS-ORG Report July 2006

Dr. Reddy's Labs

Dr. Reddy's Labs have chosen to enhance the "customer reach" strategy to build brands. The company had integrated its two marketing divisions in 1996 to create one large marketing force to increase its customer coverage. It has cut down the redundancies and expanded its customer reach effectively. The company as a result, has shown a phenomenal growth rate that is three-and-half times higher than the industry average for the next two years. To fuel the growth further, the company has also followed the brand acquisition route. It has acquired two brands from Standard Organics and one from Pfimex during 1996. It has a market share of 2.3 per cent. Later the company had acquired five brands from Dolphin Laboratories - Styptovit, Styptochrome (to enter the haemostatic market), doxt (to reinforce its These are: Styptovit, Styptochrome (to enter the haemostatic market), Doxt (to reinforce its position in the anti-bacterial segment) trichodol (a hepatic stimulant) and Styptomet to consolidate its already strong position among gastroenterologists, physicians and general practitioners. With all these moves, the company has moved up from a rank of 22 in 1998 to 11 in 2006 with a 2.3 per cent market share.

The company's marketing orientation becomes obvious when you consider that the company has, at the right time, shifted its focus to value added formulations. It has achieved a strong presence in two specialty prescriber segments: cardiovascular and gastrointestinal. The company has built a very strong franchise in these two segments. Four of the company's brands – Omez, Stamlo, Enam and Nise were among the industry's top 250 brands in 1999. The company has ten of its brands among the industry's top 500 in 2006 and these contributed to about 51 per cent of the total domestic formulations sales of DR. Reddy's.

Even in its international operations the company has been focusing on registering its branded generic formulations in overseas markets and promoting them either through the company's sales force or through distributors' sales forces.

Table 7.5 Dr. Reddy's Top Brands in India

Brand	Annual Sales Rs. Million	Brand	Annual Sales Rs. Million
1. Nise	727	6. Atocor	170
2. Omez	648	7. Clamp	125
3. Stamlo	348	8. Razo	111
4. Stamlobeta	274	9. Minitop	108
5. Enam	180	10. Gaity	107

Data derived from IMS-ORG Report July 2006

Sun Pharma

Sun Pharma has been a highly marketing oriented company right from the beginning. Dilip Shanghvi, the ebullient founder-CMD had very aptly identified the niche segments – psychiatry, neurology and cardiology as they had a narrow prescriber base and less competitive intensity in 1984 (now they are as crowded as any other segment). The company focused on these segments and introduced many new products to offer a complete product basket, a sort of precursor to the emerging disease management approach. The company provided a superior level of customer service and has maintained the leadership position in psychiatry and neurology for many years now. In the cardiology segment too the company has emerged as a leading player with many new product introductions over the years since its acquisition of Natco's brands in 1998. It has achieved the 2nd position with the acquisition of Natco's brands.

Sun's marketing mindset can be assessed from the fact that it is the first Indian pharma company to structure its entire marketing operations around two or more specific therapeutic segments. It has created dedicated stand-alone strategic business units to serve the universe of customers in these segments. Sun had eight strategic business units focusing on all major therapeutic segments in 1999. The underlying philosophy is that when customer segments are getting increasingly speciality oriented, can the marketing companies lag behind? Later, many pharma companies followed suit and are setting up separate business units to retain the focus on key segments and yet diversify into new segments.

Sun's rate of new product introduction can only be described as prolific. It has introduced as many as 30 new products in all segments during the last two years. The company is planning to launch at least twelve more before the end of this year.

Sun has doubled its market share of 1.6 per cent in 1998 to 3.3 per cent in 2006 of the Indian pharmaceutical industry and is growing faster at twenty per cent as compared with the industry's single-digit growth rate over all these years. With the acquisition of Natco's entire prescription brand portfolio, Sun improved its market share virtually over night by 0.5 per cent and moved up into the top ten club of Indian Pharma industry in 1998.

The fact that Sun had only two brands among the industry's top 250 brands contributing only one-fifth to the company's total sales in 1998 belies its marketing mindset. In specialty segments, when a company is practicing a disease management approach, share of the therapeutic segment is equally important. Sun has diversified its product portfolio later and yet retained its focus on chronic therapy areas, which have been its forte since the beginning. The company has created the maximum number of marketing teams in the country – as many as 17 to keep its focus sharply on the specialty segments of its choice. As a result Sun has in 2006, 16 of its brands among industry's top 500 brands. Table 8.9 presents details of Sun's leading brands.

Table 7.6 Sun Pharma's Top Brands in India

Brand	Annual Sales Rs. Million	Brand	Annual Sales Rs. Million
1. Glucored	317	9. Repace	145
2. Pantocid	286	10. Pantocid D	145
3. Susten	247	11. Zofer	134
4. Monotrate	195	12. Zeptol	125
5. Aztor	153	13. Cardivas	117
6. Encorate Chrono	152	14. Oxetol	105
7. Repace H	147	15. Lonazep	103
8. Alzolam	147	16. Mesacol	103

Data derived from IMS-ORG Report July 2006

Lupin

If one has to describe Lupin's strategy in one word, it is "Focus." The company has had an unwavering focus on the anti-TB segment right from the start. It has achieved, over the years, the distinction of being the world leader in its chosen anti-TB segment. Having achieved uncommon success in one segment through focus, the company has spotted another major segment, oral and sterile cephalosporins. Lupin, here too, is not viewing merely the domestic market. It has set its sights on the world cephalosporin market, in which a number of major molecules are going off patent in a few years from now. Since leadership should, like charity begin at home, it has focused on the oral cephalosporins market in India and internationally. Lupin has 14 brands among industry's top 500 brands in 2006. Having consolidated its position in cephalosporins, Lupin is extending its therapeutic coverage into other therapy areas mainly into chronic disease segments.

Table 7.7 Lupin's Top Brands in India

Brand	Annual Sales Rs. Million	Brand	Annual Sales Rs. Million
1. Odaxil	325	8. L-Cin	143
2. R-Cinex	307	9. Ramistar	137
3. AKT 4	221	10. Rablet	130
4. Cefadrox	189	11. R-Cin	112
5. Tonact	177	12. AKT 3	118
6. Ceff	164	13. Fruselac	110
7. Akonit 4	146	14. Combutol	109

Data derived from IMS-ORG Report July 2006

NPIL

Ajay Piramal has set one objective, when he entered the pharmaceutical industry. The Piramal group had to be among the top three in the industry by the year 2000. He has chosen the route of mergers, acquisitions and joint ventures to reach critical mass. Today in 2006, when you add the domestic formulations' turnover figures of all Piramal group companies including the joint venture – Sarabhai-Piramal, the group has achieved 4th position with a market share of 4.5 per cent just behind the Indian MNC Pharma firm Ranbaxy. Its market share of 2.7 of 1998 has increased to 4.5 per cent of the Indian pharmaceutical industry in 2006.

The group has a strong presence in cardiovascular, neuro-psychiatry, nephrology and antacid segments. The group has restructured its marketing operations in India to achieve a sharper marketing focus and has a total field force strength of 2,778, which makes it one of the largest in the industry. The group's marketing approach is to apply the disease management strategy, offering the total package of services – diagnostics, drug therapy options and post-treatment monitoring and care (in chronic disease areas like diabetes). The company manages its diverse product portfolio with its 15 marketing teams structured around therapy areas to sharpen its focus and stay competitive. The top ten brands of the group contributed to 29.3 per cent of its domestic formulation sales of Rs. 10.7 billion in the fiscal 2005-06. The company has 27 brands among the industry's top 500 brands in 2006 (Table 7.8).

Table 7.8 NPIL's Top Brands in India

Brand	Annual Sales Rs. Million	Brand	Annual Sales Rs. Million
1. Phensidyl	1,283	15. Ismo	147
2. Stemetil	379	16. Neomercazole	146
3. Haemaccel	275	17. Rivotril	141
4. Gardenal	268	18. Inderal	140
5. Paraxin	262	19. Nervup	139
6. Phenergan	251	20. Mazetol	139
7. Pentids	218	21. Flagyl	135
8. Supradyn	203	22. Contramal	129
9. Sorbitrate	198	23. Lobate GM	126
10. Tossex	192	24. Rovamycin	119
11. Esgipyrin	192	25. Valium	116
12. Kenacort	158	26. Bactrim	107
13. Tenormin	155	27. Becozym Forte	103
14. Actirom	154		

Data derived from IMS-ORG Report July 2006

Zydus-Cadila Healthcare

Cadila has been concentrating on brand building activity for quite some time. Even after the division of Cadila into two corporate entities, the brand building activity continues. The undivided Cadila had as many as 12 brands among the industry's top 250, which were divided equally after the split. The six top brands of Zydus–Cadila Health Care accounted for about 42 per cent of the company's domestic formulations' turnover in 1998. Zydus Cadila went on building its domestic market share with its brand building and brand acquiring strategy. As a result today in 2006, Zydus has as many as 22 of its brands featuring in industry's top 500.

Zydus Cadila today has created 10 marketing divisions to manage its diverse product portfolios. These are organized around specific therapy areas to sharpen focus at customer level. Zydus has already a wide product basket in all its therapeutic segments. The idea behind the creation of different marketing divisions is to sharpen and retain focus at the same time and to extend therapeutic coverage at the corporate level.

Zydus Cadila improved its rank from 11th in 1998 to 5th by 2006 in the Indian pharmaceutical industry. The company's market share too has grown from 2 to 3.5 per cent during the same period.

Table 7.9 Zydus Cadila's Top Brands in India

Brand	Annual Sales Rs. Million	Brand	Annual Sales Rs. Million
1. Aten	593	12. Falcigo	168
2. Deriphyllin	478	13. Nucoxia	153
3. Ocid	355	14. Penegra	151
4. Ciprobid	337	15. GRD	145
5. Primolut-N	281	16. Oxalgin DP	136
6. Pantodac	274	17. Thrombophob	133
7. Atorva	260	18. Buscopan	133
8. Dexona	252	19. Tamazac	108
9. Amlodac	237	20. Proluton	108
10. Mifegest	182	21. Losacar	107
11. Dulcolox	181	22. Formonde	103

Data derived from IMS-ORG Report July 2006

Wockhardt

Marketing has always been a priority at Wockhardt. The company first focused on pain management. The company has subsequently entered into cardiovasculars, gynaecology and paediatrics and large volume parenterals, anaesthesia and critical care biopharmceuticals. In its chase for critical mass, the company has been following the M&A (mergers and acquisitions) route. Its acquisition of Merind and Tata Pharma had given access to neuro-psychiatry among others.

Wockhardt had slipped to the 16th position in the Indian pharmaceutical industry in 2006 from its 9th place of 1998 and its market share too dropped from 2.3 per cent to 1.8 per cent during the same period. Five of its brands that accounted for about one-fourth of the company's domestic formulations' sales were among the industry's top 250 during 1998. Wockhardt today in 2006 has 15 of its brands featured among industry's top 500 brands (Table 7.10). The company retains its focus on customer segments despite extended therapeutic coverage through its 5 marketing divisions, which are structured around therapy areas.

Table 7.10 Wockhardt's Top Brands in India

Brand	Annual Sales Rs. Million	Brand	Annual Sales Rs. Million
1. Spasmo-Proxyvon	401	9. Wockadine	137
2. Dexolac	281	10. Aziwok	121
3. Decadan	162	11. Wosulin	116
4. Practin	160	12. Proxyvon	113
5. Tryptomer	149	13. Libotryp	107
6. Brozedex	143	14. Biovac B	105
7. Zedex	141	15. Winofit	104
8. Methycobol	139		

Data derived from IMS-ORG Report July 2006

Biocon

Biocon's domestic formulations marketing effort is less than two-year old. Its focus is on diabetes and cardiovascular segments. The company has a dedicated marketing team for marketing its formulations. Biocon has its own insulin brand – *Insugen,* which is promoted by the formulations marketing team. While the growth is impressive, its domestic formulations business is yet to reach the critical mass.

Glenmark

Known as a two-brand company till early 1990's, Glenmark has been able to retain its focus in its key therapeutic segment – dermatology and expanded into other rapidly growing chronic therapy areas and registered a growth rate significantly higher than the market and its major competitors to improve its market share year after year. Today the company has six of its brands in industry's top 500 (Table 7.12). The company has been pursuing a very aggressive marketing strategy in the domestic market too since the late 1990s and created 8 marketing divisions to grow faster than the market and faster than competition in Indian pharmaceutical market.

Table 7.11 Top Brands of Glenmark in India

Brand	Annual Sales Rs. Million
1. Candid B	222
2. Candid	144
3. Ascoril	138
4. Ascoril T	136
5. Altacef	122
6. Alex Cough Lozenges	112

Data derived from IMS-ORG Report July 2006

Torrent

Torrent entered the Indian pharmaceutical market through a niche strategy. Other companies such as Sun Pharma and Intas emulated Torrent and started their operations in niche areas like neuropsychiatry where competitive intensity was less in the 1980s. Torrent introduced a number of new drugs for the first time in its chosen therapeutic segments – psychiatry, neurology and cardiology. Torrent has achieved a dominant leadership position in the *cardiovascular* segment. It has also achieved leadership position in the psychiatry segment, which was seized by its one-time follower Sun Pharma. To reach critical mass faster, Torrent has diversified into the fastest growing segment, anti-bacterials, and introduced a number of products. This entry has certainly accelerated the growth of the company, catapulting it to the big league.

Torrent moved up to the 5th position torrentially by 1998 with a market share of 2.4 per cent. Five of its brands were among the Industry's top 250 then. These five brands contributed to 35.2 per cent of the company's domestic formulations' sales. Later Torrent forayed into unrelated diversification such as power, cables etc. This seemed to have diluted its focus on the Pharma business and as a result, Torrent slipped by nine ranks to 14 and dropped its market share to 1.9 per cent in 2006. The company, however, is back with renewed vigor and sharpened its focus and created 11 marketing divisions organized around therapy areas to regain its pre-eminent position in chronic therapy areas. The company has also been pursuing aggressive new product strategy for which it has been wellknown in the past.

Table 7.12 Torrent's Top Brands in India

Brand	Annual Sales Rs. Million
1. Alprax	308
2. Droxyl	302
3. Dilzem	283
4. Domstal	256
5. Topcef	222
6. Nikoran	179
7. Listril	129
8. Betacard	120

Data derived from IMS-ORG Report July 2006

Group 'B' Companies Competing for International Generics Space

Three out of the ten companies in 'Group B' do not participate in the domestic formulations business. Their focus is on APIs and dosage forms for international markets. They are single-minded in their pursuit of becoming leading international generic companies. Out of the other seven companies participating in domestic formulation market, Cipla is the leader of the Indian drug companies with a market share of 5.1 per cent and is currently ranked at number 2. The seven companies have between them about 54 brands among the top 500 brands in Indian pharmaceutical industry. The seven companies in Group B contribute close to 11 per cent of the total domestic formulation sales of 257.11 billion in 2006 (MAT July 2006, IMS-ORG). They have created 23 marketing divisions to strike an optimum balance between customer focus and diversification of productmix.

Table 7.13 Group 'B' Companies : Domestic Market Share

Company	Branded Formulations Sales in India Rs. Billion	Market Share Per cent
1. Cipla	13.07	5.1
2. Aurobindo Pharma*	No participation	
3. Matrix Laboratories	No Participation	
4. Orchid	0.30	0.1
5. Ipca Laboratories	3.32	1.3
6. Alembic	4.30	1.7
7. Claris Life Sciences**	1.40	
8. J. B. Chemicals	1.80	0.7
9. Unichem Laboratories	4.02	1.6
10. Strides Arcolabs	No Participation	

Data derived from IMS-ORG Report July 2006

** Mainly institutional sales, not reflecting on retail audit, sales figures derived from domestic share mentioned on the company's website

Table 7.14 Group 'B' Companies : Therapeutic Focus

Company	Marketing Teams (Number)	Therapeutic Focus
1. Cipla	2	Anti-asthmatic and Respiratory, Anti-infective, ARV, Diabetology, Cardiovascular, Gastro-intestinal, Pain Management, and Neuro-psychiatry, Gastroenterology,
2. Orchid	2	Anti-infectives, Neuro-Psychiatry, Cardiovascular, and Nutritional
3. Ipca	7	Anti-malarial, Anti-infective, Laboratories Cardiovascular, Diabetology, Dermatology, Neuro-psychiatry
4. Alembic	4	Anti-infective, Cardiovascular, Diabetology, Geriatric Medicine, Pain Management, Gastro-intestinal, Nutritional
5. Claris Life Sciences**	1	Critical Care, Parenterals across specialties such cardiovascular, anti-infective, Anesthesia,
6. J.B.Chemicals	3	Cardiovascular, Gastroenterology, Anti-infective, Neuropsychiatry
7. Unichem Laboratories	4	Anti-infective, Gastroenterology, Cardiovascular, Diabetology, Gynecology, Neuropsychiatry

The other 3 companies in Group 'B' – Aurobindo Pharma, Matrix Laboratories, and Strides Arco Pharma do not participate in the domestic formulations market

Table 7.15 Group 'B' Companies : Brand-Building Capabilities

Company	No. of Brands in Industry's Top 500	Annual Sales of Top Brands in 2006 Rs. Million
1. Cipla	31	7,418
2. Orchid	None	
3. Ipca Laboratories	6	1,100
4. Alembic	5	1,996
5. Claris Life Sciences**	None	
6. J.B.Chemicals	5	1,057
7. Unichem Laboratories	7	1,893

Data derived from IMS-ORG Report July 2006

Cipla

Cipla has cultivated a very strong marketing mindset over the years. The company is ranked second in the Indian pharmaceutical industry with a market share of 5.1 per cent in 2006. It has a dominant leadership position in the anti-asthmatic segment and a very strong presence in a number of therapeutic segments like anti-bacterial and anti-infectives, cardiovascular, anti-helminthic and anti-cancer etc. Cipla's customer franchise among all key prescriber segments is extremely high. It is among the top three companies in terms of number of prescriptions generated by all major speciality prescriber segments.

Cipla as an organization is a lateral thinker. The company has found unique first-time solutions for many of the common problems that would bog down any ordinary company.

The credit for exploiting the opportunities of a multiple media-mix in pharmaceutical promotion should go to Cipla. It started and developed to a very fine art what the industry refers to as a multi-media approach to marketing. In fact, Cipla is considered to be a benchmark for this innovative marketing approach to enhance brand registration, recall and prescription generation. Another first to Cipla's credit is the development of a customer database indicating users and non-users and its validation through special task forces called, "prescription-watchers." This has helped Cipla considerably in brand building through precision marketing.

Cipla had 12 of its brands among the industry's top 250, which accounted for about 53.7 per cent of the company's total domestic formulations' sales in 1998. Today in 2006, Cipla has 31 of its brands featured among industry's top 500 brands (Table 7.16).

Table 7.16 Cipla's Top Brands in India

Brand	Annual Sales Rs. Million	Brand	Annual Sales Rs. Million
1. Asthalin	826	17. Restyl	160
2. Novomox	608	18. Novaclox	147
3. Seroflo	595	19. Metolar	139
4. Ciplox	563	20. Emeset	136
5. Aerocort	467	21. Acivir	132
6. Norflox	335	22. Azee	132
7. Furacort	322	23. Montair	126
8. Amlopress AT	309	24. Atorlip	115
9. MT Pill	250	25. Cefopime	115
10. Duolin	218	26. Cefadur	112
11. Theo-Asthalin	211	27. Dytor	106
12. Budecort	197	28. Urimox	104
13. Norflox TZ	190	29. Gatipin	103
14. Ciplox TZ	176	30. Amlopress	103
15. Oflox	161	31. Misoprost	102
16. Ibugesic Plus	161		

Data derived from IMS-ORG Report July 2006

Orchid

Orchid has started as a 100 per cent export oriented unit for manufacturing and marketing bulk drugs and intermediates. Later in the mid 1990s, the company integrated forward into manufacturing and marketing formulations. The company acquired Mano Pharma a start-up firm in neuropsychiatry segment to strengthen its fledgling domestic formulations business. In domestic formulation market Orchid has yet to gain a strong foothold. The company in 2006 is ranked 103 in Indian pharmaceutical market with a market share of 0.1 per cent.

IPCA

IPCA has focused on a few brands consistently over the years. The company's major strengths have been technology and the ability to integrate backward successfully to gain control on input costs. This has helped the company in building a strong presence in bulk drug exports. The company has structured its domestic marketing operations into 7 marketing divisions to promote its growing product- mix across different specialties such as cardiovascular, diabetology, anti-infectives, neuro-psychiatry, gastro-enterology, dermatology etc.

The company's focus on a few products has paid off handsomely. Today 6 of its brands are among the industry's top 500 brands. These brands account for over 38 per cent of the company's domestic sales of formulations.

The company's rank is the same as it was in 1998 - 26th in the industry whereas its market share has marginally improved from 1.1 percent in 1998 to 1.3 percent in 2006.

Table 7.17 IPCA's Top Brands in India

Brand	Annual Sales Rs. Million
1. Lariago	402
2. Perinorm	180
3. Tenoric	150
4. Tenolol	145
5. HCQS	114
6. Glycinorm	109

Data derived from IMS-ORG Repot July 2006

Alembic

Alembic is the uncrowned king of marcrolides market in India. Its top three brands are brand leaders in the three molecules of the macrolides segment – Althrocin (erythromycin), Roxid (roxithromycin) and Azithral (azithromycin) in India. These three brands contributed to over 38 per cent of its domestic formulations sales in 2006. Alembic has five of its brands featuring in the industry's top 500. The company's current rank is 19 in the Indian pharmaceutical industry with 1.7 per cent market share. The company has started a new marketing division – Specia dedicated to geriatric health care. With this, Alembic has four marketing divisions to promote its large product portfolio to different specialty prescriber groups with focused promotion.

Table 7.18 Alembic's Top Brands in India

Brand	Annual Sales Rs. Million
1. Althrocin	700
2. Roxid	533
3. Azithral	416
4. Wikoryl	206
5. Zeet	141

Data derived from IMS-ORG Report July 2006

Claris Life Sciences

Claris Life Sciences is mainly focusing on injectables and delivery systems across a number of therapeutic segments such as enteral and parenteral nutrition, anesthesia, blood products, plasma volume expanders, anti-infectives, cardiac care, infusion therapy, dialysis and transplants, and medical disposables etc. the company is a dominant brand leader in propofol sub-segment. Currently domestic business accounts for about 45 per cent of its total sales.

J B Chemicals

J B Chemicals (known as Unique Pharmaceuticals in domestic formulations market) is ranked 35 with a market share of 0.7 per cent in 2006 in Indian pharmaceutical market. The company has five of its brands in the industry's top 500. These brands account for about 59 per cent of the company's total formulation sales in India. The company has structured its domestic formulations business around specific therapy areas into three marketing divisions. It is a leading player in amoebicidal and calcium channel blocker subsegments.

Table 7.19 J B Chemicals' Top Brands in India

Brand	Annual Sales Rs. Million
1. Rantac	317
2. Nicardia	221
3. Metrogyl	211
4. Nor-Metrogyl	156
5. OF	152

Data derived from IMS-ORG Report July 2006

Unichem Laboratories

Unichem moved up to 21st rank in the Indian pharmaceutical industry in 2006 and has a 1.6 per cent market share. Seven of its top brands feature among the industry's top 500. These brands contribute to 26 per cent to its domestic formulation sales. Domestic formulations sales contributed 69 per cent to total sales in FY 2005-06. Unichem is focusing more on the chronic therapy area, which currently accounts for 45 per cent of its domestic formulations sales. The company has structured its domestic marketing operations around four marketing divisions to retain focus on its chosen customer segments.

Table 7.20 Unichem's Top Brands in India

Brand	Annual Sales Rs. Million
1. Ampoxin	509
2. Trika	326
3. Losar H	315
4. Losar	311
5. Unienzyme	189
6. Vizylac	125
7. TG-Tor	116

Data derived from IMS-ORG Report July 2006

Group 'C' Companies Competing for CRAMS Space

Six out of the ten companies in Group 'C' do not participate in domestic formulations business reflecting their focus on the CRAMS space. Two companies have demonstrated their brand building capabilities with FDC having 9 and Dabur having 3 brands featuring among the industry's top 500. These four companies have created 13 marketing divisions to achieve the twin objectives of customer focus and a wider product portfolio at the same time.

Table 7.21 Group 'C' Companies : Domestic Market Share

	Company	Branded Formulation Sales in India Rs. Billion	Market Share Per cent
1.	Jubilant Organosys*	No Participation	
2.	Divi's Labs	No Participation	
3.	FDC Limited	3.86	1.5
4.	Shasun Chemicals	No Participation	
5.	Nectar Life Sciences	No Participation	
6.	Dabur Pharma	1.87	0.7
7.	Ind-Swift	1.18	0.5
8.	Dishman Pharmaceuticals	No Participation	
9.	Natco Pharma	0.11	
10.	Suven Pharma	No Participation	

Data derived from IMS-ORG Report July 2006

Table 7.22 Group 'C' Companies : Therapeutic Focus

	Company (Number)	Marketing Teams Per cent	Market Share
1.	FDC Limited	3	Opthalmology, Oral Rehydration, Anti-infectives, ENT,
2.	Dabur Pharma	2	Oncology, Cardiovascular, Gastroenterology,
3.	Ind-Swift	7	
4.	Natco Pharma	1	Cardiovascular,Diabetology, Anti-infectives Oncology, anti-nauseants, Anesthesia

The other 6 companies in Group 'C' – Jubilant Organosys, Divi's Labs, Shasun Chemicals,. Nectar Life Sciences, Dishman Pharmaceuticals, and Suven Pharma do not participate in the domestic formulations market

Table 7.23 Group 'C' Companies : Brand-Building Capabilities.

Company	No. of Brands in Industry's Top 500 Top Brands	Annual Sales of Rs. Million
1. FDC Limited	9	2,101
2. Dabur Pharma	3	495
3. Ind-Swift	None	
4. Natco Pharma	None	

Data derived from IMS-ORG Report July 2006

The other 6 companies in Group 'C' – Jubilant Organosys, Divi's Labs, Shasun Chemicals,. Nectar Life Sciences, Dishman Pharmaceuticals, and Suven Pharma do not participate in the domestic formulations market

FDC

FDC moved up to 22nd position with a market share of 1.5 per cent in Indian pharmaceutical market. The company has a dominant leadership position in oral-rehydration segment with its brand *Electral*. The company has three marketing divisions – Spectra, Select and Proxima to retain its customer focus and yet expand its therapeutic coverage. FDC has nine of its brands featuring among the industry's top 500. These brands contributed to about 53 per cent of its total domestic formulation business.

Table 7.24 FDC's Top Brands in India

Brand	Annual Sales Rs. Million
1. Zifi	731
2. Electral	328
3. Zoxan	197
4. Zathrin	175
5. Zo	164
6. Zodoo	117
7. Vitcofol	110
8. Zifi-LBX	108
9. Zocon	102

Data Derived from IMS-ORG Report July 2006

Dabur Pharma

Dabur's main focus is on becoming a global oncology player. Oncology business accounts for two-thirds of its total turnover. Domestic business contributes for about 56 per cent today. Dabur has three of its brands among the industry's top 500. Dabur Pharma is ranked 35 with 0.7 per cent share of the Indian pharmaceutical market in 2006.

Table 7.25 Dabur's Top Brands in India

Brand	Annual Sales Rs. Million
1. Ulgel	265
2. New Livfit	125
3. Gestofit	106

Data derived from IMS-ORG Report July 2006

Ind-Swift

Domestic sales contributed about 51 per cent to total sales in the FY2005. While the company's major thrust area is the CRAMS space, it believes that performance like charity should begin at home and is increasing its focus on the domestic formulations business too. It has structured its marketing operations in India around 7 marketing divisions to promote its diverse product portfolio and at the same time retain the customer focus.

Natco Pharma

Natco Pharma is focusing on becoming a leading oncology player globally. It is a leading player in the Indian oncology market. The company is rebuilding its domestic formulations business since it had sold its entire domestic formulations portfolio in 1988 to Sun Pharma. Natco is known for its *timed-release* formulations of oral dosage forms.

Intangible no more!

Brands are no more considered as intangible assets. "It is better to own brands than factories", thundered Larry Light rather prophetically quite sometime ago. Brand acquisitions have become the order of the day for speedy, or rather, instant growth. Ranbaxy had set up a whopping $ 150 million acquisition fund mainly for acquiring brands globally as early as in the late 1990s. Today in 2006, its war chest is much bigger. In fact, so big that it is making a bid for the much bigger generic business of the European drug major Merck KgGA. The company's stated policy has been brand acquisition rather than company acquisition. Dr. Reddy's too, have been on an acquisition spree. Sun Pharma has also made its intentions clear with its recent acquisitions in the US and Europe. These companies are also looking for brand acquisitions as they have adequate manufacturing infrastructure and what they need to reach the critical mass faster is brands. These reinforce a company's market dominance, facilitate its entry into new therapeutic segments and extend therapeutic coverage.

Brand Building or Segment Leadership?

Brand building or segment leadership is as mindless a question as egg or chick – which comes first? Before getting into the details of both, we need to first define what brand building is. The top 500 brands account for over 44 per cent of the entire industry's formulation sales. One logical way of looking at the brand building capabilities of a company is to compare the number of brands a company has among the industry's top 500 and their contribution to the total sales of the company. If it is equal to or more than the industry average that could be indicative of the company's brand building capabilities.

Companies, which are operating in speciality segments, find it difficult to build big brands. There are two main reasons for this. Firstly, the total size of the market in some of the speciality therapeutic segments is smaller than the sales of some of the industry's top brands. Secondly, companies in speciality segments are forced to introduce a wide range of products or different molecules with little or no overall sales benefits in the same therapeutic category, just to keep up with the Joneses. In a branded generic market like India, the temptation is to introduce brands of every single molecule launched by different companies for the same condition. In research-based pharmaceutical markets like North America, Europe and Japan, the innovator companies defend their respective molecules with all their might. Therefore, speciality focused companies in India defend their therapeutic segments with a range of products and aim for segment leadership position however small or narrow the segment may be. Achieving segment leadership is brand building. Size does matter in brand building, but then leadership matters even more.

Thirty Companies – A Snapshot

Out of the total thirty companies discussed, 21 companies participate in domestic formulation business whereas the rest of the 9 companies are not present in the formulation business in India as they are competing for either the international generics space or the CRAMS space. Table 7.26 presents a summary of the formulation business snapshot of these companies.

Two hundred and seventeen (43.6%) of the industry's 500 brands are from the seventeen companies discussed in this chapter. Out of the total thirty companies discussed in this book nine companies do not participate in the domestic formulation market by choice as they are focused on competing for CRAMS and International Generics spaces. Four companies – Biocon, Claris Life Sciences, Ind-Swift and Natco are yet to open their account in the industry's top 500-brand club.

All these companies demonstrate a high degree of marketing acumen. They are fiercely competitive. Each one of these companies either has a leadership position or a major presence in more than one therapeutic segment. Ranbaxy has an undisputed leadership position in the largest therapeutic segment – anti-bacterial and antibiotic. Cipla has a leadership position in the anti-asthmatic segment and a major presence in a number of therapeutic segments including anti-bacterials.

Dr. Reddy's has a major presence in gastro-intestinal and cardiovascular segments. Ipca is the country's largest anti-malarial player. Torrent and Sun Pharma have a strong speciality focus particularly in neuro-psychiatry.

The customer coverage strategies and the consequent customer franchises are naturally based on different marketing approaches. Cipla, Ranbaxy and Dr. Reddy's, for example, have a very broad coverage across large prescriber segments, whereas Sun Pharma's customer coverage has a very sharp focus on a number of speciality-based narrow prescriber segments. Cipla balances these two – broad customer base and narrow prescriber focus very effectively, though it may sound like an oxymoron. Cipla has achieved the uncommon success of being among the top three in a number of prescriber segments.

These companies have also shaped the strategic thinking of the industry itself. The strategy for not just winning in the domestic market, but for penetrating overseas markets as well. These companies account for almost all of the strategic acquisitions made by Indian drug companies in overseas markets. Ranbaxy, Lupin, Wockhardt and Sun Pharma have acquired generic companies in the US and UK for exploiting the rapidly expanding markets for off-patent generic formulations in these highly industrialized markets. These companies also account for over eighty per cent of strategic alliances to gain faster access to new products, markets, and technology and to exploit the off-patent generic markets in the West.

On all criteria which assess the marketing mindset of an organization (like market share, growth, brand building capabilities, segment leadership, new product introductions, focused approach, customer coverage strategies, customer franchise among others), these companies have demonstrated that they are capable of staying competitive in the globalized world of Pharma, and they have got what it takes to win in the WTO era of pharmaceutical product patents.

Table 7.26 Thirty Companies A Snapshot

Group	Extent of Participation in Domestic Formulations Business	No. of Brands among the Industry's Top 500 Brands	Number of Marketing Divisions
'A' Ranbaxy, Dr. Reddy's Laboratories, Sun Pharma, Lupin, Nicholas Piramal, Zydus Cadila, Wockhardt, Biocon, Glenmark, and Torrent	All the ten companies participate in domestic formulations business. The total sales of all the ten companies are about Rs. 66.2 billion, which is 25.75 per cent of the domestic formulation business in India. Domestic formulations account for 37.3 per cent of their total sales in 2006.	Nine out of these ten companies in this group have a total of 151 brands among the industry's top 500 brands. The annual sales of these 151 brands are about Rs. 32.61 billion in 2006. These 151 brands contributed to 56 per cent of the total domestic formulations sales of the 9 companies (Biocon is not included as it does not have any brand among the industry's top 500).	The nine companies that are active in domestic formulations business have created 90 marketing divisions to achieve the optimum balance between focused promotion and a widely diversified product portfolio across many therapeutic areas.
'B' Cipla, Aurobindo Pharma, Matrix Laboratories, Orchid, Ipca, Alembic, claris Life Sciences, J B Chemicals, Unichem, and Strides Arcolabs	Seven out of these ten companies are participating in domestic formulations. The rest of the three companies are focusing on the international generics space. The domestic formulation sales of the seven companies were about Rs. 28.2 billion, which is 11 per cent of total domestic formulation market. Domestic formulations accounted for 42.15 per cent of the seven companies total sales (Aurobindo, Matrix and Strides are not include as they do not participate in domestic formulations market).	The total number of brands in the industry's top 500 from the seven companies in this group is 54. The annual sales of these 54 brands are about Rs. 13.46 billion in 2006. These 54 brands accounted for about 25 per cent of the total domestic formulation sales of the four companies in this group (Orchid and Claris Life Sciences are not included for arriving at this as they do not have any of their brands in the industry's top 500).	The seven companies that are in the domestic formulations business have structured their marketing operations around 13 marketing divisions to achieve the dual objective of retaining customer focus and diversify into different therapeutic areas.

Group	Extent of Participation in Domestic Formulations Business	No. of Brands among the Industry's Top 500 Brands	Number of Marketing Divisions
Group 'C' Jubilant Organosys, Divi's Labs, FDC, Shasun Chemicals, Nectar Life Sciences, Dabur, Ind-Swift, Dishman, Natco and Suven Life Sciences	Six out of the ten companies in this group are competing for the CRAMS space. The domestic formulation sales of the other four companies(FDC, Dabur, Ind-Swift, and Natco) were about Rs. 10.84 billion in 2006. Their share of the domestic formulations market was 4.2 per cent. The other six companies in the group do not participate in the domestic formulation market and therefore were excluded in this computation.	The other four companies have a total of 12 brands in the industry's top 500 brands. The annual sales of these 12 brands in 2006 were Rs. 2.6 billion. These brands accounted for 40.3 per cent of the total domestic formulation sales of the two companies – FDC and Dabur.	The four companies in the group have their domestic marketing activity structured around thirteen marketing divisions to achieve the twin objectives of achieving customer focus and product-mix diversification.

Chapter Eight

Technology Focus

Technology drives corporate success worldwide. Even in India, it is technology that fueled the growth of the successful companies. Consider the pharmaceutical industry for example:

The pharmaceutical sector has shown the most dramatic growth among all sectors since independence - from a mere Rs. 100 million to about Rs. 446 billion in FY 2005-06. Thirty companies: Ranbaxy, Cipla, Lupin, DRL, Wockhardt, Nicholas Piramal, Aurobindo Pharma, Torrent, Cadila Health Care, Sun Pharma, Matrix, Ipca, Orchid, and others account for about 69 per cent of the total industry sales. These of course, are consolidated sales of these thirty companies and their international subsidiaries. This indicates the degree of dominance of these companies in the Indian pharmaceutical industry and studying their business strategy and behavior would give meaningful insights so that other aspiring entrepreneurs in the developing world could emulate them and replicate their success in their respective areas. What is the common strategic thread that runs through all these companies and other successful companies not mentioned here?

Technology : All these companies have been steadily investing in upgrading their technology to world class standards. Unless your products and services are world class, you have no chance of even entering international markets. The highly industrialized markets like North America,

Europe and Japan, which account for over 80 per cent of the world pharmaceutical market, have erected many entry barriers. Consider these barriers for example:

- Indian drug firms can export bulk actives only when they have a DMF (Drug Master File) for that particular drug.
- One can have a DMF only when he manufactures the drug at a facility approved by US FDA and the formulator should have his formulation approved by the FDA using the bulk from the proposed source.
- To market an off-patent generic formulation, one needs to match his formulation like a fingerprint with the innovator brand both in terms of dissolution profile and bio-equivalence.
- Even the bio-studies need to be conducted at a US FDA-approved laboratory.

Even the NICs (Newly Industrialized Countries) and some of the developing countries have been upgrading their regulatory requirements to these levels, making entry into these markets difficult.

Technology is the only key to success. Only world class technology can convert these barriers into gateways. The message is loud and clear. Upgrade technologically or be out-dated. With technology it is 'Up' or 'Out'!

Corporate success worldwide has long been fueled by technology. Wall Street calls these technology-driven companies 'techies' and tracks their success regularly. The pharmaceutical industry is essentially technology intensive and is research driven.

Of all the sectors that have seen growth, the pharmaceutical sector probably is the most dramatic. In 1947, the size of the Indian pharmaceutical industry was Rs. 100 million. Today the pharmaceutical production exceeds Rs. 446 billion and exports exceed Rs. 180 billion. Moreover, although it was controlled by multinationals till the end of 1960s, today Indian manufacturers of bulk drugs and formulations dominate the market.Ranbaxy has crossed the coveted billion dollar mark in sales three years ago and Dr. Reddy's has achieved over a billion dollars in sales very recently in December 2006. There are other companies such as Sun Pharma, Zydus Cadila, Lupin, Cipla and Aurobindo Pharma waiting in the wings to achieve this magic figure at the earliest. Ranbaxy is the most ambitious among these for it is planning to become a $ 5 billion company by 2012.

There is a common misconception that this fantastic growth has been due to pirating technology from the West, because the Indian Patent Act of 1970 recognized only process, not product patents. But the fact is exported product patents cover less than 10 per cent of the exports. The rest are off-patent drugs; hence Indian manufacturers are competing in the open market, with original discoverers, thereby proving the more efficient nature of their process technologies and control of manufacturing costs.

It is undisputed that the most important factor that will catapult India onto the global stage, in terms of competitive presence, is the state of technology available for production of bulk drugs and formulations.

In terms of technological capability for bulk drug production, India is probably the fourth major force in the world, after the US, Western Europe and Japan, particularly for synthetic drugs.

In the area of fermentation for antibiotics, steroids, enzymes and amino acids, Indian companies are enhancing their capabilities significantly to catch up with global standards.

Today, there are nearly 800 bulk drug manufacturers in India. Some of them are being wooed by multinationals for tie-ups involving manufacture, marketing and even joint research.

A large number of high-selling antibiotics, cardiovascular and other drugs are going off-patent in the next five years. There is also a growing shift towards generic drugs, particularly in the US. These new Indian 'techies' are ambitiously planning to exploit the exploding North American generic market.

To penetrate the developed markets like the US is not going to be easy, whether it is for bulk actives or for formulations. There are a number of entry barriers. Consider these for example:

Entry Barriers

1. The first barrier is that the regulatory environment in these markets is very stringent. They allow imports only from those manufacturers whose facilities are approved by their respective regulatory authorities. In the US for example, you need to have your facility approved by the US FDA. Likewise, it is MHRA, which approves for the UK and the TPD for Canada. The requirements of documentation and quality standards are very tough and expensive.
2. The second barrier is that, not only do your facilities need their regulatory authority's approval but even the bulk actives and other ingredients used in the formulations need to be sourced only from approved manufacturers. The approved sources too, need to go through the regulatory process, thus pushing the input costs high. You cannot use your own raw materials, even if you can manufacture them more economically and even if they meet the material specifications, unless your facilities are approved.
3. The third barrier is that your generic formulation of off-patent drug should match the innovator brand's formulation like a fingerprint in terms of dissolution profile and bio-equivalence. Only when your generic formulation meets these criteria will your Abbreviated New Drug Application (ANDA) get the approval of the US FDA and get a 'therapeutic equivalence' rating. And only then you will have chance of marketing your generic formulation because it can be therapeutically substituted by the pharmacist or sold to HMOs and PBMs.
4. The fourth barrier is that you have to get the bio-equivalence testing done only at the US FDA approved research laboratories. This, once again, increases costs.

5. The fifth barrier is that you have to find the right distributor to market your products. Unless you have a basket of ANDAs for your generic formulations in a given therapeutic area, that meet the emerging disease management criteria or approach, you cannot reach the large customers like HMOs and PBMs in the US.
6. The sixth barrier is that you have to achieve all this fast enough to be among the first two or three generic versions of the innovator drug soon after its patent expiry. A report by Lehman Brothers (1996) notes that, in the US, the first generic can sell at a 30 per cent discount to the branded product compared to a 75 per cent discount for later entrants. Industry experts say that 80 per cent (of profits) are milked out of a drug in the first 18 months of its genericization.
7. Costs, ever escalating costs, in achieving all these are the seventh barrier. Upgrading technology, doing bio-equivalence testing at US FDA approved laboratories, ANDA filing, finding the right distribution and marketing network in the developed markets like the US, require large up front investments. This is a major entry barrier by itself.

Gateways

The new Indian 'techies' are determined to convert these barriers into gateways. They have understood clearly that the gateways to the developed markets are:

- World-class technology
- Superior product development skills
- Quality that meets the international standards
- International regulatory approvals

That is why all these companies have been vying with each other in upgrading their manufacturing facilities to meet international standards and regulatory approvals.

Group 'A' Companies: Competing for Innovation-Led Space

The world pharmaceutical industry is research-driven. Innovation therefore rules the roost. All the ten companies in Group 'A' have been investing in upgrading their manufacturing and technological infrastructure continuously. All of them have world-class manufacturing plants for APIs and FDFs that have approvals from premier international regulatory authorities such as US FDA, UK MHRA, EDQM, TPD of Canada, MCC of South Africa ANVISA of Brazil and others. The ten companies in Group 'A' have a total of forty-four manufacturing facilities in India that have the approvals of US FDA and other international regulatory authorities in the developed markets. Further, seven out the ten companies in Group 'A' also have manufacturing facilities outside India mostly through their overseas acquisitions.

Table 8.1 Group 'A' Companies : Manufacturing Infrastructure

Company	Manufacturing Infrastructure
1. Ranbaxy	5 API manufacturing facilities in India, 3 formulation facilities in India In addition manufacturing facilities in China, Malaysia, Vietnam, Nigeria, Ireland, and the US
2. Dr. Reddy's Labs	7 API manufacturing facilities, 4 formulation manufacturing facilities and one generics manufacturing unit in India One API manufacturing facility in Mexico
3. Sun Pharma	6 API manufacturing facilities, 4 formulation manufacturing facilities in India 1 API manufacturing facility and 1 FDF manufacturing facility in Hungary 3 FDF facilities in the US and 1 FDF facility in Bangladesh
4. Lupin	10 manufacturing facilities for APIs, Intermediates and FDFs spread over five locations
5. Nicholas Piramal	6 Manufacturing facilities in India for APIs and FDFs 5 Manufacturing plants in Morpeth Facility, UK 1 plant in Canada

Company	Manufacturing Infrastructure
6. Zydus Cadila	2 API plants and 2 Formulation plant in India Healthcare
7. Wockhardt	7 Manufacturing facilities for APIs and FDFs in India
	2 Manufacturing facilities for formulations and OTC products in the UK and
	1 Manufacturing facility in Germany
8. Biocon	5 plants covering diverse technology platforms such as Submerged fermentation, Solid state fermentation, Chemical Synthesis, Recombinant therapeutic proteins, and Mammalian cell-culture based products
9. Glenmark	3 API Manufacturing Facilities in India
	3 FDF manufacturing facilities in India
	1 Manufacturing Facility for FDFs in Brazil
10. Torrent	3 Manufacturing facilities for APIs, FDFs in India

Table 8.2 Group 'A' Companies : International Regulatory Approvals

Company	International Regulatory Approvals
1. Ranbaxy	US FDA, TPD Canada, UK MHRA, TGA Australia, MCC, South Africa, ANVISA, Brazil, CRA Germany, SFDA and PDA China, WHO Geneva
2. Dr. Reddy's Labs	US FDA, TPD Canada, UK MHRA, TGA Australia, MCC, South Africa, ANVISA, Brazil, WHO Geneva
3. Sun Pharma	US FDA, UK MHRA, ANVISA, Brazil, MCC South Africa, TGA Australia, WHO Geneva
4. Lupin	US FDA, TPD Canada, UK MHRA, TGA Australia, MCC, South Africa, ANVISA, Brazil, WHO Geneva
5. Nicholas Piramal	US FDA, UK MHRA, WHO Geneva
6. Zydus Cadila Healthcare	US FDA, UK MHRA, AFFSSAPS France
7. Wockhardt	US FDA, TPD Canada, UK MHRA, TGA Australia, MCC, South Africa, ANVISA, Brazil
8. Biocon	US FDA
9. Glenmark	US FDA, TPD Canada, UK MHRA, MCC South Africa, ANVISA Brazil, WHO Geneva
10. Torrent	US FDA, UK MHRA, ANVISA Brazil, WHO Geneva

Ranbaxy

Case 8.1 Technology wins kudos, gets business and even arranges an alliance!

Ranbaxy's success with the complicated synthesis of cefaclor (one of the largest selling antibiotics in the world during its patency), has become an industry legend. The company's technological prowess was amply demonstrated when they developed their own process for cefaclor and patented it in the US.

The story goes that Dr. J.M. Khanna, Head of Research and Development at Ranbaxy, went to the US patent office with 18 different processes for cefaclor, each time failing to prove novelty. This is because, Eli Lilly made life difficult for potential competitors by patenting various intermediates as 'timebombs' that went off as each stage was reached through synthesis. Undaunted, he continued to work on the problem and produced the solution the 19th time. All that diligence and hard work is paying off. An industry observer said, If Ranbaxy could spend Rs. 350–400 million a year on R&D today, it is the money from cefaclor that they are ploughing back. Eli Lilly, the discoverers of the drug themselves buy about $ 15 million worth of cefaclor a year from Ranbaxy.

A by-product of this success was the tie-up with Eli Lilly for a multi-level joint venture that covers marketing, manufacturing and development of pharmaceutical substances and dosage forms in India and select overseas markets.

Ranbaxy has been continuously upgrading its technological infrastructure and capabilities over the year. Today, the company has five API manufacturing facilities, and four FDF facilities in Punjab, Himachal Pradesh and Madhya Pradesh states of India all practicing cGMP with international regulatory approvals such as US FDA, UK MHRA, TGA of Australia, MCC of South Africa and CRA (Cologne Regional Administration) of Germany. Furthermore, the company has manufacturing facilities in international markets like China approved by SFDA (The State Food and Drug Administration) and PDA (Provincial Drug Administration) of China,

Malaysia, Ireland and the US. Its manufacturing facility in China was awarded excellent grade in manufacturing.

Ranbaxy has implemented global supply chain management with The Advanced Planner & Optimizer program in major markets such as US, India and the UK. The company has also commissioned Quality Engineering Cells at most locations.

Dr. Reddy's Labs

DRL has been steadily investing in technology to create a world-class manufacturing infrastructure. The group's bulk drug facilities have international regulatory approvals. They have been exporting their bulk actives and intermediates to the highly regulated markets like the US, Europe and Japan. All their plants implement cGMP and conform to international standards. The company has today seven high performance multiple API production facilities that practice cGMP. All these units are successfully inspected by US FDA. The FDF of Dr. Reddy's too has international regulatory approvals such as US FDA, UK MHRA, TGA of Australia and MCC of South Africa. In addition, DRL has a US FDA approved facility in Mexico through its acquisition of Roche's API business. All these state-of-the-art facilities make Dr. Reddy's Labs a formidable player in Custom Pharmaceutical Services with end-to-end solutions.

Sun Pharma

Sun Pharma has reached the critical mass in manufacturing infrastructure in a short time through acquisitions, mergers and investments. It had in 1998 six manufacturing facilities spread over the states of Gujarat, Maharastra and Tamilnadu for manufacturing bulk actives and pharmaceutical dosage forms. All these facilities conform to the international regulatory standards. The company has US FDA and UK MCA approvals for its bulk drug facilities. Sun Pharma, in addition has an offshore manufacturing base in the US (through its equity-based alliance with Caraco Pharmaceuticals in Michigan) that is approved by FDA.

Sun Pharma has strengthened its manufacturing and technological capabilities significantly during the last five years to emerge as a leading player not only in India but also on the international generics scene. The company today has got 7 API plants two of which are US FDA approved and 9 FDF manufacturing plants (four in India, three in the US, one in Hungary, and one in Bangladesh). The Company's in house technology development capabilities are such that it scales up about 20 APIs and makes 8 – 10 DMF filings every year.

Lupin

Lupin's successful affair with technology started with the manufacture of vitamin B6. The problem with the manufacture of vitamin B6 is that it has a complex 12-stage process, where some of the intermediates are unstable. Lupin acquired the technology from National Chemical Laboratories (NCL), took up the challenge of scale-up and has mastered the technology.

Rifampicin is another success story of Lupin. They have a dominant leadership in the domestic market and also export the bulk to several countries. Cephalosporins are another area where Lupin has achieved considerable success. It is the technology strength of Lupin in manufacturing injectable cephalosporins that is instrumental in finding a strong partner like Merck Generics of Germany for marketing these in developed markets like the US, Europe and Japan once they come off-patents.

Lupin has also achieved significant success in three other areas. The company is the world leader in the production of the anti-TB drug ethambutol, accounting for 60 per cent of world production. Their ethambutol process is so efficient that even the discoverer of the drug, Lederle, started buying the bulk from Lupin. The company has a dominant share of the world market of another anti-TB drug pyrazinamide. All these achievements amplify the technology focus of Lupin. The company has ten manufacturing facilities for APIs, intermediates, and FDFs spread over five locations and are fully integrated. Nine of its manufacturing facilities have US FDA approvals and two have approval from UK MHRA.

Nicholas Piramal

Nicholas Piramal has created, in less than ten years, an impressive manufacturing infrastructure, almost entirely through acquisitions. In 1992, it had invested Rs. 200 million to build a world class manufacturing plant for formulations at Pithampur in Madhya Pradesh. The company realized that creating green field projects is expensive and time consuming and has taken the acquisition route. The company had acquired a bulk drug plant for manufacturing vitamin A at Thane near Mumbai, when it took over Roche. It spruced up the facility to meet the international standards and approvals.

Nicholas Pirmal group has acquired in 1996 the Hyderabad-based bulk drug company – Sumitra Pharmaceuticals and Chemicals, which has one of the largest multi-product bulk drug manufacturing facilities in the country. The company upgraded these facilities so that it can use its large manufacturing infrastructure to meet domestic requirements and also use it as a sourcing base for some of the overseas markets.

Nicholas Piramal continued its acquisition spree even in the new millennium to emerge as one of the leading Custom Manufacturing Organization (CMO) in the world. With its recent acquisitions of Torcan in Canada and Morpeth from Pfizer in the UK NPIL Pharma has become truly an end-to-end solution player in the CRAMS space. The company has today about 6 manufacturing facilities in India for APIs and FDFs, 5 plants in the UK for APIs and FDFs with unique technologies and one in Canada. Many of its facilities have approvals of international regulatory authorities like US FDA and UK MHRA and WHO.

Zydus-Cadila

Zydus–Cadila Health Care group built a Rs. 1-billion manufacturing facility at Moriaya in Ahmedabad. This has been one of the largest investments in a single location in Indian Pharma industry. The facility has separate blocks for biological production, antibiotic formulations and formulations for different therapeutic segments. It has received approvals of US FDA and European regulatory authorities.

Zydus has developed a number of cost-effective alternative processes for some important bulk drugs. Zydus believes that technological up-gradation to international standards is a must to compete effectively in the post-GATT era. Zydus has built state-of-the-art technology infrastructure to be globally competitive with manufacturing facilities for APIs, Intermediates and formulations and received approvals from leading international regulatory authorities from the US, UK, France, South Africa, Brazil etc.

Wockhardt

Wockhardt has constantly expanded its manufacturing technology. Over the years it has invested in building and acquiring 11 manufacturing plants in India, UK and Germany that harness six different technologies. The company's aim of matching the world players both in terms of presence and technology is being achieved through its massive modernization and structural changes. Its manufacturing facilities have international regulatory approvals from US FDA and the UK MHRA, TGA Australia etc.

Wockhardt, in addition is seeking tie-ups with the technology leaders of the world for development and manufacture of biotechnology based therapeutic proteins and vaccines. The technology thrust areas of Wockhardt are – APIs, Formulations, Biotechnology products and IV fluids. The company is leveraging its world-class technological strengths in the area of contract manufacturing. It has a number of long-term contract manufacturing arrangements with some of the global leaders in the pharmaceutical and life sciences industry.

Biocon

Biocon, the technology-driven, integrated biopharmaceutical enterprise has grown significantly during the past three years. The company has built its core fermentation expertise, acquired new skills and strengthened its research and development platforms. The company is focusing on new generation drugs like statins, recombinant human insulin and oral insulin, anti-cancer drugs, and immunosuppressant drugs used by organ transplant patients. Biocon has patented processes for manufacturing lovastatin and simvastatin. The company has tied up with the international drug major Bristol Myers Squibb to supply recombinant human insulin for use in their novel formulation.

Biocon is also focusing on monoclonal antibodies – a new class of drugs in the area of biotherapeutics to address unmet needs especially in oncology and autoimmune diseases. The company made the single largest investment in its history – Biocon Park, a Rs. 6.5 billion integrated biopharmaceutical manufacturing hub spread over 90 acres with multiple manufacturing facilities, laboratories including large-scale microbial fermentation, primary recovery, chemical conversion and purification meeting international regulatory requirements. Biocon has the largest facility in Asia for manufacturing recombinant therapeutic protein based products like human insulin. It also has the state-of-the art facility for manufacturing mammalian cell-culture based products.

Glenmark

Glenmark has been sharpening its strategic focus since 1999 to remain competitive in the product patent era. The only way to stay competitive is to build world-class technological and R&D infrastructure and capabilities in the globalized pharmaceutical world. The company accordingly followed a strategic path and quickly built and acquired manufacturing facilities that are comparable to the best in the world. It acquired GSK's API facility at Ankaleshwar and upgraded its other facilities and built one at Goa. Today, three of its six manufacturing facilities are approved by leading international regulatory authorities like US FDA, UK MHRA, TGA of Australia etc. In the shortest time, the company has also made its presence felt in the discovery space too. Because of its technological up-gradation both in infrastructure and competencies, the company has been able to establish its presence in over 70 countries across the globe. Glenmark has consolidated its presence in LATAM through its acquisition of the Brazilian firm – Klinger Laboratorios along with its ANVISA-approved manufacturing facilities.

Torrent

Torrent has embarked on a modernization plan, which incorporates the latest available technology and reorganization of the existing facilities between manufacturing locations. The company has also modified the existing layout of its Vatva plant, to enhance production capacity and storage facilities. Torrent manufactures a number of bulk drugs and drug intermediates as well as formulations across a wide range of therapeutic segments. The technology thrust areas for torrent are – APIs, Formulations including NDDS and biotechnology. Torrent made substantial investments and built three manufacturing facilities for APIs, and Formulations conforming to international regulatory standards. Its manufacturing facilities for APIs and formulations have recently received the US FDA approval. The company's quality control facility too received the accreditation - the prestigious ISO/IEC 17025 by NABL.

Group 'B' Companies: Competing for International Generics Space

International generics offer a huge opportunity for pharmaceutical firms that are vertically integrated, technologically advanced and competitive in terms of lower costs of production. These ten companies in Group 'B' have between themselves as many as 104 manufacturing facilities with multiple technological platforms and cGMP compliance. Most of them conform to international regulatory standards. The ten companies in Group 'B' have between them about 25 manufacturing facilities that have the approvals of US FDA and other leading regulatory authorities in the world such as UK MHRA, EDQM, MCC of South Africa, TGA of Australia, ANVISA of Brazil and WHO, Geneva etc.

Table 8.3 Group 'B' Companies: Investment on Technology Up-gradation

Company	Manufacturing Infrastructure
1. Cipla	34 manufacturing facilities for APIs and FDFs on multiple technology platforms across India
2. Aurobindo Pharma	12 Manufacturing facilities for APIs and FDFs in India 2 Manufacturing J Vs in the US 2 Manufacturing J Vs in China
3. Matrix	4 API Manufacturing facilities
4. Orchid	2 API Manufacturing facilities 3 FDF Manufacturing facilities
5. Ipca	3 API Manufacturing facilities 5 FDF Manufacturing facilities
6. Alembic	2 API Manufacturing facilities 2 FDF Manufacturing facilities
7. Claris Life Sciences	1 FDF Manufacturing Facility
8. J B Chemicals	11 manufacturing facilities for APIs and FDFs in India
9. Unichem	2 API Manufacturing facilities 3 FDF Manufacturing facilities
10. Strides Arcolabs	13 facilities worldwide ie., India, Poland, Brazil, USA for manufacturing APIs, specialty chemicals, FDFs, Soft gelatin capsules

Table 8.4 Group 'B' Companies: International Regulatory Approvals

Company	International Regulatory Approvals
1. Cipla	US FDA, UK MHRA, PIC Germany, MCC South Africa, TGA Australia, TPD Canada, ANVISA, Brazil, WHO Geneva, SIDC, Slovak Republic
2. Aurobindo Pharma	US FDA, UK MHRA, MCC South Africa, TGA Australia, TPD Canada, ANVISA Brazil
3. Matrix	US FDA, UK MHRA, TGA Australia, MCC South Africa
4. Orchid	US FDA, UK MHRA
5. Ipca	US FDA, UK MHRA, TGA – Australia, MCC – South Africa, ANVISA – Brazil, Who –Geneva, Oman MOH, Tanzania FDA, and NDA - Uganda
6. Alembic	US FDA, EDQM, WHO

Company	International Regulatory Approvals
7. Claris Life Sciences	UK MHRA, TGA Australia, NAM Finland, ANVISA Brazil, INVIMA Colombia, GCC
8. J B Chemicals Sciences	US FDA, UK MHRA, MCC - South Africa, ANVISA – Brazil, NCLPP – Algeria, F&DB – Ghana, NDA - Nigeria, MOH – Russia, INVIMA – Columbia,
9. Unichem	US FDA, UK MHRA, ANVISA – Brazil, MCC – South Africa, WHO - Geneva
10. Strides Arcolabs	US FDA, UK MHRA, MCC - South Africa, ANVISA – Brazil, TGA Australia, WHO - Geneva

Cipla

Cipla's core strength has been technology. The company has built world-class technology be it process development or formulation development or even a platform development over the years. As a result the company has received approvals from virtually every major regulatory agency in the world. Today, Cipla has tied up with five companies in the US for marketing a 140-strong product pipeline in the US generics market.

Cipla's technological leadership is evident from its API product portfolio of about 225 drugs covering all major therapeutic segments. The company manufactures more than half of the bulk drugs produced in the country. Further all its API manufacturing facilities at Vikhroli in Mumbai, Kurkumbh and Patalganga in Maharastra, Bangalore in Karnataka have approvals from all major regulatory authorities such as US FDA, UK MHRA, PIC Germany, TGA Australia, MCC South Africa, ANVISA Brazil, and WHO, Geneva.

Case 8.2 A Small step leads to a giant leap in the anti-asthmatic market!

Technology has been a core competence of Cipla. The company has achieved a very high degree of cost effectiveness in its process technologies for a number of bulk drugs. One of the initial successes of Cipla was with the synthesis of salbutamol, an anti-asthmatic drug discovered by the international leader, Glaxo. Cipla has marketed its salbutamol at prices much lower than the prevailing international prices. The company has never looked back since then.

That small step has indeed become a giant leap towards a dominant leadership position in the anti-asthmatic segment in India. Cipla, of course, had developed sophisticated aerosol technology and had introduced a number of therapeutic options for treating asthma and has further strengthened its position.

Case 8.3 Value addition through technology
Cipla has also achieved great success with its technological power in the anti-cancer segment in India. One of its major triumphs was the commercialization of the extraction of vinblastin from vinca rosea leaves, which was later converted to vincristine – a popular anti-cancer drug through out the world. Earlier, India used to export the dried leaves of vinca rosea and Eli Lilly used to make vincristine out of them. Cipla has scaled up the known-but-difficult process of extracting the alkaloid vinblastin from vinca rosea, converting it to vincristine and marketing it at a price slightly less than one third of the international price. That is value addition through technology.

Aurobindo Pharma

Investing over Rs. 4.95 billion, Aurobindo Pharma over the last seven years built an enviable manufacturing infrastructure and has as many as eleven plants in India approved by major international regulatory authorities like US FDA, UK MHRA, TGA of Australia, MCC of South Africa etc. The company also acquired a manufacturing facility in the US. Aurobindo's technological prowess is evident from its robust portfolio of over 188 APIs and 102 ANDAs covering six major therapeutic areas such as antibiotics, ARVs, Cardiovasculars including statins, CNS, Gastro-intestinals, anti-allergics, and respiratory etc.

Matrix Laboratories

Matrix Laboratories has built and acquired world-class technological competencies and infrastructure, which made it a very eligible and attractive suitor. Mylan Laboratories the American generic drug major made an irresistible offer and acquired a controlling stake of 71.5 per cent in Matrix. Three API manufacturing facilities of Matrix have the approvals of international regulatory authorities such as US FDA and UK MHRA etc. Matrix has a FDF manufacturing facility at Nashik in Maharastra that conforms to US FDA standards and is cGMP-compliant. Here's an example (case 8.4) that amplifies the technological capabilities of Matrix.

Case 8.4 Process Technology Paves the Way for Growth

Citalopram, the leading anti-depressant molecule with annual sales of over US $ 2.5 billion in 2002 from the innovator drug company Lundbeck was to lose its market exclusivity due to impending patent expiry in various European countries. Matrix filed a process patent for Citalopram on February 27, 2007 and never looked back. Lundbeck made an almost irresistible offer to Matrix for acquiring the process patent of Citalopram. Matrix refused it and decided to go at it alone marketing the API to generic companies and filed another patent for citalopram under Patent Cooperation Treaty (PCT) in order to remain a preferred supplier to generics companies. Citalopram contributed to 50 per cent of Matrix total turnover in 2001-02. The axiom – *fortune favours the brave* – is proven once again and Matrix went on product diversification, built a world class manufacturing infrastructure, got international regulatory approvals that matter to regulated markets and became an attractive suitor for Mylan Laboratories one of the leading US generics players who acquired it in 2006.

Orchid

Orchid has started as a 100 per cent export oriented unit for manufacturing bulk actives, with emphasis on cephalosporins. Building plants and upgrading technology to world-class standards, therefore, has been a pre-requisite and it had its facilities approved by US FDA and UK MHRA. The company practices the latest cGMP standards in its manufacturing facilities. It has its own power plant for captive generation and an effluent treatment plant that meets the international standards in terms of creating an eco-friendly manufacturing environment.

Orchid continues to upgrade its manufacturing infrastructure and capabilities and has today three of its facilities approved by US FDA, UK MHRA, EDMF, TGA of Australia and ANVISA of Brazil. The company is competing in two rapidly growing competitive spaces – International Generics and CRAMS.

IPCA

IPCA has put up its first bulk drug unit in 1985. The company has invested in technology and upgradation of manufacturing facilities over the last two decades. As a result, it had three formulation manufacturing facilities and six bulk drug plants in 1996, which certainly should indicate the technology focus of IPCA. What is even more credit worthy is that the company has US FDA approvals for nine of its bulk drugs manufactured at its plant at Ratlam in Madhya Pradesh, India. Two of its facilities have approvals from UK MHRA. It has a number of long-term contracts for manufacturing from some of the leading European Drug manufacturers.

Alembic

The hundred-year old veteran pharmaceutical company is known for its adaptation of the changing market place. Alembic is a highly respected and vertically integrated pharmaceutical company in Asia. The company has upgraded its technological infrastructure and pioneered the fermentation process in India. The company is dominant player in macrolides and has a strong presence in anti-infective segments. The company's API facility has successfully undergone inspections of US FDA and EDQM. The company is currently exporting its APIs, intermediates and formulations to about 75 countries across the world. Alembic is now focusing on regulated markets.

Claris Life Sciences

Claris Life Sciences has manufacturing facilities that are designed to produce aqueous and oil-based products and glass/PE containers and bags. The facilities are US FDA approvable and cGMP-compliant. Already a number of international regulatory authorities such as UK MHRA, TGA (Australia), NAM (Finland), ANVISA (Brazil), INVIMA (Colombia), GCC (Gulf Cooperation Council) including Saudi Arabia, UAE, and other Middle East countries have approved the sterile parenteral manufacturing facilities.

Claris has technological capabilities in multiple product platforms like parenteral FAT Emulsion technology, Micro-emulsion technology, cytotoxic manufacturing, cephalosporins, dialysis bags and accessories, APIs, Medical equipment, plastic films, components and accessories. The company's manufacturing capabilities too are versatile.

J B Chemicals

State-of-the-art equipment and instruments give J B Chemicals the edge to compete globally. The infrastructure, with its optimum installed capacities and capital costs, gives the company its sustainable competitive cost advantage. All their operations are supported by fully integrated Supply Chain practices and ERP systems (JD EDWARD- XE) enabling the company to provide a faster response and service to all our customers across the world. Three of its eleven manufacturing facilities have approvals from US FDA indicating its focus on regulated markets.

Unichem Laboratories

The sixty-three year old Unichem is taking a fresh look at the opportunities that the twenty-first century pharmaceutical world has to offer. The company has over the years built a technological infrastructure that is comparable with the best in the world as its focus is sharpening on the regulated markets. The company has also been upgrading its product developmental capabilities. The company has two API Plants and three FDF Plants with approvals from leading international regulatory authorities like US FDA, UK MHRA, MCC of South Africa, and ANVISA of Brazil. It has recently started a Pharma Technology Development Center at Goa essentially for developing FDFs for regulated markets.

Strides Arcolabs

One of the top five soft gelatin capsule manufacturers in the world, Strides Arcolabs is focusing on the new opportunities in the post product patent regime. The company has 13 manufacturing facilities located in India, Brazil, Mexico, Poland, Italy and USA. Its Indian manufacturing facilities for regulated markets have the approvals of all major international regulatory authorities like UK MHRA, MCC of South Africa, TGA of Australia and WHO. All its facilities are cGMP-compliant. Strides has filed 21 ANDAs and has a pipeline of 80 products under development. It has licensed 40 products in regulatory markets and registered its products in 37 countries so far. The company is building a world-class technological infrastructure and capabilities to become a preferred partner in the CRAMS segment too. It has already developed considerable expertise to provide its client companies services across the Pharma value chain – in product development program towards achieving their clinical and regulatory goals.

Group 'C' Companies: Competing for the CRAMS Space

The ten companies in Group 'C' have about 33 manufacturing facilities. Many of them either already have approvals by international regulatory authorities such as US FDA, UK MHRA, EQDM, TGA of Australia, MCC of South Africa, TPD of Canada, ANVISA of Brazil or conforming to their standards. As they are competing for the CRAMS space, majority of them have also built an R&D infrastructure that is comparable with the best in the world. All of these companies are preparing themselves to compete across the CRAMS value chain.

Table 8.5 Group 'C' Companies : Manufacturing Infrastructure

Company	Manufacturing Infrastructure
1. Jubilant Organosys	API facility in India API facility in the US
2. Divi's Labs	2 API Facilities
3. FDC	1 API Manufacturing facility 4 FDF Manufacturing facilities 2 Manufacturing facilities for Oral Re-hydration salts
4. Shasun	2 API Manufacturing facilities 1 FDF Manufacturing facility
5. Nectar Life	1 API Manufacturing facility 1 FDF Manufacturing facility
6. Dabur	1 API Manufacturing facility for oncology and non-oncology products in India 1 FDF Manufacturing facility in India 1 FDF Manufacturing facility in UK
7. Ind-Swift Laboratories	1 cGMP-compliant API Manufacturing facility with 5 dedicated blocks 5 Manufacturing facilities for FDFs
8. Dishman	2 API Manufacturing facilities Pharmaceuticals
9. Natco Pharma	2 API Manufacturing facilities 1 FDF Manufacturing facility for small volume and large volume parenterals covering many products 1 FDF Manufacturing facility
10. Suven Life Sciences	1 API manufacturing facility 1 Pilot plant with R&D center

Table 8.6 Group 'C' Companies : International Regulatory Approvals

Company	International Regulatory Approvals
1. Jubilant Organosys	US FDA
2. Divi's Labs	US FDA, EDQM, TPD, Canada
3. FDC	US FDA, UK MHRA, MCC – South Africa, ANVISA, Brazil, WHO, UNICEF, NDA – Uganda, MSF, France
4. Shasun	US FDA, UK MHRA, TPD Canada
5. Nectar Life Sciences	WHO
6. Dabur	US FDA, UK MHRA, TGA of Australia
7. Ind-Swift Laboratories	WHO, US FDA
8. Dishman Pharmaceuticals	WHO
9. Natco Pharma	US FDA
10. Suven Life Sciences	WHO

Jubilant Organosys

From an advanced intermediates manufacturer, Jubilant Organosys ascended to custom research and manufacturing services (CRAMS) expanding into the area of APIs and later entering the high potential segment of drug discovery and development services by investing consistently in upgrading its technological infrastructure and competencies. The company today has a US FDA approved API facility in India and another US FDA facility for API as well as FDFs in the US. The company is able to leverage its world-class technology base by providing customized services to 15 of the top 20 pharmaceutical companies spread over 50 countries.

Divi's Labs

Divi's Laboratories started as a research center supplying process technology on turnkey basis to several generic drug manufacturers and later entered into manufacturing APIs and intermediates. The company clearly positioned itself in the CRAMS space, developed several new products and ventured into the field of peptide synthesis. The company's manufacturing facility received certifications for ISO-9002, ISO-14001, OHSAS-18001 and European Certificate of Suitability (ECOS). It has also successfully completed the inspection of USFDA. Divi's with its world-class technological and research and development infrastructure offers a distinct competitive advantage to innovator companies over the entire life cycle of the products.

Divi's provides custom synthesis services to innovator companies and is currently working on more than 75 products with top twenty companies. The company is IPR-adherent and therefore not tying up with any Para IV challengers.

FDC Laboratories

The septuagenarian – FDC has made a steady progress over seventy years to become a global company. The company's manufacturing facilities have approvals from all major regulatory authorities in the world such as US FDA, UK MHRA, MCC of South Africa, ANVISA of Brazil, WHO, UNCEF among others. FDC has a dominant share of oral re-hydration salt in India and in a number of less regulated markets. The company exports its products to over 50 countries across the globe. It has a strategic alliance with Akorn Inc. in the US for marketing its sterile ophthalmic preparations.

Shasun Chemicals

Started with the manufacturing of analgin a mature API in 1976, Shasun has come a long way to be recognized as a quality producer of APIs, intermediates and more recently even FDFs in the world today. The company is exporting its products to more than 40 countries across Europe, North America, Latin America and Asia. It has entered into a number of strategic alliances with leading MNCs like Boots, Eli Lilly, and GSK among others for supplying APIs and intermediates. The company's asset base has grown from a very modest Rs. 2.6 million in 1976 to over Rs. 2.6 billion today. The company is aspiring to be a leading player in the CRAMS space and is constantly upgrading its technological and research and development infrastructure. Both of its API plants have approvals of US FDA, UK MHRA and TPD of Canada. The US FDA inspection of its FDF facility is due.

Nectar Life Sciences

Nectar Life Sciences is one of the largest manufacturers and exporters of cephalosporins and semi-synthetic penicillins. The company has modern manufacturing facilities at the foothills of Himalayas in Punjab, India. The company currently manufactures both oral and sterile (lyophilized and crystalline) range of APIs and formulations and is planning to diversify into NPNC (Non-penicillin, Non-cephalosporin) APIs as well. The company exports to over 70 countries – less regulated markets - across the globe. Nectar Life Sciences is planning to move up the value chain and to regulatory markets. It is investing Rs. 300 million in building a cGMP-compliant, US FDA-approvable facility at Baddi, Himachal Pradesh in India. The company is aspiring to be a preferred partner to international pharmaceutical companies in both the areas – contract manufacturing and contract research.

Dabur Pharma

An associate company of Dabur one of India's most respected FMCG Companies – Dabur Oncology Plc has set its sights clearly on becoming a leading international oncology pharmaceutical company. The company accordingly built a technological and developmental infrastructure. Two of its manufacturing facilities have approvals from three major regulatory authorities in the world such as US FDA, UK MHRA and TGA of Australia. The company's FDF manufacturing facility at Baddi in Himachal Pradesh in India has approvals from regulatory authorities of over thirty countries that are less regulated so far. More are on the anvil. The company is targeting mainly the generic oncology market in regulated markets and entered into alliances with some of the leading generic players such as Hospira and Abbott's Hospital products division for penetrating the hospital segment in the US. Dabur has a manufacturing facility in Bordon UK that has the approvals of both UK MHRA and US FDA. The company uses the cutting edge software to process chromatography data including LIMS system.

Ind-Swift Laboratories

Ind-Swift Laboratories has considerable process development skills. It has presence in chronic disease segments like cardiovascular, diabetology, hyperlipdemic and antidepressant segments. Its eight APIs figure in the top 20 global blockbuster drugs. The company has positioned itself in the CRAMS segment and is focusing on regulatory markets. Its major export destinations currently are Turkey, Syria, Pakistan, Korea and Greece. The company's technological capabilities can be gauged from its attractive pipeline of 20 products that would go off patent between 2007 and 2010. The company filed four DMFs in the US and 48 DMFs in Europe. The company entered into contract research agreements with two European pharmaceutical companies. It has a cGMP-compliant and US FDA-approved manufacturing facility with five dedicated blocks covering 150,000 square feet for APIs and 5 FDF manufacturing facilities. The company is gearing up to achieve over 45 per cent of its revenues from the CRAMS segment and accordingly investing in beefing up its technological and R&D infrastructure.

Dishman Pharmaceuticals

Dishman Pharmaceuticals and Chemicals Limited, a research-driven company in synthetic chemistry is focusing on CRAMS segment. It has long-term contracts for supply of intermediates on a long-term basis with Solvay Pharmaceuticals B.V. Netherlands and a few others in Europe and North America. The company embarked on building a Greenfield multi-purpose API plant that meets the international regulatory standards and cGMP-compliant. Leveraging on its process innovation experience and expertise, Dishman is focusing on meeting the developmental needs of MNCs and supply the intermediates for APIs of their NCEs.

Natco Pharma

Natco Pharma started with a differentiation when it entered the market in 1985 with its time-release formulations in different segments. The company has developed many APIs, intermediates, finished dosage forms including small and large volume parenterals and built a huge manufacturing infrastructure. The company has been a preferred partner in contract manufacturing services for many of the domestic majors. The company sold its entire basket of products in domestic market to Sun Pharma in 1997 but later it has revitalized its operations through a refocusing strategy. The company is targeting the international generic market in oncology segment and CRAMS space. Two of Natco's manufacturing facilities covering APIs and FDFs have US FDA approvals enabling the company to enter the world's largest generics market- US.

Suven Life Sciences

Suven Life Sciences has a clear focus on drug discovery and development of novel, highly-selective, potent small-molecule drugs that target G-Protein Coupled Receptors for the treatment of debilitating CNS disorders such as Alzheimer's disease, schizophrenia, depression, vascular dementia, mild cognitive impairment, Parkinson's disease, memory impairments with aging, sleep disorders, feeding disorders and obesity.

Suven gets 75 per cent of its business from CRAMS and the remaining through drug discovery support. In the CRAMS segment, the company manufactures and supplies intermediates to Innovators companies for their clinical trials. Suven offers services across a broad spectrum of the value chain – from lead development to clinical trials.

Thirty Companies – A Snapshot of Current Technology Status

The thirty companies discussed in this chapter have one thing in common. All of them have been steadily investing to upgrade their technological infrastructure and capabilities constantly. Continuous improvement or Kaizen as the Japanese say is the only way to become competitive and more importantly to stay competitive. Here is a snapshot of their technological progress and current status in 2006.

Table 8.7 Thirty Companies – Current status of Technology Infrastructure

Group	Manufacturing Infrastructure	Regulatory Approvals
'A' Ranbaxy, Dr. Reddy's Labs, Sun Pharma, Lupin, Nicholas Piramal, Zydus Cadila, Wockhardt, Biocon, Glenmark and Torrent	About 89 manufacturing facilities in India for manufacturing APIs and FDFs. Most of these are state-of-the-art, cGMP-compliant and world-class. About 22 manufacturing facilities outside in India in counties such as US, Canada, Mexico, Brazil, South Africa, Nigeria, Russia, UK, Ireland, Germany, Hungary, Romania, Spain, France, Malysia, Vietnam, China and Bangladesh.	Virtually all major international regulatory authorities such as US FDA, TPD – Canada, UK MHRA, EQDM, ANVISA–Brazil, MCC – South Africa and others approved either some or all of their facilities.
'B' Cipla, Aurobindo Pharma, Matrix, Orchid, Ipca, Alembic, Claris Life Sciences, J B Chemicals, Unichem and Strides Arcolabs	About 58 manufacturing facilities in India for manufacturing APIs and FDFs. Most of these are state-of-the-art, cGMP-compliant and world-class. About 17 manufacturing facilities outside India in countries such as US, UK, Germany, Poland, Brazil and China	Virtually all major international regulatory authorities such as US FDA, TPD – Canada, UK MHRA, EQDM, ANVISA–Brazil, MCC – South Africa and others, approved some of their facilities.
'C' Jubilant Organosys, Divi's Labs, FDC, Shasun Chemicals, Nectar Life Sciences, Dabur, Ind-Swift Laboratories, Dishman Pharmaceuticals, Natco Pharma and Suven Life Sciences	About 31 manufacturing facilities in India for manufacturing APIs and FDFs. Most of these are state-of-the-art, cGMP-compliant and world-class. Four manufacturing facilities in US, UK and Srilanka.	Virtually all major international regulatory authorities such as US FDA, TPD – Canada, UK MHRA, EQDM, ANVISA–Brazil, MCC – South Africa and others, approved the facilities of seven of these companies. For others the inspections are due as they have some of their facilities conforming to international regulatory standards.

These thirty companies have a total number of 188 manufacturing facilities in India for manufacturing APIs and FDFs across multiple technological and product platforms. In addition, these thirty companies have a total of 43 manufacturing facilities overseas. These companies have as many as 75 of their facilities approved by the US FDA as on December 2006. All these companies are focusing on creating world-class technological infrastructure irrespective of their current size as they are aspiring to be global players competing for three major opportunity areas – innovation-led space, international generics space and CRAMS space.

The more aggressive players in the Indian pharmaceutical industry are vying with each other to build a technological infrastructure that is internationally comparable and training their people to be internationally competitive. Apart from competing effectively in the post product patent regime, these companies are keen to exploit the various opportunities that the global pharmaceutical industry has to offer.

Another major opportunity area is that the European companies are looking for sourcing arrangements with Indian companies for patent-expired generic formulations. There are two reasons for this. European Union laws prohibit local pharmaceutical companies from undertaking any sort of developmental activities before the expiry of patent. They have to approach either the American companies for development prior to the expiry of patents, which can be very expensive, or exploit the scientific talent in developing countries like India and China. India can be the most favored destination because of the proven track record in process development and availability of a vast, cost-effective pool of English speaking scientific talent. Up-gradation of technology, therefore, will be a sustainable competitive advantage for Indian drug companies.

Up or Out!

Technology up-gradation is no longer a matter of choice. It is a must. It is not only vital for progress or rapid growth, but is essential even for survival. The domestic market place in the product patent regime will be a level playing field. The level of competition and intensity will be different. Companies that are upgrading technologically are the ones that are growing faster than the rest.

While combined market share of top ten multinational companies and the top ten Indian Companies in Indian Pharma market in 1998 is almost identical, in 2006 the Indian drug majors who have been constantly upgrading their technological infrastructure and competencies have leapfrogged and have a market share that is almost twice as much as the MNC sector in India at the top-ten level. Top ten MNCs have a market share of 17.8 per cent, whereas the top ten companies of the domestic sector have a market share of 33.4 per cent in 2006.

Furthermore, when trade barriers disintegrate and when the protective armour of process patents gives way to strong IPR protection, the only option is to be internationally competitive. When the competition is world class the only option is to be world class yourself. Implicit in a level playing field is the 'level' of competence and competitiveness of the players. For those who are well prepared, it is a level playing field. For others, it could as well be a minefield. In a market place that is driven by technology, it is indeed Up or Out!

Chapter Nine

Research Focus

Pharmaceutical research is expensive, time consuming and risky. The process of discovering and developing a new drug is long and complex and faces difficult odds. It takes upwards of 5,000 chemically synthesized molecules to produce just one approved drug. According to data compiled by the Tufts Centre for the study of drug development, of all the drugs that entered clinical trials between 1980 and 1984, only 18.3 per cent have entered the market and a mere 23.5 per cent are ever expected to become marketed drugs.

What is the moral of the story? Evaluate research programs thoroughly. Focus on focused research.

Given the high cost and risk of drug discovery, what with estimates ranging between $ 800–1000 million for developing a single drug from concept to commercial commercialization, can Indian companies ever think of discovering new drugs? At $ 1000 million, the total turnover of only two pharmaceutical companies for the fiscal 2006 just equals or more exceeds the amount (Ranbaxy has crossed the coveted US 1 billion mark three years ago and Dr. Reddy's have just crossed it in the first quarter of FY2007) required for developing just one new drug.

Dr. K. Anji Reddy has demonstrated that Indian drug firms can do it, despite these odds. DRL became the first Indian drug firm to license its molecules (developed by its research foundation) to international drug majors against milestone payments, sharing of further developmental and registration costs and royalty payments once the drugs are approved. He has indeed shown the way to drug firms in developing countries.

Close on the heels Dr. Reddy's is Ranbaxy, India's leading pharmaceutical company, in announcing its NCEs. Ranbaxy too is looking for partners for carrying on the further developmental activities required and for registration across the world. Torrent has become the third company to file for patents in India and the US for its NCE – TR 266, a coronary vasodilator. Wockhardt, Lupin, Sun Pharma and Glenmark too have announced their strategic intent in competing for the drug discovery space few years ago. These companies have gradually increased their R&D investment over the last few years and today in 2006 are investing around 7 – 10 per cent of their sales.

The leading Indian companies are clearly shifting their emphasis from imitative research to innovative research. There is a clear change of focus on focused research.

The relationship between patent protection and the pharmaceutical industry is closest and most direct in research and development.

The policy decisions here centre on the investment, the selection of priorities when setting up the programs and the balance between management of innovation and the management of risk. All of these are necessarily evaluated with an eye on patent protection. This is because unpatentable success in pharmaceutical R&D is rapidly devalued by imitation, eventually forcing the innovators to become less innovative in order to reduce industrial risk.

In a world where progress in drug therapy is needed and desired, the industry considers patent protection to be indispensable for innovative endeavor. Patents do not guarantee innovative success, but their absence or inadequacy will undermine the motivation to take the financial risks that are implicit in drug development.

The Cost of a New Chemical Entity

A 1994 study conducted by economists at Duke University found that only 3 out of every 10 drug products (New Chemical Entities) introduced from 1980 to 1984 had returns higher than their average after-tax R&D costs. The analysis revealed that 20 per cent of products with the highest revenues generated 70 per cent of returns during the period. In other words, given the high cost and risk of drug research, companies must rely on a limited number of highly successful products to finance R&D.

Economists have estimated the cost of bringing a new drug to market at $ 359 million. This estimate, however, captures the final costs for drugs that entered clinical trials during the late 1970s. A precise projection of what it may cost to develop a drug, beginning the research process now is difficult. Since the late 1970s, however, major drivers of development costs, including the number of required clinical trials and patients in each trial, have more than doubled.

During the 1990s the average length of time required to develop a drug has increases to 15 years. Lengthening developmental times dramatically increase the cost of bringing a new drug to market by increasing the capital needed for R&D. The cost of capital increases as companies are exposed to economic risks and uncertainties over a longer period of time.

These are the underlying reasons why pharmaceutical progress is dependent on intellectual property protection. Without strong patent protection, drug companies would not be able to attract the investment needed to conduct this high cost R&D.

Academia, Industry and Drug Research

Academic research establishments can, and often do, make important discoveries in basic research. Industrial development, however, takes upto two-thirds of the cost and risk of pharmaceutical R&D. The cost of drug discovery becomes prohibitively high, when you factor in the cost of failure. Approximately one out of ten drugs discovered enter the Phase I of clinical development. Nowhere in the world, has the public sector been able to finance the cost of drug development as a result.

As a minimum, the industry insists that research and development risk must, in the event of successful drug development, have a chance of being well rewarded by ensuring marketing exclusivity of patented drugs from the date of launch until patent expiry. The protection of intellectual property is regarded as a necessary pre-condition for industrial and economic survival.

The Prerequisites of R&D

The experience of recent decades demonstrates that, as a general rule, three prior conditions must be fulfilled for pharmaceutical R&D to flourish. They are:

1. Infrastructure in relevant science and technology.
2. Adequate industrial cash flow and profitability.
3. Watertight patent protection of the results.

Infrastructure is evidently vital, especially for pioneering advances in pharmaceutical science and biotechnology. Academic input and mechanisms to ease the flow of knowledge between 'pure' research and, applied, technology must either exist or be brought into existence.

Cash flow and profits have to be adequate in order to stimulate sustained risk and investment. That is particularly true of innovative R&D in pharmaceuticals and biotechnology, because the risk of failure is abnormally high when compared with many other research-based industries, especially during the development phase. This phase usually absorbs two-thirds of pharmaceutical R&D time and budgets.

Water-tight patent protection, the third prerequisite, is now universally accepted for pharmaceuticals in the industrialized world, for underwriting the risk of project failure and to cover the high costs of long periods of development and other costs of R&D.

Role of Government

It is now widely recognized that the real function of the government is not to carry out, or even pay for, R&D in drugs and pharmaceutical biotechnology, but to help by way of fiscal and other incentives. The government's basic responsibility is to ensure that the prerequisite conditions for innovative research, development and investment by industry are in place and the obstacles to the flow of knowledge and expertise between academic service and applied technology are removed. Only then will the ultimate purpose of such work – advances in health care and benefit to the national economy and to society – be achieved.

In the industrialized world, the role of the state in pharmaceutical and biotechnological R&D has in recent times been limited but is not unimportant. Public grants for academic research have helped to create many centers of excellence. The main function of the state has, however, been to manage economic stability and to define policies that are designed to encourage risk investment in pharmaceutical and biotech research and development.

Results in these fields have generally been closely related to government's willingness (or reluctance) and success (or failure) in creating such a climate of encouragement, both for pharmaceutical chemistry and biotechnology.

Project 1035

The government in China has played a very supportive role in the recent years to bolster the research and development activity in the country. It had earmarked $ 1.2 billion for 1996–2000 for 'Project 1035', which is aimed at producing 10 new chemical entities, 3 therapeutic mechanisms and 5 centers for synthesis, screening and testing – all in five years.

Government Support to R&D – The Indian Scenario

While the recent creation of the Technology Development Board is not comparable to the Chinese government initiative, it is certainly a welcome sign. The Indian government finally, after a twenty-five year wait, has created a Technology Development Board (TDB) in 1995 and the Technology Development Fund (TDF) in September 1996. The source of funds for the TDF is basically the 5 per cent cess levied on all payments made for technology imports – in the form of technology payments, royalties and dividends – as required under the R&D Cess ACT of 1986.

New Drug Development Process

What does it take to develop a new drug from concept to commercialization? Typically, the new drug development process involves five major stages (Table 9.1)

Table 9.1 New Drug Development Process

Stage	Process	Activity	Time taken
Stage I	Screening:	Plants and animals screened for biological activities	2 years
Stage II	Identification:	Compounds are isolated from plants concerned	2 years
Stage III	Toxicity studies:	The drug (isolated compound) is tested on animals for toxicity	1 year
Stage IV	Clinical trials:	The drug is tested on efficacy and tolerance	7 years
Stage V	NDA filing:	The drug is released in the market after FDA approval	1 year
Launch of the drug	Post-marketing surveillance	Feed back on the efficacy and side effects of the drug in actual clinical practice after launch	After FDA approval

After extensive toxicological tests and animal studies, the manufacturer must decide whether the compound should be tested on humans. If the company decides to go ahead, it must file an Investigational New Drug (IND) application with FDA. This application may run as long as 2000 pages and must include information about the pre-clinical testing and a description of the proposed clinical trials. Unless the FDA orders a hold, clinical trials may begin 30 days after the application is filed. In addition, the application must be approved by a review board of the institution or institutions, where the trials are to be conducted.

Clinical trials are conducted in three phases. In phase I, safety studies are conducted on 20 to 100 healthy volunteers. Potential side effects are identified and dosage range is determined.

Phase II clinical trials are conducted to determine the effectiveness of the drug. Approximately 100 to 300 volunteers, who have the targeted disease, participate.

Phase III typically involves 1000 to 3000 patients (and sometimes thousands more) in clinics and hospitals. They are closely monitored to assess the drug's efficacy and safety. The company compiles all the data from these trials and, if the data successfully demonstrates safety and efficacy, submits a New Drug Application (NDA) to FDA. The NDA must contain all the scientific information the company has gathered. NDAs typically, run into 100,000 pages or more. By law, FDA has six months time to review an NDA. The average review time for all NDAs approved in 1996 was 17.8 months.

Development Time

Drug development time has grown from 8.1 years in the 1960s (11.6 years in the 1970s, 14.2 years in the 1980s) to 15.3 years for drugs approved from 1990 through 1995. A large part of this increase is due to the lengthening of the clinical phase of drug development.

According to the Centre for the Study of Drug Development at Tufts University, clinical development time for drugs approved between 1990 and 1995 was 6.9 years, up from 5.5 years.

The State of R&D in India

Philip A. Roussel, Kamal N. Saad and Tamara J. Errickson of Arthur D Little Inc., one of the leading management consultancy firms in the world, have developed a frame-work for analyzing the state of R&D in their path breaking book "Third Generation R&D." According to them there are three types of research:

1. **The Incremental Research** aims at small advances in technology on the foundation of existing body of knowledge. This is similar to applied research. Most of the Indian companies like Ranbaxy,

Dr. Reddy's Labs, Lupin, Cipla, Wockhardt, Sun and Cadila have been engaging in this kind of research. The focus on incremental research is due to the absence of product patents. A number of Indian companies have demonstrated considerable skills in process research. These companies were able to compress the average time taken to launch new drugs from five years in the seventies to one year in the nineties. The advantage gained through incremental research, however, is not as long lasting as that from radical research.

2. **The Radical Research** aims at creating new knowledge on the basis of the existing body of knowledge. Some companies like Dr. Reddy's Laboratories, Ranbaxy and Wockhardt have recently become active in radical research.

   Government sponsored research institutes like Indian Institute of Chemical Technology (IICT) and Central Drug Research Institute (CDRI) are now carrying on radical research in a limited way. IICT concentrates on developing cost-effective technologies for life saving drugs and has recently shifted the emphasis from process development to product development in tune with the changing global scenario.

3. **Fundamental Research** is risky, time consuming and expensive as it falls in the domain of the discovery of new products. Prof. H. Grabowski of Duke University has analyzed R&D data of 93 new drugs from 12 US companies in 1987. His study established the cost of developing a new drug at \$ 231 million. This has risen to \$ 300 million in 1993. His other findings are equally astonishing. It took an average of 12 years to develop a new drug and only 30 per cent of the new drugs actually generate sufficient returns to cover the R&D costs. The breakeven time for a new drug was 16 to 17 years on the average.

   It is estimated that 20 substances out of 10,000 examined enter the stage of animal studies. Of these, 10 may reach clinical studies and finally one of these may gain FDA approval. These facts amply demonstrate the cost and difficulty involved in discovering new drugs. It is difficult to do fundamental research without possessing a critical mass. And the list of the top ten R&D spenders bears this out

(Table 9.2). The top ten of the big Pharma spent a whopping US $ 47.7 billion on research and development in 2005.

Table 9.2 Biggest R&D spenders in 2005

Company	R&D spending $ billion	Sales $ billion	R&D as a per cent of sales
1. Pfizer	7.4	44.3	16.7
2. J & J	6.3	22.3	28.3
3. GSK	5.7	34.0	16.8
4. Astra Zeneca	5.4	24.0	14.9
5. Sanofi-Aventis	4.8	14.9	32.3
6. Novartis	4.5	25.0	18.0
7. Roche*	4.2	15.7	26.8
8. Merck	3.8	22.0	17.3
9. Eli Lilly	3.0	14.7	20.4
10. Amgen	2.3	12.0	19.2

Source: Pharmaceutical Executive, May 2006

R&D in India : Current Scenario

For decades, the phrase 'research and development' in the Indian pharmaceutical industry parlance, meant little more than the copying of patented drugs. Since India granted no product patents, Indian drug companies could legally manufacture a drug patented abroad using a different process and market it in India and third world countries with weak or no IPR protection. But not for very much longer. Now that the country has signed the GATT agreement, that easy route to profits for Indian companies has been blocked since 2005.

That is why some of the more progressive Indian companies have been investing in building new laboratories, buying sophisticated equipment and recruiting talented scientists both at home and abroad. Indian R&D finally seems to be getting the focus it needs.

These companies seem to recognize the fact that indigenous R&D is the need of the hour, to become competitive internationally. Industry estimates put the start up cost of a basic research company at US $ 500 million, as compared to US$ 2 billion in the West.

Strategic Options for Indian Companies

New drug discovery is very expensive. It could cost around US $ 1 billion and take about 8–10 years from concept to commercialization. The cost of capital to developing one new drug is more than the annual turnover of India's largest drug company. What are the options available for Indian drug companies? Can they ever become innovative? Dr. Reddy's Labs, Ranbaxy, Wockhardt, Torrent, Sun Pharma, Lupin and more recently Glenmark have shown that it is possible to make the transition from imitative to innovative culture. It is tough, but as these companies have shown, it can be done. Indian companies are focusing mainly on two areas:

1. ***Analogue Research :*** Analogues are modifications of original molecules and thus exhibit similar activity. Analogue molecules basically are superior versions of existing drugs. An analogue typically neutralizes side effects and/or improves the therapeutic efficacy of an already patented drug. Under pressure from cost containment strategies, a number of research-based pharmaceutical companies too, are focusing on analogue research. Indian drug majors are working mainly on analogue research. An analogue may take about two years and Rs. 150–300 million to develop. Consider these initial successes that some of the leading Indian companies have achieved within a short period of launching their drug discovery programs:
    - Dr. Reddy's Laboratories has developed NCEs in therapeutic areas like diabetes and cancer. It has already filed for international patents and became the first-ever Indian drug company to license its new chemical entity to a multinational against upfront payments linked to pre-defined milestones and royalties once the drug is commercialized.
    - Ranbaxy too has filed for international patents for its NCE for treating BPH and is looking for a strategic alliance for taking this through further development to commercialization.

- Wockhardt has also developed two anti-infective compounds and is ready to file for international patents. It is also looking for a strategic alliance partner to share the further developmental effort, registration and marketing internationally.
- Torrent too has developed a new compound in the coronary vasodilator category and is filing for international patents.
- Nicholas Piramal also has identified an anti-cancer molecule at its R&D centre acquired from Hoechst. The company is planning to file global patent application for the same.
- Lupin has developed an anti-migraine product and is conducting clinical trials. It is filing for a provisional patent for this new herbal formulation. The company plans to take this product for clinical trials to Europe and US.
- Glenmark has entered into an out-licensing arrangement with Forest Laboratories in the US and Teijin Pharmaceuticals in Japan for their NCE under development.
- Suven has entered into an agreement with the global drug major Eli Lilly for pre-clinical development of certain drug candidates in CNS therapeutic area.

2. ***Novel Drug Delivery Systems (NDDS) :*** Novel drug delivery systems are superior ways of administering the drug and this requires formulation development and process development skills. It may take about three years and an investment of Rs. 1–2 billion for developing a NDDS. A NDDS could be a helper compound (polymer used to direct the drug to the target site), a polymer implant (a small polymer wafer, a capsule or a gel that allows slow and sustained release) or a micro sphere (a fatty compound or liposome, that encloses the drug to slow the release and lower the toxicity).

   A new NDDS concept is patentable. If it is an improvement, it could give a market-exclusivity for three years in the US. Ranbaxy, Wockhardt and Cipla are seriously pursuing the NDDS market in the US.

DOE – Strategy to Optimize R&D Effort

Design of experiments (DOE) ensures optimization in conducting experiments in terms of speed and dependability. It is an R&D technique developed by Sir Ronald A. Fisher, a British statistician, for systematic experimentation. It is a scientific way to analyze the causal effects. R.S. Chalapati, head of start-up quality improvement consultants, who has helped Ranbaxy implement the DOE program, highlighted the salient features of this highly useful technique in an interview with Ms. Manjari Raman of Financial Express.

At the heart of DOE lie templates for experimentation called 'orthogonal arrays'. An orthogonal array is akin to a sophisticated switching system into which many different design variables can be plugged in. With the help of an orthogonal array, even a relatively inexperienced scientist can extract the average results and thus reach reliable conclusions despite the large number of changing variables. Moreover, with an orthogonal array, the scientist has to run just eight experiments in the order prescribed in the array to reach virtually the same conclusions as he would have if he had performed up to 1024 experiments. The six steps of DOE are:

a. *Problem identification :* To define the problem more precisely, a team of scientists or design engineers needs to undertake a Pareto analysis, use a cause and effect diagram and brainstorm the possible parameters which lead to the problem.

b. *Selection of experimental design :* The team chooses the right orthogonal array depending on the number of factors (elements of a process, which have an effect on the outcome) and levels (the values the factors will take) involved in the experiment. The team after identifying the parameters needs to isolate two levels for each parameter – a high and a low – to run the experiments.

c. *Conducting the experiments :* The team has to do just eight experiments. The DOE principle can be applied to cycle time, yield, waste and cost.

d. *Analysis of variance :* Analysis of variance (ANOVA) is a statistical tool used to measure the impact of each individual factor on the variation in the final response. This step allows the team to prioritize which of the identified factors have maximum impact. The impact of each factor is ranked and only the factors with significant impact are chosen. This step invariably results in cost reduction.

e. *Determining the best levels :* The team now selects the optimum combination of factors and levels. It is critical that the team selects the right factors, levels and parameters.

f. *Conducting confirmation run :* To reassure themselves that the optimum experiment is designed by DOE does deliver, the team conducts confirmatory experiments. Comparing the actual rejection or defect levels improves the veracity of the new experiment.

Ranbaxy is the first domestic pharmaceutical company to use DOE techniques to develop new bulk drug and formulation development processes. Within eighteen months of implementing DOE techniques, Ranbaxy has achieved significantly higher yields – about 17 per cent improvement in one product. In another product, it was able to bring the costs down by slicing the quantity of one ingredient by 38 per cent. The company has been able to achieve better control over processes and has shrunk the cycle time for developing a bulk drug from the lab to the manufacturing stage from 3 years to 18 months on average.

Collaborate to Compete

Since Indian companies cannot match the MNCs for financial clout, it probably makes sense to work in tandem, either with one another or with the national laboratories. Some large Indian companies like Ranbaxy are holding discussions with the government on drug development with equal cost sharing. The infrastructure for R&D in the public sector is sizeable. There are as many as twenty-five state-owned national institutes that undertake research and development activities.

These can be broadly classified under CSIR (Council for Scientific and Industrial Research) and ICMR (Indian Council of Medical Research) as presented in Table 9.3. What needs to be done is to upgrade these to world-class standards and inject the spirit of enterprise and collaborative culture.

Table 9.3 Government research institutes

CSIR Laboratories

1. Centre for Biochemical Technology (CBT), New Delhi
2. Central Drug Research Institute (CDRI), Lucknow
3. Central Food Technological Research Institute (CFTRI), Lucknow
4. Central Institute of Medicinal and Aromatic Plants (CIMAP), Lucknow
5. Central Electro-chemical Research Institute (CERI), Karaikudi
6. Center for Cellular and Molecular Biology (CCMB), Hyderabad
7. Indian Institute of Chemical Biology (IICB), Hyderabad
8. Indian Institute of Chemical Technology (IICT), Hyderabad
9. Institute of Microbial Technology (IMT), Chandigarh
10. Indian National Scientific Documentation Centre (INSDC), New Delhi
11. Industrial Toxicology Research Centre (ITRC), Lucknow
12. National Institute of Science of Technology (NIST), New Delhi
13. National Botanical Research Institute (NBRI), Pune

ICMR Institutes

1. National Institute of Nutrition (NIN), Hyderabad
2. National Institute of Virology (NIV), Pune
3. Institute for Research in Reproduction (IRR), Mumbai
4. Tuberculosis Research Centre (TRC), Chennai
5. Central JALMA Institute for Leprosy (CJIL), Agra
6. Malaria Research Centre (MRC), Delhi
7. Institute for Research in Medical Institute (IRMI), Chennai
8. Institute of Cytology and Preventive Oncology (ICPO), New Delhi
9. Enterovirus Research Centre (ERC), Mumbai
10. ICMR Genetic Research Centre, Mumbai
11. National AIDS Research Centre (NARC), Pune

Others

1. National Institute of Pharmaceutical Education and Research (NIPER), Chandigarh
2. B.V. Patel PERD Centre, Ahmedabad

Interestingly, state owned laboratories have also begun serious work on new drug development. Consider these moves:

- Indian Institute of Chemical Technology (IICT), Hyderabad, which has turned the copying of drugs into a fine art, is taking to drug research with a missionary zeal.
- In Lucknow, the Central Drug Research Institute (CDRI), the only institution in the country to have produced new drugs so far, is updating its facilities.
- The Council of Scientific and Industrial Research (CSIR) is trying to pool and restructure its resources and expertise to start work on drug development. Considering its infrastructure and experience, the CSIR could play a significant role in the joint drug research programs being considered by the government and a section of the industry.

Key Issues

One of the key issues is that most of the new investments being made now will not yield immediate results as they are making up for the lack of R&D investments in the past years to acquire facilities that are taken for granted abroad.

Scientific expertise is another. Since they have become used to duplicating drugs, few companies have the required knowledge base and talent to create new ones. Some companies are trying to bridge the gap by bringing scientists from abroad, mainly from the US, but have had only modest success so far. Ranbaxy and Dr. Reddy's Labs had been advertising in the past in US publications but they had found that, despite the scarcity of jobs in the US, only one in every ten Indian scientists settled there is willing to come back.

Contract Research Opportunities

Pharmaceutical research is a different ball game. It is very much different from other industries. Wherever basic research is highly dependent on technology, India will not be able to be competitive enough for world business to be interested. But in pharmaceutical research, particularly at the initial end of the funnel of discovery like identifying a molecule and conducting tests, the value addition can be very high. The scientific skills of India definitely suit the business needs of pharmaceutical R&D.

Within the US there is pressure to keep costs down. In the past, research funding generally kept rising by 10 per cent each year and the salaries of research scientists also kept rising annually. There is cap on research spending now.

There are only two options in such situations. Either they would have to reduce the number of projects or get more work done with the same amount of money. One of the ways to do this is by what is called – "out-sourcing research." This is happening very quickly within the US. Contracting out to academic institutions, universities and non-profit organizations etc., has begun. This out-sourcing is increasingly being extended to countries like China and India.

The basic research costs of drug discovery are high the world over and staffing cost, in particular, is very high. It is 40 per cent in Japan and as high as 60–70 per cent in the US. Because of the high quality of R&D and qualified scientists, India can carry out the initial part (of the research funnel) at a tenth of international cost. By contracting out the basic research, they can save the costs of development and deploy these for clinical research and other areas where costs are going up significantly.

This business–research model is already becoming popular in the developed countries and will definitely usher in an era of contract research in India too. Here is what Randall L. Tobias, chairman and CEO of Eli Lilly, the global pharmaceutical major said about out-sourcing research some time ago:

> The dispersed research helps to achieve global level research capabilities by leveraging local research strengths. Each country or region is strong in certain areas of disease and drug research. Also technology has made

it possible to access and also to communicate individual and group research capabilities through a net work spanning the globe. Such a dispersed approach should bring better results cost effectively.

Fred Hassan, CEO of Schering Plough Corporation, USA said some time ago on creating a climate for scientific innovation:

> Observing that science innovation occurs best in small entrepreneurial environments, a very serious and growing challenge for our industry, is to see whether we can create a small company environment in a big company organization.

A number of technocrats sensed the opportunity and started creating drug discovery support service capabilities of world standard and are providing dedicated services through the creation of Full Time Equivalent (FTE) services.

Patents Hold the Key

Furthermore, Richard Sykes, chairman of the world's leading drug firm – Glaxo-Wellcome (Glaxo SmithKline now), in his visit to India a few years ago said:

> If all goes well with the patent bill, we would consider investment in R&D seriously as patents is one of the fundamentals governing inward investment. We would look for strengths in the science base and in the clinical base in India and that's where we would put our investments.

Intellectual Property

Business, the world over, is moving into a new era, where competitive advantage comes only from intellectual capital.

Generations of business and accounting students have been taught that value lies in 'assets'. Assets come in four forms – three of them (current, fixed and investments) are precise and measurable, and the fourth (intangible assets) is imprecise and essentially immeasurable until it is sold.

All this is changing rather rapidly. It is increasingly becoming obvious that the new source of wealth is not material – it is information, knowledge applied to work to create wealth.

How fixed are fixed assets really? Gary Hamel, a professor at London School of Business has argued that an asset is really 'only a perception of an opportunity about which, a majority of people have agreed!'

Some observers have even suggested that intellectual capital actually subsumes what we usually think of as fixed assets, which on closer observation prove to be less fixed, than we thought.

Whatever viewpoint you may agree with, it is apparent that the value of intellectual capital in the world's business is immense. Consider these facts:

- Charles Handy of London Business School has estimated that these intellectual assets may typically be worth three or four times a company's tangible book value.
- Morgan Stanley's world index estimates that the average value of companies on the world's stock exchanges is two times the book value.
- In the United States, corporate market value typically ranges from two to nine times the book value.
- Closer home in India, Price Waterhouse Coopers have done an indicative analysis of listed Indian companies with 1997-98 turnover of more than Rs. 1 billion. The study has identified 25 companies, which, even in today's depressed markets, command a market value, which is more than 4.5 times the book value of tangible assets.

Alfred P. Sloan, the legendary chairman of General Motors realized the intrinsic value and true worth of intellectual capital long before any one could even visualize it for he said:

> Take away my factories, my money and assets. But give me back my people and my organization. In five years, I will have all of them back.

That should be convincing enough even for the skeptics on the real power and value of intellectual capital.

One of the greatest challenges facing any business today is the gap between its balance sheet and market valuation. This gap, representing the bulk of a company's true value, consists of indirect assets – organizational knowledge, customer satisfaction, product innovation, employee morale, patents and trademarks – that never appear in its financial reports.

It has increasingly become obvious that the real value of the companies cannot be determined by only traditional accounting measures. The worth of any knowledge-based and information-intensive organization lies not in bricks and mortar, or even in inventories and receivables, but in another intangible kind of asset: intellectual capital.

Walter Wriston in his highly influential book, *The Twilight of Sovereignty*, writes: "Indeed, the new source of wealth is not material – it is information, knowledge applied to work to create wealth."

Welcome to the new age of intellectual capital. Rick Karlgaard, editor of Forbes ASAP, identified the importance of intellectual capital and wrote almost prophetically in a 1993 editorial:

> As an index, book value is dead as a doornail, an artifact of the Industrial Age. We live in the Information Age. Of course, though remarkably few people have come to terms with the fact. Failure to understand the declining relevance of book value – and the hard assets that form the ratio's numerator – is the proof of this. Human intelligence and intellectual resources are any company's most valuable assets.

In the pharmaceutical industry, leveraging of intellectual capital is even more important. A few years ago a huge pharmaceutical entity (Novartis) was created by the merger of two Swiss-based pharmaceutical giants – Sandoz and Ciba, mainly on the platform of intellectual capital: both companies wanted to benefit from the combined pipeline of new drugs under research once they came together.

Three Essential Elements

Intellectual capital has three essential elements. These are:

1. *Human Capital* is the combined knowledge, skill, innovative capabilities and employee competence. It also includes the company's values, culture, and philosophy. The company cannot own human capital.
2. *Structural Capital* includes the hardware, software, customer databases, patents, trademarks and infrastructure - in other words everything left at the office when employees go home.
3. *Customer Capital* is essentially the relationships built with the key customer groups.

Intellectual Capital - Future Implications

A few years from now, investors may look for things like a customer satisfaction index and employee satisfaction index. Steven M.H. Wallman, the then commissioner of the Securities & Exchange Commission (SEC), at a symposium in 1996 at Washington predicted that intangible assets and their use would become the heart of annual reports and financial statements, the way they are today, would be added as appendices.

Furthermore, a special committee on financial reporting formed by the American Institute of Certified Public Accountants (AICPA) to address a growing concern about the relevance of orthodox financial reporting and disclosure to the modern economy, in its report suggested these improvements:

1. The provision of information about corporate plans, opportunities, risks and uncertainties.
2. Better alignment of external reporting systems with internal management control and information systems.
3. Enhanced discussion of non-financial performance factors that create long term value such as non-financial performance data, have value relevance and can be effectively used by analysts as leading indicators of future financial performance.

Four Pillars of Intellectual Capital

1. ***Employee Satisfaction Index :*** There is a strong correlation between market capitalization and employee satisfaction. Human resource development (HRD) policies and practices in all relevant areas like role clarity, goal clarity, performance review mechanisms, compensation systems, training and development initiatives, transparent transactions with employees and team building activities are essential to create a performing organization. In the ultimate analysis, morale can be high where performance is high and employees enjoy what they do. Organizations should therefore, constantly benchmark their practices against the best-in-class companies and monitor their progress. Periodical employee surveys on the following areas are very useful to achieve high levels of employee satisfaction: average years of service; employee turnover; willingness to take up new projects; willingness to be relocated; and time and resources spent in training and development.
2. ***Customer satisfaction Index :*** Customer satisfaction leads to customer loyalty. It is your contented customers who will drive your market shares up. In the ethical drug business, prescription monitoring is one sure way of measuring customer satisfaction. The number and frequency of prescriptions and even the number of products prescribed can measure the relative loyalty levels of customers.
3. ***Share of Talent :*** In the new millennium, knowledge is the crucial determinant factor of success in the market place. Competition is not just between products and markets. Competition is essentially between the talents of one company versus others. Acquiring and retaining talent, therefore, is of paramount importance. Success strategies for acquiring and nurturing talent include: drawing up a list of the best available talent in the industry; acquiring them; monitoring the response to job advertisements; involving the top management in hiring; and developing and building internal commitment through empowerment.

4. ***Capturing Organizational Knowledge :*** An organization's knowledge is the sum of the knowledge of all the employees. But, when people leave companies, they usually take away whatever they have learnt with them. This vital loss is preventable. While you cannot capture whatever they have learnt entirely, you can capture a substantial part of it. The two strategies to prevent this loss are:
   A. Ensure that your employees document almost everything that they have learned while working with the company.
   B. Make sure that people work in teams that are mutually supportive so that learning is always shared among the employees.

The Only Source

What are the factors that are responsible for creating a competitive advantage? Something, which is not freely available, not easily substitutable and cannot be leveraged across the business is of competitive advantage.

Capital, which has been historically a scarce commodity, is no longer scarce. Today as markets globalized and become more efficient, it is relatively easy for companies around the world to access cash at relatively inexpensive rates from anywhere on the globe. Its access is not restricted any more with more and more countries liberalizing their economies.

Customer relationships and employee commitment are not easily replicable. One cannot leverage them across the businesses. In such a scenario, what is the only non-replicable, unique, proprietary and sustainable competitive advantage your business has? Intellectual capital of course!

How Successful Companies Build Intellectual Capital

Intellectual capital in the pharmaceutical industry comprises intangible assets like brand equity, FDA approvals, trademarks, patents, physician relationships, relationships across the supply chain, relationships with alliance partners, relationships with original patent holders and employee competence and commitment.

Research overseas has shown that customer loyalty and employee commitment are perhaps two of the most important intangible assets. A few years from now, investors may look for things like a customer satisfaction index and employee satisfaction index.

Here is how successful companies constantly work on building and strengthening their intellectual capital base and enhance the value of their intangible assets:

1. ***Customer Relationships :*** Pharmaceutical companies monitor customer contacts product category-wise and prescriber segment-wise. They track customer loyalty and customer conversion through continuous prescription monitoring. They involve their key customers like opinion makers and trendsetters in identifying new product opportunities and even formulating their product strategies to gain greater internal commitment. They build wide distribution networks of stockists and retailers and manage them effectively to ensure continuous availability of their products at the right time, at the right place and at the right price.
2. ***Relationships with Alliance-Partners :*** The key to success in any alliance is the ability to build a win-win relationship based on mutual trust and respect for each other's competence and contribution. Ability to build and manage a strategic alliance is an increasingly important intangible asset. When technology changes (it is changing rapidly), you automatically get the benefits of change through alliances, if you manage them effectively. Further, if a multinational is looking for a partner in India, it would obviously choose a company with a strong base of intellectual capital like good customer franchise, wide distribution network, product and process developmental capabilities and employee competence.
3. ***Brand Equity :*** Successful pharmaceutical companies review the health of their brands internally and take corrective action as required. They actively pursue an aggressive strategy of brand building. They track brand preferences and prescription switches through continuous prescription monitoring. Based on this, they formulate customer conversion and consolidation strategies.

4. ***Research and Development :*** They step up the R&D investment to create world class infrastructure for doing research and development work. They put up a competent and experienced research team focusing on all key aspects of research like process development, formulation development, NDDS, biotechnology and even drug discovery (analogue research, mainly). They file for international patents for the molecules developed and look for strategic alliances for sharing the further developmental work, product registration and marketing across all key markets in the world.
5. ***Management Processes :*** Winning companies are constantly looking for improvement in their management processes. They reorganize their operations around customer segments to be more competitive.
6. ***Information Technology :*** Highly successful pharmaceutical companies like Ranbaxy, Dr. Reddy's Labs and Nicholas Piramal are investing in information technology. Ranbaxy in particular is setting the pace in creating an infotech culture within the company. The company believes that there is more to Infotech than mere investment in hardware and software. Building an infotech culture involves, apart from hardware and software, top management commitment to training and development and change management. It is investing about one per cent of its sales in information technology and is convinced that infotech is an enabler of operational effectiveness.
7. ***People :*** Progressive companies realize that people are their most important asset as they create and enhance the value of their intellectual capital. Their top managements spend time in recruitment, training and development of managers. They believe that increasing levels of productivity is a direct outcome of increased hours spent on training. They also track training per employee. Some of them even put the value of their employees (Infosys, for example) on their balance sheet. There are others who track the education levels of their employees and the value added per employee.

Do it Now!

Leif Edvinsson and Michael S. Malone in their pioneering book on 'Intellectual Capital', write about its future very convincingly:

> The rise of intellectual capital is inevitable, given the irresistible historical and technological forces not to mention the investment flows that are sweeping across the modern world and driving us to the knowledge economy. Intellectual capital will dominate the way we value our institutions because it alone, captures the dynamics of an organization's sustainability and value creation. It alone recognizes that a modern enterprise changes so fast that all it has left to depend and defend.

Intellectual capital is one of the most important metric of any model for measuring corporate performance, as it pierces the surface and uncovers true value. In doing so, it restores both common sense and fairness to economics.

Make no mistake, whatever the path you choose, intellectual capital is our future. Invest in it. Build it. If you are investing in and building the intellectual capital base of your organization, you are in fact building your own future. Do it Now!

Winning Moves

A handful of Indian companies have realized the potential that research and development can offer. They have taken the initiative of investing in R&D in a bigger way. They have stepped up the R&D investment to 5 to 10 per cent plus of their sales as compared to the industry average of 1.8 per cent. These companies are shifting their focus from process development to product development. Here are the winning moves of some of the more progressive Indian drug companies:

Group 'A' Companies:

Competing for the Innovation-Led Space

All the ten companies in Group 'A' have built world-class R&D infrastructure and acquired a critical mass of scientific talent who are highly competent and qualified. Many of the scientists have experience in cutting-edge research in their earlier assignments with some of the global Pharma majors and international universities and institutions of repute. All of them are focusing on chronic disease segments for discovery research such as cardiovascular, metabolic disorders (diabetes, lipid disorders and obesity), respiratory disorders (asthma and COPD), inflammation (rheumatoid arthritis), CNS disorders and others. Infectious diseases and pain management are also on their discovery radar. NDDS and biopharmaceuticals too are a priority.

Since drug discovery is for the long term, virtually all of them are also competing for the international generic space by stepping up their ANDA and DMF filings in the regulated markets for generating the critical mass of revenue for fueling their discovery dreams.

Table 9.3 Group 'A' Companies : R&D Focus

Company	Scientists (Number)	Focus Areas
1. Ranbaxy	1,120	Process Research, Generic Research for Regulated Markets, NDDS, NCE Research, and Biotechnology Research Therapeutic Areas: Cardiovascular, Metabolic Disorders, Diabetes, Anti-infectives, Inflammation, COPD, and Biopharmaceuticals
2. Dr. Reddy's Labs	950	Process Research, Generic Research for regulated markets, NDDS, NCE Research and Biotechnology Research Therapeutic Areas: Cardiovascular, Diabetes, Metabolic Disorders,
3. Sun Pharma	500	Process Research, Generic Research for regulated markets, NDDS, NCE Research Therapeutic Areas: CNS, Cardiovascular, Respiratory, Inflammation, Diabetes and Pain management
4. Lupin	320	Process Research, Generic research for regulated markets, NDDS, Phyto-pharmaceuticals, and NCE Research Therapeutic Areas: Anti-infectives, Respiratory, Cardiovascular

Company	Scientists (Number)	Focus Areas
5. Nicholas Piramal	350	Process development, Phyto-pharmaceutical research, Generic research, NDDS, and NCE development Therapeutic Areas: Oncology, Inflammation, Autoimmunity, Diabetes and NSAIDs
6. Zydus Cadila	500	Process Research, Generic Research, NDDS, NCE Research Therapeutic Areas: Cardiovascular Diseases, Metabolic Disorders, Inflammation
7. Wockhardt	400	Process Research, Generic Cadila Research for Regulated Markets, NDDS, NCE Research, Biotechnology Therapeutic Areas: Anti-infectives, Pain Management, Cardiovascular, Biopharmaceuticals
8. Biocon	300	Process Research, Generic Research for Regulated Markets, NCE Research, Biotechnology Research Therapeutic Areas: Diabetes and Oncology
9. Glenmark	400	Process Research, Generic Research for Regulated Markets, NDDS, NCE Research, Biopharmaceuticals Therapeutic Areas: Asthma, COPD, Diabetes, Obesity and Inflammation
10. Torrent	538	Process development, Product development, NDDS Therapeutic Areas: cardiovascular, diabetes, obesity, anti-infectives

Table 9.4 Group 'A' Companies : Intellectual Property Creation

Company	R&D Investment in FY 2006 Rs. million	Intellectual Property Patents filed/Granted till FY 2006
1. Ranbaxy	6,393	791 / 198
2. Dr. Reddy's Labs	1,737	353 / 72
3. Sun Pharma	1,615	395 / 56
4. Lupin	988	240 / 53
5. Nicholas Piramal	775	214 / 200
6. Zydus Cadila Healthcare	817	108 / -
7. Wockhardt	1,040	150 / 30
8. Biocon	764	566 / 37
9. Glenmark	467	20 / -
10. Torrent	564	219 / 123

Ranbaxy

Ranbaxy is India's highest spender on research with a budget of Rs. 350 million since 1995, which was 5 per cent of sales. The company has come long way since 1978-79 when the research (lab renovation budget as it was called then) budget was only Rs. 75,000. Today Ranbaxy has over 1,125 scientists conducting research across many platforms and many therapeutic areas. Their objective is to be the first private sector company in India to bring a new drug to market.

Ranbaxy's commitment to fight the diseases of the developing world is reflected through the progress made by its scientists on their anti-malarial molecule that it is developing jointly with Medicines for Malaria Venture (MMV), Geneva. The molecule completed the proof-of-concept Phase II (a) studies and activities for Phase II (b) studies are underway with trials in India, Thailand and Africa.

Ranbaxy has probably the largest team of scientists – over 1,125 conducting its research activities over a number of platforms and therapeutic areas. There are 300 scientists directing its multi-disciplinary approach to drug discovery in various therapeutic areas like infectious diseases (anti-bacterial and anti-fungal), urology (Benign Prostatic Hyperplasia and Urinary Incontinence), metabolic disorders (Type 2 Diabetes, and Hyperlipidemia), inflammatory diseases (Asthma, and COPD), and Rheumatoid Arthritis. The company has created in-house capacities for bio-equivalence and bio-analytical studies to accelerate its ANDA filings and reduce the overall costs of innovation. The cumulative filings of ANDAS with US FDA stand at 183 at the end of FY2006.

Ranbaxy is also the leader of Indian pharmaceutical industry in creating intellectual property. The company filed 185 patent applications in various areas such as drug discovery team in India (60), NDDS team (15), pharmaceutical research team in India (35), and process research in FY 2006 alone. Ranbaxy has ten active drug candidates at various stages of development in the area of drug discovery. The NCE pipeline of the company comprises three molecules (Table 9.5).

Table 9.5 Ranbaxy's NCE Pipeline

Molecule	Screening	Pre-Clinical	Clinical Phase I II	Approval	Launch
RBX 11160	Anti-Malarial				
RBX 9861	Urinary incontinence; Asthma; COPD				
RBX 10558	Dyslipidemia				

In addition, the company has one compound in the late stage of discovery for Community-acquired Respiratory Tract Infection (CARTI).

Ranbaxy entered into a number of research partnerships with leading institutions and universities in India – with Anna University for evaluating a number of medicinal plants for potential NCE development; with NIPER in the area of respiratory diseases; and with NCL in the area of infectious diseases.

Dr. Reddy's Laboratories

Dr. Reddy's has a two-pronged strategy for research. On the research side the strategy is to continue expanding the discovery pipeline with sharper focus on creating new discovery platforms in the chosen therapeutic areas of cardiovascular and metabolic disorders. On the development side the objective is to speed up the development of the NCE assets through a combination of in-house and co-development initiatives to minimize the inherent risk in drug development and maximize the returns.

In this regard Dr. Reddy's along with ICICI Venture Capital Fund Management Company and Citigroup Venture Capital International Growth Partnerships Mauritius Limited have formed an integrated drug development company called *Perlecan Pharma Private Limited* with an equity commitment of US $ 52.5 million. Dr. Reddy's have transferred to Perlecan all rights and titles of four NCEs in the area of cardiovascular and metabolic disorders. Perlecan's mandate is to speed up the further developmental activities of these.

Dr. Reddy's have entered into another partnership with Rheoscience A/S for further development and commercialization of their most advanced NCE asset – balaglitazone for Type 2 diabetes, which is all set to move into Phase III clinical trials. The arrangement allows DRL to retain its full rights for North America, Japan and the Rest of the World except Europe (excluding Russia and CIS) and China. In addition, Dr. Reddy's have entered into another co-development and commercialization agreement with Argenta Discovery Limited for developing a novel approach in the treatment of COPD.

The company has so far filed 70 ANDAs with US FDA, which include 29 Para IV filings. Its total DMF filings are over 151 (81 in the US, 28 in Canada, and 42 in Europe). Dr. Reddy's have an interesting development pipeline in discovery research (Table 9.6)

Table 9.6 Dr. Reddy's Development Pipeline in Discovery Research

Molecule	Screening	Pre-Clinical	Clinical Phase I	Clinical Phase II	Approval	Launch
DRF 2593	Metabolic Disorders					
DRF 10945	Metabolic Disorders					
RUS 3108	Cardiovascular					
DRL 11605	Metabolic Disorders					
DRF 1042	Oncology					
DRL 12424	Metabolic Disorders					
DRL 16536	Metabolic Disorders					

Sun Pharma

What is particularly noteworthy about Sun's research and developmental effort is the fact that the company started a state-of-the-art of research centre with an initial investment of Rs. 60 million even when the company's total sales turnover was a mere Rs. 200 million.

Sun Pharma set up its first research center - Sun Pharma Advanced Research Center (SPARC) in 1993 at Baroda, which has grown in the next nine years to a world class research campus for both complex generic research and NCE research. In addition, the company created another research center at Mumbai in 1997 to develop generics for the regulated markets – mainly for marketing by its US subsidiary Caraco.

Started with two APIs developed and launched in 1995, the process development at Sun Pharma has indeed come a long way to over 100 APIs in 2006. The NDDS research at the company resulted from a single drug Lithosun SR in 1985 to a number of products (almost forty FDFs every year) covering:

- Metered Dose Inhalers
- Liposomal Drug Delivery Systems
- Biodegradable Depot Formulations
- Controlled release formulations
- Osmotic release formulations
- Nasal sprays
- Melt tabs

The company has invested so far a whopping Rs. 6 billion on research and currently committing 11 – 12 per cent of its sales. The company's 161 research labs are engaged in research activities across organic synthesis, formulation development, biotechnology, peptide synthesis, analytical method development, pharmacokinetics, bioequivalence and discovery research. Sun Pharma is geared up today to file over 20 ANDAs and about 10 DMFs in regulated markets every year. About 35 – 40 per cent of current research budget is allocated to innovation-based projects, which is expected to exceed 50 per cent over the next three years. The company recognizes that NCEs and NDDS need prioritization and pro-innovation mindset and is in the process of de-merging its drug discovery research business into a separate company with its own charter and management.

Sun Pharma filed a total of 464 patents of which 42 have been granted.

The company's drug discovery initiative is taking shape in three specific therapy areas for known therapeutic targets. Novel drug delivery systems are under development across four platforms. One NCE has completed Phase I of clinical trials in Europe, and is expected to enter Phase II soon. Two NDDS projects are likely to enter phase II trials in the US over the next few months.

Lupin Laboratories

Lupin created a world-class research facility – Lupin Research Park in Pune, India sprawling across 19 acres with a built up area of 150,000 square feet housing 320 scientists who are directing its research activities in different areas such as process research, generic drug research for regulated markets, NDDS, NCE research, and research in phyto-chemistry. Lupin filed for over 240 patents so far. Further, University of Pune has approved the Lupin Research Park for carrying out doctoral research in the faculty of pharmacy, biochemistry and health sciences.

The company is partnering with leading scientific institutions in India such as NCL in Pune, IICT in Hyderabad, CDRI in Lucknow, and RRI in Jammu for its NCE research.

Research Pipeline : Lupin has over the recent years created a creditable pipeline of four Investigational New Drugs (IND) addressing three different disease areas of migraine, psoriasis and tuberculosis (Table 9.7)

Table 9.7 Lupin's Research Pipeline

Molecule	Screening	Pre-Clinical	Clinical Phase I II	Approval	Launch
LL 2011 (Amigra)	Anti-Migraine				
LL 4218 (Desoside P)	Anti-Psoriasis				
LL 4858 (Sudoterb)	Anti-TB				
LL 3348 (Herbal)	Anti-Psoriasis				

Nicholas Piramal

Nicholas Pirmal acquired the Hoechst research facility in 1998 and upgraded it into a state-of-the-art research center which has very high throughput screening capabilities and a natural product library of over 35,000 microbial strains and 5,600 plants derived from diverse habitats in India. Currently, the research center has 350 scientists and 80 of these are PhDs. About ten per cent of its scientists have international experience at prestigious institutions, universities and global Pharma majors. The company prepared its strategic blueprint in the new millennium on four pillars. The four Pillars of research at Nicholas Piramal are:

1. Formulation Development
2. Bulk drug development: organic synthesis and process development
3. Drug discovery
4. Clinical research at the group's hospital in Parel, Mumbai

Focus Areas : Nicholas Piramal selected its therapeutic areas for continuing research based on significant unmet needs in the market place and scientifically validated therapeutic pathways in well-understood biological pathways. The company focuses on therapeutic areas such as oncology, inflammation, autoimmunity, infectious diseases and diabetes.

Research Roadmap : Currently, the company has a sustainable pipeline of lead compounds from in-house development as well in-licensing.

The strategy is to have 5 to 8 molecules in human clinical trials between 2007 and 2010 and launch at least one of its own compounds by 2010.

Research Pipeline : Nicholas Piramal has an impressive research pipeline to make this a reality (Table 9.8). The company has total nine molecules at various stages of development. Three molecules including two phyto-pharmaceuticals are in Phase I or Phase II clinical trials, five molecules are ready for filing IND and pre-clinical toxicology studies are completed for one molecule.

Table 9.8 Nicholas Piramal's Research Pipeline

Molecule	Screening	Pre-Clinical	Clinical Phase I II	Approval	Launch
P 276	Oncology				
P 1446	Oncology	Ready for IND			
P 979	Inflammation	Ready for IND			
P 1539	Inflammation	Ready for IND			
P 1736	Diabetes	Ready for IND			
PP 05 (Herbal)	Inflammation				
PP 04 (Herbal Lotion)	Anti-fungal				
K M 80 (Herbalt)	Oncology				
P M 181104	Anti-infective	Ready for IND			

Zydus Cadila Health Care

Zydus has been continuously investing over the last few years in research and development activities across process research, generic drug research for regulated markets, NDDS, NCE research and biopharmaceutical research. Currently, over 500 scientists are directing the company's developmental efforts. 230 scientists out of these are dedicated to NCE research as the company is determined to become a research-driven global Pharma major by 2020. Zydus has established a clinical research development activity in-house. Two drug discovery collaborations are also underway with IICT, Hyderabad in India. The company's R&D spend in FY 2006 was Rs. 817 million. Zydus has four molecules in various stages of development (Table 9.9) and is evaluating a number of leads in anti-thrombolytics and cardiovascular areas actively.

Table 9.9 Zydus's NCE Pipeline

Molecule	Screening	Pre-Clinical	Clinical Phase I II	Approval	Launch
ZY H1	Metabolic Disorders				
ZY H2	Diabetes	IND Filed With DCGI			
ZY 01	Obesity				
ZY 11	Inflammation and Pain, Arthritis				

Wockhardt

Wockhardt's multi-disciplinary research capabilities cover three areas - recombinant biotechnology, new drug discovery, and generic pharmaceuticals. The company invested over one billion rupees on research and development in the year 2005 alone. It created a world-class biotech facility - The Wockhardt Biotech Park in Aurangabad, India, which received

WHO GMP certification for both Wepox (recombinant erythropoietin) and Wosulin (recombinant human insulin). Wockhardt is the first Asian company to launch recombinant insulin from concept to market stage. Wockhardt's focus on biotechnology is in the area of therapeutics development through genetic engineering. It is estimated that by 2010, nearly 25 per cent of pharmaceutical products produced in the world will be through this process.

WCK 771, its proprietary compound as a parenteral MRSA agent successfully completed Phase I human clinical trials and entered phase II Proof-of-concept stage. The company's 400-strong scientific tean filed 150 patents including 3 biotech patents so far.

Biocon

The acquisition of Nobex Corporation's IP assets provided Biocon with a valuable technological platform and complete ownership of the oral insulin and BNP programs of the acquired. It also brought 300 plus patents based on oral peptide delivery in the cardiovascular and metabolic disorders segments. Biocon with this strategic acquisition has one of the industry's leading IP portfolios in the area of structural transformation of naturally occurring peptides of therapeutic activity with over 566 patents.

Syngene, Biocon's custom research arm a frontrunner in its segment and Clingene, its clinical development arm, which provides clinical development activities are poised for greater growth as the global Pharma majors are increasingly looking for outsourcing research. The company has a number of collaborations in place with some of the leading scientific institutions across the globe for its research programs:

- Partnering in product development with Vaccinex, USA
- Joint PhD studies at Karolinska Institute, Sweden
- Joint research programs between Karolinska Institute, Sweden
- Partnering in product development with Center of Molecular Immunology (CIM), Havana

Biocon has an impressive pipeline of discovery-led products (Table 9.10). It has a collaboration program with CIMAB of Cuba for a monoclonal antibody, BioMab EGFR™, which has completed a two-year clinical trial for head and neck cancers, oral insulin, oral BNP, BVX 20 and anti-CD monoclonal antibodies. The oral insulin, IN 1055 is entering into Phase I.

Table 9.10 Biocon's Discovery Pipeline

Molecule	Screening	Pre-Clinical	Clinical Phase I II III	Approval	Launch
IN 105	Diabetes				
BVX	Inflammation				
BioMab (EFGR™)					
Tlht	Oncology / Inflammation				
Oral BNP	Cardiovascular				

Glenmark

In a span of six years, Glenmark has developed a pipeline of six molecules two of which are in clinical development and four are set to enter the clinical phase. The company has also initiated research on biopharmaceuticals at its research facility in Switzerland. The company entered into strategic alliances for co-development and marketing once these are approved of its two molecules, which are in clinical development with Forest Laboratories in North America and Teijin Pharma in Japan. Glenmark would like to market these products on its own in markets across Asia, and Africa. The company's NCE pipeline is impressive with six molecules at various stages of development (Table 9.11). Glenmark is also examining several other targets and plans to bring one compound to clinical trials every year. This will further diversify the research portfolio, reducing the risk of failure and increasing the rate of success.

Table 9.11 Glenmark's NCE Pipeline

Molecule	Screening	Pre-Clinical	Clinical Phase I II	Approval	Launch
GRC 3886 (Oglemilast)	Respiratory (Asthma, COPD)				1009/10
GRC 6211	Pain, Migraine, Incontinence, and Asthma				2011
GRC 10622	Pain				2012
GRC 4039	RA and Inflammatory Disorders				2012
GRC 8200	Diabetes Type II				2010
GRC 10389	Obesity				2011

Torrent

Torrent has been adopting and updating new and latest technologies for its research process, which enabled the company to create a discovery pipeline based on multiple biological targets and also work on collaborative research projects with global Pharma majors. Currently, Torrent is working on 6 in-house NCE projects within therapeutic areas such as diabetes and its related complications, obesity, and cardiovascular disorders. The company has cumulatively filed 219 patents for NCEs from these and earlier projects in all major markets such as USA, Japan, Europe, Czech Republic, Australia, Brazil, Mexico, Argentina, China, Hong Kong, Russia, and India out of which the company received 123 approvals.

Torrent stepped up its generic research for regulated markets and increased its scientific staff to 538. The company spent 8.16 per cent of its sales on its research activities in the FY 2006. The company's collaborative research agreement with Astra Zeneca aimed at discovering a novel drug candidate for the treatment of hypertension is progressing well and is on schedule. Torrent and Astra Zeneca would jointly fund the research project in equal proportion. The agreement envisages success-based R&D milestone payments to Torrent, and royalties based on the commercialization of the drug candidate. Torrent would get co-marketing rights of the products for its home market, India.

Torrent is one of the foremost sponsors of research in universities. The company is planning to back up its research activities with strategic alliances with well-known international companies.

Torrent is working out ways to make its R&D a profitable proposition and has signed up with the likes of William Harvey Research Institute in the UK for conducting collaborative research. Complementing Torrent's advanced research infrastructure and facilities are its alliances with several leading institutions and Pharma majors such as Astra Zeneca, Sweden, Birla Institute of Technology, Pilani, M.S. University, Baroda, and University of Pune. Torrent's Research Center has accreditations from a number of international agencies such as the Brazilian ANVISA, OECD Research Certification, GLP Compliance Monitoring Unit of the Inspectorate for Health Protection, Ministry of Health, Welfare and Sport of the Netherlands and NABL. These accreditations and certifications make Torrent Research Center globally competitive.

Group 'B' Companies: Competing for International Generics Space

The ten companies in Group 'B' are actively competing for the international generics space. The prerequisites for an international generic company are vertical integration to achieve cost leadership, ability to develop non-infringing processes, FDF developmental capabilities, analytical chemistry skills and regulatory capabilities. These companies have been steadily increasing their investment on R&D over the years and built world-class manufacturing facilities and many of them have received approvals from international regulatory authorities such as US FDA, UK MHRA, South Africa's MCC, Australian TGA, Canadian TPD, ANVISA of Brazil, WHO, Geneva and EQDM of Europe. Many of these companies have partnership arrangements with leading American and European generic firms for marketing their generic formulations in the regulated markets. Their research focus too is clearly on process research, generic product development for regulated markets, NDDS for creating the product differentiation. There is a very high degree of commonality in the therapeutic areas of their focus. The focus areas are infectious diseases, cardiovascular, metabolic disorders, oncology, pain management, inflammation, respiratory disorders, CNS disorders and some are focusing in addition on biopharmaceuticals.

Table 9.12 Group 'B' Companies : R&D Focus

Company (Number)	Scientists	Focus Areas
1. Cipla	450	Process Research, Generic Research for Regulated Markets, and NDDS Therapeutic Areas: Anti-infectives, Cardiovascular, Diabetes, Oncology, CNS and Gastroenterology
2. Aurobindo	400	Process Research, Generic Research for Regulated Markets, NDDS, NCE Research Therapeutic Areas: Antibiotics, ARVs, CVS, Statins, Diabetes, CNS, Anti-allergics, and Respiratory
3. Matrix	150	Process Research, Generic Research for Regulated Markets, NDDS Therapeutic Areas: Anti-infectives, Cardiovascular, Diabetes, ARVS, Pain management, CNS, Oncology, PPIs, and Anti-asthmatics
4. Orchid	450	Process Research, Generic Research for Regulated Markets, NDDS, NCE Research and Biotechnology Research
5. Ipca	240	Process Research, Generic Research for Regulated Markets, NDDS
6. Alembic	125	Process Research, Generic Research for Regulated Markets
7. Claris Life Sciences	100	Process Research, NDDS, LDDS, Sciences Film and Device Development, Biotech Research

Company (Number)	Scientists	Focus Areas
8. J B Chemicals	150	Process Research, Generic Research for Regulated Markets, NDDS and NCE Research Therapeutic Areas: PPIs, Antifungals, Antibacterials, and NSAIDS
9. Unichem	100	Process Research, Generic Research for Regulated Markets, NDDS, and Biotechnology Therapeutic Areas: Cardiovascular, Diabetes, Inflammation, and Anti-infectives
10. Strides	200	Process Research, Generic Drug Development for Regulated Markets on multiple platforms such as patented Matrix Technology and Nano Suspension Technology in Softgels Therapeutic Areas: Oncology, Immunosuppressants, ARVs, Anti-TB, Anti-malarials, Hormones, and Biopharmaceuticals

Table 9.13 Group 'B' Companies : Intellectual Property Creation

Company	R&D Investment in FY 2006 Rs. Million	Intellectual Property Patents Filed / Granted Till FY 2006
1. Cipla	1,554	NA / 112
2. Aurobindo Pharma	770	205 / 29
3. Matrix	599	54 / -
4. Orchid	613	360 / 42
5. Ipca	379	95 / 5
6. Alembic	301	89 / -
7. Claris Life Sciences	100*	NA
8. J B Chemicals	144**	114 / 43
9. Unichem	242	NA
10. Strides Arcolabs	262	NA

*approximate figure as the company spends @2.5 per cent of its sales on R&D

**approximate as the company spends

Cipla

Cipla's product developmental capabilities can be gauged from the fact that the company has achieved the distinction of developing the first ever oral drug for the treatment of thalassaemia. The company has been at the forefront of process development for a long time. It has developed over the years, innovative processes for over 120 pharmaceutical bulk actives. Many more new molecules are at various stages of development.

Yet another feather in the cap of Cipla's innovative process is that it has developed a number of new drug delivery systems and products employing new technologies including the micro-emulsion form of cyclosporin. Development work continues on new formulations in dispersible and sustained-release forms as well as CFC-free aerosols.

Cipla has four R&D centers and all of them continue to have the approval of the Ministry of Science and Technology, Government of India. The company works closely with the CSIR laboratories and other research and educational institutions. Cipla's multi-disciplinary approach to research has so far produced over 125 monographs to British, European, US and international pharmacopeias.

Aurobindo Pharma

The research prowess of Aurobindo is evident from its massive product portfolio of over 120 APIs, 102 ANDAs, 136 DMFs and COS all of which are developed in-house. The company is actively competing in the international generics and CRAMS spaces and has already become a force to reckon with over 50 ANDA approvals in regulated markets such as USA and Europe. Aurobindo's 400 scientists have so far filed over 205 patents of which 29 are granted so far. The company's research spend in FY 2006 was 5.2 per cent of sales at Rs. 770 million and the research focus is on anti-infectives, ARVs, cardiovascular diseases, statins, diabetes, gastrointestinals, respiratory diseases and anti-allergics.

Matrix Laboratories

Research and development certainly has been the backbone of Matrix. The company has two distinctive competencies – one is the ability to innovate across therapeutic segments and technology platforms like synthetic chemistry, fermentation, Bio-Catalysts and High Potency manufacturing technology. The other is a young team of knowledge associates – the scientists at Matrix who have a combined experience of filing over 250 ANDAs. In the FY 2006, the company's research spend was about 9 per cent of sales at Rs. 599 million. Its API product portfolio is around 169 of which 140 are developed and 29 are under development. Matrix filed its first ANDA on March 27, 2006. The company today is geared up to file 30 ANDAS and 30 DMFs in FY2007. When it comes to generating intellectual property, Matrix has filed 54 patents, 88 DMFs and one ANDA till end March 2006.

Orchid

Orchid's R&D infrastructure comprises a world-class drug discovery center and pre-clinical facility conforming to GLP. In addition, Orchid's drug discovery subsidiary in the US Bexel Pharmaceuticals Inc. is engaged in exploratory chemistry and leading edge biology and clinical development management. The therapeutic focus of Orchid-Bexel programs is on orally active small molecules covering diabetes, obesity, inflammation, and oncology. The company's pipeline comprises BLX-1002, an anti-diabetes molecule in human proof-of-concept studies and out-licensing discussions. It has a total of 16 lead molecules in discovery and pre-clinical stages. Orchid is planning to bring 3 molecules to Phase I and double its pipeline of drug leads over the next three years. The company has been committing 6 to 7 per cent of turnover on R&D, a significant portion of which is committed to discovery research.

Orchid has so far filed 360 patents worldwide of which 42 have been granted, 221 have been published and the balance are under examination. Over 27 per cent of all patent applications relate to new drug discovery, NDDS and biotechnology.

IPCA

The focus of Ipca's research center is on generics in regulated markets specially in Europe and USA. The center has developed expertise over the years in APIs, drug intermediates, and formulation development including NDDS and ANDA. As an international generic company Ipca is concentrating on innovative chemistry-driven process research for developing non-infringing routes for APIs and drug intermediates and intellectual property. In the area of NDDS Ipca is concentrating on therapeutic segments such as cardiac care, anti-infectives and anti-diabetics. Ipca has an ultramodern research facility with the latest technology required for conducting high quality research for getting into regulated markets.

Alembic

Alembic's research facility – BioArc is the nucleus of all its research endeavors spanning generic research, contract research, clinical research, bioequivalence, biological studies, process research and fermentation research, which it pioneered in India. The company's focus areas of research are patentable non-infringing processes for APIs, NDDS in formulations development research. Alembic's focus on generic research is targeted at penetrating the regulated markets.

The company has invested over Rs. 300 million on this facility. The acceleration of patentable research at Alembic is evident from its 45 filings in FY 2006. Till date, the company filed 89 patents in India, US and other countries.

Claris Life Sciences

Claris Research Foundation (CRF) has pioneered a number of technologies in the last few years. Consider these for example:

- Developed Lipid Drug Delivery Systems to manufacture its flagship product, propofol in the anesthesia segment
- Developed expertise Liposomal Drug Delivery Systems (LDDS)
- Triple and double chamber nutrition system
- Developed a proprietary multi-layer film for bag manufacturing

The company is one of the very few companies in the world to develop processes for developing specific APIs such as hydroxyethyl starch, iron sucrose and pamidronic acid. Claris forayed into biotechnology research with Monoclonal Antibodies (MAB) and recombinant technology.

J B Chemicals

J B Chemicals believes that R&D is the lifeblood of a pharmaceutical company and has been focusing on research for quite sometime. Its research efforts over the years have so far resulted in 24 international patents, and 15 Indian patents. In addition, it has already developed 20 NCE candidates in NSAID therapeutic area. It has two state-of-the-art R&D laboratories at Mumbai and Ankaleshwar and is planning one more at Pune with an investment of Rs. 400 million at Pune. The company is focusing on development of generic products for regulated markets, NDDS dosage forms in therapeutic segments such as cardiac care, anti-infectives and anti-diabetics. The company introduced a Novel Insoluble Drug Absorption Technology (NIDAT) for their nifedipine formulation - Nicardia CD. It has also received a patent for ranitidine controlled release tablets in the US and for nifedipine sustained released tablets in South Africa and Kazakhstan.

The company launched its drug discovery program and has some initial success with 20 patentable molecules some of which have already been granted. For three prioritized molecules out of these pre-clinical studies are in progress.

Unichem Laboratories

Unichem has created a state-of-the-art research and development facility that is ISO 9001-2000 certified and approved by Department of Science and Technology. The company has research facilities for Chemical R&D and Biosciences R&D. Its biosciences research facility is located at the Indian Institute of Science Campus, Bangalore. The major focus of its bioscience research is on biologically active peptides of therapeutic value. The chemical research facility at Mumbai has developed novel and innovative processes for new generation molecules in various therapeutic areas such as anti-hypertension, anti-inflammatory, anti-depressant, and anti-histaminic. It has also started recently working on statins and similar drugs. The company is also planning to enter the drug discovery area soon.

In addition, Unichem has started a Pharmaceutical Technology Development center that is cGMP-compliant at Goa, India, for conducting contract research for generic product development for regulated markets such as US, Canada, Europe etc.

Strides Arcolabs

Strides Technology and Research (STAR) has over 200 researchers striving to break new ground in pharmaceutical research in areas such as process development, clinical supplies manufacturing, and generic product research across various dosage forms. The core competence of Strides is softgel capsule manufacturing. The company is developing a number of generic products in a wide range therapeutic areas such as immunosuppressants, hormones, controlled substances and oncology products. Strides has filed a total of 657 dossiers across the world which includes regulated markets as well as semi-regulated markets. The focus of the company however is on regulated markets.

Strides commenced CRAM supplies to GE, Ciba Specialties, Abbott among others. The company is setting up a new FTE lab (Food Technology and Engineering) for offering global Pharma companies a wide range of capabilities in select therapeutic areas and clinical manufacturing. Medgene, the biotech arm of Strides is the first company in India that commenced r-hGH (recombinant human growth hormone) in softgel dosage form. Strides has an oncology pipeline of 36 formulations in softgels. Strides spent Rs 242 million on R&D in FY 2006.

Group 'C' Companies

While all the ten companies in Group 'C' are competing in the CRAMS space, some of them like Dabur and Natco are also competing in the international generic space. Dabur, in addition is focusing on drug discovery area particularly in oncology. All of them are IPR-compliant and follow a non-competing strategy which is essential for any firm aspiring to become the partner-of-choice for the global drug majors. All these companies have either already built a world-class manufacturing and research infrastructure or are in the process of building one. Some of them have approvals from international regulatory authorities that are required to enter the regulated markets. These companies are actively working towards building and improving their capabilities in all relevant areas of research such as process research, generic product development for regulated markets, NDDS, NCE research in order to become competitive across the Pharma value chain.

Table 9.14 Group 'C' Companies : R&D Focus

Company	Scientists (Number)	Focus Areas
1. Jubilant	885	Process Research, Generic Organosys Research for Regulated Markets, NDDS, and NCE Research
2. Divi's Labs	200	Process Research Peptide Synthesis
3. FDC	100	Process Research, FDF Research and Generic Research for regulated markets
4. Shasun	150	Process Research, FDF Development, Generic Research for regulated markets, NCE Development, and Clinical Research
5. Nectar Life Sciences	200	Process Research, and FDF Development
6. Dabur Pharma	270	Process Development, Generic development, Molecular diagnostics, Vaccines, NDDS, NCE development Therapeutic Areas: oncology, anti-diabetics, cardiovascular,
7. Ind-Swift Laboratories	85	Process Research, FDA Development
8. Dishman Pharmaceuticals	100	Process Research, Generic Research for Regulated Markets
9. Natco Pharma	45	Organic Synthesis, Generics for Regulated markets, NDDS, NCE development Therapeutic Areas: Oncology, Anti-Hypertensives, Anti-migraine, G I Disorders, Anti-depressants,
10. Suven Life Sciences	190	Discovery Research, Clinical Research and CRAMS Therapeutic Areas: CNS

Table 9.15 Group 'C' Companies : Intellectual Property Creation

Company	R&D Investment in FY 2006 Rs. Million	Intellectual Property Patents Filed / Granted
1. Jubilant Organosys	1,050	NA
2. Divi's Labs	872	NA
3. FDC	54	8 / 4
4. Shasun	264	NA
5. Nectar Life Sciences	120	NA
6. Dabur Pharma	269	350 / 120
7. Ind-Swift Laboratories	217	9 / -
8. Dishman Pharmaceuticals	245	NA
9. Natco Pharma	11	135 / 18
10. Suven Life Sciences	220	39 / -

Jubilant Organosys

Jubilant Organosys has been able to forge sustaining relationships with global Pharma and biotech majors as its accent is on collaborating rather than competing with them. The key enabler in this effort is its research focus. As an aspirant of becoming one of the leading players in the CRAMS Space, Jubilant invested in research and development consistently over the last ten years and transformed itself from a commodity chemicals player into an integrated pharmaceutical industry player competing across the Pharma value chain. The company today has a 885-strong scientific team to give it the necessary edge in research area. It has state-of-the-art facilities for conducting research in process development, generic drug development for regulatory markets discovery research right from informatics, medicinal chemistry, biology, pre-clinical, clinical up to supply of the APIs and formulations. The company has a 52-bed facility in India for conducting bioequivalence studies. There are over 200 employees in India and the US dedicated for clinical research activity.

Divi's Labs

Divis Labs has become a preferred supplier to some of the global Pharma majors due to its research and developmental capabilities and technological infrastructure. The company, by following a strategy of collaboration rather than competition, is able to improve its share in the custom synthesis segment. Divi's Labs has 117 research stations in the five research centers manned by a competent team of over 200 scientists and have completed more than 300 projects successfully. The company's focus is clearly on APIs and drug intermediates. Its IPR compliance enables partnership with some of the leading Pharma MNCs right from the early stage of the product life cycle. Divi's facilities have approvals and from leading international regulatory authorities such as US FDA, EDQM and ISO 9001, ISO 14001, and OHSAS 18001. The company has developed a portfolio of over 106 products. The company's research focus is on carotenoids, chiral chemistry, organic synthesis, peptides, nucleotides and marketing focus on regulated markets.

FDC Laboratories

FDC is surely shifting gears to get into the global generics market. The company has a modern research center with state-of-the-art instrumentation. The areas of research are – process research, generic drug development for regulated markets, NCE research and biopharmaceutical research. For its NCE research, FDC is collaborating with National Chemical Laboratories (NCL) and universities and clinical laboratories. The company has filed so far 8 patents internationally out of which 4 have been granted. The company invested about 1.5 per cent of its sales on R&D during the year.

Shasun Chemicals

Shasun continues to invest in R&D to improve its product pipeline. The company is focusing on custom synthesis, contract research, generic product development and would like to become a partner of choice for the global drug majors. The company is, accordingly building its capabilities to provide services from the lab to the API plant ending up with development and manufacturing of FDFs and indeed provide services through out the life cycle of the product. Shasun's UK subsidiary at Dudley has about 45 scientists with significant experience in route identification, process development, process industrialization and analytical method development.

The company is having partnership arrangements with the New Jersey-based Alpharma Inc (now a part of the Actavis group) and Glenmark, USA for marketing its select generic formulations in cardiovascular and CNS therapeutic areas. Shasun's R&D spend in FY 2006 was Rs. 264 million.

Nectar Life Sciences

Nectar Life Sciences is currently focusing on developing new technologies, non-infringing processes. The company is setting up a modern R&D center at a cost of Rs 150 million with a strength of about 200 scientists to step up its efforts in chemical research, analytical research, product development research and clinical research to enter the regulated markets. Nectar is currently spending 3.88 per cent of its turnover on research and development.

Dabur Pharma

Dabur established Dabur Research Foundation, a premier research organization in 1979 with a clear focus on innovative products in the therapeutic segment of oncology, today more than 270 scientists are engaged in research and product development at Dabur. The center has developed strong capabilities in NDDS and NCE research that resulted in a robust pipeline of 16 novel anti-cancer molecules at various stages of development. The company developed a novel polymeric Nanoparticle delivery system that has the potential to become a super generic. Its NDDS formulation of paclitaxel is in a very advanced stage of clinical development. Another drug, which is at a very advanced stage of clinical development is its novel therapeutic product for adenocarcinomas, including cancers of the ovary, lung, colon, pancreas and breast.

DRF filed more than 350 patent applications worldwide with 120 patents granted. The company has invested about Rs. 269 million, which is 10 per cent of its turnover in FYE March 2006.

Ind-Swift Laboratories

Ind-Swift Laboratories invested over Rs. 478.5 million over the last five years in research and development. The company tied up with national institutes like NIPER (National Institute of Pharmaceutical Education and

Research), Chandigarh for facilitating an easy access to critical insights into process and product development. Further, it is setting up a Rs 250-million R&D center focused on developing generic products for regulated markets in Mohali, Punjab, India. Ind-Swift is the first generic company in the world to develop clarithromycin and roxithromycin granules. The company has a pipeline of 20 products that would go off patent between 2007 and 2010. The company's 85-member strong scientific team filed nine patents out of which one is granted so far.

Dishman Pharmaceuticals

Dishman Pharmaceuticals has an unique capability of offering a single-point contact for R&D - process development, and production outsourcing facility – a seamless flow of technology and production from discovery through clinical production to launch. The company's research activities can be broadly classified into four categories:

1. Contract research and process implementation of contract manufactured molecules
2. Pilot studies of new molecules for clients
3. Process optimization and improvement, and
4. Research for in-house applications.

Dishman focuses only on APIs and intermediates. The company is stepping up its research effort and has over 100 scientists. The company spent 11.4 per cent of sales at Rs. 245.1 million on R&D in FY 2006.

Natco Pharma

The resurgent Natco Pharma is sharpening its focus on research in therapeutic areas such as anti-migraine, anti-hypertensives, anti-depressants, anti-neoplastics, CNS, and G I disorders. The company also collaborated on some of the research projects with national institutes like CCMB and IICT. It also developed the capabilities of developing advanced intermediates for experimental drugs. Natco has an ANDA pipeline of 15 products of which two are filed. Its API product portfolio is 159 DMFs across the world (128 in Europe and 8 in the US filed). Eight more are under preparation at the end of FY2006.

The company has two molecules in oncology, which it is developing in association with Temple University in the US – NRC/An/015 and NRC/An/019 both of which are showing promise in combating myeloid leukemia. These two have successfully completed in vivo and in vitro studies and animal studies are ready for further studies. Natco is planning to file a IND soon for these two molecules.

Suven Life Sciences

Suven has metamorphosed itself from a contract manufacturer to drug discovery support services provider to drug discovery partnership with global Pharma majors. The company recently signed an agreement with Eli Lilly, one of the leading international Pharma companies to collaborate on pre-clinical research of molecules in the therapeutic areas of CNS disorders. Suven will receive milestone payments if the identified drug candidates are selected by Lilly for further development. About 190 scientists are working on the research programs at Suven. The company's R&D spend in FY 2006 was 26.59 per cent of its turnover.

Thirty-Companies – A Snapshot of R&D Focus

Research and development is the key competency for success in pharmaceutical industry. The thirty companies discussed in the book realize this more than others in Indian pharmaceutical industry. The combined R&D spend of all the thirty companies was Rs. 23.25 billion in FYE March 2006. The average R&D spend by these companies is about 7.5 per cent of sales, which is at least seven times more than the average spend on R&D by other companies in India. There seems to be a pecking order too clearly indicating the respective competitive space. Companies in Group 'A' competing for the innovation-led space accounted for close to two-thirds of the total R&D spend (65%) whereas companies in Group 'B' competing for the international generics space accounted for a little over one-fifth (21%) and companies in Group 'B' competing for the CRAMS space accounted for the rest (14%).

The total number of patents filed by these thirty companies is close to five thousand of which nearly a fourth are granted. These companies account for over 80 per cent of all progress made by the Indian pharmaceutical industry in creating intellectual property, be it patents, ANDAs, DMFs, brands of generic formulations, strategic alliances covering process and product development activities or the world class R&D infrastructure. The NCE pipeline of these thirty companies is over 40 compounds in various stages of clinical development phase. A snapshot of their progress, activities and achievements is presented in Table 9.16.

While all these moves and progress indicate the right direction, the one question keeps coming back to the skeptics is that is really possible to develop a blockbuster drug from India? After all, there are only two companies in India that have crossed the volume one billion dollars in annual sales, which is the cost of developing a single new drug from concept to commercialization. Is it a dream or is it really possible?

A Possible Dream!

Dr. Anji Reddy, Chairman of Dr. Reddy's Laboratories, is very confident, even inspiring when he talks of research and development. He believes that Indian companies will do well in the post GATT era. He says, "There have been many occasions when small companies have done outstanding research. So why can't we? Consider the classic example of Kyorin, a small Japanese company, which has discovered norfloxacin (anti-bacterial drug) in the mid eighties. And he adds rather prophetically:

> It is true that no Indian company is capable of taking an idea all the way up to the market, which involves an expenditure of hundreds of millions of dollars. But as Dr. Reddy's Labs have proved, it is within the realm of Indian industry to undertake pre-clinical research and license it out for upfront payments and royalties. Unless a handful of Indian pharmaceutical companies come forward to undertake this, even in the next 100 years, we will not see a 'Merck' or a 'Pfizer' from India.

Table 9.16 Thirty Companies - A Snapshot of R&D Focus

Group	R&D Investment, Focus and Capabilities	Intellectual Property	NCE Pipeline
'A' Ranbaxy, Dr. Reddy's Labs, Sun Pharma, Lupin, Nicholas Piramal, Zydus Cadila, Wockhardt, Biocon, Glenmark, and Torrent	The total R&D investment by the ten companies in the group is about 8.85 per cent (Rs. 15.6 billion) of their sales in FY 2006 as compared to the industry average of less than 2 per cent. The total number of research scientists in these ten companies is over 5,028.	The total number of patents filed by all the companies in the group are over 3,056 of which 769 are granted.	The total number of products under various stages of development by all the ten companies in this group are over 38 many of which are in either late preclinical or clinical development. This does not take into account the number of drug candidates in the early pre-clinical development.
'B Cipla, Aurobindo, Matrix, Orchid, Ipca, Alembic, Claris Life Sciences, J B Chemicals, Unichem, and Strides Arcolabs	The ten companies competing for the international generics space have invested Rs, 4.96 billion on R&D in FYE March 2006, which is approximately of a third of the companies in Group 'A'. The total number scientists engaged in the research and development activities are about 2,265. The research areas of focus are virtually common for all these companies indicating a very intense competition among themselves even in many of the international markets.	The total number of patents filed by all the companies in this group is close to one thousand of which 231 have been granted so far.	As all these companies are predominantly competing in the international generics space, and drug discovery is not their priority, J B Chemicals, however, has three molecules in pre-clinicals.

Group	R&D Investment, Focus and Capabilities	Intellectual Property	NCE Pipeline
'C' Jubilant Organosys, Divi's Labs, FDC, Shasun, Dabur, Ind-Swift, Dishman, Natco, and Suven Life Sciences	The total investment in research and development by all the companies in this group was about Rs. 3.13 billion in FYE March 2006. The total number of scientists involved in R& D activities of these ten companies are around 2,225 currently. Jubilant Organosys is competing in both international generics and CRAMS spaces. Almost all these companies are gearing up their infrastructure and enhancing their capabilities to be competitive across the CRAMS value chain.	The total number of patents filed by these ten companies are more than 546 while 141 are granted so far.	Many companies in this group are actively into custom research rather than discovery research as they have a long way to reach the critical mass required for NDDR. Two companies have about five compounds in late stage pre-clinical and one in clinical.

Chapter Ten

Global Mindset

There is more to the phrase-'internationalization', than mere semantics. The transition from exports to internationalization is not simple. It is an arduous journey, which requires determination and an uncompromising attitude. Above all it needs a change of mindset to view the world as a whole. The transition from an export-oriented company to an international company broadly involves five phases:

1. Domestic operations with some exports
2. Strongly export oriented
3. Regional operations with core domestic strengths
4. International operations with strong headquarter control
5. Global operations

Ranbaxy is one company that has been working hard to internationalize its operations. It started its exports in 1975 and has evolved as the first Indian multinational drug company through a well crafted strategy, matched by impeccable execution. Other leading Pharma companies like Dr. Reddy's Lupin, Wockhardt, Cipla and Sun too have been aggressively pursuing a course of internationalization. The degree of aggression of course varies from firm to firm.

The key success factors for an internationalization strategy are:

1. Creating, developing and upgrading to world class in manufacturing technology, product development, packaging and marketing.

2. Building manufacturing facilities that conform to international regulatory standards and getting them approved. Without these approvals, one cannot export formulations or bulk actives to the industrialized world which accounts for over 80 per cent of the total pharmaceutical market.
3. Reach a critical mass and economies of scale in time through whatever means it takes to achieve - brand, business or company acquisitions.
4. Collaborating to compete. Improving synergies and market and product access through strategic alliances. Convert entry barriers into gateways through joint ventures.
5. Formulating country-specific strategies.
6. Establishing manufacturing presence to improve market access and logistics.
7. Moving closer to customers by setting up regional operations across various countries.

Going global has become a catchphrase for many companies across industries worldwide and the pharmaceutical industry in India is no exception to this. The Indian drug industry has earned a net exporter status for over ten years now, mainly due to the spectacular effort by a handful of companies. The main reasons for this pursuit of the greener pastures abroad are:

- The market outside your home market is much larger, however big your domestic market might be.
- India for example accounts for just two per cent of the world pharmaceutical market in value terms and over 8 per cent of world production in terms of volume. The market is thus low priced and realizations are lower. In fact, even neighboring countries like Bangladesh, Pakistan and Sri Lanka have higher prices.
- The global market is higher priced and offers better realizations. Globalization, therefore, is the natural choice for any company that wants to expand in terms of value and volume.

- Drug industry is technology-driven and research intensive. Both technology and research need huge up front investments. Revenues and profits generated in the domestic markets are not adequate in funding to fuel growth.
- International operations enable an organization to develop world-class technological and marketing competence.

The Indian drug industry has come a long way from the status of a 'necessary evil' during the license raj of the early 1980s to the export-led growth stage in the early nineties and now towards internationalization of the business.

In the early eighties, exports were seen as unprofitable but necessary if one wanted an import license as they were linked. Ranbaxy was perhaps the first Indian pharmaceutical company, which thought otherwise; that exports could be profitable. After all, prices of pharmaceutical products were much higher all over the world. It is this winning mindset that has been responsible for keeping Ranbaxy ahead of other companies in India since the late 1980s.

What separates the thirty companies under our study from the rest of the companies in Indian pharmaceutical industry is that they are all following a well crafted strategy of internationalizing their respective businesses. The total revenues from international operations of these thirty companies in FYE March 2006 was over a whopping Rs. 162 billion. All these companies are at various stages or phases of the internationalization process depending on their chosen competitive spaces. What is common among all their strategies is that each company would like to achieve over fifty per cent of their sales from overseas markets within two to three years. Some of them have already achieved more than this. Let us briefly examine their game plans for international markets.

Group A' Companies – International Operations

Four of the ten companies in Group 'A' have over fifty per cent of their revenues generated from international markets. The rest of the six companies too are aiming to generate more than one-half of their revenues from international markets. All the ten companies in Group A' have built world-class manufacturing and R&D infrastructure to remain competitive. Every one of these companies have their facilities approved by leading international regulatory authorities which is mandatory for exporting to regulated markets. The companies in this group account for maximum number of ANDA (over 540) and DMF filings with US FDA as compared to the filings by pharmaceutical companies from any other country.

Table 10.1 Group 'A' Companies : International Sales

Company	Rs. Billion	Contribution to Total Sales (%)
1. Ranbaxy	38.77	76.00
2. Dr. Reddy's Laboratories	16.03	66.00
3. Sun Pharma	6.95	38.48
4. Lupin	7.63	46.00
5. Nicholas Piramal	3.38	21.40
6. Zydus Cadila Healthcare	2.24	14.86
7. Wockhardt	8.88	63.00
8. Biocon	3.57	52.00
9. Glenmark	3.18	42.00
10. Torrent Pharma	4.19	45.00

Ranbaxy

Ranbaxy decided to export in 1975–76. The company has never looked back since then. Today in 2006 about 76 per cent of their sales come from their international operations. How did Ranbaxy achieve what it did? By focusing. Through a well defined strategy. Above all by effectively implementing it.

Ranbaxy wanted to be an international company that stands on its feet against stiff competition in overseas markets. The only way to achieve this was through building competitive advantages both in terms of strategy and implementation. The key elements of Ranbaxy's internationalization strategy are:

- Developing and upgrading to world class level in manufacturing technology, product development, packaging and marketing.
- Creating and building infrastructure that support the strategy. In other words, building manufacturing facilities conforming to international standards and getting them approved by international regulatory authorities for both pharmaceutical substances and dosage forms.
- Reaching the critical mass and economies of scale through acquisition of brands, businesses and companies that fit into the overall game plan of the company.
- Improving synergies and market access to difficult-to-penetrate markets through joint ventures.
- Formulating country-specific strategies.
- Establishing manufacturing presence to improve market access and logistics.
- Moving closer to customers by setting up regional operations across various countries.
- Moving closer to customers by setting up regional operations across various countries.

Ranbaxy had set its sights on the global market way ahead of its peers in the Indian drug industry. The company had taken an approach to exports in the late 1970s that is significantly different from what was then prevalent in the industry. While the industry was convinced that exports were not profitable (as they had to be done on a marginal costing basis), Ranbaxy thought otherwise. The company had seen, much before the others, that exports could be profitable as price realizations in international markets for pharmaceutical products are much higher.

Ranbaxy has always been ahead of the competition by continuously revitalizing its strategy. Today, the company has achieved the distinction of being one of the major international generic companies with a turnover of close to two billion dollars. There is no other company except for perhaps

Teva, an Israeli company the numero uno of the world's generic drug industry, that has a presence in as many markets as Ranbaxy. Further, it has a distinct competitive advantage over many overseas generic companies. It is one of the most integrated generic companies in the world.

Many overseas generic companies out source their bulk drug requirements, whereas Ranbaxy is vertically integrated and can use its low-cost API manufacturing base in India for generic launches overseas. The fact is that if you control bulk, you also control cost, quality and availability. Ranbaxy, therefore, is likely to derive more value addition than its peers in the US generic markets, as it controls costs throughout the value chain.

Ranbaxy has become a top-ten global generic player with a growing presence in 23 of the top 25 markets. The company is among the largest ANDA filers with US FDA. The cumulative ANDA filings of Ranbaxy are 170 (including 10 ARVs under PEPFAR) making it the second largest pipeline in the US, the world's largest generics market. U S contributed to 28 per cent of the company's total sales at $ 328 million in FY 2006. Ranbaxy competes in three market segments in the US – generic pharmaceuticals, Private label, OTC formulations and Ranbaxy Labeled products. The company improved its market share in the covered market of generic pharmaceuticals in the US to 13.9 per cent during the year.

The company has also commenced operations in Canada, the eighth largest Pharma market in the world with the introduction of eight products. Eight more products are in the pipeline for the Canadian market. In Mexico, the company registered 45 products during the year.

The company is also pursuing the generics market in the European Union aggressively. Europe contributed 17 per cent of its turnover at US $ 204 million. The company has two Day-1 launches of sertraline and lansoprazole in the U K representing a market size of US $ 430 million at innovator prices in 2005. The company extended its product portfolio with the launch of 12 new products including two Day-1 launches of simvastatin and sertraline in France during the year leading to 100 per cent coverage of the top 20 molecules. Ranbaxy is present in 21 of the top 25 E U countries and expanded its presence by starting wholly owned subsidiaries in Hungary, Portugal, Italy and a representative office in Bulgaria. The company moved up to the 30th position in the generic segment in Germany and had two Day-1 launches of cefpodoxime and sertraline. The company improved its overall position in the EU through some strategic acquisitions – Terapia, the largest independent generic company in Romania, Ethimed, an established generic company in Belgium, a large un-branded generic product portfolio of Allen S.p.A in Italy, and 18 generic products from a leading Pharma company in Spain.

Ranbaxy is ranked seventh among generic companies and is placed at 29th position among pharmaceutical companies in South Africa with sales of US $ 24 million during the year. In Brazil Ranbaxy is the fifth largest generic player. Ranbaxy is one of the very few vertically integrated international generic pharmaceutical companies. The global sales of the top ten molecules of the company were over US $ 405 million in FY ending in December 2005. Sales from International markets contributed 76 per cent to the total turnover of the company during the same period. The region-wise break-up (Table 10.2.) of the company's revenues indicates its international character.

Table 10.2 Ranbaxy's International Sales

Region	FYE December 2005 Sales in US $ (Million)
US	328.00
India	222.00
European Union	204.00
Africa	68.00
CIS	65.00
Latin America	40.00
South Africa	24.00
The Middle East	15.80
China	14.60
Malaysia	14.00
Thailand	8.00

Dr. Reddy's Labs

About two-thirds of total sales of Dr. Reddy's Labs are from their international operations making the company truly an international Pharma company.

The company has a reasonable presence that is growing steadily with each passing year in the US, the world's largest generics market. The key driver is having a critical mass of product-mix. Dr. Reddy's have filed a total of 70 ANDAs of which 21 are approved. They have 49 ANDAs pending approval with US FDA, which includes 29 Para IV filings. In APIs too, the company has a pipeline of 81 cumulative DMFs in the US, 42 in Europe and 28 in Canada. The company's recent acquisition of Roche's Mexican plant gives instant access to major customers, products and markets beefing up its Custom Pharmaceuticals Services business. The betapharam acquisition in Germany, and the products acquisition in Spain strengthened its presence in Europe.

Dr. Reddy's entered into an agreement with the global Pharma major, Merck to sell the authorized generic versions of their brands - Zocor, and Proscar if the 180-day marketing exclusivity is granted to the first filer on either product.

International sales contributed to two-thirds of the total company's revenues with Europe accounting for 18 per cent, US 16 per cent, Rest of the World 17 per cent and India 34 per cent.

Sun Pharma

Sun Pharma is increasingly recognized as an international company in 26 markets across South East Asia, Russia, China, The Middle East, and Africa where it has a trained field force of 250 in addition to agents' representatives. International sales contributed to about 38.5 per cent of the company's turnover in FY2006 with a total of 740 products marketed in 26 countries. The company has commenced operations in countries like Mexico, Brazil, Peru, and Columbia in FY 2006.

The company's US subsidiary, Caraco in the US recorded $ 82.5 million in FY 2006 with 21 products. Forty-four ANDAs are pending approval with the US FDA and these include some Para IV filings. Sun Pharma's acquisition of ICN in Hungary enabled the company to enter the controlled substance API manufacturing space, one of the few sites in the world with approvals for such products. The company has a war chest of US $ 450 million for international acquisitions.

Sun Pharma has currently built capabilities and capacities to scale up 20 APIs, and file 8-10 DMFs and 8-10 ANDAs per year. The company has already a strong pipeline of over 100 APIs across various therapeutic categories.

Lupin

Lupin is beefing up its international marketing operations through a market-specific mix of strategies. The company has its marketing team in key international markets to promote its products directly. In addition, the company also entered into some of the leading international generic companies such as Baxter, and Henry Schein in the US to distribute its select products exclusively to the US Hospital segment and Physician Office segment respectively. Lupin launched 7 generic formulations and filed 18 ANDAs in FY 2006.

In the US Lupin has a focused team of 50 national pediatric force to promote its branded generic formulation - Suprax- (cefixime) and Atopiclair- (a non-steriodal cream to pediatric patients for relieving atopic dermatitis and allergic contact dermatitits).

In CIS markets, Lupin has a dedicated team of 80 people to promote its products in countries such as Russia, Belarus, Ukraine, Kazakhstan, Uzbekistan and Azerbaijan. In Asia, Africa, Middle East, and Latin America the company adopts a strategy of entering into alliances, JVs, and synergistic partnerships with some of the leading players in the respective markets. In addition, the company is capitalizing on its R&D strengths to enter Japan, Australia, Mexico and Brazil.

Nicholas Piramal

Exports contributed to a little over a fifth (21.4 per cent) of the total company's sales in FY 2006. The company is focusing on custom manufacturing space for global markets and has emerged as one of the top ten custom manufacturing service companies in the world with total revenues of about US $ 250 million of which US $ 100 million are from formulation development and manufacturing services. The company's recent acquisitions of Avecia in UK, and Pfizer's manufacturing site at Morpeth, UK have further consolidated its position as one of the leading

CRAMS players in the world. The company is launching its integrated formulation services from pre-clinical formulations to launch commercial formulations in regulated markets such as North America, Europe and hopes to be among the top-three players in the world in CRAMS space.

Zydus

Zydus Cadila Health Care built a robust regulatory pipeline, filed total 25 ANDAs and 40 DMFs with the US FDA in a short span of three years. The company has already received approvals for 12 ANDAs turning its US operations profitable in the very first year. Zydus has achieved this by an immaculate execution of a multi-pronged strategy. The company marketed its products in alliance with Mallinckrodt, the seventh largest generic player in the US under the joint label 'ZyPharma.' The Company, in addition extended its reach by servicing select customers directly under the label 'ZyGenerics.' Zydus plans to launch 10-12 products this year and plans to triple its top line.

The focus of Zydus in France is on pure generics business to drive growth. The company sold the branded business of Zydus France SAS to Aerocid of France for € 7 million, which it acquired from Alpharma, France for € 3.7 million. The deal with Evolupharm in France gives Zydus an instant access to a network of 2,250 pharmacies. The company launched 76 generic presentations in France till FYE 2006 including three blockbuster products - simvastatin, omeprazole and sertraline.

In Brazil, Zydus launched its products through its subsidiary Zydus Healthcare Brasil Limitada and so far filed 23 pure and branded generics dossiers so far. The company launched four products so far and is planning to launch eight more this year with Venture Pharm as its marketing partner. The company's global contract manufacturing operations earned Rs. 500 million this year. Zydus has signed 11 contracts with innovator and generic companies with a peak revenue potential of $ 23.6 million.

Although international sales contributed only 14.85 per cent during FY 2006, the company is bullish on international sales and aggressively pursuing an expansion strategy both in terms of products as well as markets.

Wockhardt

European Union is the single biggest region for Wockhardt and it accounts for over forty per cent of its total sales while the US and the Rest of the World contributed eleven per cent each. Wockhardt UK is amongst the top ten generic companies in the UK. The company has two first-day launches (on the first day of patent expiration) – generic version of terbenafine in the UK and lamotrigene generic formulation in Germany through its subsidiary, Esparma GmbH. Wockhardt is pursuing an aggressive strategy for the US generics market too. The company has eleven ANDAs approved by the US FDA. Wockhardt has also filed 16 ANDAs in FY 2006 nine of which are for injectables. The company is exploring ways to increase its presence in five regions for rapid growth in the years to come – South East Asia, Asia Pacific, Middle East, South America and Africa.

Wockhardt is building a war chest of $ 800 million for strategic acquisitions in the US and Europe to achieve even a faster growth in international markets.

Biocon

Exports (Rs. 3.58 billion) accounted for 58.2 per cent of Biocon's sales during FY 2006. The company currently exports simvastatin to Europe, Japan, Canada and pravastatin to the European markets. Biocon is currently exporting mycophenolate mofetil (MMF), sirolimus and tacromus to semi-regulated markets and recently filed a DMF for these products with the US FDA.

Glenmark

Exports and international sales contributed to about 42 per cent of Glenmark's total turnover in FY 2006. The company exports and markets branded generic and generic formulations in 70 countries and APIs in 45 countries across the globe. Glenmark has so far filed 491 dossiers internationally and received 151 approvals.

Glenmark's focus is on regulated markets. The company's strategy covers all possible options for accelerated growth such as co-development, in-licensing and out-licensing. Glenmark is filing ANDAs aggressively and has filed so far 38 ANDAS with US FDA. The company is planning to file

15-20 more ANDAs in FY 2007. Glenmark has entered into a strategic alliance with Merck Generics for developing eight generic formulations in the dermatology segment for European market where both the companies will market the products once approved. The company has also entered into another agreement with Lehigh Technologies Inc. for marketing seven products in the US market. Lehigh Technologies would develop, manufacture and register the generic formulations under the Glenmark name to be marketed by Glenmark exclusively in the US. These include controlled substances for which the competition is rather very limited.

The company has been strengthening its presence in the LATAM region through the acquisition route and has acquired two companies – one in Brazil and another in Argentina in the last two years. It has filed 19 dossiers and is planning 8-10 more this year.

Geographical region-wise contributions of international sales to total sales of Glenmark at the end of December 2006 are presented in Figure. 10.1.

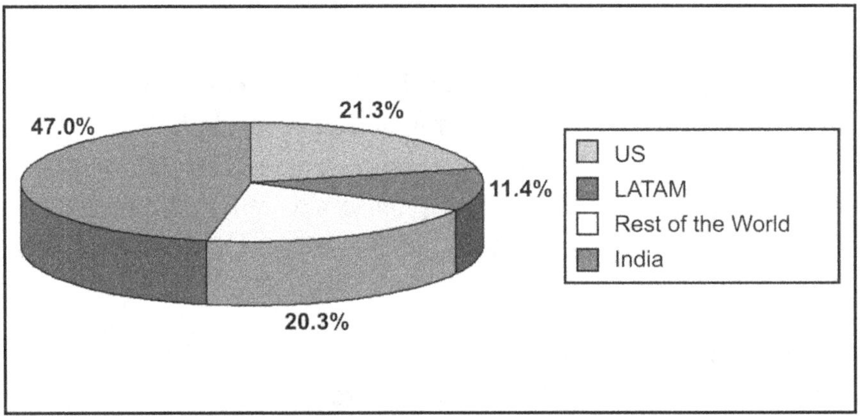

Figure 10.1 Glenmark's International Sales

Torrent

International sales of Torrent grew by 45 per cent and contributed to (including the consolidated sales of its German subsidiary, Heumann) about 45 per cent of its total turnover. These comprised branded generics, unbranded generics and APIs. The region-wise breakup of the company's international sales is presented in Figure 10.2.

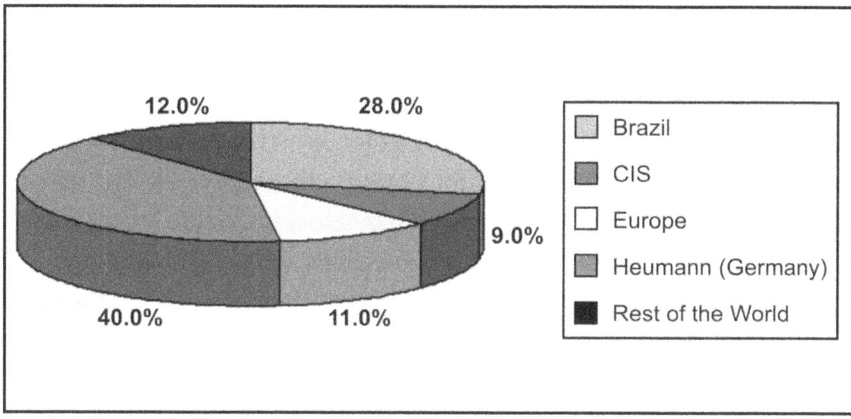

Figure 10.2 Torrent's International Sales

Group 'B' Companies – International Operations

The total exports from the ten companies in Group 'B' during the FY 2006 were over Rs. 51.04 billion. Seven out of these ten companies earned one-half of their total revenues from exports. Cipla and Aurobindo lead the pack in terms of total exports sales. Aurobindo has one of the largest product portfolios in both APIs as well as ANDAs. All the companies have either already forged alliances with international generic players or in the process of forming tie-ups for marketing their products in the regulated markets.

Table 10.3 Group 'B' Companies : International Sales

Company	Rs. Billion	Contribution to Total Sales (%)
1. Cipla	15.15	48.13
2. Aurobindo Pharma	8.27	55.06
3. Matrix Laboratories	8.45	72.90
4. Orchid	6.76	76.12
5. Ipca Laboratories	4.01	53.25
6. Alembic	1.23	18.49
7. Claris Life Sciences*	2.00	50.00
8. J.B.Chemicals	0.91	19.00
9. Unichem Laboratories	0.93	19.62
10. Strides Arcolabs	3.33	95.00

* Approximate figures as per the company's website

Cipla

Cipla exports APIs and Formulations nearly to 170 countries across the world. The company filed over 80 DMFs in the US and over 60 DMFs in Europe. In addition, Cipla as a part of its focus on regulated markets has entered into partnerships with eight leading international generic players for 140 ANDA projects. It has received regulatory approvals for marketing salbutamol MDIs in Denmark, and budesonide inhalers in Germany and Portugal. Further nine additional inhaler products are in various stages of regulatory submissions. The company is initiating clinical trials on multi-dose DPIs for the European markets. Cipla has established strategic partnerships for other important international markets across the globe and has registered over 4,000 products in various countries.

Exports contributed to Rs. 15.6 billion, which is fifty per cent of the company's total turnover in FY 2006. Here are the details of its exports region-wise (Figure 10.3).

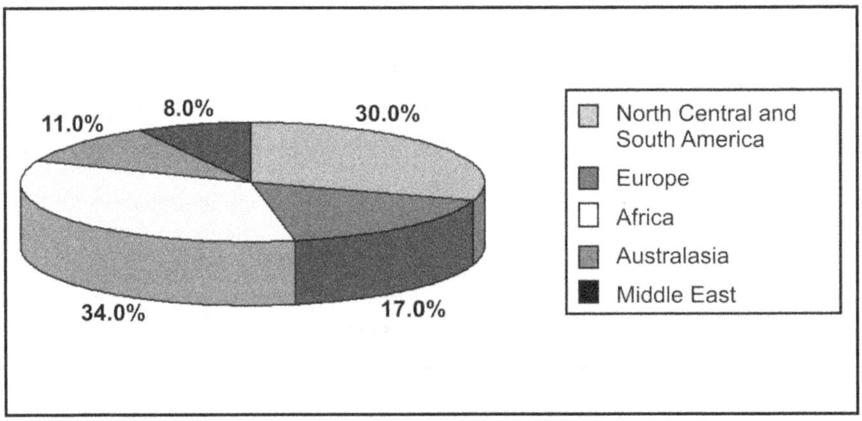

Figure 10.3 Cipla's Exports

Aurobindo Pharma

Aurobindo exports its products to over one hundred countries across the world. International sales contribute approximately one-half of its total sales. The company has till date filed over 337 DMFs of which 102 are with US FDA, 133 in European Union including EQDM and 102 in other countries. This is one of the highest filings in the industry. Aurobindo is also active on the formulation front and has filed significant number of ANDAs – 75 with

US FDA, 26 in European Union and received approvals for 35 from US FDA and 5 from UK MHRA and one from EQDM.

Aurobindo has geared up on the ARV segment and received approval for 18 products under PEPFAR. The company has also registered its ARV products with WHO and in other countries like South Africa.

Matrix Laboratories

Matrix enhanced its exposure in the high-margin regulated markets and entered into long-term supply contracts. Exports contributed to about 73 per cent of its total sales in FY 2006. Europe is the single biggest market for matrix contributing almost fifty per cent of its total sales. The region-wise break up is presented in Figure 10.4.

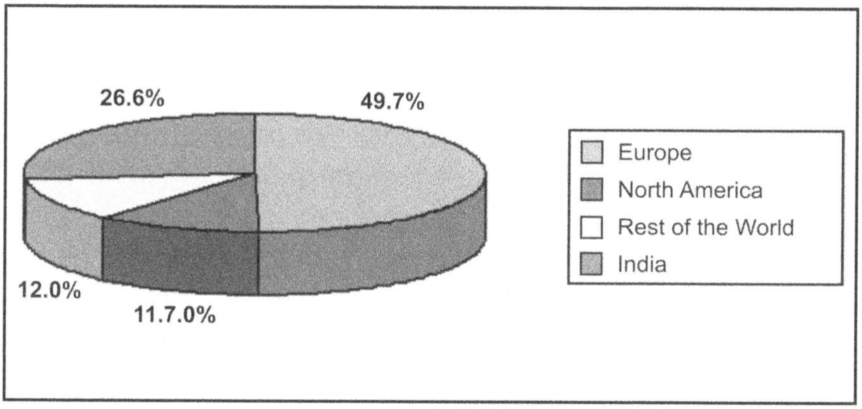

Figure 10.4 Matrix - Region-wise sales

Orchid

Orchid has undergone a mammoth strategic transformation that expanded the scope and scale of its business with a focus on the FDF and its business from an API supplier to FDF developer, manufacturer, CRAMS player and an NCE developer. The company's main focus is on regulated markets and has filed 30 DMFs and 25 ANDAs with US FDA. The company is also expanding into non-penicillin and non-cephalosporin product space with the filing of 5 DMFS and 2 ANDAs in the US. Orchid has one of the largest portfolios in the antibiotics domain among the global generic players with 25 DMFs and 23 ANDAs with US FDA.

The company's strategy is to develop products and look for appropriate partners for the front-end marketing through distribution alliances. Orchid has tied up with global distribution majors such as Apotex Inc, Apotex Corp, Par Pharmaceuticals Inc, Actavis, Stada, IVX and Mayne Pharmaceuticals for distributing 41 products (21 antibiotics and 20 NPNC products) in the US, Europe and other regulated markets.

Over three-fourths (Rs. 6.96 billion) of Orchid's total sales are from international markets. Orchid exports APIs to regulated markets such as US, Canada, and Europe and formulations to 28 countries. The company has over 305 product registrations and entered new markets such as Malaysia, Brazil, Sudan, UAE, and GCC countries.

IPCA

Ipca exports its products – both APIs and generic formulations to over 100 countries across the world. Exports contributed to over one-half of its turnover (53.25 per cent) in FY 2006. The company developed 36 generic formulations dossiers for registration in UK out of which 12 are already registered. Twenty-five more generic formulations are under various stages of development for the European market. Ipca mainly exports APIs to USA, Canada and Latin America and formulations to Panama, Brazil and West Indies. The company's wholly owned subsidiary in the US is coordinating generic drug registration activities and filed 3 ANDAs for which it holds DMFs in the US. The company has also singed agreement with a marketing partner for the distribution of generic formulations in the US on a profit sharing basis.

Ipca markets branded generic formulations through its own field force in Russia, Ukraine, Kazakhstan and a number of countries in Africa such as Uganda, Sudan, Tanzania, Kenya and Nigeria. The company is expanding both geographically and product-mix-wise in CIS region. The company exports formulations and APIs in Asia to countries like Sri Lanka, Myanmar, and Vietnam. Ipca markets its range of branded generic formulations through dedicated field force. In the final quarter of the FY 2006 Ipca began exporting formulations to Australia. It has registered 4 generic dossiers in Australia. Here is the geographical region-wise breakup of Ipca's exports (Table 10.4)

Table 10.4 Ipca's Exports

Region	Exports (Rs. Million)	Contribution (%)
Europe	174.4	43.40
Americas	46.79	11.64
CIS	57.45	14.30
Asia	49.67	12.36
Africa	62.75	15.62
Australasia	10.77	2.68

Alembic

Alembic is redefining its game plans for the WTO era. The highlights of its competitive strategy are:

- Introducing NDDS for existing molecules
- Rational combinations of existing products
- In-licensing of products
- Launching of non-IPR products like nutraceuticals
- Co-marketing opportunities
- Co-development of APIs, FDFs and NCEs

Till now Alembic has been focusing for its generic and branded generic formulations on markets such as Russia, Ukraine, Nigeria, Tanazania, Keny, Vietnam, Myanmar and European traders. The company is now focusing on regulated markets and filed 8 DMFs with US FDA and is gearing itself to file a minimum of 5-6 DMFs every year from now. Exports of formulations and APIs contributed about 18.5 per cent in FY 2006 to the company's total sales.

Claris Life Sciences

Claris Life Sciences has a presence in more than seventy countries across North, Central and South Americas, Europe, China, CIS, Asia Pacific, Africa through its own sales force and local teams. Exports contributed to one half of its total sales in FY2006. The company has filed 9 ANDAs with US FDA and 40 MAAs in Europe and Australia.

J B Chemicals

Exports contributed to 57 per cent of the total revenues of J B Chemicals in FY 2006. The company entered the new markets such as Ivory Coast, Peru, and Venezuela during the year. J B chemicals has a strong presence in Sri Lanka, South East Asia, and Africa with its branded generic formulations. It is among the top-twenty companies in Sri Lanka, Vietnam and Thailand. The company is sharpening its focus on the regulated markets and commenced the shipment of ciprofloxacin tablets, its maiden FDF export to the US during the year. It has entered into a marketing alliance with Lannet Company Inc. USA to market its generic formulations through Neo JB LLC (a J V between J B Chemicals and Spectrum Pharmaceuticals Limited).

Unichem Laboratories

Exports earned Rs. 935 million and contributed to about a fifth (19.62%) of Unichem's total sales in FY 2006. The company has so far filed 690 dossiers and received approvals for 377 in over twenty-five countries that it is exporting. The company is increasing its focus on regulated markets and has filed its maiden ANDA and entered into a development and marketing alliance with two generic companies in the US, Pliva Inc, and Lannet Company for marketing generic formulations under joint labels. Unichem has eleven product registrations in South Africa and two products in Brazil through its wholly owned subsidiaries.

Strides Arcolabs

The Strides strategy is to avoid front-end marketing activity and partner instead with strong players in the respective regions for marketing in all the fifty countries that it is making rapid strides. South and Central Americas contribute about 36 per cent of its total sales. Exports accounted for over 95 per cent of Strides' total sales in FY 2006. The company follows a differentiated strategy based on its distinctive competence in all of its export markets. Here is sneak preview of its winning moves:

- Supply retail and hospital generics in niche injectable products and softgels

- Development and long-term supply arrangements in Europe
- Supply of softgel products and high value added manufacturing for leading Australian Pharma companies
- Forging alliances with a reputed MNC as a contract manufacturing partner to support their initiatives to provide free treatment to the poor TB patients as part of WHO's 'Stop TB Programs'

Group 'C' Companies - International Operations

Six out of the ten companies in Group 'C' competing in the CRAMS segment earn more than half of their total revenues from overseas markets. The total value of exports by the ten companies in this group was Rs. 18.38 billion during FY 2006. Every one of these companies is sharpening their focus on the regulated markets. All of them are upgrading themselves in every which way they can to become globally competitive and more importantly to remain across the Pharma Value Chain. Many of them have formed strategic alliances with the global Pharma majors for long-term supply of APIs, intermediates and FDFs through out the product life cycle.

Table 10.5 Group 'C' Companies : International Sales

	Company	Rs. Billion	Contribution to Total Sales (%)
1.	Jubilant Organosys	5.19	76.00
2.	Divi's Labs	3.52	90.00
3.	FDC	0.81	21.48
4.	Shasun Chemicals	2.23	64.00
5.	Nectar Life Sciences	0.87	28.00
6.	Dabur Pharma	1.17	43.51
7.	Ind-Swift	1.61	50.00
8.	Dishman Pharmaceuticals	1.64	75.92
9.	Natco Pharma	0.80	38.67
10.	Suven Pharma	0.64	77.11

Jubilant Organosys

International markets especially regulated markets are the key drivers of growth for the Pharma business of Jubilant Organosys. International business contributed 76 per cent of the company's net sales in FY 2006. Sales to the regulated markets of North America, Europe and Japan contributed 51 per cent, and sales to China contributed 20.7 per cent.

Jubilant Organosys is strengthening its presence across the value chain during the year by entering the generic pharmaceutical market of the US through the acquisition of Trinity Laboratories Inc. (rechristened as Trigen Laboratories Inc) and its wholly owned subsidiary (renamed Jubilant Pharmaceuticals Inc) has US FDA approval for oral solid dosage forms manufacturing facility at Maryland, USA. In pursuant with its strategic vision, the company through its subsidiary Jubilant Biosys entered in one of its kind deal acquired 100 per cent equity in the US-based clinical research organization, Target Research Associates Inc (renamed Clinisys Inc). This strategic acquisition provides the company strong customer relationships with large global Pharma companies and helps optimally utilize the strengths in the area of clinical research and clinical data management.

Divi's Labs

Divi's Labs is an export-driven company. Exports constituted to 90 per cent of its total sales in FY 2006. The company is constantly working towards enhancing its business to advanced markets. Here's the break up of its region-wise contribution (Figure 10.5):

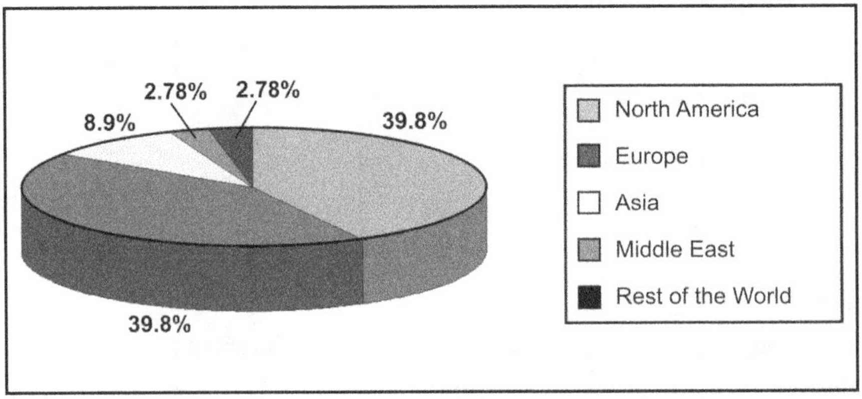

Figure 10.5 Divi's International Sales

FDC Limited

FDC is increasing its focus on international markets and expanded its formulation exports to 97 countries. Exports earned Rs. 800 million and contributed to 21.48 per cent to its total sales in FY 2006. With over 300 product registrations in place across the Americas, CIS, Africa, Asia and the EU, FDC is sharpening its competitive edge for the product patent era.

FDC has filed 10 ANDAs with US FDA and entered into a marketing alliance with Akorn Inc. for marketing its products in the US. The company has four products registered in the European Union. In addition, FDC is a preferred supplier to global customers including non-profit organizations like UNICEF, IDA, MSF, and PSI.

Shasun Chemicals

Shasun's existing presence in New Jersey and London with the addition of marketing team of Shasun Pharma Solutions Limited, has enhanced the competitiveness of the company. Shasun has been able to enhance the share from its existing customers and also add 15 new customers during the FY 2006. Top ten customers contribute to over 60 per cent of the sales. The company's customer list reads like a who's who list of the global Pharma industry with companies like Aventis, Boots, Eli Lilly and GSK among others. Shasun has entered into strategic alliances with Alpharma Inc. US (now a part of Actavis Group) and Glenmark USA Inc for marketing select generic formulations in CNS and cardiovascular therapeutic categories.

Exports contributed to 74 per cent of Shasun's sales in FY 2006.

Nectar Life Sciences

Nectar Life Sciences currently exports to over 70 countries across five continents which comprise China, Korea, Hong Kong, South East Asia, Eastern Europe, Syria, Jordan, Egypt, Pakistan, Bangladesh, and to certain countries in Africa and South America. Sales from international markets contributed to over 28 per cent of its net sales in FY 2006. The company is planning to enter regulated markets with an aggressive strategy of filing DMFs.

Dabur Pharma

Dabur has clearly focused on the global oncology market. The company is already recognized as the Number One Oncology generics player in Thailand, Malaysia, and Philippines. International sales at Rs 1.17 billion contributed to about 44 per cent of total sales in FY 2006. APIs constituted 44 per cent of international business. Dabur has registered 45 oncology products in over 40 countries – LATAM (14 countries), Africa (8 countries), Europe (2 countries), CIS (5 countries), Asia Pacific (11 countries), Australia and New Zea Land. Dabur is concentrating on the regulated markets and has an exclusive alliance with Hospira (a company spun-off from Abbott Hospital Products) for the US market for marketing 15 oncology products in the US. The company has already filed 3 ANDAs in the US and all the three are vertically integrated.

Ind-Swift Laboratories

Ind-Swift is the second largest manufacturer of clarithromycin, an antibiotic API in the world. The company forged alliances with reputed international pharmaceutical companies in the US, UK, Germany, Spain and Greece, and Mexico for servicing their requirements of four major products - clarithromycin, fexofenadine, atorvastatin, and clopidogrel exclusively once they go off patent. The company has in its portfolio of APIs eight of the top twenty blockbusters with a market size of US $ 25 billion. Ind-swift has successfully completed the US FDA inspection for its clartithromycin manufacturing facility towards the end of 2006. Exports currently contribute Rs 1.61 billion, which is about fifty per cent of the company's turnover. The company is all set to start sales and marketing operations in the major pharmaceutical markets of over 30 countries in the regions of Africa, CIS, Asia and Latin America in FY 2007.

Dishman Pharmaceuticals

Over three-quarters of Dishman's total revenues were from exports in FY 2006. The company is strengthening its competitive quotient as the US FDA inspection is successfully completed for its Bavla facility which is a 100 per cent EOU to manufacture eposartan mesylate, an anti-hypertensive drug to be supplied to Solvay Pharmaceuticals BV, a Fortune 500 company. Dishman is one of the two companies in the world with whom Solvay has entered into a long-term supply agreement of newly developed molecule whose patent is due to expire in 2013.

Natco Pharma

Exports contributed to about 39 per cent of the total sales of Natco Pharma in FY 2006. Natco has established itself as a reliable contract manufacturer in India and is now pursuing aggressively international markets. The company is planning to register its products in countries such as Ukraine, Cambodia, Vietnam, Myanmar and Sri Lanka in 2007. Natco is focusing on regulated markets particularly the US generics market and has tied up with a US-based company to commercialize two ANDA injectable products – one in each – anti-emetic and anti-cancer therapeutic segments. The combined market size for both these products is currently around US $ 875 million. Natco is following a strategy for the US market that is significantly different from many generic players. It has acquired a retail pharmacy - Nick's Drugs in New Jersey, which has an annual revenue US $ 22 million. The company is planning some more acquisitions in the retail route and would like to market its generic products directly through these stores when approved.

Suven Pharma

Suven's export turnover virtually doubled to Rs. 636.98 million (94 per cent growth over the previous year) in FY 2006. Income from international markets accounted for over 77 per cent of total sales. Here is the region-wise break-up (Figure 10.6):

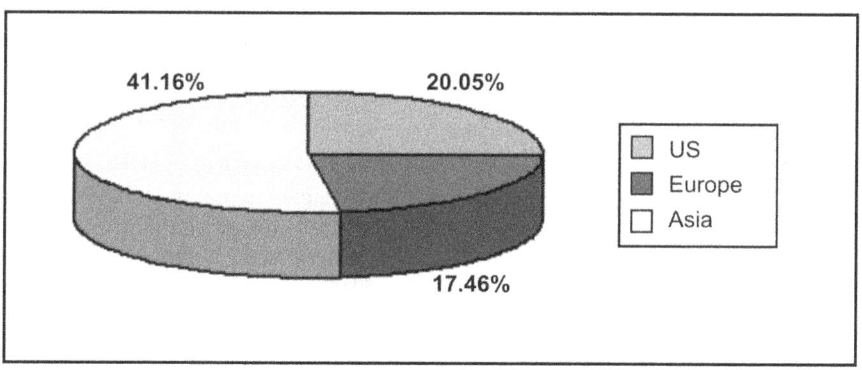

Figure 10.6 Suven's Exports

Thirty-Companies – A Snapshot of International Operations

The total sales of all the thirty companies from international markets was about Rs 164.24 billion which contributed 53.25 per cent to their total revenues of Rs. 308.44 billion in FY 2006. When you compare this with the total exports of Rs. 210 billion by the Indian pharmaceutical industry during FY 2006, the dominance of these thirty companies and the significance of their contribution to the progress of the Pharma sector in India becomes evident. The sales of these companies include the consolidated sales of their international subsidiaries and therefore cannot be considered as exports from India. Even without taking into account the consolidated sales of their wholly owned subsidiaries in international markets these thirty companies account for over fifty per cent of the total exports of pharmaceuticals from India. A snapshot of their presence in international markets and their contribution to exports is presented in Table 10.5.

Table 10.5 Thirty-companies - A Snapshot of International Operations

Group	Sales from International Markets	Extent of Internationalization
A Ranbaxy, Dr. Reddy's Labs, Sun Pharma, Lupin, Nicholas Piramal, Zydus Cadila, Wockhardt, Biocon, Glenmark and Torrent	Total sales value from internation markets of all the ten companies In FY 2006 was Rs. 94.82 billion. 53.45 per cent of the total sales of the group as a whole was from international markets in FY 2006	Six of the ten companies have manufacturing facilities in some of the major international markets. Ranbaxy is the most internationalized of all the companies with manufacturing facilities in six countries. All the ten companies have international acquisitions in some form or the other. Seven of these ten companies have their own marketing teams promoting their branded generics and generic formulations in select international markets. The companies in the group either export to or have their operations in over 170 countries across the globe.

Group	Sales from International Markets	Extent of Internationalization
B Cipla, Aurobindo, Matrix, Orchid, Ipca, Alembic, Claris Life Sciences, J B Chemicals, Unichem, and Strides Arcolabs	Total sales value of all the ten companies. from overseas markets in FY 2006 was R.51.04 billion. 51.65 per cent of the total sales of the group as a whole was from international markets in FY 2006	The first five companies in the group have significant presence in international markets and are keen contenders to be among the leading international generic companies in the foreseeable future. Matrix, which is now a part of the international generic major Mylan Laboratories is already there, although not entirely by itself. Cipla has the widest market coverage exporting to over 170 countries across the five continents its APIs and generic formulations. Close on heels is Aurobindo with probably one of the biggest portfolios of APIs and ANDAs among international generic players with an ever-increasing presence in regulated markets.
C Jubilant Organosys, Divi's Labs, FDC, Shasun, Nectar Life Sciences, Dabur Pharma, Ind-Swift Laboratories, Dishman Pharmaceuticals, Natco Pharma, and Suven Life Sciences.	Total sales value of all the ten companies from overseas markets in FY 2006 was Rs. 18.38 billion. 57.03 per cent of the total sales of the group as a whole was from international markets in FY 2006.	Six out of the ten companies in the group focus clearly on the CRAMS space. Dabur is competing in international generics space and drug discovery space as well with a clear focus on oncology segment. Jubilant Organosys, the biggest player in the group is aggressively pursuing a strategy of competing in CRAMS space by builiding up competencies across the Pharma value chain including clinical research and clinical data management. Divi's laboratories, and Shasun are striving to be perhaps the most preferred partner for innovator companies across the Pharma Value Chain. Suven Life Sciences, although the smallest in terms of present turnover is very big on dreams. The company's recent strategic alliance with the international drug major, Eli Lilly in the co-development of NCEs in Neurology segment belies its small size.

Common Thread

What are the common factors in the strategies for internationalization of all these leading Indian pharmaceutical companies? Virtually all these companies are keenly pursuing a strategy of progressing from export of bulk actives and intermediates to exports of more value added formulations. The strategic objective of each of these firms, which are preparing themselves to effectively compete in the post-GATT era, is to become an integrated, international generic firm. On closer examination, it is clear that Ranbaxy has been the role model for most of these companies, in terms of strategy. The evolutionary process of some of the leading Indian drug firms in internationalizing their businesses seems to have a common pattern. The steps or the milestones in this evolutionary process are:

1. Exports of bulk drugs to developing countries.
2. Exports of generic formulations to third world countries.
3. Exports of bulk drugs and intermediates to developed countries.
4. Marketing of branded generic formulations in developing countries through agents or distributors.
5. Marketing of generic formulations through company's marketing teams in developing countries.
6. Marketing of generic formulations of patent-expired drugs in developed countries.
7. Marketing of branded generic formulations of patent-expired drugs in developed countries.
8. Licensing of own NCEs to MNCs in developed countries.
9. Marketing own NCEs in developed countries through company's marketing teams.
10. Having a full-fledged joint venture with a local partner covering product development, manufacturing and marketing in developed countries.

Paradigm Shift

There is more to internationalization of business than mere export turnover. What is needed to make the real transition from exports to internationalization is a paradigm shift or a change in mindset. A change in attitude from patent busting to respecting intellectual property rights. This can be seen from the recent licensing arrangements that some of the Indian Pharma companies like Ranbaxy, Wockhardt and Nicholas Piramal have entered into for introducing the molecules of MNCs. If you want to be a global player, you cannot have two sets of rules - one for domestic market and another for overseas markets.

Acquisition of a true international character is more important than the acquisition of manufacturing facilities or even brands in overseas markets. Ranbaxy is the first Indian drug company to acquire an international character. It has manufacturing bases in six regions and has marketing operations in 26 countries. Over 15 per cent of its entire work force is non-Indian indicating the international nature of the company.

Whom do you benchmark against is another important aspect that companies wanting to internationalize should consider seriously. You cannot achieve global competitiveness if you benchmark your operations against your domestic rivals. You need to benchmark against the global players – the best in class. Ranbaxy has been benchmarking its operational targets against global generics manufacturers like Teva, the world's leading generic player and Mylan of the US, Tofa of Italy – to become cost competitive. Small wonder then, that it has become the 9th generic company in the world. It had planted the seeds for international business as early as 1968 and it has worked relentlessly at it.

Many of these companies, whose approaches we have discussed here, have achieved significant success in terms of export turnover and have contributed to the domestic industry's net exporter status. But internationalization of business is a different ball game. It requires world class skills and capabilities, relentless pursuit of excellence, international character, respect for intellectual property rights and a winning mindset. Above all a global mindset, which means an openness to change.

Chapter Eleven

Winners and Spectators

The pace of change in the Indian pharmaceutical industry ever since the government has joined WTO by signing GATT and implementing product patents can only be described as 'radical'. How else can you explain the recent spate of mergers and acquisitions of all sizes and shapes and types – brand, business, facilities and even research centers?

In any radically altered environment what is put to the test is one's ability to adapt and cope up with the change. The peculiar characteristic of any change is that it gives only one option for dealing with it. Either you master the change or you will be mastered by the change.

Mastering change involves anticipation. It calls for a proactive approach. You have to visualize the change before it arrives. That is what strategic vision is all about. The detailed accounts of thirty of the leading Indian drug companies competing in the three major competitive spaces – innovation-led, international generics, and CRAMS are presented here. These companies have visualized the likely aftermath of GATT and the inevitable product patent era. They have been preparing thoroughly and proactively to meet the challenges of a strong IPR protection regime – a virtual about turn from the highly protected process patent environment of the present.

These thirty companies are ranked in order of their readiness and preparedness to compete effectively in the WTO era. They have been taking a number of initiatives to build sustainable competitive advantages into their strategies. Their workouts too, have been far more strenuous than those of their peers. It is said that there are three basic types of companies:

A. Companies that make things happen,

B. Companies that let things happen and

C. Companies that wonder what happened.

These thirty companies obviously belong to the first category. They are distinctly ahead and are planning to stay ahead. Consider for example that these thirty companies collectively account for:

A. Over a third of the industry's turnover,

B. About 40 per cent of the industry's exports,

C. Close to 90 per cent of manufacturing facilities in the country that are approved by international regulatory authorities like US FDA, UK MCA and others,

D. Over 90 per cent of acquisitions – brands, businesses, facilities and research centres- in the industry and

E. Over 90 per cent of all strategic alliances in the industry both in India and abroad.

The marketing environment of the Indian pharmaceutical industry is changing radically. Analysts and pundits predict that the industry is in for a major shake-out. The symptoms and the telltale signs are already there for the discerning observer to see. How else can you explain the recent spate of mergers and brand acquisitions? Consider for example the ever-increasing and never-ending spate of mergers, acquisitions of all types, shapes and sizes such as brands, facilities, and companies and the numerous strategic alliances. All these portend a strong and positive consolidation phase for the industry.

How do you decide, select and identify the winners in such a rapidly and constantly changing scenario? Picking up winners against such a backdrop is not an easy task. You cannot just evaluate them on mere performance indicators. Current performance does not necessarily guarantee future success. Neither can you judge based on the potential. Potential is only a promise on the evaluation sheet till it is realized.

Apart from the current performance indicators, it is important to assess how the companies are preparing themselves for competing in the impending product patent regime.

Based on the international experience of countries like Italy and Japan which have embraced product patents in the late sixties, ten strategic elements can be isolated as criteria for evaluating the degree of preparation by Indian pharma companies to meet and beat competition in the product patent era:

a. Strategic Vision
b. Reaching the Critical Mass
c. Marketing Focus
d. Technology Focus
e. Research Focus
f. Strategic Integration
g. Internationalization of Business
h. Alliance Attractiveness
i. Intellectual Capital
j. Operational Excellence

For each of these strategic elements, a set of evaluation criteria is developed. All these companies are assessed on a ten-point scale qualitatively where a rating of 'high' means 'ten' points, a 'medium' rating 'five' points and a 'low' rating 'one' point. The assessment, although qualitative in nature, is backed by quantifiable evidence wherever possible. Here is the rationale for the ratings:

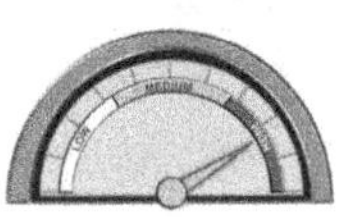

High : Significant evidence that the company has made substantial progress towards its strategic objectives and has reached the predetermined milestones. Clearly the leader of the pack.

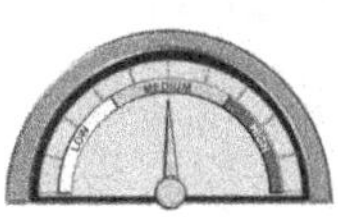

Medium : Adequate evidence that the company is making progress on its strategic objectives. There are also clear indicators that the company is investing its efforts and money in critical areas to stay competitive in the future. Not a leader, but a competent and competitive follower.

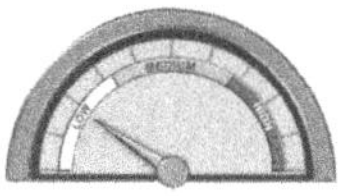

Low : Evidence to suggest that the company is on its way to reach the critical mass in all key areas. Growth rate usually higher than the industry average. The company has started investing its effort or is yet to invest significantly in critical areas to effectively compete in the product patent era.

Evaluation Criteria # 1: Strategic Vision

How does one evaluate a company on a criterion like strategic vision? Strategic vision essentially means building the best possible assumption base about the future and thereby develop intuitively proactive strategies that shape the industry evolution. Competition for strategic vision, therefore, is to establish one's company as the intellectual leader in terms of anticipation and influence over the direction of industry progress. It is virtually seeing the future before it arrives. Ranbaxy, viewed against this background, certainly emerges as the intellectual leader of the Indian drug industry. It has always been ahead of the competition. The company over the years has been able to develop the much-needed prescience to anticipate changes almost intuitively and was virtually able to see the future before it arrived. Its strategy is almost a model for many aspirants in the Indian pharmaceutical industry for survival and growth in the WTO era.

The criteria considered for qualitatively assessing a company's strategic focus are:

A. Industry foresight and strategic focus
B. Ability to spot, anticipate changes
C. Translating strategic vision into detailed action plans and ability to implement

Evaluation Criteria # 2: Critical Mass

Critical mass is the market share, which a firm must obtain in order to become fully competitive on price and cost. This calls for an ability to assimilate the start-up costs and then build on direct cost base large enough to absorb competitively the indirect costs of business. Timing is of essence in terms attaining the critical mass. It is important to reach it within a reasonable span of time, comparable to normal developmental lead-time in the relevant industry. Failure to build up quickly creates strong pressures even to abandon the venture itself and may even lead to bankruptcy.

Making realistic estimates of the critical mass is indeed critical. A number of firms in Indian pharmaceutical industry apparently with out having anticipated the very high start-up costs, the critical mass required to sustain and the very large development, marketing and debt servicing costs have paid very dearly. Natco's failure to anticipate these and to reach the critical mass quickly enough has forced the company to sell its established over-the-counter medicine brand in the Russian Federation to Ranbaxy and to put its most profitable domestic formulation business on the block in 1998. Divi's Labs on the other hand, has reached the critical mass in real quick time and has been a darling of the investing community almost since inception.

Here are some of the successful companies that have reached the critical mass to be competitive in the post-GATT era. These companies are preparing actively to progress in the strong intellectual property protection regime of the future. Here are the criteria used in assessing these companies on their race to reach the critical mass:

A. Sales turnover, growth rate
B. Rank in the industry
C. Size of the field force and total number of employees
D. Strategic routes taken to reach the critical mass – organic growth? Acquisition of brands? Companies?

Evaluation Criteria # 3: The Marketing Focus

The marketing orientation and focus of an organization are crucial for its success. Marketing orientation is synonymous with customer orientation. Understanding the needs and perceptions of the customer should be the starting point of any business.

The criteria used for a qualitative assessment of a company's marketing focus are:

A. Market share and growth rate
B. Size of the participated market

C. Degree of dominance in key therapeutic segments

D. Extent of customer franchise

E. Width and depth of distribution

F. Brand building capabilities

G. New product introductions

Evaluation Criteria # 4: Technology Upgradation

The pharmaceutical industry is technology-driven. Technology upgradation, therefore, is essential just to keep pace with the changing industrial scenario. To lead the change, development of technology should be of even higher order. Technology gives a firm its distinctive competitive advantage. High labour costs, for example can be offset by superior technology. Take the case of Glaxo's microprocessor controlled continuous process plant at Singapore for manufacturing the bulk drug ranitidine, the world's largest prescribed drug during its patency. It has very few operators. The production costs compare favorably with some of the world's low-cost producers. Technology can increase productivity considerably.

Consider the opportunity horizon for Indian drug companies in the post-GATT era. A number of leading drug manufacturers from India are vying with each other to exploit the huge opportunity in the fast growing off-patent generic formulations market in North America and the European Union. Technological upgradation to international standards is a prerequisite for exporting to those markets. The regulatory authorities from these markets allow imports only from the plants they approve. Without their approval of your manufacturing facilities, you cannot even think of exporting your generic formulations. You have to upgrade your facilities to their standards to get the due approvals. Technology upgradation holds the key that can convert these entry barriers into gateways.

To be globally competitive, you need to have world class technology. That explains why so many Indian companies are making a beeline to upgrade their plants and to get approvals from international regulatory authorities like US FDA. UK MCA etc.

Here are the criteria used for qualitative assessment of technology upgradation by the front runners of the Indian pharmaceutical industry:

A. Manufacturing infrastructure.

B. State of quality – conforming to WHO, GMP, cGMP guidelines?

C. Approvals from international regulatory authorities like US FDA, UK MCA, Canadian HPB and South African MCC etc.

D. Investment pattern in technological upgradation.

E. Manufacturing facilities overseas

Evaluation Criteria # 5: Research Focus

Pharmaceutical industry, the world over is research-led. Under a strong IPR regime, no pharma company can progress without significant R&D effort. Otherwise, it may end up as a supplier of products and services, if it has a core competency in any relevant area like manufacturing, marketing and distribution. The bigger firms may even gobble it up if it has good manufacturing capability or brand equity.

Even to assimilate and absorb the new technologies, a critical mass of product and process developmental skills are needed.

Some of the more determined Indian drug majors have been stepping up their R&D investments and efforts. They are setting up world class research facilities and formulating focused research strategies. Some companies like DRL and Ranbaxy have even been successful in developing new lead compounds and started filing INDAs. Others like Wockhardt and Lupin have started building infrastructure required for launching their drug discovery programs.

The criteria for a qualitative assessment of a company's research focus are:

A. R&D infrastructure

B. Number of scientists and their qualifications

C. Areas of research focus

D. Investment in R&D as a per cent of sales

E. Collaborations in research

F. Progress or breakthroughs in research

Evaluation Criteria # 6: Strategic Integration

In the Indian pharmaceutical industry extensive vertical integration is taking place. Bulk drug firms are integrating backwards into intermediates. At the same time, they are also integrating forward into value-added finished dosage forms. This very significant trend is greatly raising economies of scale as well as the amount of capital necessary to compete in the industry. This in turn is erecting barriers to entry. This trend, which is likely to continue, may drive smaller competitors out of the industry once the growth levels off. If the smaller players have efficient plants and processes of operations, they may become the prime targets for acquisitions by the larger firms, which are on a consolidation spree.

Some of the leading Indian drug firms, Ranbaxy, Lupin, Wockhardt, Sun, Torrent, Ipca, Orchid and more recently Glenmark, have been actively pursuing the strategy of vertical integration for some time. Their efforts are more intensified now, since vertical integration offers some key benefits and gives the firms distinct and sustainable competitive advantages. Some of the commonly cited benefits of vertical integration are:

A. Achievement of economies of scale.
B. Cost savings across the firm's operations like coordinated production.
C. Purchasing controls and leverage.
D. Control on quality.
E. Timely availability.

Here are the factors considered for a qualitative assessment of a company's strategic integration:

A. Nature and extent of integration
B. Level of integration
C. Bulk drug portfolio

Evaluation Criteria # 7: Alliance Attractiveness

With alliances, we can do more with less, remarked by a Managing Director of a large corporation, known for its penchant for alliances.

That is the basic purpose of allying with some one. To do more with less. To achieve synergy. Strategic alliances will help you gain access to new products, markets, and technology. Alliances buy time, save costs.

Alliances will become even more important in an environment that strongly protects intellectual property rights. Once product patents are in place in the country, unless you are the original innovator, your access to new products and technologies will be limited to your current products. It is only through alliances and licensing arrangements you can get access to new products.

That is the reason why there are a spate of alliances among the leading players in the Indian drug industry and some of the leading international companies over the last few years.

Consider these criteria for evaluating qualitatively the alliance attractiveness of the more progressive Indian pharma companies:

A. Alliance attractiveness
B. Number and nature of strategic alliances – marketing, manufacturing tie-ups, technical collaborations, joint ventures with equity participation finalized

Evaluation Criteria # 8: Internationalization of Business

Internationalization of business for Indian drug firms is no longer a matter of choice. In the product patent era, every company needs to be research oriented. Pharmaceutical research is expensive and risky. The costs of developing a drug have gone up phenomenally. The risks and costs of developing new drugs cannot be borne by any one national market. One has to graduate from exports to internationalization of business like Ranbaxy has.

Consider these factors for assessing qualitatively a company's approach to internationalizing its business:

A. Exports turnover and their contribution to total sales.
B. Quality of exports.
C. Number of product registrations in overseas markets.
D. Number of marketing offices abroad.
E. Number of off-shore manufacturing bases.
F. Number of employees overseas.
G. Investment in international operations.
H. Number and nature of strategic alliances abroad.
I. Number and nature of acquisitions in overseas markets.

Evaluation Criteria # 9: Intellectual Capital

In an open economy that is increasingly stock market oriented, one tends to look at indicators with greater relevance to day-to-day investment. A company may have a high but unproductive asset base. Likewise, sales turnover alone does not mean much unless it is remunerative. Finally, the profits generated have to be perceived by the market to be of an enduring nature. When all these factors fall in place, the firm enjoys a high market capitalization.

Market capitalization assumes greater importance when a company decides to raise finance in the global market. Accurate pricing of the shares of a company, which in turn is a function of the total market capitalization of the company becomes very important in a competitive environment. Moreover, the Government of India would allow only companies with high economic performance and market capitalization to approach international investors.

A firm's intellectual capital, therefore, becomes more important than ever before. Consider these criteria for a qualitative assessment of a company's intellectual capital:

A. Intangible assets
B. Investment in R&D
C. Investment in training and development
D. Investment in information technology
E. Number of patents filed and approved
F. Number of DMFs, ANDAs and INDAs filed and approved
G. Total number of product registrations globally

Evaluation Criteria # 10: Operational Excellence

Implementing a strategy is as important as formulating it in the first place. Elementary as it may seem, the best of strategies cannot produce even acceptable results let alone the planned ones, if they are not implemented effectively.

Operational excellence is the firm's ability to execute its strategic plans. It spans the entire gamut of functions that a firm is engaged in.

A firm can achieve leadership position in the market place, only when it excels in its operations. That is a cardinal principle.

Here are some of the important criteria used for assessing qualitatively a company's operational excellence:

A. Key financial indicators like PAT, ROCE, RONW and PE ratio etc.
B. Degree of professionalization
C. Strength of top line and second-line management
D. Acquisition of talent in all functions and in all markets
E. Performance measurement and reward systems
F. Investment in training, development and succession planning

Survival of the Fittest!

Why do some companies survive and grow while others stagnate and perish? It is the balanced power of both brain and brawn. The power of strategic thinking and the ability to execute the action plans. In other words, it is intellectual capital that has always been a decisive factor in the rise of civilizations, organizations and people. Rich Karlgaard, editor of Forbes ASAP, puts it so succinctly in his foreword to Leif Edvinsson and Michael S. Malone's book on intellectual capital:

> For at least 60,000 years our ancestors, the Cro-Magnons, lived side by side with the Neanderthals. Then, about 30,000 years ago, the Neanderthals disappeared.
>
> Why did one species survive and the other perish? Both used tools and language, but the Cro-Magnons had a lunar calendar. Soon they correlated the passing days with the migratory patterns of bison, elk and red deer. This insight was dutifully recorded on cave-wall paintings.

In retrospect the reasons for their perishing seem quite simple. Even obvious. The authors explain:

> Hungry for meat, the Cro-Magnon was taught all that he had to do was wait at a river crossing on certain days, spear in hand. In the meantime the Neanderthals appear to have unwisely scattered their men and their scarce resources in search of random encounters. They allocated their resources poorly. They perished.

Industry experts predict that the number of companies in the post-GATT era will dwindle considerably. Industry will consolidate itself during this period. Some would even suggest that the number of companies operating in the Indian pharmaceutical industry would be around three hundred by the time dust settles. While it is difficult to say how many companies would win, how many will survive and how many will remain as mute spectators, watching these rapid changes, the portents are clear that the consolidation phase has commenced and will continue. It is also difficult to predict who will be predators and who will be the prey. Today's predators can as well be tomorrow's prey to some other larger, more powerful predators, who will be on the prowl.

Fiercely competitive or not, the market place is ruthless and merciless. In such an environment only the fittest survive.

Corporate Dashboard

At any time, having the ability to know how well the business is doing is based on a set of key performance indicators. In today's world of hyper-competition precise yet concise information helps the top executives who need accurate dependable information in a quick capsule. The corporate dashboard provides a snapshot of the thirty companies discussed through out this book, as they are constantly working out to improve their competitive quotient to move ahead of competition. The ten criteria for qualitatively assessing their competitiveness are covered in the six categories presented in Table 11.1 (Corporate Dashboard) – critical mass, market focus, technology focus, research focus, global mindset and operational excellence.

Table 11.1 Corporate Dashboard

Rank	Company	Score
1	**Ranbaxy**	
	A. **Critical Mass :** Ranbaxy is clearly the leader of the pack of global aspirants from India with over Rs. 51 billion in annual sales achieved through a dexterously crafted strategy and meticulous execution over the years. The eight acquisitions the company made in the five years since 2002 clearly provide the synergy and reinforcement in leading international generic markets such as France, Germany, Spain, Netherlands, Romania and South Africa.	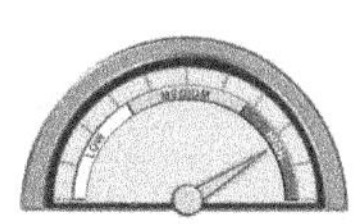

B. **Market Focus:** Ranbaxy has a very wide and deep product portfolio in the Indian pharmaceutical market competing aggressively in many therapeutic segments. 25 of its brands are fully integrated, which it markets in a number of international markets. The company recorded Rs. 13.2 billion in sales for FYE December 2005, the second highest among Indian companies in India. Ranbaxy is also in the forefront in brand building in the Indian pharmaceutical market with as many as 33 of its brands featuring among the top 500 pharmaceutical brands in India. These thirty-three brands contributed to over 67.5 per cent of the company's total sales during the year. The company retains its marketing focus across the many therapeutic categories and prescriber segments in both acute and chronic therapy areas with its 9 specialty focused marketing divisions.

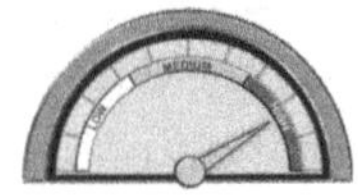

C. **Technology Focus:** Ranbaxy has built a world-class technological infrastructure that spans eight countries in the world such as China, Ireland, India, Malaysia, Nigeria, Romania, Vietnam and the US. Many of these facilities have approvals from International regulatory authorities like US FDA, UK MHRA, Australian TGA, Canadian TPD, South African MCC, Brazilian ANVISA, and the Middle Eastern GCC etc. The company is one of the few totally integrated international generic pharmaceutical companies in the world covering intermediates, APIs, FDFs and across multiple technology platforms.

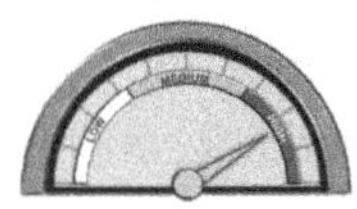

D. **Research Focus:** Ranbaxy, one of the top-ten international generic companies in the world has built world-class research infrastructure. The company has a total of 1,120 scientific staff engaged in research and development activity covering various areas such as process research, generic research for regulated markets, NDDS and NDDR. Ranbaxy invested Rs. 6.40 billion on R&D in FY 2006. The company has been building up its intellectual property too steadily but surely. The company has filed a total of 791 patents internationally and been granted 198 till FYE March 2006. Ranbaxy is among the top filers of ANDAs with US FDA. The cumulative ANDA filings of the company stand at 183. Two of the company's NCEs completed Phase I and Phase II respectively. The company filed an additional IND with DCGI.

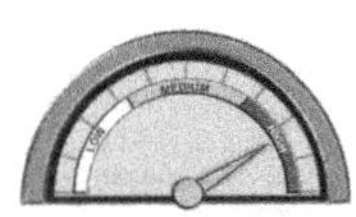

E. **Global Mindset:** International sales contributed to over three-fourths of Ranbaxy's total sales in FYE December 2006. The regulated markets such as US (28 per cent) and the European Union (17 per cent) contributed to 45 per cent of total sales. BRICS (Brazil, Russia, India, China and South Africa) contributed to 31 per cent and the Rest of the World (ROW) and the API business contributed to 24 per cent. Ranbaxy is the most internationalized of all the pharmaceutical companies from India.

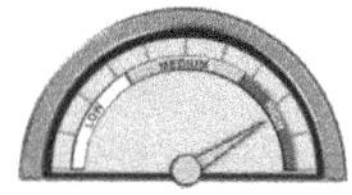

F. **Operational Excellence:** The overall financial performance of Ranbaxy is not as high as it is on other criteria or parameters probably due to its aggressive pursuit of building market share in overseas markets through acquisitions and investment in ANDA submissions including the Para IV filings. The company had a PAT to sales Ratio of 5 per cent, ROCE of 6.1 per cent, and RONW of 10.4 per cent during FYE December 2006.

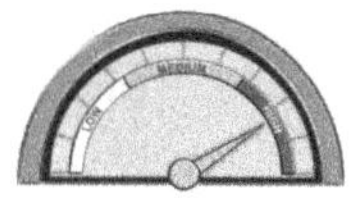

2 **Dr. Reddy's Laboratories**

A. **Critical Mass:** Dr. Reddy's Labs has become the second Indian pharmaceutical company to cross the coveted landmark of the US $ one billion mark in December 2006. The company's five international acquisitions in the last five years contributed to this significantly by bolstering its European generics sales, CPS business and API business in regulated markets.

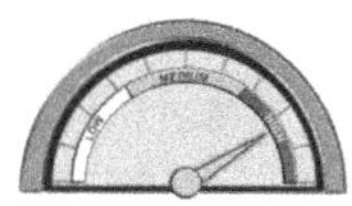

B. **Market Focus:** Dr. Reddy's Laboratories registered Rs. 5.91 billion in the branded generic formulation segment of the Indian pharmaceutical market. The company has ten brands among the industry's top five hundred contributing 47 per cent to its total sales during FYE March 2006. The company retains its marketing focus among the different therapeutic and prescriber segments with 7 specialty-marketing teams.

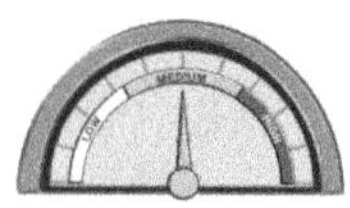

C. **Technology Focus:** Dr. Reddy's Labs has built over the years a technological infrastructure that is among the best in the world and is vertically integrated covering drug intermediates, APIs, FDFs across multiple technological platforms. Many of the company's manufacturing facilities have approvals from almost all the international regulatory authorities. Dr. Reddy's have about twelve manufacturing facilities These facilities are located in India, Germany, and Mexico.

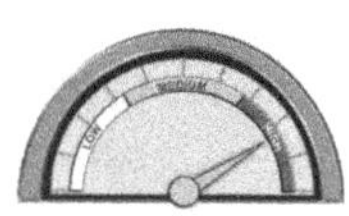

D. **Research Focus:** Dr. Reddy's Laboratories has pioneered the co-development strategy in India with its landmark agreement with Novo Nordisk the leading anti-diabetic player in the world. Dr. Reddy's have 950 scientists working on research and development activity across the whole spectrum from process research to drug discovery research and NDDS. The company has invested Rs. 1.73 billion on R&D in FYE March 2006. The company has been building intellectual capital and filed 353 patents of which 172 are received till now. The cumulative filings of DMFs stand at 151. Dr. Reddy's have also filed 70 ANDAs so far including 29 Para IV filings. The company's NCE pipeline too is impressive with two NCEs completing Phase II and three NCEs completing Phase I so far. Dr. Reddy's have formed a joint venture company in yet another innovative strategic move – Perlecan for research and development with ICICI Venture Capital Fund Management Company and Citi Group Venture Capital International Growth Partnerships Mauritius Limited fund as a de-risking strategy of innovation.

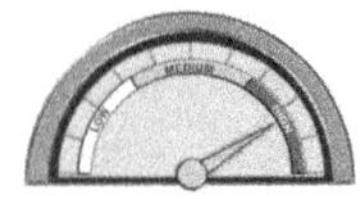

E. **Global Mindset:** Dr. Reddy's Labs today has become a force to reckon within international generics business. Overseas sales contributed to two-thirds of the total sales of the company in FYE March 2006. Regulated markets such as the US (16 per cent) and Europe (18 percent) contributed a major chunk to 34 per cent to total sales in the year.

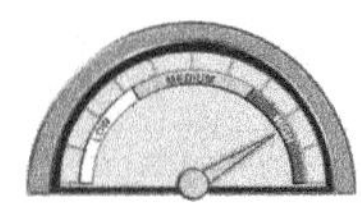

F. **Operational Excellence:** The company's PAT in FYE March 2006 was Rs. 1.63 billion which was 6.7 per cent of total sales. The EPS increased significantly this year to Rs. 21.24 from Rs. 2.76 of last year.

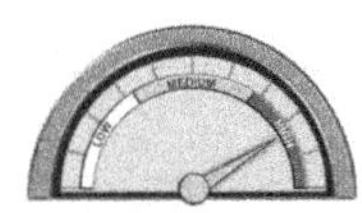

3 **Cipla**

A. **Critical Mass:** Cipla has recorded over Rs.32 billion in sales for the year ending March 2006. About fifty per cent of its total sales were from international markets, which the company forayed into only a few years ago. Cipla has been at one of the top two positions in the Indian branded generic formulations market for over two years.

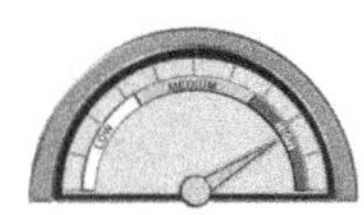

B. **Marketing Focus:** Cipla has been one of the frontrunners in the Indian pharmaceutical market for many years. The company was ranked second with Rs. 13.07 billion in sales for FYE March 2006. Cipla has thirty-one brands featuring among the industry's top 500 contributing to 56.7 per cent of its domestic formulations sales during the year.

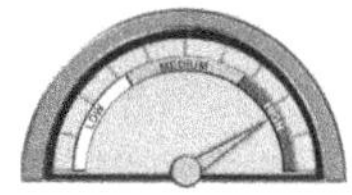

C. **Technology Focus:** Cipla's technological competence and infrastructure are widely acknowledged in the Indian pharmaceutical market. The company has thirty-four manufacturing facilities across India many of which have approvals from almost all major international regulatory authorities in the world such as US FDA, UK MHRA, Canadian TPD, South African MCC, Brazilian ANVISA, South African MCC etc. In all the strategic alliances that Cipla entered into so far, the company's role and contribution are clearly defined as a technology provider while the local partners have essentially the marketing responsibility.

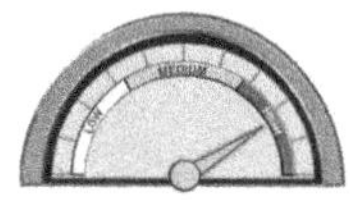

D. **Research Focus:** Cipla has 450 scientists of which 268 are PhDs engaged in process research, formulation development, NDDS research and generic research for the regulated markets. The company invested Rs. 1.55 billion in FYE March 2006, which is over five per cent of sales. Cipla has 80 API patents and 32 formulation patents to its credit.

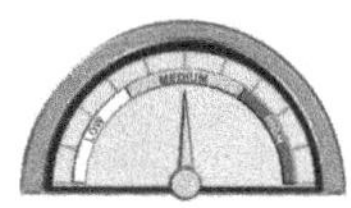

E. **Global Mindset:** International sales contributed to over 48 per cent of Cipla's total turnover at Rs. 15.15 billion in FYE March 2006. Regulated markets accounted for 47 per cent of total international sales with the US contributing 30 per cent and the Europe 17 per cent. Africa contributed to 34 per cent of total international sales during the year.

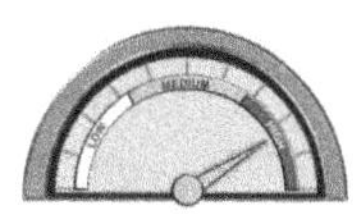

F. **Operational Excellence:** Cipla's PAT in FYE March 2006 was Rs. 6.08 billion which was 19 per cent. The company's RONW was 30.66 per cent during the year.

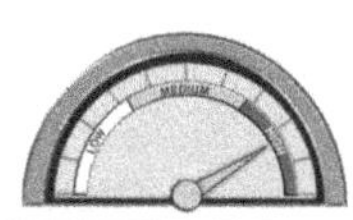

4 Sun Pharma

A. **Critical Mass:** The specialty focused Sun Pharma was ranked fifth in the year ending March 2006 in the Indian pharmaceutical market. The company's total sales were over Rs. 18 billion in the year ending March 2006. The

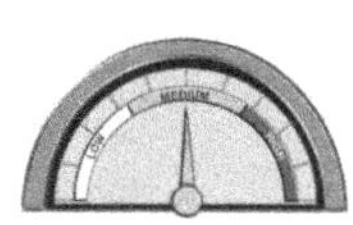

four acquisitions that the company made over the last three years in the US and Hungary enhanced its presence in international markets and contributed significant percent of its total sales.

B. **Marketing Focus:** Sun Pharma seems to have perfected the art of specialty marketing in India with leadership in a number of chronic therapy areas with 17 different specialty-marketing teams that function as SBUs. The company achieved Rs. 8.39 billion in branded formulation sales in India, which is 52.4 per cent of its total sales during FYE March 2006. Sun Pharma has 16 brands among the industry's top 500 which contributed to about 30 per cent of its domestic formulation sales at Rs. 2.52 billion during the year.

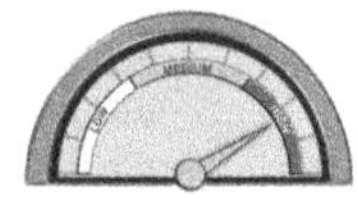

C. **Technology Focus:** Sun Pharma has built a technological infrastructure that caters to the world's most stringent regulated markets. The company has seventeen manufacturing facilities for manufacturing APIs, and FDFs covering multiple technology platforms. The company has its manufacturing facilities in India, US, and Hungary.

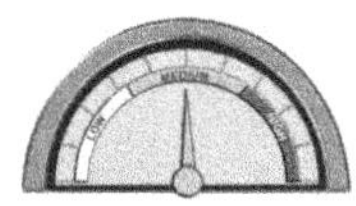

D. **Research Focus:** Sun Pharma Advanced Research Center (SPARC) has over 500 scientists today working on research and development across the whole spectrum of pharmaceutical research. The company invested Rs. 1.61 billion in FYE March 2006, which is 8.9 per cent of sales. The total number of patents cumulatively is 464 of which 42 have been granted so far. The company has geared up to file 10 DMFs and 20 ANDAs every year. The company is planning to de-merge its discovery research activity as a separate company in 2007. One of Sun Pharma's NCEs has completed Phase I in Europe and two NDDS products have completed Phase II in the US.

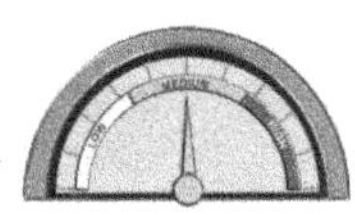

E. **Global Mindset:** International sales contributed to Rs. 6.95 billion, which is about 38.5 per cent of the company's total sales. Fifty five per cent of Sun Pharma's international sales were from the company's generic arm in the US – Caraco Pharmaceuticals. With the recent acquisition of ICN Pharma in Hungary, Sun's presence in the EU would also increase significantly in the foreseeable future.

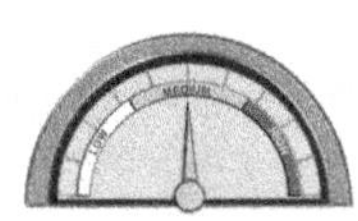

F. **Operational Excellence:** Sun Pharma has earned a PAT of Rs. 4.61 billion, which is a very healthy 25.5 per cent in FYE March 2006. The Company has increased its net worth considerably from 11.3 billion last year to 15.9 billion during the year under review.

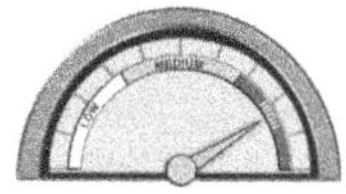

5 Lupin

A. **Critical Mass:** The leading anti-TB player in the world is diversifying its product portfolio and Lupin's sales turnover of RS. 16.6 billion during the FYE March 2006 clearly reflects that strategic shift. Lupin is looking for strategic acquisitions to accelerate its growth. The company forged six alliances during the past few years to gain and improve market access, out-license some of its products and long-term supply arrangements with some of the leading global players.

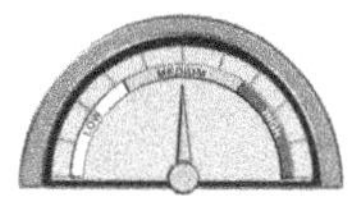

B. **Marketing Focus:** Lupin is a dominant leader in the anti-TB market in India and internationally. The company has achieved Rs. 5.9 billion in the Indian branded generic formulation market in 2006. Fourteen of the company's brands are among the industry's top 500 and contributed to over forty per cent of its total domestic formulation sales. Lupin has six marketing divisions to promote its products across therapeutic areas in a focused manner.

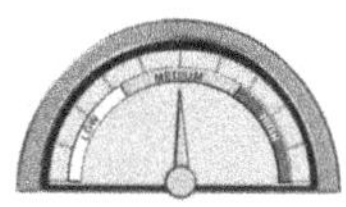

C. **Technology Focus:** Lupin has ten manufacturing facilities of which nine have approvals from US FDA and two from UK MHRA. In addition many of these have approvals from other international regulatory authorities across the world. Lupin has over two hundred molecular entities in its product mix.

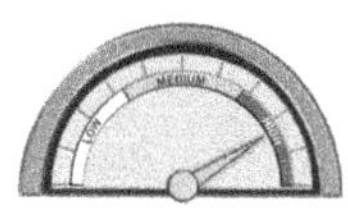

D. **Research Focus:** Lupin Research Park, the state-of-the-art epicenter for all research and development activity of Lupin has 320 scientists from multiple disciplines. The company invested Rs. 988 million in FYE 2006, which is 6 per cent of sales. The company has so far filed 240 patents of which 53 have been granted. Lupin has two NCEs in Phase I and two more in Phase II.

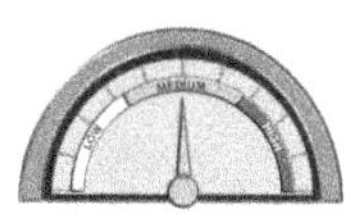

E. **Global Mindset:** International sales contributed to Rs. 7.63 billion, which is 46 per cent of total sales in FYE March 2006. US formulation sales contributed to over 28 per cent of total international sales.

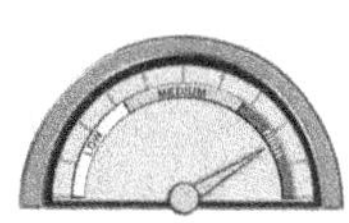

F. **Operational Excellence:** Lupin earned a PAT of Rs. 1.83 billion, which is 11.02 per cent in FYE March 2006. The EPS was Rs. 44.59 during the year.

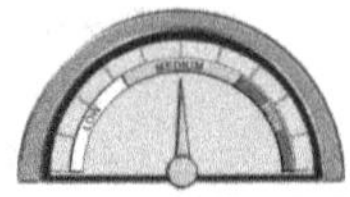

6. Wockhardt

A. **Critical Mass:** Wockhardt, one of the consistent performers in the Indian pharmaceutical industry has consolidated its position in the European generics market, which is the single largest region for the company contributing over 45 per cent of the total sales of Rs. 14.1 billion in FYE March 2006. The company reinforced its position in the European Union with four acquisitions during the last three years in United Kingdom, Germany, Ireland and France. In addition, Wockhardt entered into eight strategic alliances for contract manufacturing and in-licensing.

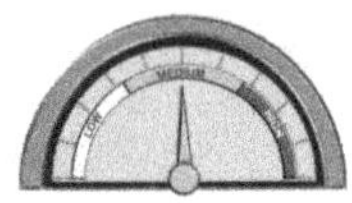

B. **Marketing Focus:** Wockhardt is a well-known brand in India and the company featured in the Interbrand's *Indian Business Super Brands* 2005 report. The company recorded Rs. 4.61 billion in domestic formulations sales with 15 of its brands finding place among the Industry's top 500. These fifteen brands contributed to about 51.6 per cent of the company's total domestic formulations sales during the year.

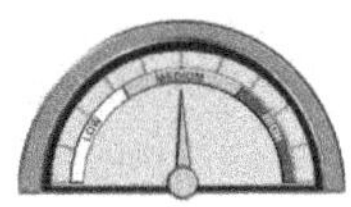

C. **Technology Focus:** Wockhardt has nine world class manufacturing facilities in India and the UK many of which have approvals from international regulatory authorities from regulated markets such as US FDA, UK MHRA, South African MCC, Brazilian ANVISA, Canadian TPD etc. The company is vertically integrated and has capabilities across multiple technology platforms.

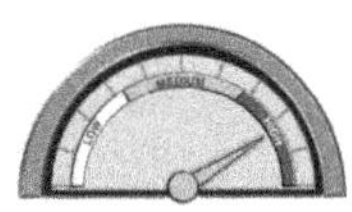

D. **Research Focus:** Wockhardt has 400 scientists working on research and development activity on all aspects of pharmaceutical research including biopharmaceutical research and discovery research. The company invested Rs. 1.04 billion in the fiscal 2006, which is 7.4 per cent of sales. Wockhardt filed 150 patents so far globally of which 37 have been granted so far. The company's NCE has entered Phase II clinical trials.

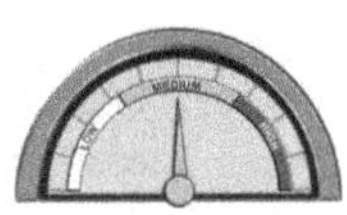

E. **Global Mindset:** Wockhardt achieved close to two-thirds of its total sales in international markets (Rs. 8.88 billion or 63 per cent) in FYE March 2006. Europe was the

company's single largest market contributing 41 per cent of its total sales during the year.

F. Operational Excellence: Wockhardt earned an impressive PAT of Rs. 2.9 billion, which is 20.56 per cent of turnover during FY March 2006. The EPS was Rs. 23.55 during the year.

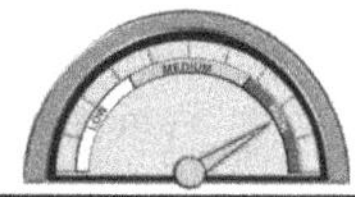

7. Aurobindo Pharma

A. **Critical Mass:** In a short span of over five years Aurobindo Pharma has metamorphosed itself from a low-cost API supplier into a prominent international generic player with a sales turnover of about Rs. 15 billion for FYE 2006. The company in the process made three strategic acquisitions in the US and the UK to gain and strengthen market access to regulated markets.

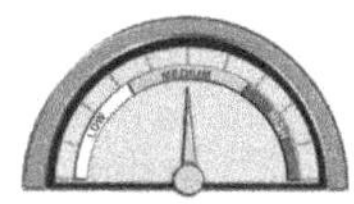

B. **Marketing Focus:** Aurobindo Pharma does not participate in the domestic formulations market. While the company has proven technological prowess, its marketing activity is planned through partnerships and alliances in overseas markets.

C. **Technology Focus:** Aurobindo Pharma has achieved cost leadership and became a completely integrated player across many therapeutic areas and molecules. The company's infrastructure comprises twelve world-class manufacturing facilities for APIs, FDFs across multiple technology platforms. Aurobindo, in addition has two JVCs in the US and China.

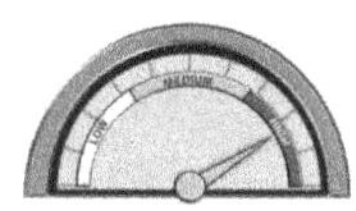

D. **Research Focus:** Aurobindo Pharma has invested Rs. 770 million in fiscal 2006, which is 5.1 per cent of sales. Over 630 scientists are working on research and development covering all areas of pharmaceutical research. The company filed 205 patents till date of which 29 have been granted. The company has developed 120 APIs and filed 136 DMFs and COS and 120 ANDAs till now.

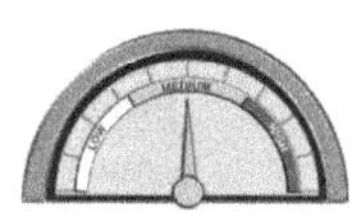

E. **Global Mindset:** Aurobindo Pharma improved its international presence during the year with its aggressive ARV strategy and DMF and ANDA filings in the regulated markets. Exports contributed to about 55 per cent of the company's total sales in FYE March 2006.

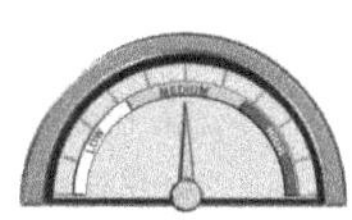

F. **Operational Excellence:** Although there has been a significant increase in PAT over the last year it is still low at 4.7 per cent of sales. This is probably because of low margins on ARVs under PEPFAR and APIs. When the company starts leveraging the huge ANDA pipeline through marketing tie-ups the PAT could increase considerably in the foreseeable future.

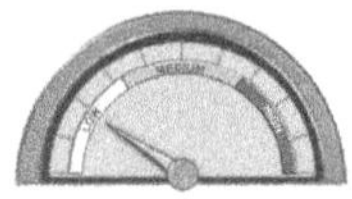

8. **Nicholas Piramal**

A. **Critical Mass:** Nicholas Piramal, one of the keen contenders for the top slot in the CRAMS space recorded a sales turnover of over Rs. 15.82 billion in FYE March 2006. The takeover tycoon continues to be on an acquisition spree and made eight more acquisitions during the last six years to gain access to new technology platforms, new B2B customers and generics business in regulated markets. The company has also entered into eleven strategic alliances to gain market access, supply arrangements and out-licensing.

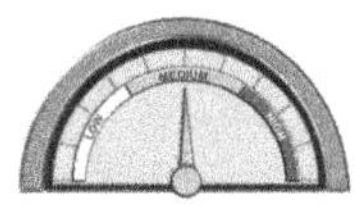

B. **Marketing Focus:** Nicholas Piramal has successfully integrated its six acquisitions in India and created 15 marketing teams to stay focused and grow and revitalize its many mature brands. The company achieved Rs. 11.15 billion in formulation sales in India. Nicholas Pirmal has 27 brands among the industry's top 500 brands contributing about 53 per cent of its total domestic sales at Rs. 5.9 billion.

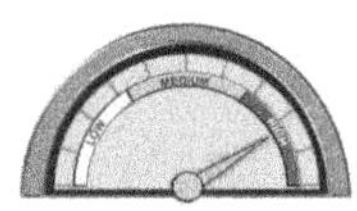

C. **Technology Focus:** Emerging as one of the leading CRAMS players in the world, Nicholas Piramal has been creating a technological infrastructure that compares with the best in the world through brown field ventures and sewing up alliances with international drug majors for long-term supply arrangements. The company has twelve manufacturing facilities in India, UK and Canada for manufacturing APIs, FDFs across multiple technology platforms.

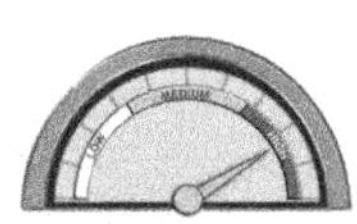

D. **Research Focus:** Nicholas Pirmal has bolstered its R&D effort with the acquisition of Hoechst (now Aventis) in India. Today the company has 350 scientists working on all aspects of pharmaceutical research including discovery research. Nicholas Piramal has invested Rs. 775 million in the fiscal 2006, which is 5.1 per cent of

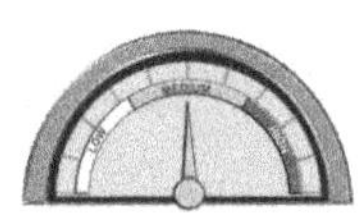

sales. The company filed 214 patents of which 200 are already granted. The company has an impressive NCE pipeline with 9 compounds at various stages of development with two in Phase I and two more in Phase II.

E. **Global Mindset:** Global sales and custom manufacturing services contributed to 21.5 per cent of company's total sales in FYE March 2006.

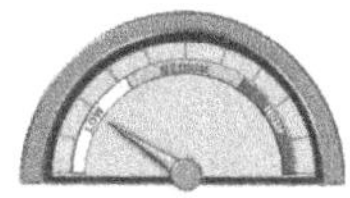

F. **Operational Excellence:** Nicholas Pirmal earned a net profit of Rs. 1.2 billion, which is 7.85 per cent of sales in FYE March 2006. The ROCE was 14.3 per cent, RONW 12.2 per cent and EPS was Rs. 5.8 for the year under review.

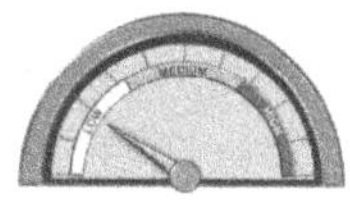

9. Zydus Cadila

A. **Critical Mass:** Zydus has reached a critical mass of Rs. 15.07 billion in FYE March 2006. The company made three acquisitions in India and France between 2001 and 2003 to extend its therapeutic coverage in the domestic formulations market and to gain access to the French and European generic markets. Zydus has also entered into eight strategic alliances covering contract manufacturing, co-marketing and co-development areas.

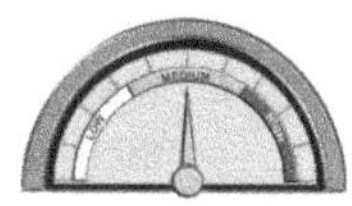

B. **Marketing Focus:** Zydus Cadila recorded Rs. 8.98 billion in formulation sales in India during 2006 with 22 of its brands featuring among the industry's top 500 contributing to 57.9 per cent of the total company's sales. The company has 10 marketing teams to stay focused on the different prescriber segments and grow its brands across the many therapeutic categories.

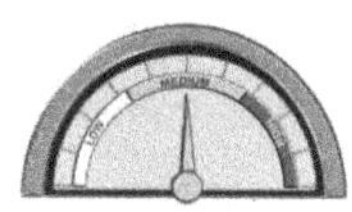

C. **Technology Focus:** Zyus Cadila has four manufacturing facilities for APIs, and FDFs and is a totally integrated company. The company has received approvals from all major international regulatory authorities in the world such as US FDA, UK MHRA, EQDM etc.

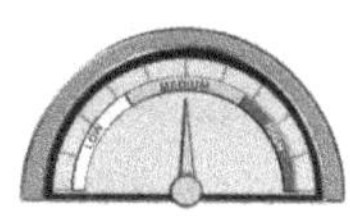

D. **Research Focus:** The 500 scientists in Zydus Cadila's research center filed 108 patents. The company invested Rs. 817 million on R&D in FYE March 2006, which is 5.4 per cent. The company's NCE pipeline comprises four products targeted at metabolic disorders, diabetes, cardiovascular and inflammation. In addition, Zydus filed 36 ANDAs and 40 DMFs in the last three years.

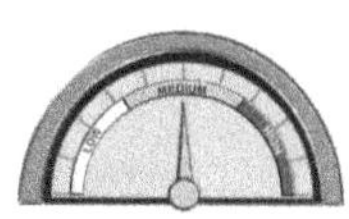

E. **Global Mindset:** International sales contributed for 14.9 per cent at Rs 2.25 billion in FYE March 2006.

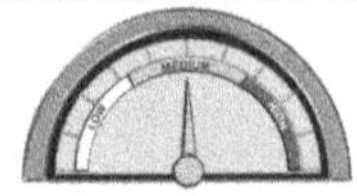

F. **Operational Excellence:** Zydus earned a PAT of 12.6 per cent during the year under review. The ROCE was 17.02 percent.

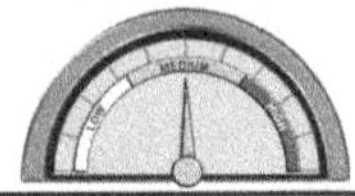

10. Glenmark

A. **Critical Mass:** Glenmark, the new kid on the block leapfrogged into the big league in a short span of five years with four acquisitions and twelve strategic alliances covering all key areas such as market access, product access, in-licensing, out-licensing and co-development. The company is on a springboard to further growth having reached a critical mass of Rs. 7.57 billion in FYE March 2006.

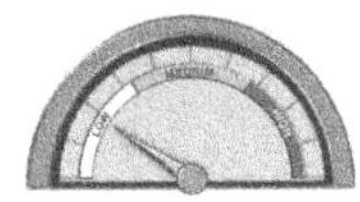

B. **Marketing Focus:** Known for its focus on dermatology for a long time, Glenmark is diversifying rapidly into other therapeutic areas and recorded Rs. 3.16 billion in domestic formulations sales FYE March 2006. The company has six of its brands among the industry's top 500 contributing to about 27.7 per cent of its formulations sales in India during the year. Glenmark has eight marketing divisions to sharpen its focus on different therapeutic as well as prescriber segments.

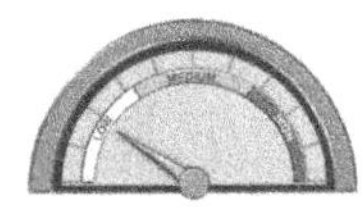

C. **Technology Focus:** Glenmark has seven manufacturing facilities for APIs, FDFs and is vertically integrated. The company's facilities are located in India and Brazil. The company has received approvals from major international regulatory authorities in the world.

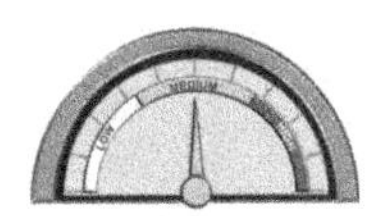

D. **Research Focus:** Like a bolt out of the blue, Glenmark within a short span of five years or so catapulted itself into the big league of pharmaceutical research including NDDR. The company today has 400 scientists working on all aspects of pharmaceutical research and development making Glenmark even more competitive. Glenmark invested Rs. 467 million on R&D in the fiscal 2006, which is about 6.17 per cent of sales. The company filed 20 patents so far and has an impressive NCE pipeline with three in Phase I, one in Phase II and two more ready for Phase I.

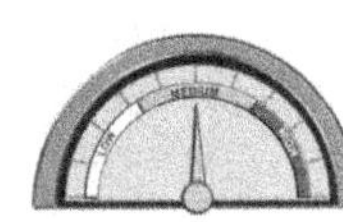

E. **Global Mindset:** International sales contributed to about 42 per cent of Glenmark's total turnover at Rs. 3.18 billion in FYE March 2006. The company is focusing on regulated markets.

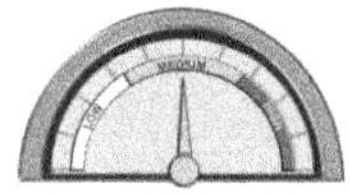

F. **Operational Excellence:** Glenmark earned a PAT of Rs. 879.8 million, which is 19.87 per cent of the ompany's turnover during FYE March 2006. The EPS was Rs. 5.54 in the same period.

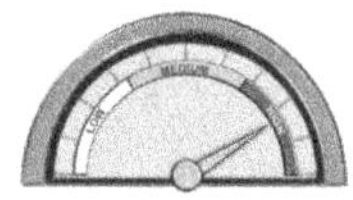

11. Torrent

A. **Critical Mass:** Once a niche-market player, who pioneered specialty focused approach in Indian pharmaceutical industry, Torrent Pharma is regaining focus and the lost leadership position and reached a critical mass of Rs. 6.92 billion FYE 2006. The company made a key strategic acquisition in Germany, the largest generics market in Europe in 2005 to gain access to the European generics market. The company also forged four strategic alliances in the areas of co-development, co-marketing, and out-licensing.

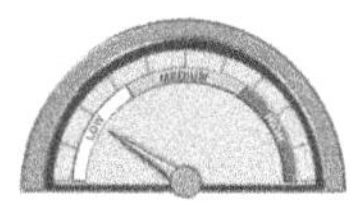

B. **Marketing Focus:** Torrent Pharma, fighting back for regaining its once-pioneer of the specialty segment status in chronic therapy areas recorded close to Rs. Five billion in sales for FYE March 2006. Torrent has created eleven marketing teams to focus on different therapy areas and specialty prescriber segments. The company has eight brands among the industry's top 500 contributing to 36 per cent of its domestic formulations sales during the year.

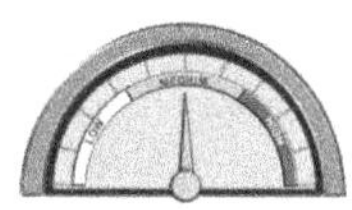

C. **Technology Focus:** Torrent has three manufacturing facilities that are cGMP-compliant. The company has received approvals from major international regulatory authorities including US FDA. The company has manufacturing capabilities across multiple technology platforms and is vertically integrated.

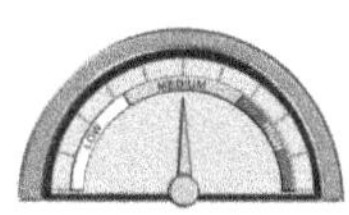

D. **Research Focus:** Torrent has been stepping up its research and development effort. The company invested 8.15 per cent of sales in FYE March 2006 at Rs. 564 million. The company filed 214 patents of which 123 are granted. The company entered into a co-development strategic alliance with the global drug major Astra Zeneca. Torrent has 6 NCEs at various stages of development.

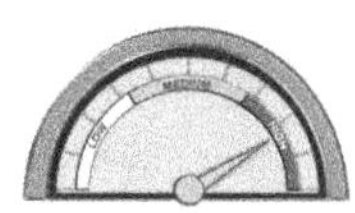

E. **Global Mindset:** International sales contributed to 45 per cent of total turnover in FYE March 2006 thanks to Heumann's acquisition in Germany, which accounted for 40 per cent of total international sales. Brazil, which contributed 28 per cent is the second biggest international market for Torrent.

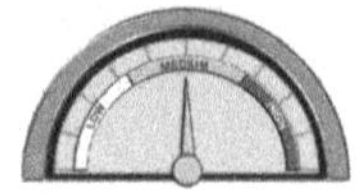

F. **Operational Excellence:** Torrent earned a PAT of Rs. 658.3 million, which is 9.5 per cent of sales in FYE March 2006. The EPS was Rs. 6.01 during the year under review.

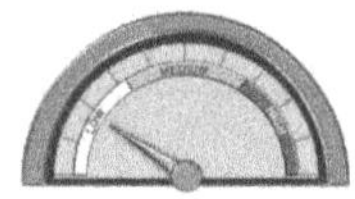

12. Orchid

A. **Critical Mass:** The fully integrated cephalosporin player aiming for a leading position in the international generic cephalosporin space is diversifying its product portfolio and achieved a critical mass of Rs. 8.88 billion in FYE March 2006. The company has also made three acquisitions in the recent years and sued up eight alliances to strengthen its research and development capabilities and for marketing its generic formulations in the US.

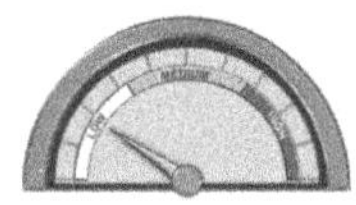

B. **Marketing Focus:** Orchid has a small token presence with Rs. 300 million in domestic formulations sales during FYE M arch 2006. The company's domestic acquisition of Mano Pharma did not make any significant impact yet.

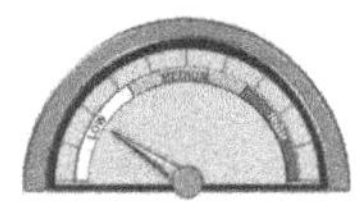

C. **Technology Focus:** Orchid, one of the most completely integrated cephalosporin players in the world has been expanding its manufacturing infrastructure and capabilities to non-cephalosporin, non-penicillin therapeutic areas. The company has built state-of-the-art technological infrastructure for manufacturing APIs, and FDFs across multiple technology platforms.

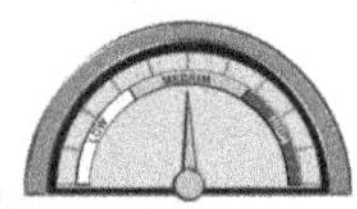

D. **Research Focus:** Orchid has 450 scientists and filed 360 patents of which 42 have been granted. Twenty seven per cent of patents are in the area of NDDR and NDDS and biotechnology indicating the shift from process research to product research. Orchid invested over 6 per cent of sales on research and development in the fiscal 2006. The company has 16 lead molecules at various stages of development.

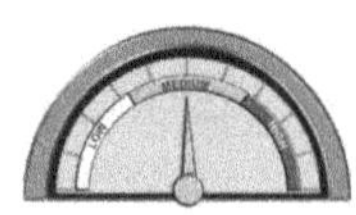

E. **Global Mindset:** Exports contributed to over three-fourths (76.12%) of Orchid's total turn over in FYE March 2006. The company's major focus is on regulated markets and has tied up with generic distributors like Apotex, Par, Actavis, Stada and Mayne for marketing its generic formulations in the US, Europe and other regulated markets.

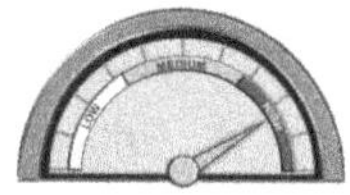

F. **Operational Excellence:** Orchid has earned a PAT of Rs. 829 million, which is about 10 per cent of its sales in FYE March 2006. The EPS was Rs. 14.85 during the same period.

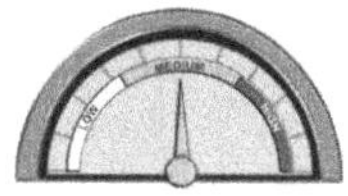

13. Jubilant Organosys

A. **Critical Mass:** With two acquisitions in the US and considerable experience in organic synthesis, Jubilant Organosys is bracing itself to make most of the CRAMS space having already reached a critical mass of Rs. 7.89 billion in FYE March 2006.

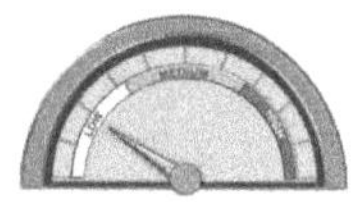

B. **Marketing Focus:** Jubilant Organosys has no participation in the domestic formulation business.

C. **Technology Focus:** Jubilant Organosys has two manufacturing facilities for APIs – one in India and one in the US with approvals from leading international regulatory authorities from the world. The company has tied up with some of the international drug majors for long-term supply of drug intermediates and APIs based on its technological capabilities.

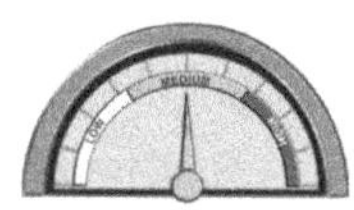

D. **Research Focus:** Jubilant Organosys has 885 scientists of whom 680 are engaged in drug discovery and clinical research. The company invested 1.05 billion on research and development activities in pharmaceutical and life sciences research which is 13.3 per cent of the pharmaceutical sales of the company or 6.98 per cent of the total turnover of the company in FYE March 2006.

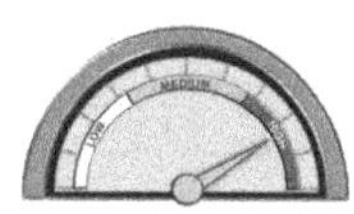

E. **Global Mindset:** Exports contributed to 76 per cent (Rs. 5.99 billion) of the pharmaceutical business of Jubilant Organosys during FYE March 2006.

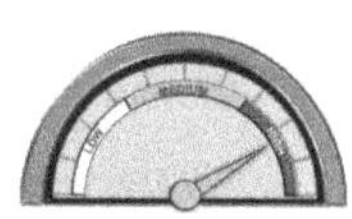

F. **Operational Excellence:** The company has earned a PAT of 8.6 per cent of sales during the same period. The EPS was Rs. 10.15. The ROCE was 14.1 per cent.

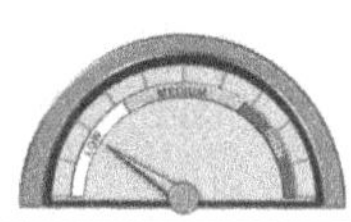

14. Biocon

A. **Critical Mass:** Biocon, the biotech major from India having reached a critical mass of Rs. 7.93 billion in FYE March 2006 is pursuing the classical strategy of acquisition and collaboration to emerge as a leading player of global distinction in biopharmaceuticals.

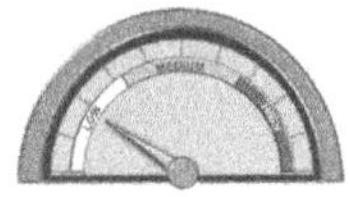

B. **Marketing Focus:** Biocon has a very small presence in the domestic formulations as of now with Rs. 90 million in sales for FYE March 2006.

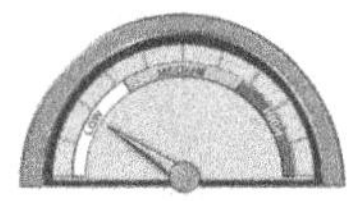

C. **Technology Focus:** Biocon, the leading biopharmaceutical company from India has built a world-class manufacturing infrastructure for APIs and FDFs covering multiple technology platforms. The company has five manufacturing plants and has received from approvals from all leading international regulatory authorities.

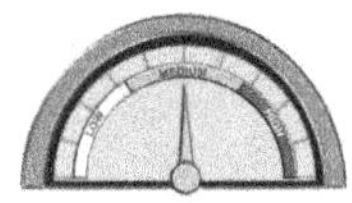

D. **Research Focus:** Biocon invested 9.63 per cent of sales on R&D in the fiscal 2006. The company has 300 scientists working on research and development across the Pharma value chain. The company has a total of 566 patents filed, many of which are a result of Nobex acquisition. Biocon's NCE pipeline has two molecules in Phase I and one in Phase II.

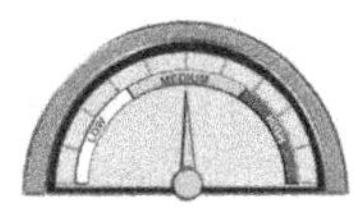

E. **Global Mindset:** Exports contributed to 52 per cent of Biocon's total turnover at Rs. 3.58 billion in FYE March 2006.

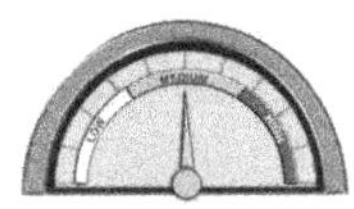

F. **Operational Excellence:** Biocon earned a healthy PAT of Rs. 1.34 billion, which is 19.26 of its turnover during FYE March 2006. The EPS was Rs. 18.20 in the same period.

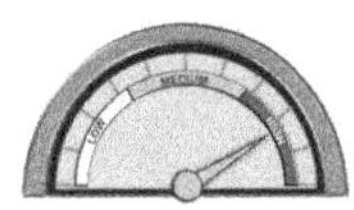

15. Ipca Laboratories

A. **Critical Mass:** A leading player in anti-malarials and anti-nauseants in India, Ipca has a strong international presence with its APIs and reached a critical mass of Rs. 7.53 billion in FYE March 2006.

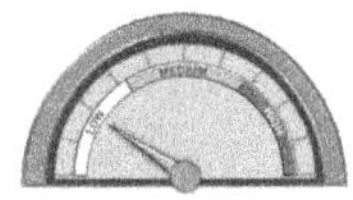

B. **Marketing Focus:** Ipca, the dominant anti-malarial player has achieved Rs. 3.32 billion in sales for FYE March 2006 in domestic formulations market. The company has entered many other therapy areas with seven marketing divisions and has six of its brands featuring among the industry's

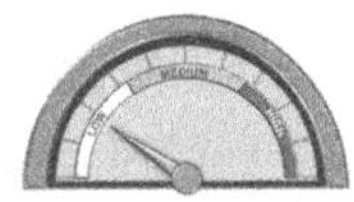

top 500 contributing about 33 per cent to its domestic formulations sales.

C. **Technology Focus:** The leading anti-malarial player in India, Ipca has three manufacturing facilities for APIs and five for FDFs in India. Many of the company's facilities have approvals from leading international regulatory authorities such as US FDA and UK MHRA and others.

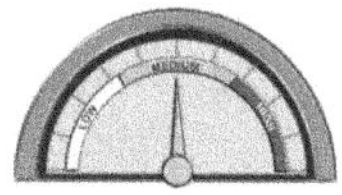

D. **Research Focus:** Ipca's R&D spend in FYE March 2006 was 5.05 per cent of its turnover. The company filed over 95 patents till now covering novel processes for manufacturing APIs and formulations in India, USA and other countries.

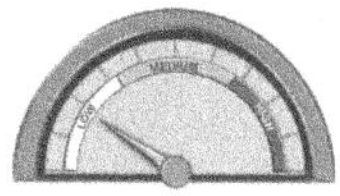

E. **Global Mindset:** Exports contributed to 53.6 per cent of Ipca's total sales at Rs. 6.39 billion in FYE March 2006. Europe was the largest market for the company with 43 per cent of its international sales.

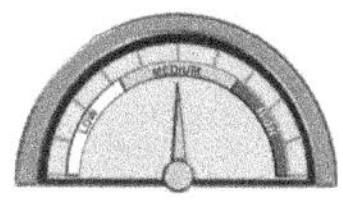

F. **Operational Excellence:** Ipca recorded a PAT of 639 million, which is 8.49 per cent of its turnover. The EPS was Rs. 25.59 during the year.

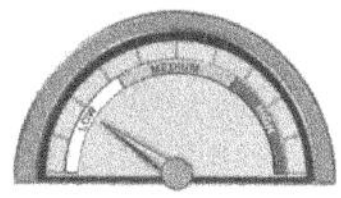

16. Divi's Labs

A. **Critical Mass:** The highly focused Divi's Labs is determined to become a leading player in the CRAMS and custom synthesis space. The company has long-term supply agreements with some of the global pharmaceutical majors. The total turnover of Divi's Labs in FYE March 2006 was Rs. 3.92 billion.

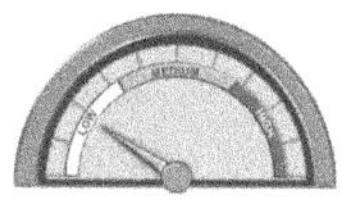

B. **Marketing Focus:** Divi's Labs has no participation in the domestic formulations business as it is competing in the CRAMS space and aiming to be a preferred partner of global Pharma majors.

C. **Technology Focus:** Divi's Labs has two CGMP-compliant API manufacturing facilities in India that have approvals from leading international regulatory authorities such as US FDA and UK MHRA. The company has entered into long-term supply agreements with some of the international drug majors based on its technological capabilities.

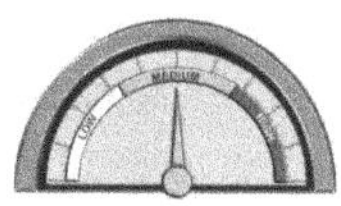

D. **Research Focus:** Divis Labs has a product portfolio of 106 products. The company has 200 scientists engaged in research and development activity to make it a preferred

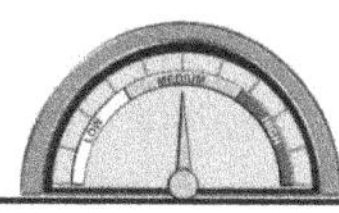

partner for global majors across the value chain in the Pharma product life cycle. Divis invested Rs. 872 million, on R&D which is 22.2 per cent of its sales in FYE March 2006.

E. **Global Mindset:** Exports contributed to 90 per cent of total sales of Divi's Labs in FYE March 2006. About 80 per cent of the company's exports during the year were to regulated markets such as North America and Europe.

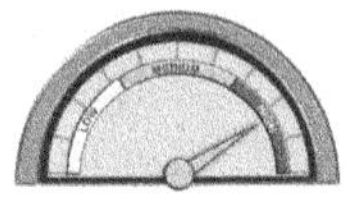

F. **Operational Excellence:** Divi's Labs has earned a PAT of Rs. 700 million, which was 17.86 per cent of sales in FYE March 2006. The RONW was 20.68 per cent and EPS of Rs. 55 during the same period, made the company a darling of the investors.

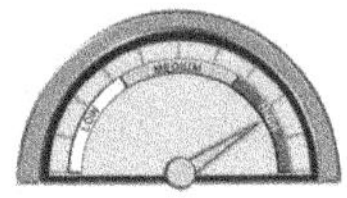

17. Dabur Pharma

A. **Critical Mass:** Dabur with a sharp focus on global oncology market has achieved Rs. 2.68 billion in FYE March 2006. Dabur has already achieved the distinction of a leading oncology generics player in some of the South East Asian countries.

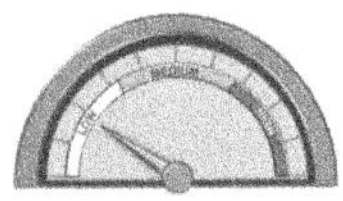

B. **Marketing Focus:** The oncology-focused Dabur Pharma recorded Rs. 1.87 billion in domestic formulations sales with three of its brands among the industry's top 500 contributing to 26.5 per cent in FYE March 2006. The company has two marketing divisions in India.

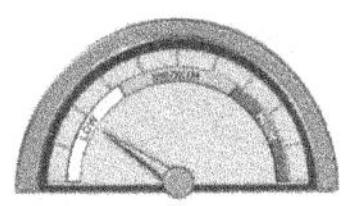

C. **Technology Focus:** The oncology focused and vertically integrated Dabur Pharma has two manufacturing facilities – one in India and one in UK. The company has forged alliances for marketing its generic oncology formulations in the US with two leading American Generic companies.

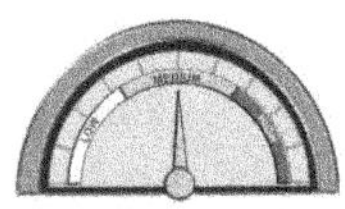

D. **Research Focus:** Dabur Pharma has 160 scientists working on all aspects of pharmaceutical research and filed 130 patents internationally till date of which 40 have been granted.

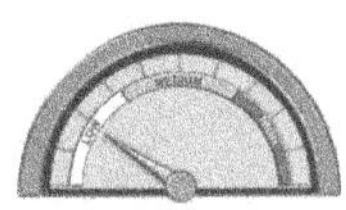

E. **Global Mindset:** International sales accounted for about 43.7 per cent of Dabur Pharma's total sales in FYE March 2006. The company is focusing on regulated markets and on oncology generics.

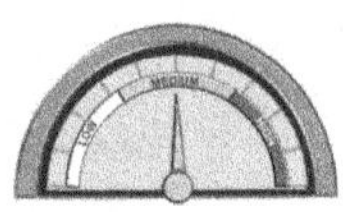

F. **Operational Excellence:** Dabur has earned a PAT of Rs. 220 million, which was about 6.77 per cent of the company's total income in FYE March 2006. The key financial ratios such as ROCE and RONW were 6.66 and 6 per cent respectively.

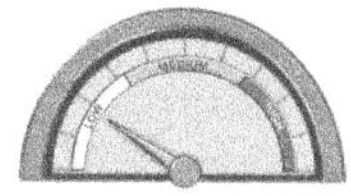

18. Matrix Laboratories

A. **Critical Mass:** With four acquisitions and two strategic alliances in the last three years Matrix has augmented its manufacturing and technological capabilities and recorded sales of over Rs. 11.58 billion in FYE March 2006. Consequently the company became even a more attractive suitor for the American generic major Mylan Laboratories, which acquired it in the last quarter of 2006.

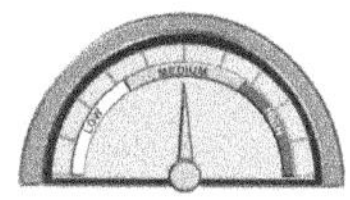

B. **Marketing Focus:** Matrix does not participate in the domestic formulations business.

C. **Technology Focus:** Matrix with its world-class manufacturing infrastructure of five plants – four for APIs and one for FDFs has become an attractive suitor for Mylan the American generic major which acquired it recently. The four API plants of Matrix have approvals from leading international regulatory authorities such as US FDA, UK MHRA, EQDM and South African MCC.

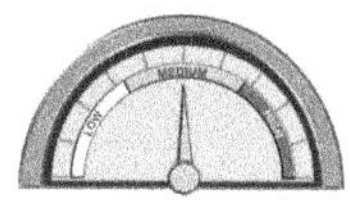

D. **Research Focus:** The 150 scientists engaged in the research and development activities at Matrix have combined experience of filing 250 ANDAs. The company filed 54 patents, 88 DMFs and one ANDA till now. Matrix invested Rs. 599 million on R&D in FYE March 2006, which is 5.17 per cent of sales.

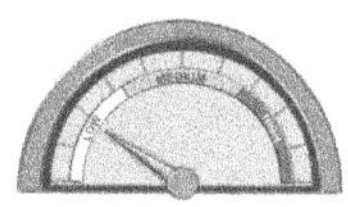

E. **Global Mindset:** Matrix achieved close to three-fourths of its total sales (72.9%) from international markets during FYE March 2006. Europe was the single largest destination of the company's exports accounting for 49.7 per cent and North America accounting for 11.7 per cent during the year.

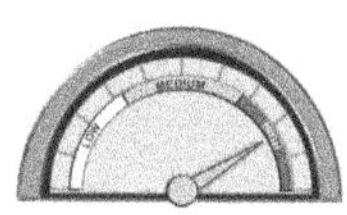

F. **Operational Excellence:** Matrix achieved net profit of Rs. 1.99 billion, which is 17.18 percent during the year under review. There has been an improvement in other key financial ratios such as ROCE (17.75%), RONW (20.94%) and the EPS was Rs. 12.11 during the same period.

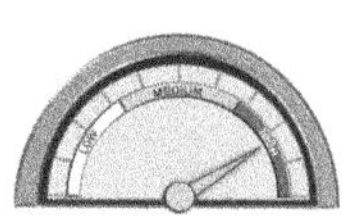

19. Shasun Chemicals

A. **Critical Mass:** Shasun Chemicals is bent on transforming itself from an API supplier to a preferred partner for global majors across the whole spectrum of CRAMS and reached a critical mass of Rs. 3.49 billion in FYE March 2006.

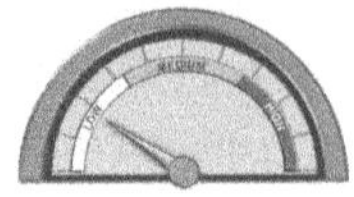

B. **Marketing Focus:** Shasun does not participate in the domestic formulations business as its strategy is committed to become a preferred partner to international and domestic Pharma majors.

C. **Technology focus:** Shasun has threee manufacturing facilities – two for APIs and one for FDFs that are c-GMP-compliant. The company's two API plants have approvals from all major international regulatory authorities including US FDA and UK MHRA. Shasun has proven technological capabilities across multiple platforms.

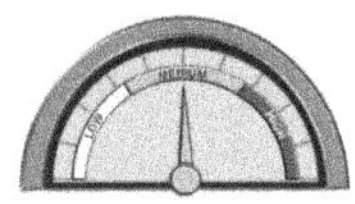

D. **Research Focus:** The R&D spend of Shasun in FYE March 2006 was Rs. 263.6 million, which was 7.55 per cent of its turnover. Due to the company's unique partnership positioning with emerging companies, the company has an enviable pipeline of 14 molecules in Phase II and Phase III.

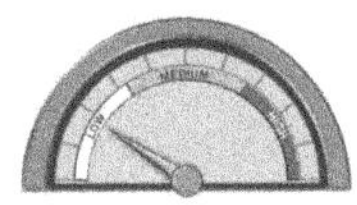

E. **Global Mindset:** Exports contributed to 74 per cent of the company's turnover during FYE March 2006.

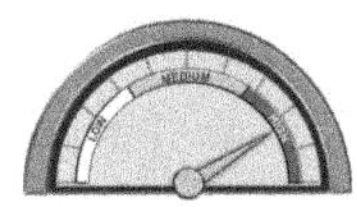

F. **Operational Excellence:** Shasun earned a PAT of Rs. 365.4 million, which is 10 per cent of total sales in FYE March 2006. the Company's ROCE and RONW were 16 and 20 per cent respectively. The EPS during was Rs. 7.75.

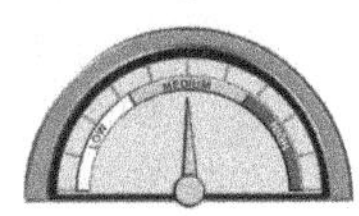

20. Strides Arcolabs

A. **Critical Mass:** With presence in over sixty countries across the world and a leading position in Latin America Strides Arcolabs achieved a critical mass of Rs. 3.49 billion in sales for FYE March 2006 with two acquisitions and six strategic alliances in the last few years.

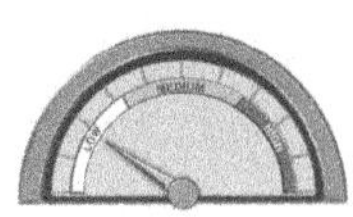

B. **Marketing Focus:** Strides Arcolabs does not participate in the domestic formulations business.

C. **Technology Focus:** The softgel specialist from India, Strides Arcolabs has created a world-class technology infrastructure with thirteen manufacturing facilities worldwide. The company's facilities are located in India, USA, Brazil and Poland and have approvals from all major international regulatory authorities.

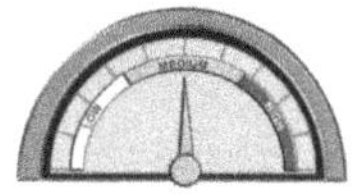

D. **Research Focus:** 200 scientists are working on research and development at Strides Arcolabs today. The company has filed a total of 657 product dossiers globally till date and has a pipeline of 36 softgel-FDFs in Oncology.

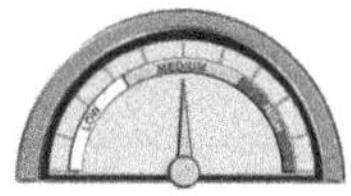

E. **Global Mindset:** International sales contributed to 95 per cent of total sales of Strides in FYE March 2006. South And Central Americas accounted for about 43 per cent and North America and Europe accounted for 35 per cent of total sales during the year.

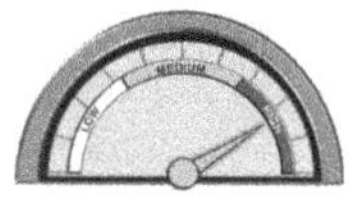

F. **Operational Excellence:** Strides earned a PAT of Rs. 461.09 million, which is 13.8 per cent of its turnover in FYE March 2006. The EPS was Rs. 11.53 during the same period.

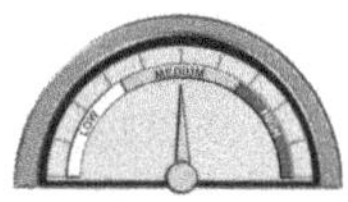

21. J B Chemicals

A. **Critical Mass:** Ranked 38 in the Indian pharmaceutical industry JB chemicals recorded Rs. 4.81 billion in sales for FYE March 2006. The company is competing for the international generics space and CRAMS space for its future growth.

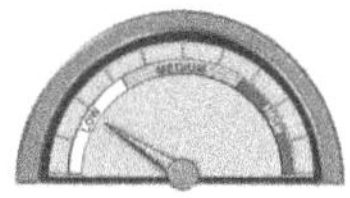

B. **Marketing Focus:** J B Chemicals has achieved Rs. 1.8 billion in domestic formulations sales for FYE March 2006 with five of its brands featuring among the industry's top 500 contributing about 58.9 per cent. The company has three marketing divisions to promote its products to physicians in different specialty segments in India.

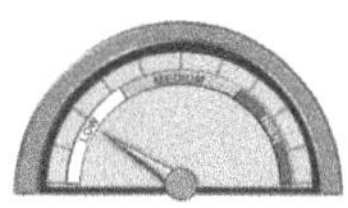

C. **Technology Focus:** J B Chemicals has eleven manufacturing facilities for manufacturing APIs and FDFs in India. The company has approvals for many of its facilities from all major international regulatory authorities such as US FDA and UK MHRA and EQDM.

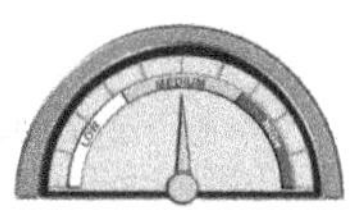

D. **Research Focus:** The R&D spend of J B chemicals is between 2.5 to 3 per cent of sales currently.

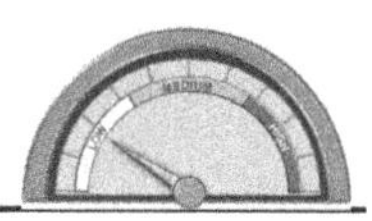

E. **Global Mindset:** Exports accounted for about 56 per cent of total sales of J B Chemicals in FYE March 2006. The company is sharpening its focus on regulated markets.

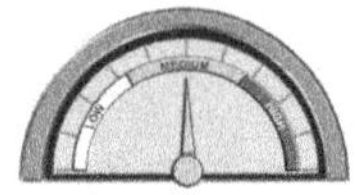

F. **Operational Excellence:** J B Chemicals has earned a PAT of Rs. 709 million, which was 14.74 of total revenues in FYE March 2006. Other key financial indicators for the year such as ROCE were 19.97 per cent, RONW 21.29 per cent, and EPS Rs. 8.83.

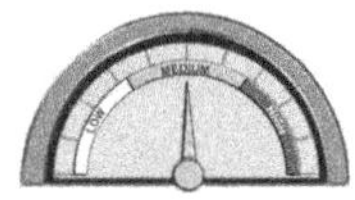

22. Unichem

A. **Critical Mass:** One of the oldest pharmaceutical companies, Unichem is bullish on its future and is aspiring for a prominent position in the international generics space. The company has achieved Rs. 4.66 billion in sales during FYE March 2006.

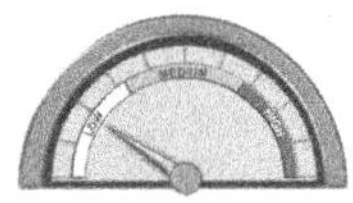

B. **Marketing Focus:** Unichem Laboratories achieved Rs. 4.02 billion in domestic formulations sales for FYE March 2006. The company's four marketing divisions pushed seven of its brands into industry's top 500. These seven brands contributed to 47 per cent of the company's domestic formulations sales.

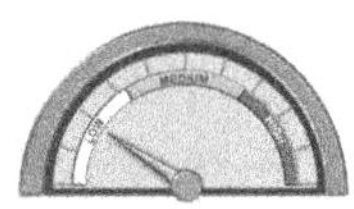

C. **Technology Focus:** Unichem has five manufacturing facilities – two for APIs and three for FDFs. The company has received international regulatory approvals for two of its facilities.

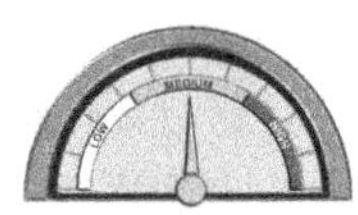

D. **Research Focus:** Unichem's R&D spend in FYE March 2006 was Rs. 123.25 million, which was 2.58 per cent of its turnover. The company has about one hundred scientists engaged in research and development activities.

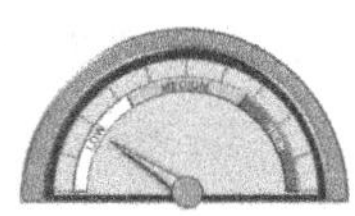

E. **Global Mindset:** Exports contributed close to a fifth of the total sales for Unichem in FYE March 2006. The company is focusing on regulated markets and forged strategic marketing alliances with two generic companies in the US for marketing their generic formulations.

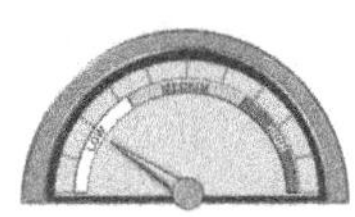

F. **Operational Excellence:** Unichem earned a PAT of Rs. 818.6 million, which is 17.8 per cent of sales during FYE March 2006. The company's key financial rations such as ROCE, RONW were 27.8 per cent and 23.7 per cent respectively while the EPS was Rs. 23.8 during the same period.

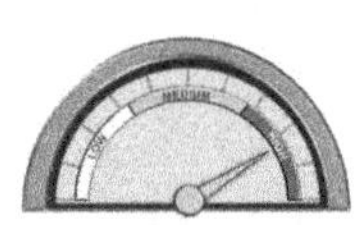

23. Alembic

A. **Critical Mass:** The centurion among the Indian pharmaceutical companies, Alembic stood the vicissitudes of changing times and is gearing itself to stay competitive in the product patent era. The company recorded Rs. 6.65 billion in sales for FYE March 2006.

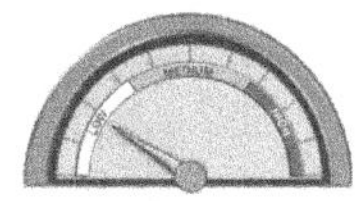

B. **Marketing Focus:** Alembic, recorded Rs. 4.3 billion in domestic formulations market with five of its brands (sales Rs. 1.99 billion) featuring among the industry's 500. The company has four marketing divisions.

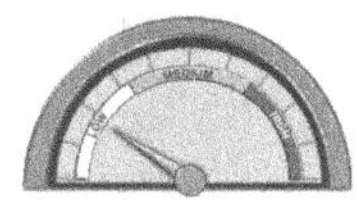

C. **Technology Focus:** Alembic, one of the oldest pharmaceutical companies in Asia has four manufacturing facilities covering multiple technology platforms and is vertically integrated across its major product lines. One of the company's API plant has US FDA approval while its other facilities are c-GMP-compliant and have approvals from some of the leading international regulatory authorities.

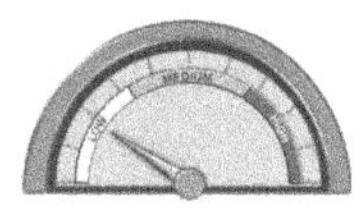

D. **Research Focus:** Alembic has over 125 scientists in its research arm – BioArc, which is also pursuing contract research opportunities. The company invested Rs. 301 million on R&D which is 4.5 per cent of its sales in FYE March 2006. Alembic filed a total of 89 patents till now.

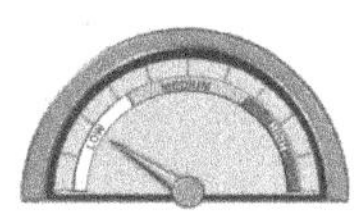

E. **Global Mindset:** International sales contributed to 18.45 per cent of the total turnover of Alembic at Rs. 1.23 billion during FYE March 2006.

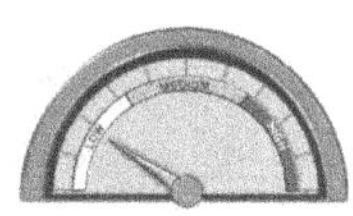

F. **Operational Excellence:** Alembic earned a PAT of Rs. 785.2 million, which is 12.06 per cent of turnover during FYE March 2006. The EPS was Rs. 28.56 during the year.

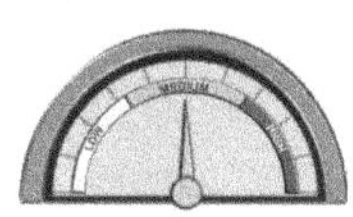

24. Claris Life Sciences

A. **Critical Mass:** Claris Life sciences is clearly focused on hospital products covering many therapeutic areas. The company recorded about Rs. 4 billion in sales for FYE December 2006.

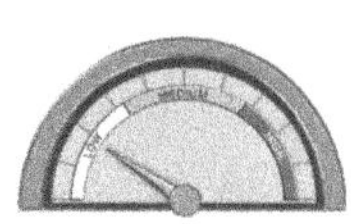

B. Marketing Focus: Claris Life Sciences is focused on the hospital segment and recorded Rs. 1.4 billion in sales for FYE December 2006.

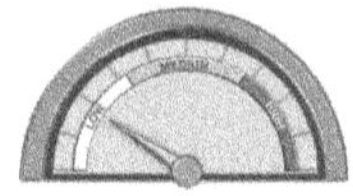

C. Technology Focus: Claris Life Sciences is focusing on hospital products including small and large volume parenteral preparations covering major therapy areas and multiple technology platforms. The company's manufacturing facility has major international regulatory approvals.

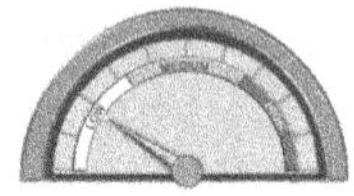

D. Research Focus: Claris Life Sciences has 100 scientists working on research and development activities focusing on LDDS, NDDS and biotechnology. Claris filed 9 ANDAs with the US FDA and 30 MAAs in Europe and Australia.

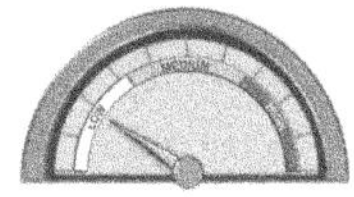

E. Global Mindset: Claris Life Sciences recorded fifty per cent of its total sales from international markets during FYE December 2006.

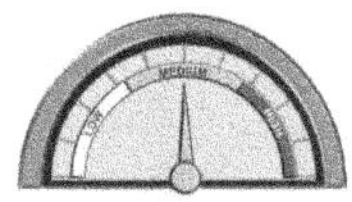

F. Operational Excellence: Claris is actively preparing in registering its products and tying up marketing alliances with overseas partners. The potential for future financial performance seems to be brighter as the activities are in the right place at the right time.

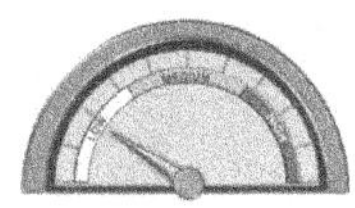

25. FDC Laboratories

A. Critical Mass: FDC Limited, the septuagenarian which has reached a critical mass of Rs. 3.77 billion in FYE March 2006 is becoming young again to stay competitive in product patent era.

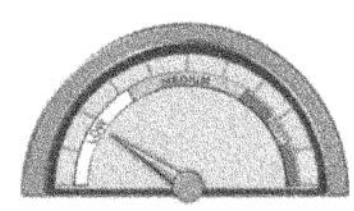

B. Marketing Focus: FDC Laboratories achieved Rs. 3.86 billion in domestic formulations market in FYE March 2006. The company has 9 brands, which contributed to 55 per cent of its domestic formulations sales. FDC has three marketing divisions in India to retain its promotional focus in different prescriber segments.

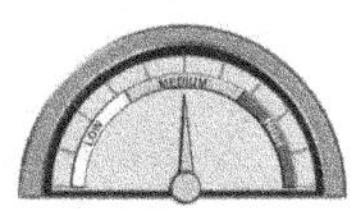

C. Technology Focus: FDC laboratories, the leading player in oral re-hydration segment has four FDF plants and one API manufacturing facilities. The company has major international regulatory approvals including US FDA and UK MHRA.

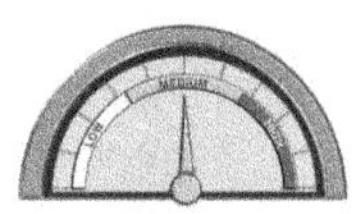

D. Research Focus: The R&D Spend of FDC per annum is over 1.5 per cent of sales.

E. **Global Mindset:** Exports of FDC were Rs. 800 million, which accounted for 21.5 per cent of total sales in FYE March 2006. The company is now focusing on regulated markets and filed 9 ANDAs with US FDA and has four products registered in UK.

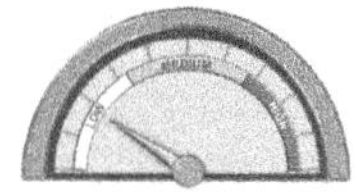

F. **Operational Excellence:** FDC has earned a PAT of Rs. 694.3 million, which was 18.39 per cent of total sales in FYE March 2006. The EPS was Rs. 3.63.

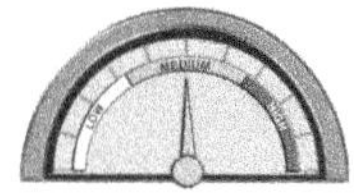

26. Ind-Swift Laboratories

A. **Critical Mass:** Primarily a supplier of APIs to markets with little or no regulation, Ind-Swift Laboratories is slowly but surely graduating into regulated markets and achieved annual sales of Rs. 3.23 billion FYE March 2006.

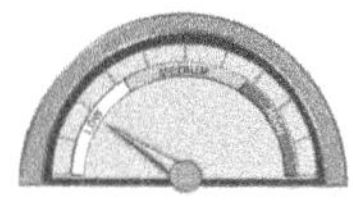

B. **Marketing Focus:** Ind-Swift has seven marketing divisions in India and recorded sales of Rs. 1.87 billion in domestic formulations market.

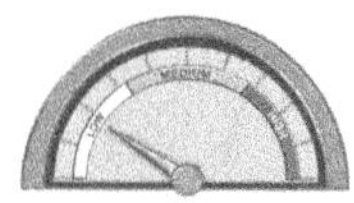

C. **Technology Focus:** Ind-Swift has five FDF plants one cGMP-compliant API manufacturing facility with five dedicated blocks. The company's clarithromycin API facility has recently completed the US FDA inspection successfully.

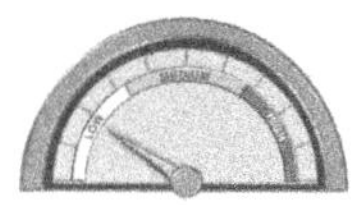

D. **Research Focus:** Ind-Swift invested Rs. 217 million in FYE March 2006 on R&D activity, which is 6.6 per cent of sales. The company has 85 scientists engaged in research and development activity currently.

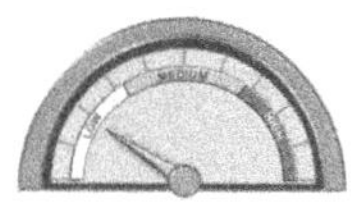

E. **Global Mindset:** International sales at Rs. 1.61 billion contributed to 50 per cent of Ind-Swift's total sales in FYE March 2006.

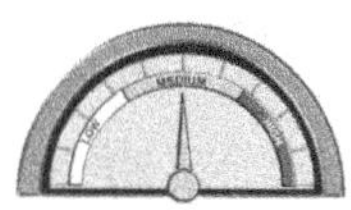

F. **Operational Excellence:** Ind-Swift has earned a PAT of Rs. 347.87 million, which was 10.74 per cent of the company's total sales in FYE March 2006. The EPS was Rs. 17.00 during the same period.

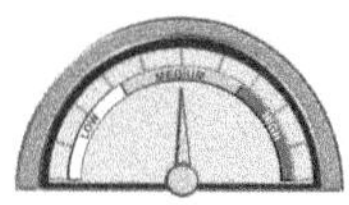

27. Natco Pharma

A. **Critical Mass:** The resurgent Natco Pharma is becoming more competitive across the Pharma value chain and achieved Rs. 2.07 billion in sales for FYE March 2006.

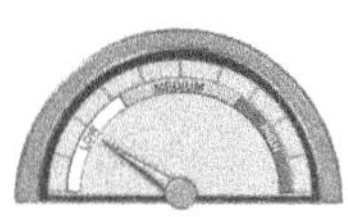

B. **Marketing Focus:** Natco Pharma has recorded Rs. 110 million in domestic formulations sales for FYE March 2006.

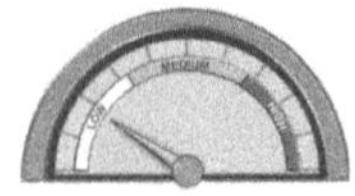

C. **Technology Focus:** Natco Pharma has built a huge manufacturing infrastructure with two very large API facilities one FDF facility for small and large volume parenterals and one FDF facility for other dosage forms. The company has received US FDA approval for its API facility. Its other facilities have approvals from some of the leading international regulatory authorities.

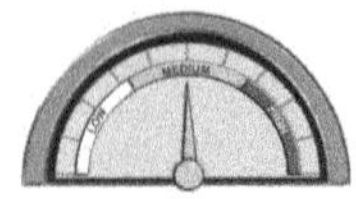

D. **Research Focus:** Natco invested Rs. 74.28 million, which is 4.62 per cent of its sales on R&D in FYE March 2006. The company's total DMF filings stand at 159 and ANDA filings at 2 with eight more under filing.

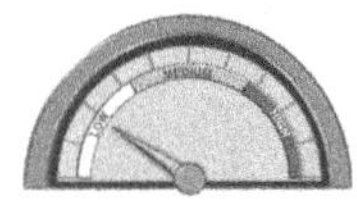

E. **Global Mindset:** Exports contributed to about Rs. 805 million, which is 39 per cent of total Natco's turnover in FYE March 2006.

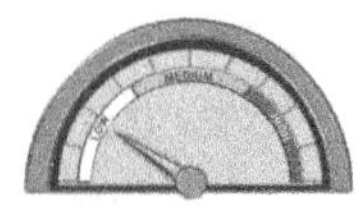

F. **Operational Excellence:** Natco has earned a PAT of Rs. 237.93 million, which is 12.8 per cent of its turnover in FYE March 2006. The EPS was Rs. 8.76 in the same period.

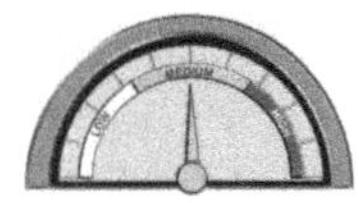

28. Nectar Life Sciences

A. **Critical Mass:** Nectar Life Sciences, originally an integrated cephalosporin player is diversifying into non-cephalosporin and non-anti-biotic product competitive spaces without losing focus on cephalosporins. The company has achieved Rs. 3.1 billion in sales FYE March 2006.

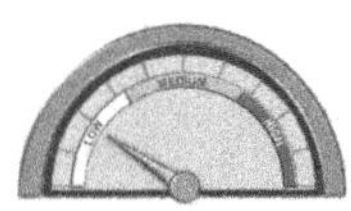

B. **Marketing Focus:** Nectar Life Sciences has no participation in domestic formulations market currently.

C. **Technology Focus:** Nectar Life Sciences has two c-GMP-compliant manufacturing facilities – one for APIs and one for FDFs. The company is a vertically integrated cephalosporin player.

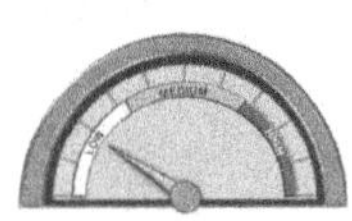

D. **Research Focus:** Nectar Life Sciences is setting up a modern research and development facility with a cost of Rs. 150 million manned by 200 scientists for conducting process research, formulation development research for regulated markets. The company currently spends about 3.8 per cent on R&D activity.

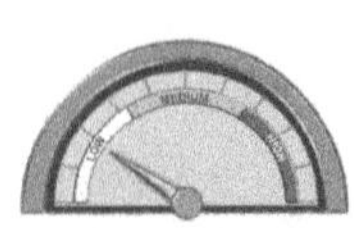

E. **Global Mindset:** Exports contributed to Rs. 2.53 billion, which is 81.6 per cent of the total turnover of the company in FYE March 2006.

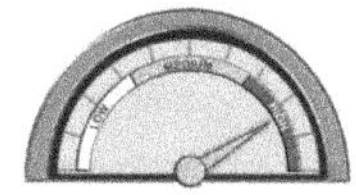

F. **Operational Excellence:** Nectar has earned a PAT of 255.5 million, which is 8.2 per cent of the total sales. The EPS was Rs. 18.21 in the same period.

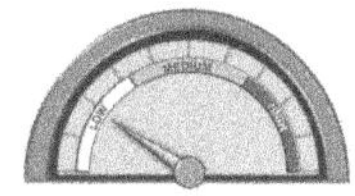

29. Dishman Pharmaceuticals

A. **Critical Mass:** Dishman Pharmaceuticals is changing gears to grow faster and has positioned itself as a preferred partner of global pharmaceutical companies in the CRAMS space. The company clocked Rs. 2.16 billion in sales for FYE March 2006.

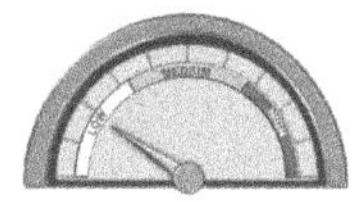

B. **Marketing Focus:** Dishman Pharmaceuticals has no participation in domestic formulations market currently.

C. **Technology Focus:** Dishman Pharmaceuticals has two API facilities one of which has approval from the US FDA.

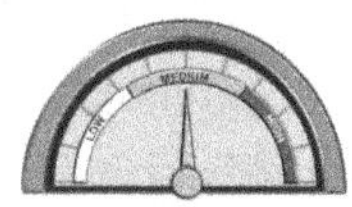

D. **Research Focus:** Dishman invested Rs. 245 million in FYE March 2006, which is 11.3 per cent of sales.

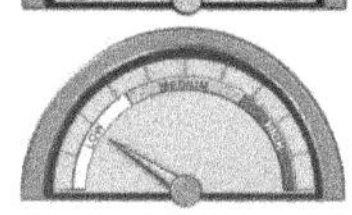

E. **Global Mindset:** Exports at Rs. 1.64 billion contributed to 75.92 per cent of Dishman's sales in FYE March 2006.

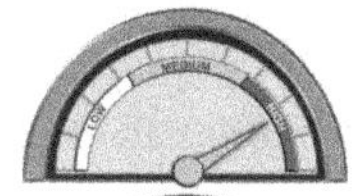

F. **Operational Excellence:** Dishman has earned a PAT of Rs. 456 million which was 21 per cent of sales in FYE March 2006. The EPS was Rs. 6.6.

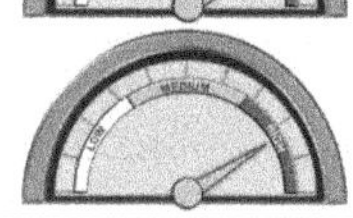

30. Suven Life Sciences

A. **Critical Mass:** With an aspiration to emerge as one of the leading players from India providing full spectrum of services in discovery related services, Suven Life Sciences has achieved Rs. 830 million in FYE March 2006.

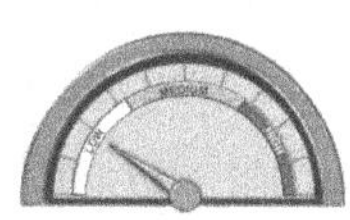

B. **Marketing Focus:** Suven Life Sciences does not participate in the domestic formulations market.

C. **Technology Focus:** Suven has one API facility that is c-GMP-compliant.

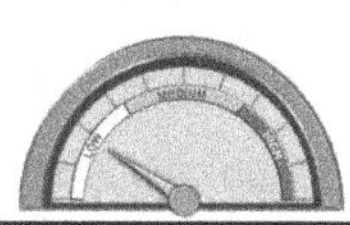

D. **Research Focus:** Frost and Sullivan, a global consulting firm has awarded Suven Life Sciences the partner of choice in drug discovery for CNS from India in 2005. Suven has 190 scientists engaged in drug discovery research. The company invested Rs. 220 million on R&D which is 26 per cent of its sales in FYE March 2006. The company signed a co-development agreement with Eli Lilly, the international drug major for CNS therapeutic area.

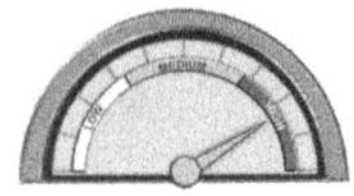

E. **Global Mindset:** Exports accounted for over three-fourths (76.7 per cent) of Suven's turnover at Rs. 636.98 million in FYE March 2006.

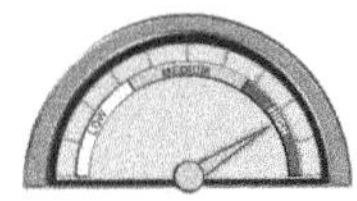

F. **Operational Excellence:** Suven earned a PAT of Rs. 85.68 million which is 10.3 per cent of turnover in FYE March 2006. The EPS ws Rs. 2.55 during the same period.

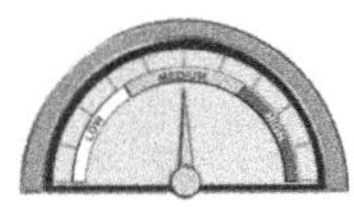

Ten More Global Aspirants

Here is a brief account of ten more Indian pharmaceutical companies, whose game plans are similar to the ones we have discussed throughout this book. Although some of these companies are bigger in size, they are not included for a detailed study as they are closely held companies and not publicly traded. The information about their moves and results is difficult to validate, as they are not listed. A broad perspective of what they are aiming at, their capabilities and competencies could be presented with a reasonable degree of clarity and dependability. These companies are – Hetero Drugs, Cadila Pharmaceutials, Intas, Panacea Biotech, Emcure, Indoco Remedies, Neuland Pharmaceuticals, Granules India, Gland Pharma, and GVK Bio Sciences. Seven out of these ten companies have invested in upgrading their technology and received approvals from major regulatory authorities such as US FDA. Virtually all of them have tied up with more than one strategic partner either for market access, product access or technology access. Some of them have entered into long-term supply arrangements. Others have entered into co-development or clinical research alliances. Table 11.2 presents a brief account of the game plans of these ten global aspirants.

Table 11.2 The Other Global Aspirants

1. **Hetero Drugs:** In a relatively short period of time, Hetero Drugs carved a niche for itself in the pharmaceutical industry in India. The company has been investing in building intellectual capabilities as well as capital to stay competitive in the product patent era. The Rs 12-billion Hetero group is involved in manufacturing and marketing of APIs and FDFs, Contract Research, Custom Synthesis and Contract Manufacturing.

2. **Intas Pharmaceuticals:** Intas Pharmaceuticals is a specialty focused pharmaceutical company from India with global aspirations. The company is among the top 3 companies in the Neuro-psychiatry segment in India. Intas has recorded a total turnover of Rs. 6.24 billion in FYE March 2006. Exports contributed to 25 per cent of the company's total sales in the year. The company currently exports to over fifty countries in South East Asia and Africa. The company is now focusing on regulated markets such as US and Europe. Intas has earned a PAT of Rs. 803 million, which is 12. 87 per cent of sales during the year. The EPS was Rs. 98.29.

3. **Cadila Pharmaceuticals :** The Strategic Vision of Cadila Pharmaceuticals is to be a leading pharmaceutical company in India and to become a significant global player by the year 2010. Cadila Pharma recorded a turnover of Rs. 6.9 billion in FYE March 2005. The company has strategic collaborations and operations spanning over 90 countries across the globe. Cadila Pharma is a totally integrated company in life sciences from intermediates to APIs to FDFs and biopharmaceuticals. The company's state-of-the-art R&D center houses over 400 scientists and is also engaged in contract research services. The company has earmarked a US $ 55 million up-gradation during this year. The company's manufacturing infrastructure comprises five cGMP-compliant facilities in India and has received international regulatory approvals from US FDA, UK MHRA, ANVISA of Brazil, MCC of South Africa, TGA of Australia and WHO, Geneva. The company has filed 9 patent applications in 2004 and has filed 9 DMFs with US FDA. Cadila Pharma has a JV in Ethiopia.

4. **Panacea Biotech Limited:** Panacea biotech Limited is a vaccine focused pharmaceutical and biotechnology company from India. Vaccines accounted for close to three-fourths (74.48%) of the company's turnover of Rs. 5.53 billion in FYE March 2006. The company's R&D spend during the year was 6.14 per cent of sales with about 200 scientists manning its R&D center. The company has five marketing divisions to market its formulations across the various therapeutic areas to multiple specialty prescriber segments. Panacea has a 50:50 J V with the UK-based Chiron Vaccines. The company has earned a Pat of 592.5 million, which is 10.69 per cent of sales during the year. The EPS was Rs. 7.36 and ROCE was 24.09 during the same period.

5. **Emcure Laboratories:** Established in 1983, Emcure has become a preferred contract manufacturing partner to many a multinational pharmaceutical companies in India. The company has subsequently set its sights on the world stage and built up its technological and developmental capabilities to become competitive in the CRAMS space. Ranked currently twenty-fifth in the Indian branded generic formulations market Emcure has been one of the fastest growing companies for a few years now. The

company has a US FDA approved manufacturing facility and tied up with a number of American generic companies such as Actavis, Pliva and Ivax among others for API supplies and marketing generic formulations. The company also forged a developmental alliance with the international drug major BMS.

6. **Indoco Remedies:** Started exactly after a week of India's Independence, Indoco Remedies has taken rather a long time to reach where it has reached today, but it looks like that it would go places. Indoco has recorded a turnover of Rs. 2.69 billion in FYE March 2006. The PAT was 12.94 per cent of total income at Rs. 314.9 million. The EPS was Rs 26.64 and ROCE was 22.72 per cent during the year. Exports contributed to about 48 per cent of sales during the year. Indoco is active in the domestic formulations business with five marketing divisions promoting its diverse product mix to multiple specialty prescriber segments. The company invested Rs. 246.9 million, which was 10.14 per cent of sales during the year on research and development activity. The company has eight manufacturing facilities some of which have received approvals from leading international regulatory authorities such as US FDA, UK MHRA, ANVISA of Brazil and MCC of South Africa among others. Every which way you look at Indoco's arrival in the brave new Pharma world was delayed but not denied!

7. **Neuland Laboratories :** Neuland Laboratories is one of the reputed API manufacturers from India with global aspirations. The company has invested right from the inception on upgrading technology and process research. The company's manufacturing facilities are state-of-the-art and received approvals from major international regulatory authorities such as US FDA, EQDM, UK MHRA among others. Neuland clocked a turnover of Rs. 1.7 billion in FYE March 2006 with a net income of Rs. 62 million. Exports contributed to about 70 per cent of the company's total sales of which regulated markets such as the US and Europe contributed to two-thirds of total exports.

8. **Granules India :** Granules India has positioned itself differently to emerge as a winner in the product patent era of pharmaceutical world. The company wants to become a large- scale consumer healthcare focused service provider and achieve a global breadth in the delivery of service. The company has invested in cutting edge infrastructure and technologies to support strong partnerships with industry leaders. Granules today has achieved the distinction of being the only company to commercially manufacture combination pharmaceutical formulation intermediates (PFIs of multiple APIs). Granules has recorded a turnover of Rs. 1.76 billion in FYE March 2006.The company has earned a PAT of 92.5 million during the same period. International sales contributed to 82 per cent of the total turnover with North America accounting for a major chunk of 44 per cent of the total.

9. **Gland Pharma Limited:** Started as a Heparin manufacturing company twenty-five years ago, Gland Pharma has redefined its vision to become a global injectable player providing value-added services. The company accordingly invested in technology, research and developmental activities. Today, Gland Pharma has an injectable

manufacturing facility that has international regulatory approvals from leading international regulatory authorities such as US FDA and ANVISA of Brazil. Gland Pharma seems determined to cross the important milestone of US $ 100 million dollars in two to three years.

10. **G V K Bio Sciences :** GVK Bio Sciences is the new kid on the block in among the ever-growing CROs. GVK Bio has created a world-class infrastructure for contract research development support services covering the whole spectrum such as informatics, biology, process R&D, clinical pharmacology, and clinical research. The company has entered into a strategic development alliance with the global drug major John Wyeth wherein GVK Bio would dedicate a discovery chemistry site with about 150 scientists. GVK Bio has 460 scientists and has top ten pharmaceutical and biotech companies on its clients list.

On the Right Track

The game plans of these companies are similar to the thirty companies we have discussed in this book. Some of them are competing for the international generics space and almost all of them are competing for CRAMS space in some way or other. Once a company reaches a critical mass in terms of investible surplus it expands its competitive space by competing across other components of the Pharma value chain. GVK Bio Sciences is only company that is clearly focused on Contract Research. Seven out of these companies have already approvals from all major regulatory authorities in the world such as US FDA, UK MHRA, Brazilian ANVISA and South African MCC among others. Consider their achievements and contributions to the growth of the Indian pharmaceutical industry so far:

- The combined turnover of these companies is in excess of Rs. 40 billion in FYE March 2006
- Seven companies have one or more approvals from US FDA of their manufacturing facilities
- The total value of exports by these ten companies was around Rs. 12.5 billion in FYE March 2006
- The total number of scientists engaged in R&D activity in these ten companies is around 1,500
- These ten companies have a total of about thirty-five manufacturing facilities

A Disclaimer

The analysis and the ranking presented in this chapter is a qualitative assessment of their strategic actions and performance as of now (FYE March 2006). Purists take qualitative assessment either with a pinch of salt or with unadulterated skepticism. But then, the qualitative assessment presented in this book is evidence based. Evidence of their actions and performance based on the published reports, the annual reports of the respective companies, and informal discussions with a number of senior managers of various pharmaceutical companies over the last twelve months. Therefore it is dependable as a pointer or indicator of the likely course charted by these companies and the progress they are likely to make. But then, current potential and performance do not certainly guarantee future performance. Also differences in current sizes are not certainly indicative of future performance in these turbulent times as an acquisition here and a merger there could virtually change the position and picture of the company and its competitors as it were on a board game of snakes and ladders.

Chapter Twelve
Winners' Checklist

It would be hard to find out a company that can do business in the 'product patent regime' as it did in the 'process patent raj'.

A few companies have responded effectively. Many are not able to respond adequately. One reason for the ineffectual response is that business leaders simply have not appreciated the rate and pace of change - how the 'has become' is becoming.

The key to success is in anticipating change before it arrives, and evolve, plan strategies to ride it, to master it.

The winners' checklist is about asking some of the important questions that should signal to a company how the change is taking place and how much 'it' needs to change.

The Major drivers of change are in areas like:

- Information technology
- Global perspective for global markets
- Ethical corporate behavior
- Responsibility to society at large, not just shareholders
- Total customer solutions

Here then, are twenty key questions every business leader should ask (and answer). Here's the winners' checklist. Check it out!

The rate of change in the Indian drug industry is so high that incremental improvements will not work, let alone maximize your potential. Gone are the days when you could gain a competitive edge by developing a slightly better way of doing things. The pace of change is so rapid that it is almost like a gale force wind. If you aim to take a small step or two you will probably end up going backwards. You need to take a big step into the teeth of the gale merely to hold your position. To move forward, you have to take more than one big step at a time. The change has to be revolutionary, not evolutionary.

Consider what Gary Hamel said while talking about strategy as revolution:

> Let us admit it. Corporations around the world are reaching the limits of incrementalism. Squeezing another penny out of costs, getting a product to market a few weeks earlier, responding to customers' inquiries a little bit faster, ratcheting quality up by one or more notch, capturing another point of market share - these are the obsessions of managers today. But pursuing incremental improvements, while rivals reinvent the industry is like fiddling when Rome burns.

When the usual is no longer usual, a business-as-usual approach is sure to fail. Moreover, the rate of change offers opportunities for competition to exploit if you fail to do so. John O' Keefee, Group Vice President, Proctor & Gamble, in his highly stimulating and thought provoking book on 'Business Beyond the Box - Applying Your Mind for Breakthrough Results' says that, "too many organizations use the past as a sofa. The past should be used as a springboard and not as a sofa". The key question to ask is - how does your organization use the past - as a sofa or as a springboard?

Here are twenty such questions, which act as a checklist for arriving at the big steps that are needed to move forward in this era of cataclysmic change. All the successful companies have found answers to these and planned their strategies accordingly. Here is the winners' checklist:

1. Do we have a well-defined Mission (not just statement) that is understood by all team members? Do our senior management team members see themselves as revolutionaries or evolutionaries in our industry? Are they contented with the

status quo? Or do they want to re-write the rules for the industry? What is our leadership quotient? What is our industry foresight?

2. Do we have a clear vision and a detailed blue print for action as to how we are going to achieve what we want to achieve? How detailed are our action plans? Do they indicate responsibility centers and time lines for each key objective?

3. Do all our employees share the organizational optimism and aspirations? Do they have a clear sense of urgency for accomplishment? Do they have a sense of ownership of our organizational goals and objectives?

4. Is our top management allocating as much time for pre-market competition as to market competition? How much of their time goes into running and managing current business as compared to that spent to visualize, anticipate changes and plan for future business opportunities? How much time do they spend in maintenance as opposed to building our business?

5. Do we have a clear and collective agenda for building core competencies in all key areas and key markets? Do we have market-specific strategies? What are our competencies in regulatory area? What are our capabilities in filing DMFs and ANDAs in regulatory markets? What is the depth and breadth of our product portfolio?

6. What is the stretch involved in our aspirations? What is our current level of performance? Where do we stand right now? Where do we want to go? What do we need to reach where we want to reach? How do we bridge the gap? What is our action agenda for acquiring the resources we need and for building the infrastructure that our growth plans require?

7. What is our manufacturing infrastructure? Do our plants conform to international regulatory requirements? How many of our facilities for manufacturing bulk actives and formulations are approved already by international regulatory authorities like

US FDA, UK MHRA and others? What is the level of preparation required and by what time frame can we have our facilities approved?

8. What is our R&D infrastructure? What is our investment on research and development? How does it compare with our major competitors and with the industry average? What are the areas of our research focus? What is the quality of our scientific talent and temper? What is our acquisition agenda for scientific talent? What is our NCE pipeline like?

9. Global markets require a global perspective and posture. What is our stance towards IPR? Do we respect IPR protection? Companies like Nicholas Piramal, Ranbaxy, Cipla, Wockhardt, Glenmark and Zydus, among others who are actively seeking strategic alliances with prospective partners are already entering into licensing and co-marketing arrangements for gaining access to new products, markets and technology. Many of these companies are also chasing acquisition targets overseas to accelerate their growth. Attitude towards intellectual property rights and their protection is vital to form strategic alliances and to build relationships internationally. One cannot have two different sets of rules – one for the domestic market and another for overseas markets, when a company wants to go global.

10. How have we embraced information technology? Corporations in the new millennium will increasingly reorganize around information technology. To be competitive, companies must use high-tech tools of information technology like ERP (Enterprise Resource Planning), digitalization of communication across its units in all its operating markets, RFID technology , SCM, CRM, web presence, and strategic databases of customers and datamining.

The Key Questions to ask are:

- What is our investment in information technology? In hardware? In software?
- What is our investment in training and development of our teams?

- Are we planning innovative strategies to reach our customers by exploiting the revolutionary developments that are taking place in information technology? And manufacturing technology covering multiple platforms? And in research development areas?
- What are our plans to graduate into electronic marketing and database marketing?

11. Can we thoroughly introspect our leadership and style of management? Has it changed over the past ten–twenty years? Or has it remained pretty much the same? If there is change, is the change marginal, moderate or radical? Have we accepted the idea of change frequent if not constant? Here is what Lawrence A. Bossidy, the Chairman of Allied Signal spoke on 'Reality Based Management', at The Economic Club of Washington in June 1996:

> Today's leaders take nothing for granted. They know that greater the market share and their margins, the harder other people are working to take it away from them. Their only hope is a perpetual sense of insecurity that inspires them to try to discern winds of change in the market, to come out with new and improved products and services and try to stay two or three steps ahead of their competition.

12. Are we providing a climate for nurturing innovation and entrepreneurship? The large organization needs to be more innovative and entrepreneurial. Do we have employees who can make decisions and accept responsibility? More importantly, do we allow them to take decisions? Do we empower them?

13. Successful organizations worldwide are realizing the need to have less hierarchical, flatter and cross-functional structures. They are adopting the matrix model of organization. What is our organization structure? Or are we like a big pyramid? Are we a more horizontal organization? How many layers does our organization structure have?

14. What do our employees really think of our company? Are they proud to work for our company? Do they feel that they are in control of their professional lives? Do they feel they have it within their power to make a difference in the success and failure of the organization? Are they able to balance the demands of their careers with those of their personal lives?

15. What is our level of integration? How far are we from becoming a fully integrated pharmaceutical company? Vertical integration does give sustainable competitive advantage to a drug firm. It gives the firm the much-needed control on costs, quality and strategy. Are all our ANDAs are totally integrated?

16. Where do we stand in the process of internationalizing our business? Are we still exporting only pharmaceutical substances, drug intermediates and generic formulations? Do we have a clearly laid out strategic action plan for graduating from exports to internationalization in the next three to five years?

17. How attractive are we as an alliance partner for prospective suitors from overseas? Successful companies world wide are switching from competition to a collaboration mode. Successful partnership is both a science and an art. To be an attractive alliance partner, one needs to have:

    - A dominant presence in more than one therapeutic segment
    - Manufacturing facilities approved by international regulatory authorities
    - Strong customer franchise
    - Product and process development capabilities
    - Wide distribution network
    - Competent medical detailing force

    What is our strategy to build and acquire these in the next three to five years?

18. How responsive are we? What is our speed of response? Andrew S. Grove, the Chairman of one of the world's most competitive corporations, says that, "ultimately, speed is the only weapon we have". In the international generics business, speed is the critical determinant factor for success. The 'first mover' advantage is vital even for survival. A 1996 report by Lehman Brothers notes that, in the US, the first generic entrant can sell at a 30 per cent discount to the innovator brand, compared to a 75 per cent discount for the later entrants.

19. How do we benchmark? What are our benchmarking practices? Whom do we benchmark against? Within the industry? Or across industries?

20. How sharp is our customer focus? Are we structuring ourselves around the customer or we still hierarchical? The winning corporations today are organizing around the customer, not the hierarchy. In today's fiercely competitive market, it is the customer who calls the shots. Companies, which can create customer solutions and total good experience only will succeed. Ted Levitt of Harvard Business School advised us as long as forty-seven years ago, through his landmark paper 'Marketing Myopia' that a thoroughly customer-oriented management can keep a growth industry growing, even after the obvious opportunities are exhausted.

Winning Leadership for an Era of Change

Lawrence A. Bossidy suggests four action steps for making a company a winner in an era of change through effective leadership:

1. One, determine the task at hand by honestly assessing where you stand with customers, employees and competitors.
2. Two, articulate a vision of where you want to be and values for how you want to behave. Set aggressive goals and keep everyone focused on achieving them.

3. Three, fill your company with people who are bursting with energy and creativity; people with diverse talents, who nonetheless can work together in a team setting. Give people constant, candid feedback, and let them know that their highest career aspirations can be fulfilled at your company.

4. And finally, create a culture that is obsessed with customers, and build your organization and incentive systems around the interests of the customer.

Index

D

E

Q

R

S

T

U

V

W

X

Z